TEXAS WOMAN'S UNIVERSITY
3 4351 00013023

D1047377

DATE DUE
5-31-85
MAR 19 2013

TEXAS WOMAN'S UNIVERSITY
LIBRARY
DENTON, TEXAS
DEMCO

Linguistics and Literacy

TOPICS IN LANGUAGE AND LINGUISTICS

Series Editors:
Albert Valdman and Thomas A. Sebeok
Indiana University, Bloomington, Indiana

ISSUES IN INTERNATIONAL BILINGUAL EDUCATION
The Role of the Vernacular
Edited by Beverly Hartford, Albert Valdman, and Charles R. Foster

LINGUISTICS AND LITERACY
Edited by William Frawley

Linguistics and Literacy

Edited by
William Frawley
University of Delaware
Newark, Delaware

PLENUM PRESS • NEW YORK AND LONDON

Library of Congress Cataloging in Publication Data

Delaware Symposium on Language Studies (3rd: 1981: University of Delaware)
Linguistics and literacy.

(Topics in language and linguistics)
Proceedings of the Third Delaware Symposium on Language Studies, held October 15–17, 1981 at the University of Delaware, Newark, Delaware.
Bibliography: p.
Includes index.
1. Written communication—Congresses. 2. Linguistics—Data processing—Congresses. 3. Reading—Congresses. 4. Language and languages—Study and teaching—Congresses. 5. Literacy—Congresses. I. Frawley, William, 1953–   . II. Title. III. Series.
P211.D4 1981   001.54′3   82-18535
ISBN 0-306-41174-1

Proceedings of the Third Delaware Symposium on Language Studies, held October 15–17, 1981, at the University of Delaware, Newark, Delaware.

Printed in the United States of America

CONTENTS

COMPUTERS AND LITERACY

LINGUISTICS AND READING

SECOND-LANGUAGE LITERACY

INTRODUCTION

William Frawley

University of Delaware

Several years ago, I performed a kind of perverse experiment. I showed, to several linguistic colleagues, the following comment made by Walker Percy (in *The Message in the Bottle*): language is too important a problem to be left only to linguists. The linguists' responses were peculiarly predictable: "What does Percy know? He's a mercenary outsider, a novelist, a psychiatrist! How can he say something like that?" Now, it should be known that the linguists who said such things in response were ardent followers of the linguistic vogue: to cross disciplines at whim for the sake of explanation---*any* explanation. It was odd, to say the least: Percy was damned by the very people who agreed with him!

Fortunately, the papers in this book, though radically interdisciplinary, do not fall prey to the kind of hypocrisy described above. The papers (from the Third Delaware Symposium on Language Studies) address the question of literacy---a linguistic problem too important to be left only to linguists--but many of the authors are not linguists at all, and those who are linguists have taken the care to see beyond the parochialism of a single discipline. The subsequent papers have been written by psychologists, linguists, anthropologists, computer scientists, and language teachers to explain the problem of how humans develop, comprehend, and produce extended pieces of information (discourses and texts).

Of course, whenever researchers from various disciplines assemble to discuss such a topic, there is the inevitable risk of more opinions than arguers. This was not the case, it seems to me, in the Symposium and in the papers which this book contains. Some clear statements have emerged from the conference:

1. There is a close connection between oral discourse and written discourse: two forms of language normally thought of as extremely divergent.

2. The comprehension and production of discourse can be predicted and understood if tools outside the mainstream of text analysis are employed.

3. The computer is a useful (but often unused) tool for attacking traditional literacy problems.

4. The computer, itself, poses a new kind of literacy problem.

5. Reading is not as simple as linguists often make it out to be, especially if one considers the processes involved in verbal reasoning and in the acquisition of standard written English by speakers of non-standard English.

6. The ontogenesis of reading skills is connected both to drawing skills and to early parent/child interactions.

7. The acquisition of a second language is a peculiar literacy problem: the structure, comprehension, and production of discourses and texts are critical not only for explaining second language performance but also for the development of new methodologies for second language instruction.

These seven statements should, however, be understood as statements only, not as final answers; they are the threads which hold the book together. If final answers to the problem of literacy could be spelled out in a book of this length, we would have the eighth wonder of the world on our hands. This book is a compendium of approaches, innovations, and some answers. Perhaps, given these findings, linguists and their non-linguist colleagues can finally come to understand what it means for a human to be literate.

* * *

This book would never have been possible without help from numerous sources. The College of Education of the University of Delaware provided a generous grant for the symposium. Lisa Vallett did excellent proofreading and editorial work; Larry Spivey and Philip Biechler were pressed into service on artistic matters; Susan Cross meticulously typed a difficult manuscript; Robert DiPietro provided his usual clear-headed advice. I thank them all.

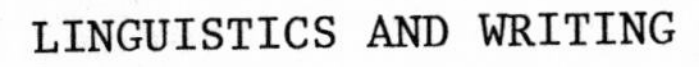

LINGUISTICS AND WRITING

THE LITERATE WRITES AND THE NONLITERATE CHANTS: WRITTEN LANGUAGE AND RITUAL COMMUNICATION IN SOCIOLINGUISTIC PERSPECTIVE[1]

F. Niyi Akinnaso

University of Ife, Nigeria

INTRODUCTION

Recent research by discourse analysts and students of literacy has shown a major consequence of literacy to be the dichotomization of language into two relatively distinct varieties: oral and written (see, for example, Goody and Watt, 1963; Greenfield, 1972; Goody, 1977, 1980; Olson, 1977a, 1977b; Ochs, 1979; Tannen, 1979, 1980a).[2] For more than half a century, the lexical and structural differences between the two varieties have been the subject of rigorous study by linguists and language teachers (Woolbert 1922; Harrell 1957; Drieman 1962; DeVito 1964, 1967; Golub 1969; O'Donnell 1974; Poole and Field 1976; Ochs 1979; Chafe 1979). The two varieties can be distinguished according to several criteria, including (1) modes of acquisition and transmission; (2) mechanisms and contexts of production; (3) the kinds and degree of planning required; (4) language structure and degree of complexity; and (5) the social and cognitive functions specific to each modality. When these criteria are applied to written language, we find a preponderance of the following: conscious learning (often through special schooling); modality-specific processes of production; the detachment of the writer from his/her audience; conscious planning and systematic organization; permanency of text and accurate reproduction of knowledge; the elevation of text through decontextualization and depersonalization; lexical elaboration and syntactico-semantic complexities (see Akinnaso, 1981, for a review).

Drawing on resources from anthropology, folklore, and linguistics, this paper demonstrates that these features are not peculiar to writing, so that it is not only in literate societies that language can be dichotomized according to them. In nonliterate (traditional) societies, ritual communication (for example, ritual chants and divination verses) is different from everyday talk in much the same way that written language differs from ordinary conversational language in literate societies. Using data from sixteen-cowry divination in Yoruba and applying the defining characteristics of written language to ritual communication, we find that the differences between the two modes of communication are more matters of degree than of kind.[3] It is argued that if we examined their socio-historical functions within the broader context of language evolution, we would find that oral ritual communication and written language are more similar than they are different.

THREE TYPES OF LINGUISTIC SITUATION

In developing the argument of this paper, it is useful to distinguish three major types of linguistic situation.[4] I shall characterize them as (1) the "oral language" situation, (2) the "written language" situation, and (3) the "classical language" situation. Ordinarily, these represent three chronological stages in the evolution of language.

The first situation is where language takes a purely oral form, and that is where writing has not been introduced. This can be regarded as the primitive stage in the evolution of language since all natural languages were originally of this form. Swadesh (1971) and Kay (1975) characterize purely oral languages as "local languages," while Ong (1980) describes the local language situation as one of "primary orality." According to Kay (1977), local languages are characterized by restricted vocabulary and nonautonomous (context-bound) usage (cf. Greenfield, 1972).

The second situation, which corresponds to Swadesh's and Kay's "world languages," is where language exists in two relatively distinct and modality-specific varieties, oral and written, for some or all of the population. The written variety is usually considered somewhat "elevated" and more complex than the spoken. It is assumed to be characterized by what Bernstein and Kay respectively call "elaborated code" and "autonomous speech style." And because it is often based on the dialect of the upper or ruling class, the written variety is normally accorded higher prestige than the spoken. With the spread of literacy within a given population, such elevated forms often spread across the population to the extent that (some) speakers begin to "speak a written language" (Greenfield, 1972), causing or perpetuating such distinctions as those between "oral" and "literate" speech style (Collins and Michaels, 1980) or between "standard" or "supralocal" and "non-standard" or "local" varieties. According to Ong (1980), this kind of linguistic situation often gives rise to what he describes as "secondary orality."

The third kind of linguistic situation corresponds to Swadesh's "classical language" situation, where language exists only in written form, either because of the death of the oral form, as with Latin (Ong, 1971), or because it never existed in oral form, as with classical Chinese (Rosemont, 1974). Ferguson's (1959) "high" form in a diglossic situation corresponds to the minimal stage of the classical language situation.

Considerable attention has been given to situations of the second and third kind especially by students of literacy and classical philology, respectively. The written language situation has been extensively studied by Goody (Goody and Watt, 1963; Goody, 1968, 1977, 1980) and Olson (1977a, 1977b, 1980a, 1980b), especially with respect to the cognitive and linguistic consequences of writing. Although these workers continue to make interesting references to the oral language situation, major work on the subject has been done by folklorists and "oral theorists" (Lord, 1960; Finnegan, 1973, 1977, 1981) and by sociolinguists using folkloristic material (Bauman 1977; Sherzer, 1977a, 1977b; Fox, 1981; Peek, 1981). But while students of the oral language situation have highlighted many interesting aspects of ritual communication in non-literate societies, none has systematically examined the effects of such communicative processes on language structure, nor the social functions of ritual communication vis-à-vis those of written language. As such is the goal of this paper, a sample of Yoruba ritual communication is presented in the following section, with a brief analysis of its structure. By "ritual communication" is meant the use of language in conventionally specified contexts in which patterns of interaction and of linguistic choices are restricted along certain definable directions and set apart from those of ordinary conversational interaction.

SIXTEEN-COWRY DIVINATION IN YORUBA

I want to illustrate here the key aspects of ritual communication through a brief discussion of one verse taken from Bascom's recordings or èrìndínlógún "sixteen-cowry divination" in a Yoruba village in 1951, a period when the diviner's language was still relatively unaffected by literacy.[5] I shall concentrate on the structure and content of the verse rather than on the divinatory process as a whole.

Like Ifa (see Bascom, 1969; Abimbola, 1969, 1977), sixteen-cowry divination is both a body of knowledge and a system of social, emotional, and pathological control, employing relevant historical and mythological precedents contained in the special divination verses to be recited, chanted, or sung by the diviner. It is, however, a simpler system than Ifa both in its repertoire of verses and in its range of applications.

Sixteen-cowries, known as owó ẹ̀rọ̀ mẹ́rìndínlógún, are cast on a basketry tray, and the number of shells lying mouth up are counted. There are only 17 configurations, from zero to sixteen, each corresponding to an odù or "figure" with an associated body of verses. For example, when there are eight cowries facing mouth up and eight down, the configuration is known as Èjì Ogbè, with which 49 verses are associated.[6] Once the figure has been determined by the first toss of the cowries, the diviner begins to recite the verses associated with it until he is stopped by the client who ordinarily selects the verse that is relevant to his own case. From the point of interruption, the divinatory process begins to alternate between ritual and conversational language, depending on how many additional casts of cowries and explanations are required. Usually, more specific information can be obtained by additional casts of the cowries, choosing between specific alternatives on the basis of the rank order of the 17 figures, although choice is heavily restricted. There are only two alternatives, between "left hand" and "right hand." The choice between more than two alternatives is made only by asking them in sequence and receiving "Yes" or "No" answers on specific predictions. In general, predictions are of two categories: ire ("blessing") and ibi ("evil"). Each category is composite and its members are rank ordered.[7] Further inquiries can be made about the specific recipient of the blessing or evil among the client, relations, and friends.

After all specifics are ascertained, the client may then ask what is necessary to ensure the promised blessing or to avert the predicted evil. In each case a specific form of sacrifice is recommended. Recipients of the sacrifice may vary from ritually significant trees (e.g., the ìrókò tree) to recognized divinities; further information can be obtained about the ingredients of the sacrifice, as well as where, when, and how it is to be made. The latitude of the diviner's recommendations is, however, in all cases, heavily constrained by the historical or mythological precedent contained in the relevant verse(s) which indicates the present predictions.

Below is a verse from Èjì Ogbè, one of the 17 figures.[8]

1. Ọ̀tọwútọwutọ́wú,
   Ọ̀tọwútọwutọ́wú,
2. Ọ̀rọwúrọwurọ́wú,
   Ọ̀rọwúrọwurọ́wú,
3. Ọ̀tọ̀ọ̀tọ̀ làá j'ẹ̀pa,
   One by one we eat peanuts,
4. Ọ̀tọ̀ọ̀tọ̀ làá j'ìmumu;
   One by one we eat tiger nuts;
5. Lọ́tọ̀lọtọ̀ ni wọ́n ọ́n sọ olú etutuú s'ẹ́nu;
   One by one we throw queen ants into the mouth;
6. Bi èrún jà, bí èrún ta,
   When driver ants fight, when driver ants sting,
7. Wọ́n á fi ìrù ba ara wọn télétèlètélé
   They touch each other lightly with their tails;
8. Dá fún 'Kúgbàgbé tíí ṣe ọmọ àgbà Òòsà Wújì.
   The diviner cast for 'Kúgbàgbé, who was the child of old Òrìṣà Wújì.

9. Ikú wá gbàgbé mi lóòní
   Death, forget me today;
10. Àgbẹ̀ rokoroko, wọn kò sàì gbàgbé ewé kàn.
   Farmers hoe and hoe, they still forget one weed.
11. Ikúgbàgbé ní òún ti le ṣe tí òun kò fi níí le kú?
   Ikúgbàgbé asked, what could he do so that he would not die?
12. Wọ́n ní kò níí kú
   They said he would not die.
13. Kíni òun yío haa ṣe?
   What should he do?
14. Wọ́n ní kó rúbọ
   They said he should offer a sacrifice.
15. Kíni òun yío haa rú?
   What should he sacrifice?
16. Wọ́n ní kó rú ẹgbàá mẹ́jọ
   They said he should offer 16,000 cowries;
17. Wọ́n ní kó rú àgbébọ̀ adìẹ kan
   They said he should offer a hen;
18. Kó rú ẹyẹlée kan;
   He should offer a pigeon;
19. Wọ́n ní kó rú aṣọ araa rẹ̀;
   They said he should offer the clothes he was wearing;
20. Wọ́n ní kó ní igbiń mẹ́jọ,
   They said he should take eight snails,
21. Kó máa lọ̀ọ́ bọ̀Ọ̀sà.
   And go and sacrifice them to Òrìṣà.
22. 'Kúgbàgbé ṣáà kó ẹbọ, ó rúbọ,
   'Kúgbàgbé collected the sacrifice, he offered the sacrifice;
23. Ó k'érù, ó tùu nuu
   He collected them, he appeased the gods,
24. Ó sì lọ̀ọ́ bọ̀Ọ̀sà
   And he sacrificed to Òrìsà.
25. Ni 'Kúgbàgbé ò bá lee kú mọ́.
   Subsequently, 'Kúgbàgbé did not die.
26. Ní wáà ńjó ní nyọ̀;
   And he was dancing, he was rejoicing;
27. Ni ó wáà ńyin àwọn awo,
   He was praising the diviners,
28. Ni àwon awo ńyìn 'ìṣà,
   And the Diviners were praising Òrìṣà,

29. Pé bẹ̀ẹ̀ ni àwọn awo t'ǒun nṣẹ'nu rereé wí.
    That his Diviners were always speaking the truth.
30. Ọ̀tọwútọwutọ́wú,
    Ọ̀tọwútọwutọ́wú,
31. Ọ̀rọwúrọwurọ́wú,
    Ọ̀rọwúrọwurọ́wú,
32. Ọ̀tọ̀ọ̀tọ̀ àá j'ẹ̀pà;
    One by one we eat peanuts;
33. Ọ̀tọ̀ọ̀tọ̀ àá j'ìmumu;
    One by one we eat tiger nuts;
34. Lọ́tọ̀lọtọ̀ ní wọ́n ọ́n sọ olú etutu s'ẹ́nu;
    One by one we throw queen ants into the mouth;
35. Bí èrún jà, bí èrún ta,
    When driver ants fight, when driver ants sting,
36. Wọ́n á fi ìrù ba ara wọn télétèlètélé
    They touch each other lightly with their tails;
37. Dá fún 'Kúgbàgbé tíí ṣe ọmọ àgbà Òòṣà Wújì.
    Cast for 'Kúgbàgbé, who was the child of old Òrìṣà Wújì.
38. Ó ní "Ikú wá gbàgbé mi lóònì,
    He said, "Death, forget me today,
39. Àgbè rokoroko, wọn kò ṣàì gbàgbé ewé kàn;
    Farmers hoe and hoe, they still forget one weed;
40. Àrùn gbàgbé mí lóònì,
    Sickness, forget me today,
41. Àgbè rokoroko, wọn kò ṣàì gbàgbé ewé kàn,"
    Farmers hoe and hoe, they still forget one weed."
42. Èjì Ogbè ni.
    This is Èjì Ogbè.

In commenting on this text, I shall focus on certain aspects of its organization and special uses of language that set it apart from social communication--that is, the everyday use of language for purposes of interpersonal relations. First of all, by recognizing the text as verse, we have introduced an unusual element of language structure. Verse differs from prose and everyday conversational language in that the former is normally built around regularly recurring structural units, while the latter normally lacks this quality (see Norman, 1980). Such formal units may be manifested on the phonological level as alliteration, rhyme, fixed patterns of tone or pitch of voice, syllable quantity, etc. at the grammatical level, such recurrent structures may be manifested as parallelisms of syntactic and semantic structures.

Let us illustrate this point with two examples, one phonological and the other grammatical. Undoubtedly, the best way to appreciate the phonological qualities of divinatory speech is to listen to one. As with our sample data, the verses are recited, chanted, or sung in a special "voice," using stylized intonation contours. In our sample text, the formulaic portions (lines 1-7; 30-42) were partly recited and partly chanted with a rhythmic quality unparalleled in colloquial Yoruba. Although the verses run into each other with more than usual speed, each information or idea unit is presented as a distinct tone group and separated from the surrounding idea units by pitch variation, assonance, alliteration, rhyme, and rhythm

The distinctiveness of each idea unit is further enhanced by the preponderant use of grammatical parallelisms, a common example of which is the pairing of lexical items (usually content words) in a similar syntactic environment. This means that, as Norman (1980:393) points out for Quiche ritual language, "both members of the pair must bear the same syntactic relation in their respective clauses, and there must be word-for-word identity between other lexical items occupying corresponding positions in the two clauses" (for further illustration of this organizational principle in ritual texts, see T'sou, 1968; Sherzer, 1977b). For example, in the sample text above, parallelisms of this kind are abundant in lines 1-6; 16-20; 22; 26-35; 36-41. In lines 3 and 4, for instance, the paired terms ẹ̀pà ("peanuts") and ìmumu ("tiger nuts") are both direct objects, and the other syntactic slots common to the two clauses are filled by identical lexical items. Similarly, in line 6, the shared syntactic slots are filled by identical lexical items except the paired terms jà ("fight") and ta ("sting"), both of which are intransitive verbs occupying an identical structural position in both clauses. In addition to differentiating ritual from social communication, these phonological and grammatical devices provide useful cues for the analysis of the text, especially in the separation of the lines in a verse as we have done with our sample data.

In addition to phonological and grammatical features, sixteen-cowry divination is distinguished from colloquial Yoruba by special, often archaic, words or expressions, some of which are unique to particular verses or figures. An example in our sample text is the pair _Ọ̀towútowutówú/ Ọ̀rọwúrowúrowú_ (lines 1-2; 30-31), which appear in only three out of 210 verses (see Bascom 1980), all occurrences being in the _Èjì Ogbè_ figure. Norman (1980) and Sherzer (1977b) have pointed out similar retentions of esoteric and archaic vocabulary in Quiche ritual language and in _kapur ikar_, a Cuna curing chant respectively. David Parkin (personal communication) has made similar observations about Giriama ritual texts. Such archaic or "classical" expressions are retained partly to enhance the authority of the text, partly to serve as a major mnemonic memorization device, and partly to elevate the semantic structure of the text. Such archaisms contribute to the unintelligibility of ritual texts, reinforcing Gumperz's (1964:95) observation about ritual communication in a local Indian village: "the language of the chants is, as a rule, unintelligible to uneducated members of the audience."

The organization of ideas within each verse is in itself a major mnemonic device. As in our sample text, nearly all the verses in sixteen-cowry divination follow the same pattern, although there are considerable variations in length and content. The general format manifests a three-part structure, as follows.[9]

Part I A formulaic opening (1-7).

Part II An account of the historical or mythological case which serves as a precedent for the present consultation, stating some or all of the following:

a. the personae (diviner and/or client) involved (8)
b. the occasion for the divination, mentioning the client's requests or problems (9-11);
c. the prescription (12-21);

d. the client's (non)compliance (22-24);

e. the resolution or outcome of the case the client's reaction (25-29).

Part III A formulaic closing (30-42).

Parts I and III are formulaic and fixed, while Part II is essentially narrative and so improvisatory. This means that while reciting or chanting any verse, the diviner is required to keep as close as possible to the original forms of Parts I and III as he learned them, whereas a great deal of creativity is allowed in Part II so long as the main plot, theme, and characters of the story are retained. Thus divinatory verses are composed partly before and partly during performance. It is in the composition of the improvisatory portion of the verse that the diviner's cognitive and linguistic skills are at stake, for it must share the phonological and grammatical characteristics of the rest of the verse.

An important consequence of the structural organization of our sample text is the highly integrated structure of ideas within it. The entire text hangs together with an internal cohesion that is absent from ordinary conversational language. For example, the first pair of parallel terms in Part I establishes the ground for the series of parallelisms that follow, heightening expectations about the nature of the message. The parallelisms eventually culminate in a statement about the mythological client involved (line 8). The first sequence-final intonation in the text appears at the end of this statement which, in turn, establishes the validity of the consultation reported in Part II. Closure is signalled in Part III by the repetition of the opening formulaic parallelisms. The final line, This is Èjì Ogbè, serves as (1) a stamp of authority; (2) a statement of the diviner's detachment from the entire message; and (3) a strategic cue for the client that he may now indicate the relevance (or otherwise) of the verse to his own case before the diviner moves on to the next. Although they vary in length and in the range of information contained, all the verses of sixteen-cowry divination are united by the structural organization just described and by the poetic, often musical, qualities of divinatory texts. Above all, like Ifá text, all the verses are based in Yoruba history, mythology, philosophy, religion, folk medicine, and world view.

Application of Bauman's (1977) performance model of verbal art shows that Yoruba divinatory speech exhibits major "keying" features: special codes, figurative language, special formulae, special paralinguistic features, and appeal to tradition, all of which set it apart from ordinary oral conversation. Making use of these formal and conventionalized devices, the diviner is able to convince his clientele with "the power of words" (Peek, 1981). Indeed, as Bauman (1977:32) points out, these distinctive features give ritual communication their "appropriate form [which] must be rendered in the appropriate way by the appropriate functionary."

Another major feature of ritual communication illustrated by our sample text is that its formalized language involves a different relation between the speaker and the message from that in ordinary conversation (cf. Bloch, 1975; Olson, 1980b). For one thing, the reciter is not expressing his personal views; rather, he is acting as a spokesman for the ancestors and the gods. Although his utterances constitute a distinctive register interpretable only within ritual contexts, the meaning of what he says does not depend on the immediate situation, because each verse he recites is context-free, applying to a vast range of problems beyond spatio-temporal specificity. Furthermore, the diviner is detached from the client while the verses are being recited. Although the recitation is for the client's benefit, the verses are not directly addressed to him. Mediating the interaction is the set of divining instrument placed between the diviner and the client, and which the diviner consults from time to time. While the verses are being recited, the diviner and the client look at the divining instrument rather than at each other, in the belief that the recited verses emanate from there. This parallels kapur ikar ritual chants, which are addressed to symbolic "stick dolls" rather than the patient for whose benefit the chants are recited (Sherzer, 1977b). The absence of self-reference words, e.g., first person pronouns, and phrases like "I think," "in my opinion," etc., attests to the depersonalization of the diviner's utterances, whereas the third person pronoun, wọ́n ("they"), is used throughout to place what is said within the general context of ancestral usage.

This separation of the speaker from the message is a pervasive feature of ritual utterances. For example, in Estrada's recent book, "Maria Sabina: Her Life and Chants," the Mazatec shaman concludes almost every line with a word meaning "says" as:

> I am the woman who looks into the inside of things and investigates,
> says,
>
> Lady mistress of the shade and of the house, says.

This practice is viewed as acknowledgement of the transmission of supernaturally generated messages: "Her qualification of each line with the word tzo, 'says,' is a testimony to that: that it isn't Maria Sabina but the unspoken he/she/it whose words these are" (Estrada, 1981: 9).[10]

Altogether, the cultural, linguistic, and paralinguistic features of divinatory speech give it a distinctive stamp of authority which makes it inappropriate, if not impossible, for anyone to challenge it. This authoritarian status of divinatory speech is further enhanced by its unquestionable mythological source and its appeal to tradition and ancestral sanctions. Thus, to question or disagree with a diviner in the process of divination is to challenge the established social order. As Bloch (1975) remarks of religious songs, one cannot argue with a chant or a recited verse. In his analysis of the circumcision ritual of the Merina of Madagascar, Bloch also argues that the formalized language of religious chants is partly responsible for their esoteric and authoritatian nature.

In order to understand fully the defining characteristics of ritual communication, it is necessary to see them in relation to those of social (colloquial) communication. By social communication is meant the everyday use of language for purposes of interpersonal relations, employing a variety of language otherwise known as the vernacular or local dialect. Social communicative strategies are acquired and commonly used in informal situations (home, playground, street, etc.). Such language use forms the core of regional or ethnic-based dialects, is perpetuated in social networks (cf. Gumperz, 1982), and has been extensively studied by sociolinguists. Labov, for example, studied Black English Vernacular largely from this perspective. Most social communication of this type is "unplanned" and "unplannable"; that is, it lacks forethought and prior organization, and so it is impossible to predict its form and content well in advance (Ochs, 1979).

In contrast, ritual communicative strategies are normally specially acquired and used primarily in formal settings, most commonly at the "shrine." They are characterized by elaborate structural organization and "elevated" linguistic structures, and their usage is relatively independent of both the subjective experience of the users and of their (the users') immediate social networks.

However, most students of literacy, discourse, and cognitive development have bypassed ritual communication, describing spoken language largely in terms of colloquial, social communication. They emphasize context-dependency, fragmented grammatical structure, and illogicality as the major characteristics of spoken language, treating written language as its antipode (Vygotsky, 1962; Goody and Watt, 1963; Bruner 1966; Greenfield, 1972; Poole and Field, 1976; Goody, 1980; Ochs 1979; Chafe, 1979). Although this body of work has been based largely on data taken from literate societies, the implication of the findings is that language in nonliterate societies must lack the functional and grammatical possibilities of writing. The argument of the present paper is that such a conclusion needs reexamination in the light of the close parallels between written language and ritual communication in nonliterate societies.

WRITTEN LANGUAGE AND RITUAL COMMUNICATION IN SOCIOLINGUISTIC PERSPECTIVE

The focus here will be on some major ways in which ritual communication in nonliterate societies compares to written language in literate societies, showing how they both differ from ordinary social communication or colloquial language. First of all, ritual and written language share similar social processes of acquisition. Unlike colloquial language, both are acquired within institutionalized settings and over a long period of time, possibly spanning an individual's lifetime. Writing is normally acquired in school settings; similarly, ritual communicative strategies are normally acquired through special initiation into the relevant cult, which functions more or less like the school system. In both cases, the learner is usually separated from home and placed under distinct authority, although the forms of negotiation are somewhat different. A statement about the acquisition of sixteen-cowry divinatory system is in order here.[11] It takes seven days to undergo the special initiation ritual, three years to learn how to use divination cowries, and another three to learn some of the important verses. Later, the apprentice-diviner learns the uses of leaves and herbs; after he begins his career as a diviner, he continues to learn new verses by listening to other diviners. Bascom (1980:11), in fact, summarizes it all when he concludes that in sixteen-cowry divination, "learning continues throughout a diviner's lifetime."

When we look at the conditions under which ritual communication and written language are produced, another major similarity between them becomes evident. The solitude of a writer (as characterized by Ong, 1980) is paralleled by the detachment of the diviner or ritual performer from his audience. Although both communicators become actively involved in stylizing their language as appropriate, none depends on immediate feedback from the audience, as both are engaged more or less in a monologue. In neither case is the communicative activity as such important, as in phatic conversation; rather, it is the outcome of the communicative activity that is important to the diviner or the writer.

Another common characteristic between ritual and written language is their permanency and reproducibility. Like written documents (laws, encyclopedias, books, etc.), ritual texts are retained and reproduced from generation to generation for their value. This characteristic is especially evident in the sphere of religion where the same texts are transmitted across time and space. For example, it has been argued that the traditional efficacy of the Bible and the Quran is due to the fact that written texts provide literate religions with a fixed point of reference and therefore a special mode of supernatural communication (Goody, 1968). But the fact that nonliterate religious texts are not written does not deprive them of fixity of reference or spiritual efficacy. Smith (1977), for example, has demonstrated that fixity of reference is not unique to literate religions by using data from Pābūjī oral epic to illustrate how the use of formulaic, musical, and other patterning devices gives oral religious texts a relatively permanent form and content. Evidence from Yoruba divinatory texts also shows that the basic content, form, and style of ritual and religious texts in nonliterate societies remain constant from performance to performance, despite individual and other variables that may affect the performance (Abimbola, 1977; Bascom, 1969, 1980; Olajubu 1978).[12] The permanency and reproducibility of ritual texts further promote the formalization and integration of ritual language, thus contrasting it with the fragmented quality of spontaneous oral conversation.

Recently, Olson (1980a, 1980b) highlighted another major similarity between oral ritual and written texts: they both serve an important archival function in "preserving what the society takes to be 'true' and 'valid' knowledge, knowledge from which rules of thought and action may be derived" (Olson, 1980b:106).[13] I have argued elsewhere (Akinnaso, 1981c) that, like poetry in classical Greece (as evidenced by the works of Homer), the memorized divination verses constitute an instrument of "preserved communication" among the Yoruba, providing a kind of reference library on history, mythology, religion, politics, folk medicine, and the educational mechanisms of the society (cf. Havelock, 1963). Like archival written texts, ritual texts "help to preserve the social order by minimizing dispute" (Olson, 1980b:106). Both are cited with equal authority to validate ongoing social action or behavior. Although they achieve their effects in quite different ways, the two modes of communication are vital to their users for the preservation, retrieval, and transmission of knowledge and for the reproduction of social and cultural capital (cf. Bourdieu, 1973). Looking at ritual in the extended sense of a symbolic system of communication, Barth (1975) and Leach (1976) have also examined the role of ritual communication in the replication of cultural messages. Their analyses show that the

Bible, a written text, and Baktaman oral ritual are equally effective in the performance of this function.

The use of oral ritual texts to validate ongoing social action has been vividly demonstrated by Gumperz (1964). In his study of the social functions of religious performances in a village in North India, Gumperz shows how ritual texts are used to validate social messages:

> "In one performance a Doom actor inserted a long plea for Hindi-Muslim amity into the mythological story of Nal and Damayati. Even as a government official, he would never have been accorded the attention he received nor the audience, had he attempted to make a prose speech" (Gumperz, 1964:95).

This is reminiscent of an incident I witnessed in Ajegunlẹ, a Yoruba village near the rocky city of Idanre, in 1978. A middle-aged and apparently unsuccessful man had been prevented from contributing to the settlement of a dispute between his sister and her husband. Genuinely upset, he was about tọ leave the gathering when hẹ muttered in Ìdanre dialect, *Òjij'e b'ẹ̀rọ̀'fẹ̀n*, *ṣè bi'gbi obì dó kọ̀*, *dó fìí ghẹn ẹn f'éwé má*, *ǒ ghọ́n bẹ̀ẹ sií gbáa rè ín* ("The shadow has no fear for the deep pit; is it not true that when Kolanut divorced Leaf, she started to dry up?").[14] These lines happened to have come from a particular *Ifá* verse, and as soon as they were recognized as such, the man was called back, given a hearing, and was subsequently able to initiate the final settlement of a year-old dispute between his sister and her husband.

The value and authority accorded oral ritual texts in nonliterate societies and written texts in literate societies derive partly from their "elevated" linguistic forms, partly from their archival function, and partly from their utility in validating ongoing social action (see Gumperz, 1964; Bloch, 1975; Olson, 1980b). Both derive from a transcendental source and both have distinctive styles which help to set them apart from ordinary oral conversational language.

In addition to the storage and transmission of knowledge, ritual texts perform another major function that has been attributed largely to writing: list making. The list in our sample text consists of the following sacrificial items in consecutive lines (16-20):

ẹgbàá mẹ́jọ	16,000 cowries
àgbébọ̀ adiẹ kan	1 hen
eyelee kan	1 pigeon
aṣọ ara	clothes (currently worn)
ìgbín mẹ́jọ	8 snails

The syntactic frame in which the list occurs makes it possible to detach the items from the entire verse and rehearse them in rapid succession as a nominal list, such as administrative, property and shopping lists.[15] This syntactic frame, in itself a major mnemonic memorization device, allows the listed item to occur as the object NP at the end of a formulaic sentence, producing the following pattern:

(They said) he/they should offer a
b
c
etc.

After (a) relevant verse(s) has/have been identified by the client, the diviner usually goes over the list of sacrificial items contained in the verse(s), disembedding the items from the syntactic frame. The items vary (both quantitatively and qualitatively) from verse to verse and from _odù_ to _odù_. Lists of this kind (items offered in sacrifice) were among the earliest uses of writing, as evidenced by early Sumerian tablets. For example, Nesbit (cited in Goody, 1977:88) cites the following ritual list from early Sumerian records:

4 fattened kids
26 fattened goat-heifers
319 pastured sheep
64 pastured he-goats
98 pastured ewes
66 pastured goats
33 weaned lambs

That lists of this kind should feature prominently among the earliest uses of writing suggests a close historical relationship between ritual communication and writing, reinforcing Hodge's speculations about the origin of Egyptian hieroglyphs (Hodge, 1975).

CONCLUSIONS

The preceding argument and analyses have several implications for sociolinguistic theory, two of which will be highlighted here. One centers on the "linguistic discontinuity hypothesis," and the other on the origin and process of language specialization. Bernstein (1961, 1962, 1971) has discussed the former in terms of a distinction between "restricted" and "elaborated" codes. Parallel distinctions, based on different (but related) theoretical premises, have recently been made by students of literacy, discourse, and language evolution, such as "orality" vs. "literacy" (Goody, 1977, 1980; Ong, 1980; Collins and Michaels, 1980) or "nonautonomous" (context-dependent) vs. "autonomous" (decontextualized) language (Greenfield, 1972; Kay, 1977; Olson, 1977a, 1977b).

These dichotomous distinctions have been used to explain the underachievement of speakers of "oral" (nonliterate) languages or dialects vis-à-vis the assumed superior capabilities of speakers of "written" (literate) languages or dialects (Bernstein, 1961, 1962; Greenfield, 1972; Collins and Michaels, 1980). Yet most research on the distinction between oral and written language has been based either on maximally contrastive data (e.g., formal academic papers vs. dinnertable conversations) or on informants from disparate cultural and socioeconomic background, so that several other variables were confounded with whatever differences may exist between spoken and written language. The tendency to equate the status of oral languages to that of context-dependent (e.g. dinnertable) conversations has led to the view that language in nonliterate societies must lack the formal, functional, and grammatical possibilities of written language.

The preceding discussion of Yoruba ritual language demonstrates the inadequacy of such a view. Indeed, Ruth Finnegan has recently argued, after reviewing a wide range of oral literatures in multifarious nonliterate societies, that (1) oral and written literatures are equally rich and complex both in language and content, and that (2) "the further assumption that nonliterate cultures and individuals necessarily lack the insight and inspirations--the modes of thought--that we associate with written literature seems on the basis of present evidence an unjustified conclusion" (Finnegan, 1973:144). Part of the linguistico-cognitive skills involved in oral ritual communication has been demonstrated by Sherzer (1977a, 1977b) in his account of kapur ikar, a Cuna curing chant. The chant is in itself a complex psycholinguistic activity involving the projection or playing out of a lexical taxonomy onto a parallelistic verse pattern. Sherzer (1977b:284) goes on,

> One characteristic of Cuna curing chants is that they are extremely long, often lasting several hours at a time. In addition to phonological, morphological, and syntactic features distinguishing the [chants] from colloquial Cuna, there are special lexical items used in the chants, lexical items which are often particular to single chants or even versions of them.

Evidence from a single verse demonstrates the applicability of Sherzer's observations to Yoruba divination. Yet neither the cognitive nor the linguistic skills involved in ritual communication of this type were systematically investigated before conclusions were made about the supremacy of written language and the impoverishment of orality.

Another shortcoming of contemporary comparative work on oral and written language is that explanations of language evolution have been tied to the use of writing, the general argument being that writing promoted unique linguistic structures. Yet there is abundant evidence in the sociolinguistic literature which shows that special registers of language, some with their own unique styles and grammatical structures, usually develop in response to situationally specific topics or communicative activities. Once such specialized topics or communicative activities get well-defined, appropriate register peculiarities or communicative strategies are developed around them. Such innovations often lead to lexical, grammatical, and stylistic elaboration.

In their investigation of linguistic differentiation in two nonliterate societies (the Menomini and the Zuñi), Bloomfield (1927) and Newman (1964) found that linguistic differentiation has individual and cultural dimensions. Thus, in his analysis of lexico-semantic differences between "sacred" and "slang" usage among the Zuñi, Newman (1964:402) observes that

> [although] there is no specialized tradition of esthetic writing to give an aura of prestige to its distinctively literary forms and no contrast with the vulgate of forms used only in speech[,] ... a comparable differentiation is applied in Zuni to its cultural situations; the verbal usage characteristic of sacred places and practices is marked as the dignified level of vocabulary, in contrast to the usage distinctive of the movies, the school playground, and the practices of taunting and teasing (1964:402).

Consequently, Newman (1964:402) concludes, "words acquire connotative gradations in accordance with the cultural values assigned to ideas, status groups, and situations." In reviewing this and related work, Hymes (1964:388) asserts, "variations in speech are recognized and evaluated in <u>every</u> community ... even a small and tight-knit hunting or horticultural society will recognize differences in linguistic competence and prestige and distinct levels of usage (original emphasis)." It is no wonder then that in ritual contexts, peculiar phonological, lexical, and grammatical devices are developed partly to formalize the communicative activity at hand, and partly to obfuscate the uninitiated. The "formula," incantations, lexical archaisms, and grammatical parallelisms serve such purposes, in addition to their mnemonic functions.

The division of labor and the subsequent professionalization of social, economic, religious, and political activities came to promote the development of numerous registers which remain esoteric to nonmembers.[16] While special registers may have developed to give necessary information to in-group members, their consequence is obfuscation for the uninitiated. Of special importance in this developmental process is the academic profession whose practitioners, Goody speculates, "probably spend more time reading and writing than they do speaking and listening" (Goody, 1980:120-121). The major consequences of their conscious attention to language are lexical and syntactico-semantic elaboration and the development of numerous register peculiarities.

But the diviner is no less concerned with the linguistic structure of his verses than the writer is with his language. Historically, diviners were among the first group of professionals in nonliterate societies, functioning as "the physicians, psychiatrists, historians, and philosophers of the communities to which they belonged" (Abimbola, 1977:11). They were also among the first group to develop a professional language which remains evident today in the divinatory verses, chants, and songs. A major consequence of this development is that the language of ritual became far removed from ordinary conversational language, becoming not only elevated but also esoteric. The history of writing manifests a similar process of linguistic differentiation (cf. Gelb, 1952; Cipolla, 1969; Oxenham, 1980). Like the restriction of divination to a few, literacy was historically restricted to priests or professional groups, and written language was subjected to conscious refinements in the attempt to separate it from oral language (Gleason, 1961; Gelb, 1952). Thus, the lexical and structural complexities of ritual and written language began as attempts to maintain their distinctiveness.

The implication of the position taken here is that the language of the home has always been different from the language of specialized communicative activity, so that linguistic discontinuities are not peculiar to literate societies. This means that the distinction between ordinary social communication and ritual language in nonliterate societies is as important as that between oral and written language in any discussion of language evolution, especially in accounting for lexical and syntactico-semantic complexities. In both oral and written language situations, learners encounter discontinuities between "elevated" and "lower" or stigmatized varieties, the social control mechanisms perpetuating the discontinuities being probably more crucial for the learner than the structural differences between the varieties (Akinnaso, 1981d).

I would like to conclude on a historical note. My earlier comparison of list-making in Yoruba divination and in early Sumerian writing suggests a close historical relationship between writing and ritual communication. Recent work by Hodge (1975) attests a major historical affinity between the two modes of communication. Following Jensen (1969), who contends that writing began quite suddenly rather than as a slow, gradual process, Hodge argues that Egyptian hieroglyphic writing may have been originally motivated by the ritual texts it was used to preserve. Through an analysis of Egyptian Pyramid Texts (see Faulkner, 1969), Hodge proposes that the striking parallelisms between the nature of "ritual word play" in both Egyptian culture and their writing system suggests that Egyptian writing was created on the pattern of ritual texts. Hodge (1975:344) concludes,

> The word plays and other phenomena discussed above are precisely the kinds of factors which must have been involved in the development of writing and which are reflected in the usage of the hieroglyphs by the Egyptians. As some of the Pyramid Texts appear to antedate writing in the Nile Valley, it is safe to assume that along with these, like texts existed. It would thus have been among the priests who composed and recited the spells, full of constant linguistic manipulation, that writing arose, reflecting the same associations made verbally. The Egyptians referred to writing as 'the words of the god' *mdw nčr*, indicating the association with magic and religion. The word *mdw* is that used when a magic spell is to be recited: *ǧd mdw* 'says the words ...!"

This historical relationship between writing and ritual texts, between early Egyptian hieroglyphs and "ritual word plays," seems to be replicated today in the sociolinguistic parallels between the two modes of communication.

NOTES

1. This paper is humbly dedicated to the memory of William R. Bascom, late Professor Emeritus of Anthropology

at the University of California at Berkeley, who kindly made available to me, shortly before he died, all his tape-recordings of ẹ̀rìndínlógún, "sixteen-cowry divination" on which this paper is based. His invitation that I do a sociolinguistic analysis of the ẹ̀rìndínlógún corpus and his comments and suggestions on my subsequent research design on Yoruba divination are all gratefully acknowledged.

For comments and other assistance in connection with the paper, I would like to thank Berta Bascom, John J. Gumperz, David Parkin, Steve Murray, and participants at the Third Delaware Symposium on Language Studies, especially Deborah Tannen and Judith Orasanu.

2. For a review of research on the consequences of literacy on language, thought, and society, see Akinnaso (1981a).

3. Although the modality-specific differences between speech and writing remain, there are no basic formal, functional, or structural differences between written language in literate societies and oral ritual communication in nonliterate societies.

4. These three types of linguistic situation have previously been recognized by Swadesh (1971), Kay (1977), and Goody (1977). Swadesh conceived of the three situations as sequential stages in the evolution of language, while Kay uses internal linguistic evidence to characterize the movement from the oral to the written language situation as one of increasing autonomy in the use of language. Goody has focused on the implications and effects of the written language situation.

5. Transcriptions of the recordings have been published in Bascom (1980).

6. The number of verses associated with a particular odù ("figure") varies from diviner to diviner according to their knowledge and length of training. Bascom's informant had been a diviner all his life, and, at 70, he must have optimized his repertoire of the verses. His text and manner of recitation are absolutely consistent with Yoruba divinatory practice (see Abimbola, 1969, 1977; Bascom, 1969).

7. For example, ire varies from ire gbogbo ("all blessings") to specific blessings, e.g., ire àìkú ("blessing for long life"), ire ọmọ ("blessing for children"), etc.

8. This verse can be found in Bascom (1980:68-71), where it is labelled "Eji Ogbe/A7." I have modified the transcription (1) to reflect modern Yoruba orthographic conventions, and (2) to indicate the tones. Bascom's free translation has been retained with one modification (line 10/39), where his translation missed the polarity of the original and so the import of the incantation.

9. The line references in parenthesis refer to our sample data only. However, the three-part structure outlined here remains constant, varying mainly in the amount of details included.

10. I am grateful to Steve Murray for drawing my attention to this book.

11. This account is based on the actual experience of Salakọ, Bascom's knowledgeable informant (Bascom, 1980:11). The acquisition process involves not simply contextual learning, as is often thought of nonliterate education, but a great deal of decontextualized learning. In addition to memorizing and rehearsing the verses out of context, training involves systematic discussions of Yoruba history, mythology, philosophy, metaphysics, etc., and series of question-and-answer exchanges between the master and the trainee.

12. Looking at the other side of the argument, Goody's point is valid that oral religious texts are flexible and so can be easily retooled to new social realities. It should be noted, however, that "fixity" is a relative term and that written religious texts are not wholly fixed. Take the Bible as an example. First of all, the recording of the incidents was not simultaneous with their happening, so that the major source of biblical information was memory in the first place. Secondly, in the course of transmission of primitive biblical records, several changes were introduced in the process of "copying," particularly before the advent of printing. Even today, changes continue to occur

with the publication of new editions and in the process of translation. Furthermore, the historicity of doctrinal values is always demonstrated by changes in the interpretation of relevant texts, oral or written. Ultimately, then, and with particular reference to fixity of doctrinal texts, we can only talk of differences in degree rather than in kind. (I am indebted to S. Murray for insight into the argument presented here.)

13. It is interesting to follow the development of Olson's argument about the linguistico-cognitive consequences of writing, as he moved from the advocacy of rigid dichotomies ("utterance" vs. "text," "nonautonomy" vs. "autonomy," "common-sense knowledge" vs. "scientific knowledge") to the recognition of basic functional similarity between oral ritual and written language. Tannen's work demonstrates a similar shift of emphasis from unique oral vs. literate discourse strategies (Tannen, 1979, 1980a) to a recognition of the myth in the dichotomy between orality and literacy (Tannen 1980b, and this volume). The basic role of orality, especially in regard to verbal reasoning and the mental reproduction of knowledge, is thus gaining well-deserved attention as current research findings are utilized (Orasanu, this volume).

14. These lines, taken from a major odu of *Ifá* (also replicated in *ẹ̀rìndínlógún*) provide an etiological explanation for why, till today, the Yoruba use fresh (plantain) leaves to preserve kolanut. To "divorce" your kolanut from leaf is to ruin your harvest. Apparently, the utterer of these lines had reasons for thinking that they are relevant to the case at hand. As he later explained to one of the arbitrators, his sister needed her present husband for her survival. He argued that his sister was so lazy that he feared no other man would be willing to care for her than her present husband, whom he described as "*eni pípé*" (a "complete gentleman"--perhaps an "Everyman").

15. It seems likely that, cognitively, written nominal lists are based on an underlying syntactic frame of this type, so that a shopping list will be based on an underlying syntactic pattern as

I would like to/have to/should/must buy (the following items) a
b
c
etc.

16. Although his ultimate argument is that the direction of language evolution is from nonautononous to an autonomous system of communication, Kay (1975) agrees that the process of linguistic differentiation described above characterizes the development of register peculiarities and of subsequent lexical and syntactic elaboration.

REFERENCES

Abimbola, Wande, 1969, "An Exposition of Ifa Literary Corpus," Ph.D. Dissertation, University of Lagos.

Abimbola, Wande, 1977, "Ifa Divination Poetry," Nok Publishers, N.Y.

Akinnaso, F. Niyi, 1981a, The consequences of literacy in pragmatic and theoretical perspectives, _Anth. Educ. Q._, 12:163-200.

Akinnaso, F. Niyi, 1981b, On the differences between spoken and written language, Ms., Language Behavior Research Laboratory, University of California, Berkeley.

Akinnaso, F. Niyi, 1981c, Elevated language in nonliterate societies, Kroeber Anthr. Soc.

Akinnaso, F. Niyi, 1981d, Research on minority languages and educational achievement: a synthesis and an interpretation, Am. Anthr. Assoc.

Barth, Fredrik, 1975, "Ritual and Knowledge among the Baktaman of New Guinea," Yale U. Press, New Haven.

Bascom, William, 1969, "Ifa Divination: Communication Between Gods and Men in West Africa," Indiana U. Press, Bloomington.

Bascom, William, 1980, "Sixteen Cowries: Yoruba Divination from Africa to the New World," Indiana U., Bloomington.

Bauman, Richard, 1977, "Verbal Art as Performance," Newbury House, Rowley, Mass.

Bernstein, Basil, 1961, Aspects of language and learning in the genesis of the social process, _J. Ch. Psych. and Psychiatry_, 1:313-24.

Bernstein, Basil, 1962, Linguistic codes, hesitation phenomena and intelligence, Lang. and Sp., 5:31-46.
Bernstein, Basil, 1964, Elaborated and restricted codes: their social origins and some consequences, Am. Anthr., 66:55-69.
Bernstein, Basil, 1971, "Class, Codes, and Control, Vol. 1," Routledge and Kegan Paul, London.
Bloch, Maurice, 1975, "Political Language and Oratory in Traditional Society," Academic Press, London.
Bloomfield, Leonard, 1927, Literate and illiterate speech, Am. Sp., 2:432-39.
Bourdieu, P., 1973, Cultural reproduction and social reproduction, in: "Knowledge, Education and Cultural Change," R. Brown, ed., Tavistock, London.
Bruner, J. S., 1966, On cognitive growth, I & II, in: "Studies in Cognitive Growth," J. S. Bruner, R. R. Oliver, and P. M. Greenfield, eds., Wiley, N.Y.
Chafe, Wallace L., 1979, Integration and involvement in spoken and written language, Int. Ass. for Semiotic Stds.
Cipolla, Carlo, 1969, "Literacy and Development in the West," Pelican, Harmondsworth.
Collins, J. and Michaels, S., 1980, The importance of conversational discourse strategies in the acquisition of literacy, Berkeley Ling. Soc.
DeVito, Joseph A., 1964, "A Quantitative Analysis of Comprehension Factors in Samples of Oral and Written Technical Discourse of Skilled Communicators," Ph.D. Dissertation, U. of Illinois.
DeVito, Joseph A., 1967, Levels of abstraction in spoken and written language, J. of Comm., 17:354-61.
Drieman, G. H. J., 1962, Differences between written and spoken language: an exploratory study, Acta Psych., 20:36-57, 78-100.
Estrada, Álvaro, 1980, "María Sabina: Her Life and Chants," Ross-Erikson, Santa Barbara.
Faulkner, Raymond O., 1969, "The Ancient Egyptian Pyramid Texts," Clarendon Press, Oxford.
Ferguson, C. A., 1959, Diglossia, Word, 15:325-40.
Finnegan, Ruth, 1973, Literacy versus nonliteracy: the great divide? in: "Modes of Thought: Essays on Thinking in Western and Non-Western Societies," R. Horton and R. Finnegan, eds., Faber and Faber, London.
Finnegan, Ruth, 1977, "Oral Poetry: Its Nature, Significance and Social Context," Cambridge U. Press, Cambridge.

Finnegan, Ruth, 1981, Literacy and literature, in: "Universals of Human Thought: Some African Evidence," B. Lloyd and J. Gay, eds., Cambridge U. Press, Cambridge.
Fox, James J., 1981, Adam and Eve on the island of Roti: a conflation of oral and written traditions, Conf. on Transmission in Oral and Written Traditions.
Gelb, I. J., 1952, "A Study of Writing," U. Chicago Press, Chicago.
Gleason, H. A., 1961, "An Introduction to Descriptive Linguistics," Holt, Rinehart and Winston, N.Y.
Golub, L. S., 1969, Linguistic structures in students' oral and written discourse, Rsrch. Tchng. Eng., 3: 70-85.
Goody, J., 1968, Introduction. in: "Literacy in Traditional Societies," J. Goody, ed., Cambridge U. Press, Cambridge.
Goody, J., 1977, "The Domestication of the Savage Mind," Cambridge U. Press, Cambridge.
Goody, J., 1980, Thought and writing, in: "Soviet and Western Anthropology," E. Gellner, ed., Columbia U. Press, N.Y.
Goody, J. and Watt, I., 1963, The consequences of literacy, Comp. St. in Soc. and Hist., 5:304-45.
Greenfield, P. M., 1972, Oral and written language: the consequences for cognitive development in Africa, the United States and England, Lang. and Sp., 15:169-78.
Gumperz, John J., 1964, Religion and social communication in a village in North India, J. As. St., 23:89-97.
Gumperz, John J., 1982, "Discourse Strategies," Cambridge U. Press, Cambridge.
Harrell, L. E., 1957, "A Comparison of the Development of Oral and Written Language in School-Age Children," Child Dev. Pub., Lafayette, Ind.
Havelock, E., 1963, "Preface to Plato," Harvard U.Press, Cambridge.
Hodge, Carleton T., 1975, Ritual and writing: an inquiry into the origin of Egyptian script, in: "Linguistics and Anthropology," M. D. Kinkade, K. L. Hale, and O. Werner, eds., Peter De Ridder, Lisse.
Hymes, Dell, ed., 1964, "Language in Culture and Society: A Reader in Linguistics and Anthropology," Harper and Row, N.Y.
Jensen, Hans, 1969, "Sign Symbol and Script," Putnam, N.Y.
Kay, Paul, 1977, Language evolution and speech style, in: "Sociocultural Dimensions of Language Change," G. Blount and M. Sanchez, eds., Academic Press, N.Y.

Leech, Edmund, 1976, "Culture and Communication: The Logic by which Symbols are Connected," Cambridge U. Press, Cambridge.

Lord, A. B., 1960, "The Singer of Tales," Harvard U. Press, Cambridge.

Newman, S., 1964, Vocabulary levels: Zuni sacred and slang usage. In Hymes (1964).

Norman, William M., 1980, Grammatical parallelisms in Quiche ritual language, Berkeley Ling. Soc.

Ochs, Elinor, 1979, Planned and unplanned discourse, in: "Discourse and Syntax," T. Givon, ed., Academic Press, N.Y.

O'Donnell, Roy C., 1974, Syntactic differences between speech and writing, Am. Sp., 49:102-10.

Olajubu, Chief Oludare, 1978, Yoruba verbal artist and their work, J. Am. Folklore, 91:675-90.

Olson, David R., 1977a, From utterance to text: the bias of language in speech and writing, Harvard Ed. Rev., 47:257-81.

Olson, David R., 1977b, Oral and written language and the cognitive processes of children, J. of Comm., 27:10-26.

Olson, David R., 1980a, On the language and authority of textbooks. J. of Comm., 30:186-98.

Olson, David R., 1980b, Some social aspects of meaning in oral and written language, in: "The Social Foundations of Language and Thought, Essays in Honor of Jerome S. Bruner," D. R. Olson, ed., Norton, N.Y.

Ong, W., 1971, "Rhetoric, Romance and Technology: Studies in the Interaction of Expression and Culture," Cornell U. Press, Ithaca.

Ong, W., 1980, Literacy and orality in our times, J. of Comm., 30:197-204.

Orasanu, Judith, this volume, Verbal reasoning: pragmatic, operational, and schematic aspects.

Oxenham, J., 1980, "Literacy: Writing, Reading and Social Organisation," Routledge and Kegan Paul, London.

Peek, Philip M., 1981, The power of words in African verbal arts, J. of Am. Folklore, 91:675-90.

Poole, Millicent E. and Field, T. W., 1976, A comparison of oral and written code elaboration, Lang. and Sp., 19:305-11.

Rosemont, H., 1974, On representing abstractions in archaic Chinese, Phil. East and West, 24:71-88.

Sherzer, Joel F., 1977a, Cuna Ikala: literature in San Blas, *in*: "Verbal Art as Performance," R. Bauman, ed., Newbury House, Rowley, MA.

Sherzer, Joel F., 1977b, Semantic systems, discourse structures, and the ecology of language *in*: "Stud. in Lang. Variation," R. Fasold and R. Shuy, eds., Wash. D.C., Georgetown.

Smith, John D., 1977, The singer or the song? A reassessment of Lord's oral theory," *Man*, 12:141-53.

Swadesh, Morris, 1971, "The Origin and Diversification of Language," Aldine, Chicago.

Tannen, Deborah, 1979, What's in a frame? Surface evidence for underlying expectations, *in*: "New Directions in Discourse Processing," R. Freedle, ed., Ablex, Norwood.

Tannen, Deborah, 1980a, A comparative analysis of oral narrative strategies: Athenian Greek and American English, *in*: "The Pear Stories: Cognitive, Cultural, and Linguistic Aspects of Narrative Production," W. L. Chafe, ed., Ablex, Norwood.

Tannen, Deborah, 1980b, Spoken/written language and the oral/literate continuum, Berkeley Ling. Soc.

Tannen, Deborah, this volume, The myth of orality vs. literacy.

T'sou, Benjamin K., 1968, Some aspects of linguistic parallelism and chinese versification, *in*: "Studies presented to Professor Roman Jakobson by his Students," C. E. Gribble, ed., Slavica Pub., Cambridge.

Vygotsky, L., 1962, "Thought and Language," MIT Press, Cambridge.

Woolbert, C. H., 1922, Speaking and writing--a study of differences, *Q. J. of Sp. Ed.*, 8:271-85.

THE MYTH OF ORALITY AND LITERACY

Deborah Tannen

Georgetown University

In my research on discourse over the last few years, I became aware that theoretical work done in the fields of anthropology, rhetoric, and psychology on oral and literate tradition sheds light on a variety of discourse phenomena. In investigating how this is so, I concluded that it is not orality and literacy per se that accounts for the findings of the oral/literate research, but rather that typically oral and typically written discourse reflects relatively more focus on interpersonal involvement and content, respectively. However, there is something very tantalizing about dichotomies, and something catchy about the notion of orality *versus* literacy. People continued to walk away from my talks and my articles with the oral/literate split more prominent in their minds than what I intended as my main idea: that it is not orality vs. literacy per se that is the key distinction, but relative focus on involvement vs. content.

That is why I have titled this paper "The *Myth* of Orality and Literacy," hoping to make more memorable the observation that, though research on orality and literacy underlies many of the observations I am going to make, findings of that research nonetheless reflect phenomena cutting across spoken and written modes. In particular, here I will trace my thinking about spoken and written language and orality and literacy and then show that many features that have been associated exclusively with literacy are rhetorical strategies found in spoken discourse. I will suggest that one major hypothesis about literacy and written language -- the decontextualization hypothesis --

is indeed a myth, but another -- the cohesion hypothesis -- is not.

HOW I DISCOVERED ORALITY AND LITERACY

I "discovered" orality vs. literacy as a theoretical framework when I was stumped by my own data. I was working on a project analyzing narratives told by people who had seen a film. On this project,[1] we had a short film made which had sound but no dialogue, showed it to twenty women between the ages of 18 and 26, had each one tell another woman of roughly the same age what she had seen in the film, and tape-recorded and later painstakingly transcribed the narratives. This process was repeated in many different countries in order to introduce a cross-cultural component to the research. I took the film to Greece and showed it to twenty women in Athens, repeating the procedure of the experiment there. Then I set about comparing the narratives told by Greek and American women about the same film.

I found that the American women in our study tended to approach the telling about the film as a memory task, whereas the Greek women tended to approach it as a story-telling task. The Americans seemed to struggle to recall as many details as possible, and to get them in correct chronological order ("Let's see is it while he's up in the ladder? or ... or before"). They also tended to talk about the film as a film, using cinematic jargon ("camera angle," "soundtrack," "the scene shifts"). When they exercised their critical acumen, it was directed at the filmmaker's technique. They criticized the soundtrack ("it was REALLY LOUD"), the costumes ("they were supposed to be farmerish and really just had clothes like a person with like ... store levis and a new red bandana around his neck"), and the acting ("He'd never make it as a fruitpicker").

In contrast, the Greeks told better stories. They included only those details which contributed to some main point they were building toward, and that main point was never about the film as a film, but about the film's message -- for example, that it showed the beauty of agricultural life. As a result, the Greek narratives were significantly shorter, an average of 84 "idea units"

(Chafe, 1980). Moreover, the Greeks interpreted more; they ascribed social roles and motives to the characters, and they offered explanations, judgments, and even philosophization about their actions. The Greek tendency to interpret more showed up on every level of discourse, from the broadest (for example, the "main point" of the narrative or the addition of a long soliloquy about the meaning of the film) to the narrowest (such as lexical choice, whereby, for example, with striking uniformity, the Greek speakers referred to the man in the film as a _farmer_ or _worker_, whereas the Americans referred to him as a _man_ or a _pearpicker_). The former categorizations entail the interpretation of the man's status and role, whereas the latter do not.

I was intrigued by these findings, but I was not sure what to make of them. At this point of consternation, John Gumperz suggested that I look at the literature on oral vs. literate tradition.

I turned once again to the classic article by Goody & Watt (1963), and to Goody's more recent book (1977), _Domestication of the Savage Mind_; to Walter Ong's (1967, 1977) work, and Havelock (1963), who inspired him. I turned as well to an article by David Olson which was then being passed around in manuscript and which finally appeared in the _Harvard Educational Review_ (1977). In addition, an article by Paul Kay (1977) deals with similar issues from the point of view of the evolution of language.

A number of hypotheses run through these sources. One is that the introduction of writing (although perhaps one should say "print") introduced new attitudes toward knowledge and information. It made possible and set value on rote memory as opposed to constructive memory, the former aspiring to slavish accuracy of detail, the latter aspiring to accuracy of spirit but not of detail. (Here the work of Lord, 1960, on oral formulaic tradition was inspirational. Lord, and his teacher, Parry, determined that oral epics were not memorized but recreated at each telling by stitching together formulaic expressions, and draping them over the skeleton of a familiar plot). Olson summarized, catchily, that in writing "the meaning is in the text" and in speaking "the meaning is in the context."

In these primary sources, and in much writing about language and in particular about composition that has been inspired by these sources, there has developed a decontextualization hypothesis: that in literate discourse the accuracy of detail is valued, and that literate discourse is decontextualized or text-focused rather than context-focused.

In a sense, the Americans in my cross-cultural narrative study were approaching the film narrative as a more decontextualized task, as they struggled to achieve accurate recall of details, whereas the Greeks strove for an effective story and were more inclined to omit or alter details. In this sense, the Americans used more literate strategies in their tellings. However, there is another sense in which the Americans' narratives were not decontextualized at all. They were not approaching narrative as a task contextualized in interpersonal interaction, but rather as a task contextualized in school. They were using strategies that seemed appropriate to the context they in fact were in: a university setting.

This perspective reflects a growing dissatisfaction with the notion that any discourse can be decontextualized (for example, Rader, 1982), and that what has been thought "literate" is in fact associated with formal schooling. (This conclusion is elaborately and meticulously demonstrated in Scribner and Cole, 1981). The emphasis on correct memory for detail, chronological sequence, and getting facts straight without personal evaluation, which the Americans in this study exhibited, is associated with this kind of literate or school-based strategy. The Greeks, on the other hand, being less concerned with slavish accuracy of detail and more concerned with telling a good story, were approaching the task using strategies learned in everyday interaction. Indeed, there is indication that Greeks (and members of many other cultures as well) employ such interactive strategies more regularly, in both school and business settings, where many Americans think it more appropriate to conventionally ignore interpersonal concerns and focus on content.

The point here is not that the Greeks are oral and the Americans literate. That is the misconception I specifically want to caution against. Quite the contrary, the findings of the study demonstrate that these oral and literate strategies all appear in oral language.

Thus we have exploded two myths about literacy: (1) that writing is decontextualized and (2) that text-focused discourse is found only in writing.

Another strand of my research (Tannen 1982a; 1982b) brought me face to face with a second hypothesis about literacy and orality which I believe is not a myth -- what I call the <u>cohesion</u> hypothesis: that spoken discourse establishes cohesion through paralinguistic features, whereas written discourse does so through lexicalization.

THE COHESION HYPOTHESIS

In speaking, everything that is said must be said in some way: at some pitch, in some tone of voice, at some rate of speed, with some expression or lack of expression in the voice and on the face. All these nonverbal and paralinguistic features reveal the speaker's attitude toward the message and establish cohesion -- that is, show relationships among ideas, highlight relative importance, foreground and background information, and so on. Just as Bateson (1972) observes that in a social setting one cannot not communicate (the act of keeping silent is a communication within the frame of interaction), just so, one cannot speak without showing one's attitude toward the message and the speech activity.

In contrast, in writing, the features of nonverbal and paralinguistic channels are not available. A person may wrinkle his or her face up until it cracks while he or she writes, but this will not show up on the written page. He or she may yell or whisper or sing while composing sentences, but the words as they fall on the page will not reflect this.

Therefore, in writing, the relationships between ideas and the writer's attitude toward them must be lexicalized. This can be done by stating outright (one thinks of the contrast between laughing while saying something, or writing "humorously;" by winking while speaking, or writing "I don't mean this literally"), by careful choice of words with just the right connotation, by complex syntactic constructions and transitional phrases, and so on. Thus a number of linguists have found that in spoken narrative (and I think the genre narrative is important), most ideas are strung together with no conjunctions or with the minimal conjunction "and" (Chafe, 1982; Kroll, 1977; Ochs, 1979). In contrast, in written narrative, conjunctions are chosen which show the relationship between ideas ("so," "because"), and subordinate constructions are used which do some of the work of foregrounding and backgrounding which would be done paralinguistically in speaking.

Thus we have the second hypothesis: that typically spoken discourse relies on paralinguistic and nonverbal channels, whereas written discourse relies on lexicalization for the establishment of cohesion.

ORAL AND LITERATE STRATEGIES IN DISCOURSE

The idea that spoken discourse can exhibit strategies associated with orality or literacy (that is, with typically spoken- or written-like discourse) can be traced back to what Bernstein (1964) called restricted and elaborated codes. Bernstein found that children's discourse, as elicited by experimental tasks, fell into two stylistic types, which he identified as different "codes." The two codes might be represented by something like this: in describing a picture, a child using restricted code might say, "They hit it through there and he got mad"; a child using elaborated code might say, "The kids were playing ball and hit the ball through the window. The man who lived in the house got mad at them." Now a person will have found the second version easier to understand, only because he or she does not have the picture in front of him or her.

Bernstein did not associate these two codes with orality and literacy, but this connection is observed by Kay (1977). Furthermore, Cook-Gumperz and Gumperz (1981) point out that the overt lexicalization of background material which is perfectly obvious in the context of interaction is akin to literacy. (See Michaels and Collins, 1982, for a demonstration of how primary school teachers prepare children to use literate strategies in speaking).

ORAL AND LITERATE STRATEGIES IN CONVERSATIONAL STYLE

I would like to turn now to my own research on conversational style. By tape-recording and transcribing two and a half hours of naturally occurring conversation at Thanksgiving dinner among six participants of various ethnic and geographic backgrounds, I was able to describe the linguistic and paralinguistic features that made up participants' speaking styles in this setting. I focused on such features as pacing, rate of speech, overlap and interruption, intonation, pitch, loudness, syntactic structures, topic, storytelling, irony, humor, and so on (Tannen 1979b). Many of these features turned out to cluster in the styles of participants such that three of them seemed to share what might be called one style, while the other three clearly did not share this style. I have called the "dominant" style "high-involvement," since many of the features which characterized it could be understood as placing emphasis, or what Gumperz calls the "signalling load," on interpersonal involvement, or the interpersonal dynamic of the interaction. In this sense, this style can be associated with oral strategies. The others who did not share this style expected strategies that may be seen as more literate-like in style, for they placed more of the signalling load on content.

One way in which this pattern emerged was in attitude toward and tendency to use overlap or simultaneous speech. Three of the participants in the conversation I studied were what I have called cooperative overlappers. That is, two or more of them often talked at the same time, but this overlapping speech did not mean that they were not listening to each other, and it did not mean that they wanted to grab the floor -- that is, to interrupt each other. Often, a listener talked at the same time as a speaker to show encouragement, to show understanding by uttering "response cries" (Goffman, 1981), even by telling little mini-stories to show understanding, to finish the speaker's sentences to demonstrate that the listener knew where the sentence was headed. All of this overlapping gives the speaker the assurance that he or she is not in the conversation alone. The active listener often asked questions of the speaker which the speaker obviously would have answered anyway, not to indicate that they thought the speaker was not going to tell, but to assure the speaker that the information was eagerly awaited. (Space does not permit the presentation of examples to demonstrate this, as they require detailed discussion of line-by-line explication. However, such examples and analysis can be found in Tannen 1979b; 1981a; 1981b; in press).

The preference for overlapping talk in some settings has been reported among numerous ethnic groups (Armenian-American, Black-American, West Indies, Cape Verdean-American, to name just a few). The preference for overlapping talk sacrifices the clear relay of information for the show of conversational involvement. In that sense, it is typically interactive or oral as opposed to literate in style. The effect of overlapping or "chiming in" with speakers who share this style is to grease the conversational wheels. But when speakers use this device with others who do not expect or understand its use, the effect is quite the opposite. The other speaker, feeling interrupted, stops talking. (The paradoxical aspect of this style clash is that the interruption is actually created by the one who stops talking when he or she was expected to continue). This is the obvious and natural reaction of anyone who assumes that in conversation only one person speaks at a time. Such a strategy is literate in style in the sense that it puts emphasis on content: uttering a complete message, a kind of elaborated code. (It is important to note however that this is simply one kind of elaboration, that of the message channel. The other style is using elaboration of another channel: the emotive or interpersonal one. This is discussed in Tannen, 1980b, 1981c).

Another aspect of the oral/literate strategy differences that emerged in this study of conversational style is how speakers got to the point of their stories (i.e. when they told about experiences) and what the point of their stories was likely to be. Speakers of the style I have characterized as using oral strategies (1) told more stories, (2) were more likely to tell stories about their personal experiences, (3) were more likely to have the point of their stories about their own feelings about those experiences, and, finally, perhaps most important, (4) generally did not lexicalize the point of their stories but dramatized them by recreating the speaker's own reaction or mimicry of the characters in the narrative.

These differences in storytelling styles left all participants feeling a bit dissatisfied with the narratives told by those who used a different style. Both tended to react to stories told in the other style with a variant of "What's the point?" -- the rejoinder Labov (1972) has aptly called "withering."

Only the briefest examples can be given here, but detailed examples and discussion can be found in Tannen 1979b (with somewhat fewer examples reproduced in Tannen, 1980b).

Following is an example of a story by Kurt told during Thanksgiving dinner.

(1) K: Í have a little sèven-year-old student ...
a little gírl who wears those. ..... Shé ..
is too → p

(2) T: [She wears those? [chuckle]

K: múch. Can yóu imagine? She's séven years
acc
old, and she síts in her chair and she goes...
acc———]
[squeals and squirms in his seat.]

(3) T: Oh:: Go::d. ... She's only SEVen?

(4) K: And I say well .. hów about let's dò sò-and-
so. And she says ... [Ókay. ... Jùst like thát.
acc ———] [squealing]

(5) T: [Oh:::::
p

(6) D: [What does it méan.
p, acc

(7) K: It's just so ... [She's acting like such a
p
little girl already.

K = Kurt
D = David
T = DT (the author)

Transcription conventions:

p = pianissimo (soft)
acc = accelerando (fast)
: indicates lengthening of vowel
⌈indicates high pitch. ⌈⌈indicates very high pitch.
⟶ indicates speech continues uninterrupted (look for continuation on next line).

It is clear from the transcript that the two listeners, David and I (represented in the transcript as D and T respectively), have different reactions to the story. In (3) and (5) I show, through paralinguistically expaggerated responses, that I have appreciated it. In contrast, David states in (6) that he does not understand what the story is supposed to mean. When I played this segment of the taped conversation to David later, he said that Kurt had not said what it was about the girl's behavior that he was trying to point out. Moreover, when Kurt answered David's question in (7), he did not explain at all; David said that "such a little girl" to him means "such a grownup," whereas what Kurt meant was "such a coquette." David seemed to feel that Kurt was not telling the story right: he should say what he means. To Kurt, the point was obvious and should not be stated.

At other times in the transcript David tells stories, and there the reactions of Kurt and the other oral-stylists indicate that they feel David is unnecessarily stating the obvious and not getting to the point quickly enough (see Tannen, 1979b, for detailed analysis).

By expecting the point of a story to be made explicit, and by finding events more important than character's feelings, some of the participants in this conversation were exhibiting expectations of literate-like strategies in speech. By expecting the point of a story to be dramatized by the speaker and inferred by the hearer, and by finding personal feelings more interesting than events, the other speakers were exhibiting oral-like strategies.

It is particularly significant that the speakers in my study who used what I am calling oral strategies were highly literate. Many of the studies which have distinguished between oral and literate strategies in spoken style have done so to explain the failure of children of certain ethnic groups to learn to write and read well. The speakers I have found using oral strategies in speaking are New Yorkers of East European Jewish background, a cultural group that has been documented as having a highly oral tradition (Kirschenblatt-Gimblett, 1974) as well as a highly literate one. Thus, individuals and groups are not _either_ oral _or_ literate. Rather, people have at their disposal and are inclined to use, based on individual habits as well as social conventions, strategies associated with either or both in speech and in writing.

ORAL AND LITERATE BASED FLUENCY

I would like to present one final example of how both oral and literate strategies surface in spoken discourse, suggested by recent work by Fillmore (1979) on fluency. Fillmore distinguishes four different types of oral fluency, the abilities to:

1. talk at length with few pauses
2. have appropriate things to say in a wide range of contexts
3. talk in semantically coherent, reasoned, and dense sentences
4. be creative and imaginative with language

I would suggest that the first two of these types of fluency are associated with strategies that have been called oral. They grow out of interactive or social goals, to keep talk going, where the message content is less important than the fact of talk. In contrast, the last two are literate-like types of fluency, since they depend on the intra-textual relationships (as in (3)) and build on words as carrying meaning in themselves rather than triggering social meaning (as in (4)).

CONCLUSION

In conclusion, then, both oral and literate strategies can be seen in spoken discourse. Understanding this, let us not think of orality and literacy as an absolute split, and let us not fall into the trap of thinking of literacy, or written discourse, as decontextualized. Finally, the examples presented of conversational style make it clear that it is possible to be both highly oral and highly literate. Thus, let us not be lured into calling some folks oral and others literate.

NOTE

[1]The project was funded by NIMH Grant 25592 to Wallace Chafe, at the University of California, Berkeley. Findings of this project are reported in papers collected in Chafe (1980), as well as in Tannen (1979a). The specific research discussed here, comparing Greek and American narratives, is presented and discussed in Tannen (1980a). Other parts of the present chapter are adapted from Tannen forthcoming.

REFERENCES

Bateson, Gregory, 1972, "Steps to an Ecology of Mind," Ballantine, N.Y.

Bernstein, Basil, 1964, Elaborated and restricted codes: their social origins and some consequences, Am. Anthr., 66:55-69.

Chafe, Wallace, 1980, "The Pear Stories: Cognitive, Cultural, and Linguistic Aspects of Narrative Production," Ablex, Norwood.

Chafe, Wallace, 1982, Integration and involvement in speaking, writing, and oral literature, in: "Spoken and Written Language: Exploring Orality and Literacy," D. Tannen, ed., Ablex, Norwood.

Cook-Gumperz, Jenny, and Gumperz, John J., 1981, From oral to written culture: the transition to literacy, in: "Variation in Writing," M. Whiteman, ed., LEA, Hillsdale.

Fillmore, Charles J., 1979, On fluency, in: "Individual Differences in Language Ability and Language Behavior," C. Fillmore, D. Kempler, and W. S.-Y. Wang, eds., Academic Press, N.Y.

Goffman, Erving, 1981, "Forms of Talk," U. of Penn. Press, Philadelphia.

Goody, Jack R., 1977, "Domestication of the Savage Mind," Cambridge U. Press, Cambridge.

Goody, Jack R. and Watt, Ian, 1963, The consequences of literacy, Comp. Stds. Soc. Hist., 5:304-45.

Kay, Paul, 1977, Language evolution and speech style, in: "Sociocultural Dimensions of Language Change," B. Blount and M. Sanchez, eds., Academic Press, N.Y.

Kirshenblatt-Gimblett, Barbara, 1974, The concept and varieties of narrative performance in East European Jewish culture, in: "Explorations in the Ethnography of Speaking," R. Bauman and J. Sherzer, eds., Cambridge U. Press, Cambridge.

Kroll, Barbara, 1977, Combining ideas in written and spoken English: a look at subordination, in: "Discourse across time and space," E. Keenan and T. Bennet, eds., Ling. Dept., USC.

Labov, William, 1972, "Language in the Inner City," U. of Penn., Philadelphia.

Lord, Albert, 1960, "The Singer of Tales," Harvard U. Press, Cambridge.

Michaels, Sarah and Collins, Jim, 1982, Oral discourse style: Classroom interaction and the acquisition of literacy, in: "Coherence in Spoken and Written Discourse," D. Tannen, ed., Ablex, Norwood.

Ochs, Elinor, 1979, Planned and unplanned discourse, in: "Discourse and Syntax," T. Givón, ed., Academic Press, N.Y.

Olson, David, 1977, From utterance to text: the bias of language in speech and writing, Harvard Ed. Rev., 47:257-81.

Ong, Walter J., S. J., 1967, "The Presence of the Word," Yale U. Press, New Haven.

Ong, Walter J., S. J., 1977, "Interfaces of the Word." Cornell U. Press, Ithaca.

Rader, Margaret, 1982, Context in written language: the case of imaginative fiction, in: "Spoken and Written Language: Exploring Orality and Literacy," D. Tannen, ed., Ablex, Norwood.

Scribner, Sylvia, and Cole, Michael, 1981, "The Psychology of Literacy," Harvard U. Press, Cambridge.

Tannen, Deborah, 1979a, What's in a frame? Surface evidence for underlying expectations, in: "New Dimensions in Discourse Processing," R. O. Freedle, ed., Ablex, Norwood.

Tannen, Deborah, 1979b, "Processes and Consequences of Conversational Style," Ph.D. Dissertation, University of California, Berkeley.

Tannen, Deborah, 1980a, A comparative analysis of oral narrative strategies: Athenian Greek and American English, _in_: "The Pear Stories," W. Chafe, ed., Ablex, Norwood.

Tannen, Deborah, 1980b, Implications of the oral/literate continuum for cross-cultural communication, _in_: "Current Issues in Bilingual Education," J. Alatis, ed., Georgetown U. Press, Washington, D.C.

Tannen, Deborah, 1981a, New York Jewish conversational style, _Int. J. of the Soc. of Lang._, 30:133-49.

Tannen, Deborah, 1981b, The machine-gun question: An example of conversational style, _J. of Pragmatics_, 5:forthcoming.

Tannen, Deborah, 1981c, Indirectness in discourse: ethnicity as conversational style, _Discourse Proc._, 4:221-38.

Tannen, Deborah, 1982a, Oral and literate strategies in spoken and written narratives, _Lang._ 58:forthcoming.

Tannen, Deborah, ed., 1982b, "Spoken and Written Language: Exploring Orality and Literacy," Ablex, Norwood.

Tannen, Deborah, in press, When is an overlap not an interruption? _in_: "First Delaware Symposium on Language Studies," R. DiPietro, W. Frawley, and A. Wedel, eds., U. of Delaware Press, Newark.

Tannen, Deborah, forthcoming, Oral and literate strategies in spoken and written discourse, _in_: "Literacy in the 1980's," R. Bailey, ed., U. of Michigan Press, Ann Arbor.

SOVIET PSYCHOLINGUISTICS: IMPLICATIONS FOR TEACHING OF WRITING

James Thomas Zebroski

The Ohio State University

In the last decade the work of Lev Semyonovich Vygotsky has finally begun to receive the attention in the United States that is so rich deserves. The genius of Vygotsky shines through his work despite the years of suppression in the Soviet Union, despite the frequent behavioristic misinterpretations placed on his work in this country, and despite the mistaken identification of his approach and concerns with those of Jean Piaget. Vygotsky's *Thought and Language* and *Mind in Society* have been widely read, and his insights into inner speech, the zone of proximal development, the dialectics of thought and language, and the development of word meanings and scientific concepts have proven significant, especially for those of us who are concerned with the learning and development of reading and writing abilities. Yet increasing acceptance has its own dangers.

While interest in Vygotsky and in his work in the fields of psychology and psycholinguistics is high, less attention is being paid to the context from which Vygotsky's work comes. This is particularly true of the philosophical, semiotic, and historical grounds of Vygotsky's theory. Vygotsky's work is, in this country, generally viewed to be comparable to that of Jean Piaget and is generally categorized as that of a cognitive psychologist. Yet Vygotsky viewed his work in much broader terms than these. His study of the classics of Marxism-Leninism is highly original and deeply philosophical. His application and extension of Marx's basic concept of activity is itself new. His interest in signs and sign theory foreshadows the recent development of the field of semiotics (see Wertsch, 1980; 1981). Vygotsky's attempt to forge the basis of a unified social science that connects history and sociology with psychology and pedagogy belies the narrow view of Vygotsky as a cognitive psychologist.

Not only has the current popularity of Vygotsky created a tendency to overlook the larger dimensions of his work, but this popularity, especially in the field of composition, has not been accompanied by the necessary study of the elaboration and development of Vygotsky's theory in the work of his colleagues and students. This work of the "Vygotskian school" is of critical importance if we are to understand Vygotsky's work itself. Scholars such as A. R. Luria and A. N. Leontiev, who were both co-workers with Vygotsky back in the late 1920's and early 1930's, continued his work for over forty years after Vygotosky's premature death and during the subsequent public suppression of that work (see Luria, 1979). P. Ya. Gal'perin, V. V. Davydov, and A. Markova, among many others, have continued this approach specifically in the area of the teaching and mastery of reading and writing (Markova, 1979). Except for the research of a few Americans, many of whom studied in the Soviet Union with these colleagues of Vygotsky, current reference to Vygotsky in the composition field is more perfunctory than exhaustive, reflecting more an awareness of the existence of Vygotsky's English works than an in-depth understanding and application of his theory.

With concerns such as these in mind, a small group of individuals in the Department of Humanities Education at The Ohio State University first came together over four years ago to try to make sense out of Vygotsky in some deeper way. Meeting regularly ever since, this group has attempted to get as clear an understanding of Vygotsky's theories as possible, given the restrictions of availability of translations of works from that tradition. Our specific interest has been to apply these concepts to our understanding of the development of writing processes in secondary and college level students. We believed then, as now, that to understand Vygotsky's work clearly, one must understand the work of the Vygotskian school as a whole. Further, to understand the work of the Vygotskian school, one must deal with that theory on its own terms. One must understand its ontology and epistemology, and must be careful not simply to strip mine Vygotsky for what presently appears to be of value.

James Wertsch, one of the leading Vygotskian scholars in this country, cautions us about this. Wertsch warns:

> This all adds up to saying that one should not assume that it is usually possible to tap the Soviet literature for results about a particular phenomenon that is already being investigated in the West. Studies will occasionally be found that can provide such information, but it is much more often the case that the Soviet literature will approach a problem area in a new way and that one can benefit from it most by trying to understand this new theoretical approach rather than by trying to assimilate it into one's pre-existing ideas (Wertsch, 1977: viii-ix).

Thus, my aim here must, of necessity, be limited. It is undesirable simply to pull out some quotations from Vygotsky and apply them to current U.S. theories in composition. Yet it is impossible to present the theory of activity in its entirety, placing Vygotsky's insights into their proper context. Instead what I hope to do is to suggest the comprehensiveness and the richness of this theory of activity in Soviet psycholinguistics. To do this I shall sketch out three qualities of this theory that I find especially distinguish it from many current approaches to the study of composition. In addition, I shall speculate about possible implications this approach may have for the teaching and the study of the writing process.

Three qualities, in my mind, distinguish the Soviet theory of activity, and its application to the study of speech activity specifically, from corresponding U.S. alternatives in the field of composition. First, human beings are viewed as essentially active participants in both their world and in their learning. They, surprisingly enough, are seen as the creators of their world, of history, rather than simply as products of that world and history. Second, language and culture are viewed relationally. This means that language processes are always studied not simply in terms of themselves, but also in terms of their use, their history, their connections to the other parts of social life. Third, language and cognitive processes are viewed dynamically, that is, as always in change. The focus of study, then, becomes what changes and how it changes both in language and in cognitive processes, rather than what "is." Thus for the time being, we can describe this Vygotskian view of the composing process as highly reconstructionist, relational, and dynamic.

It is this first quality of much of the work of the Soviets that attracted me to their interpretations of language processes. Vygotsky is what I might call a realistic optimist. He and his colleagues base their work on the premise that, although we are in one sense products of our history and culture, we are more importantly producers of that world. For a teacher, it seems difficult to hold any other view. From a Vygotskian perspective, instruction can make a difference, just as what people do does make a difference in history and in one's society. One of the best testimonies to this Vygotskian sense of the changes human beings make in their world, in their language, and in their own conceptions of themselves, is an article titled "The Social and the Individual in Language" (Leontiev and Leontiev, 1959). In this short but extremely dense article, the Leontievs discuss how, in several ways, language is "a product of...active reconstruction." (Leontiev and Leontiev, 1959:193). In composing studies in this country, the only approach that I have discovered that comes close to this sense of active creation and mastery of one's world and one's language is that approach that has been termed an epistemic approach to composition (see Dowst, 1980; Elasser and John-Steiner, 1977). Here, as in the writings of the Vygotskian school, we find a belief in writing as not only a means of message transmission, but as also a generative, meaning creating process. Writing and language thus not only describe and "transmit" our world, but they also create it. The Leontievs, in this article, describe in detail how this process comes about. Again, I stress that like much else out of this school of thought, this article makes for difficult reading. Yet it is one of the best attempts at explaining what the best U.S. theories of composition have always assumed--the power of the generative quality of writing. And at its heart is the basic assumption of the active nature of so-called language acquisition, of second language learning, and of student learning of the writing/reading processes. The importance of this assumption of the active reconstruction by the student, of his/her "world" will become evident later in this paper when we discuss the crucial role the Soviets attribute to reflection and metalinguistic awareness in the teaching and mastery of reading and writing.

The second characteristic of much of the work that comes out of the Vygotskian tradition is the understanding of language and thought in relational terms. What I mean by this is that the Soviets tend not to study or discuss language without also bringing in social context. Yet a relational view of language goes even further than this. It assumes that not only does social context add to our understanding of language and its use, but also that it is at the _very center_ of such a study. Context thus is not simply some additional details that one attaches to findings about language; rather context provides the very vantage point from which to observe and study language (compare, e.g., Hymes', 1974, approach to linguistics). In fact, the very name that scientists in the Vygotskian school attach to this field of study suggests the importance they place on a relational view. A. A. Leontiev prefers to call this field that of _speech activity_ rather than psycholinguistics (see Wertsch, 1977). When he uses this term, he is not simply reducing thinking and writing to speech. Rather, Leontiev uses the word _speech_ in a very broad way to emphasize that the focus of study ought to be on the relations _between_ various language processes like speaking, listening, thinking, reading, and writing instead of on isolated static linguistic behaviors. Leontiev's use of the term _activity_ indicates that these language processes must be understood not simply in terms of themselves, but also in their connections with the social context. The use of this term also relates speech and other language processes with other activities, like labor, which characterize human life. In addition, the use of the term _activity_ intimately ties speech and language processes to the broader framework of the theory of activity and its consideration of actions and operations (for the notion of activity, see Leontiev, 1977). Finally, the term indicates that to understand psycholinguistic processes, one needs to go beyond individual mental activity to search for the interrelations between these processes and social relations.

This is because Vygotsky contended that all higher psychological processes originate as shared interpsychological functions and are later internalized as intrapsychological functions in the individual. To understand these processes, therefore, one must trace their history back to the point at which they were shared and observe the transitions these processes undergo as they are internalized. All of these ideas are implicit in the term speech activity, and they all stem from the basic assumption made by the Vygotskian school that language must be studied relationally.

S. L. Rubinshtein, a contemporary of Vygotsky who developed his own psychological theory and tradition of scholarship, emphasizes the importance of keeping this relational view in mind. He notes:

> All phenomena in the world are interconnected. Every action is an interaction; every change of one entity is reflected in all others and is itself an answer to the change of still other phenomena acting upon it. Every external influence is refracted by the internal properties of that body, of that phenomena to which it is subjected... Each phenomenon is in a certain degree 'a mirror and echo of the universe.' At the same time, the result of this or that influence on any entity is conditioned by the very nature of the latter; the internal nature of phenomena is that 'prism' through which single objects and phenomena are reflected in others (Rubinshtein, quoted by Graham, 1972: 385).

Now once more we must emphasize the active nature of human mastery of psychological functions. The Vygotskian approach is quite clear about not arguing that we simply reproduce these shared functions. While the Vygotskian approach is highly contextual and ecological, and does insist that a full understanding only comes through a primary examination of context, it does not reduce human activity to behavior that is simply derived from the environment. Rather, we reconstruct our environment and ourselves, making of both something essentially new. The real focus of this work of the Vygotskian school, therefore, is on the transitions, on the interactions between the individual and environment, between nature and nurture, for each transition involves a transformation that necessarily alters the entire set of relations (see Wertsch, 1981:30-32). These transformations occurring at points of transition are critical to the Vygotskian theory, yet most readers of Vygotsky in this country tend to overlook or downplay the changes that must occur as functions are internalized.

That "prism" that Rubinshtein speaks of is extremely important, for it is one such transition. This "prism" of experience in human beings is gradually and increasingly regulated and reconstructed by the individual. Yet this individual's experience always entails interaction in a social context. Thus, mind can never be separated or studied in isolation from society; nor can the individual ever be considered apart from his culture, or that culture ever be separated from its history. Mind and society are not identities; they are a unity. The individual is not a little version of society, nor is society simply the sume of all individuals. Rather, the individual reconstructs and is reconstructed by his culture.

As if this all were not complicated enough, work out of the Vygotskian school insists that speech activity must not only be studied relationally at one point of time, but it must also be investigated <u>across</u> time in relational terms. As Blonsky (in Wertsch, 1981:27) notes, "Behavior can be understood only as the history of behavior." The relations between a person's early activity and those later developments and transformations of that activity are as critical as the study of simultaneous relations of speech to thought or of thought to writing. One needs both a synchronic and diachronic relational analysis to develop explanations of activity rather than simply descriptions of behavior (see Vygotsky, 1978:62-63). Thus, for example, if I really want to understand the writing activity of one of my current college freshmen, I need at some point to go back and trace out formative writing experiences of that student. Luria himself studied the roots of literacy in the scribbling of pre-schoolers. Clearly, this is a task that I as a teacher can only initiate. Yet it is an important one that I can encourage students themselves to engage in, in the context of my course. I will have more to say about this shortly.

This insistence on a developmental or genetic explanation applies not only to the study of the development of the individual, but also to the development of a culture and of specific activities within a culture, like literacy. The Vygotskian tradition, taken to its logical conclusion, argues that literacy here and now cannot be equated with literacy in other cultures or in other times. The contexts are different, so, regardless of the apparent similarities, the very acts of reading and writing must necessarily be different. Literacy in the U.S. in 1981 differs from literacy in the U.S. in 1971 or 1921 or 1821. Literacy changes because culture changes, and culture changes because goals and motives change. Therefore, from a Vygotskian perspective, a search for only universals of literacy impoverishes the understanding of the reading and writing processes and makes literacy programs less effective as well.

Clearly, we have already been discussing the third and final quality that is characteristic of the work of the Vygotskian school. This is the dynamic quality that is observed in mind, society, and literacy. Change, rather than stasis, is viewed as the norm. In fact, Wertsch (1979) notes that Vygotsky's book might be more accurately titled <u>Thinking and Speaking</u> to emphasize this dynamic aspect. Vygotsky himself characterizes this dynamic quality in his description of development.

> Our concept of development implies a rejection of the frequently held view that cognitive development results from the gradual accumulation of separate changes. We believe that child development is a complex dialectical process characterized by periodicity, unevenness in the development of different functions, metamorphosis or qualitative transformation of one form into another, intertwining of external and internal factors, and adaptive processes which overcome impediments that the child encounters. ... Scientific thought... sees revolution and evolution as two forms of development that are mutually related and mutually presuppose each other. Leaps in the child's development are seen by the

> scientific mind as no more than a moment in the general line of development (Vygotsky, 1978:73).

As a heuristic, Vygotsky, following the sense of this statement, might suggest that if one were to find those spans of writing development where the least seems to be occurring, what one might discover on closer examination are complex reconstructions and the origins of revolutionary leaps in development. This becomes an especially useful concept when we consider writing instruction since what are often mistaken for plateaus or even regressions in writing ability occurring in midcourse, might, from a Vygotskian perspective, be viewed as an indication of forward writing development. From this perspective, one would be very suspicious of student writing that began with abundant errors yet that did not show an increase in errors or at least a change in error types midway since it might imply students were more interested in playing it safe than in recognizing and mastering their error patterns. Shaughnessy's excellent Errors and Expectations gives ample illustration of the regularity and logic behind student errors. A Vygotskian finds much to his liking there, but would suggest that the logic and change in error patterns need to be placed not only in a synchronic analysis as Shaughnessy does in her study, but also in a diachronic analysis. Errors not only reveal a logic about them now; they show a pattern of evolution and development over time.

Now, what is the importance of all of this? How does this Vygotskian view of language as an active, relational, and dynamic process affect our view of writing and our approach to writing instruction? At least the following conclusions seem warranted.

First, if literacy development is in change, both socially and individually, we should not be surprised if methods of reading and writing instruction also vary from culture to culture and from time to time. In fact, we ought to be very suspicious of any searches for the universal method for the teaching of writing. Effective literacy instruction must, according to this approach, above all else be historically and culturally concrete. The method of writing instruction, then, needs to be derived from the ecology of the students. Just as language and thought are intimately connected to culture, so too are reading and writing derived from the culture rather than imposed on it. Writing and reading instruction can be no less organic.

Second, it follows from a Vygotskian perspective that it is the interrelations of the literate processes that must be stressed. As teachers, we ought to be quite suspicious of a course of instruction that separates reading from writing, and both from speaking and listening, and literacy itself from other artistic activities. While, clearly, speaking and writing follow different paths of development and display many contrasting qualities, they are nonetheless interrelated through their social motive and origins. Inner speech plays a critical role in thought, speech, and writing, and it is the researcher's task to more clearly trace out these interrelations between inner speech, speaking, writing, and reading. Similarly it is the teacher's task to understand more clearly how these different functions reinforce and feed back on each other. In addition, the teacher's task is to create a context that nurtures these interconnections, that encourages students to use these different functions, more completely elaborating them. Thus, it seems clear that certain types of discussion and thinking will have important effects on reading and writing.

Third, Vološinov (1973) argues that dialogue is the critical tie between these language activities. External dialogue is internalized to varying degrees as inner speech. Inner speech is then externalized as writing. There are thus at least two transitions and changes here that remove spoken dialogue from written "dialogue," not even considering the important influence of reading. Nevertheless, the unity between these forms remains. In the terms of the Vygotskian school, writing can be viewed as the "transformed form" of inner speech, which itself can be seen as the "transformed form" of external speech. If we were to think of writing in this way, even our consideration of the very products of writing would change. Again, Vološinov notes:

> Were we to probe deeper into the linguistic nature of paragraphs, we would surely find that in certain crucial respects paragraphs are

> analogous to exchanges in dialogue. The paragraph is something like a vitiated dialogue worked into the body of a monologic utterance. Behind the device of partitioning speech into units, which are termed paragraphs in this written form, lie orientation toward listener or reader and calculation of the latter's possible reactions. The weaker this orientation and calculation are, the less organized, as regards paragraphs, our speech will be (Vološinov, 1973:111-12).

Thus, if we were to try to create a sequence of writing assignments based on this Vygotskian sense of the primacy and continuity of dialogue, we would expect to begin with those kinds of writing most explicitly related to dialogue with others and move towards writing more related to dialogue (at this end point of the transformation, monologue) with self. Ironically, this is actually just the opposite of the order of most instructional sequences in composition that tend to begin with personal, monologic reflections and move towards persuasive and argumentative modes.

Fourth, the Vygotskian school as noted above attributes great importance to reflection in the instructional process. Reflection both in terms of group discussions and in terms of individual consideration of one's own use of language is dialogue about dialogue and represents an important force in directing learning. In Markova's (1979) report on language curriculum reforms in the Soviet Union, based on Vygotskian perspective, reflection is given an important place in class and individual activities. As noted above, it is usually not possible for teachers to do much of the kind of historical analysis of the development of literacy abilities that is required. Rather it becomes more important for the teacher to encourage students to follow up this kind of analysis for themselves. Practically speaking, this means having students talk, write, and think about the development of their own writing abilities and written products. Students can begin this reflective activity by writing papers about their writing, as well as commenting in writing about written teacher comments that they do not understand or agree with. The idea here is to encourage a kind of metalinguistic awareness in students.

Students need to learn about their own writing both in their own terms and in the teacher's language.

Fifth, and finally, as researchers we need to be aware of Vygotsky's arguments against Piaget's concept of egocentricity in speech and thought of young children. These arguments seem sound when applied to the development of writing abilities. Collins and Williamson (1981:23) rightly note that, "Recent research suggests that egocentrism as an explanation for abbreviated meaning in student writing deserves to be questioned." A close reading of Vygotsky would suggest that, if anything, the writing of beginning writers may appear egocentric because it is *overly* socialized, because it is *too* much for others, because it is not individuated *enough*. The problem of the so-called egocentric writer may be one of incomplete internalization of writing activities due simply to a lack of experience with the medium. This incomplete internalization, this failure to make the writing act one's own, may actually be encouraged by overemphasis on external social expectations concerning the writing. This is where reflection and encouraged metalinguistic awareness come in. The student needs not so much another external theory of writing, but rather needs to recreate and make explicit his or her own personal theory of writing derived both from personal experience with writing and from experience and knowledge obtained from other real writers. Reflection thus encourages the student to explicate and to reconstruct his or her own "grounded" theory of writing. One's own real activity becomes the basis from which one creates the object of study.

REFERENCES

Collins, James and Williamson, Michael, 1981, Spoken language and semantic abbreviation in writing, *Rsrch. Tchng. Eng.*, 15:23-35.

Dowst, Kenneth, 1980, The epistemic approach: writing, knowing, and learning, *in*: "Eight Approaches to Teaching Composition," T. Donovan and B. McClelland, eds., NCTE, Urbana.

Elasser, Nan and John-Steiner, Vera, 1977, An interactionist approach to literacy, *Hvd. Ed. Rev.*, 47:355-69.

Graham, Loren, 1972, "Science and Philosophy in the Soviet Union," Knopf, N.Y.

Hymes, Dell, 1974, "Foundations in Sociolinguistics," U. of Penn., Philadelphia.

Leontiev, A. N., 1978, "Activity, Consciousness, and Personality," Prentice-Hall, Englewood Cliffs.

Leontiev, A. N., and Leontiev, A. A., 1959, The social and individual in language, Lg. and Sp., 2:193-204.

Luria, A. R., 1979, "The Making of Mind," Harvard, Cambridge.

Markova, Ailita, 1979, "The Teaching and Mastery of Language," Sharpe, White Plains.

Vološinov, V., 1973, "Marxism and the Philosophy of Science," Seminar Press, N.Y.

Vygotsky, Lev, 1978, "Mind in Society," Harvard, Cambridge.

Wertsch, James (ed.), 1977, "Recent Trends in Soviet Psycholinguistics," Sharpe, White Plains.

Wertsch, James, 1979, From social interaction to higher psychological processes: a clarification and application of Vygotsky's theory, Hu. Dev., 22:1-22.

Wertsch, James, 1980, The significance of dialogue in Vygotsky's account of social, egocentric, and inner speech, Cont. Ed. Psych., 5:151-54.

Wertsch, James (ed.), 1981, "The Concept of Activity in Soviet Psychology," Sharpe, White Plains.

UNIVERSAL GRAMMAR AND COMPOSITION: RELATIVIZATION, COMPLEMENTATION, AND QUANTIFICATION

William Frawley

University of Delaware

INTRODUCTION

The purpose of this paper is to report the findings of an extensive study, in progress, of the applicability of a recent theory of syntax to writing. I am looking, in general, at how relational grammar, or _universal grammar_ (as it is commonly called), can predict and explain the syntactic differences in the prose of sophisticated and unsophisticated writers. In this paper in particular, I focus on how the range of usage of relative clauses, sentential complements, and quantifiers by sophisticated and unsophisticated writers adheres to the predictions of universal grammar for these syntactic phenomena. In what follows, I present a brief outline of universal grammar and its applicability to writing, a direct application of universal grammar to prose, and some closing commentary on what the use of universal grammar in writing suggests about a new definition of writing sophistication.

UNIVERSAL GRAMMAR

A Sketch of the Theory

Universal grammar has arisen as a theory in opposition to transformational grammar because, it is claimed, transformational grammar is unrealistic on two fundamental counts: (a) transformational grammar says little about syntax (i.e., does not address what it is supposed to address); (b) transformational grammar says little about how actual languages work (i.e., does not make universal claims). As to (a), universal grammar theorists argue that transformational grammar does not focus on the basic notions of syntax: namely, the systematic relations, such as "subject of," "direct object of," "indirect object of," "object of preposition," etc., which are responsible for combining words into sentences. Thus, the claims of universal grammar are claims about syntax as a combinatorial process, not as a system of derivations or transformations. As to (b), universal grammar theorists give evidence for their claims from extensive surveys of languages, which transformational grammar has generally been accused of not doing. In this sense, universal grammar deserves the title "universal" since its purpose is to specify the combinatorial rules of syntax (relations) which all human languages must share and to justify such claims with extensive empirical evidence.

To illustrate the mechanisms of this theory, let me describe the work in universal grammar that has been done on relativization, complementation, and quantification. Keenan and Comrie (1977), in their now famous article on relativization, found that there was a universal hierarchy of grammatical phenomena which could undergo relativization. From an elaborate survey of the syntactic operations in hundreds of languages, they discovered that all languages relativize subjects (i.e., can create relative clauses whose subjects are relativized: e.g., the boy who is here...), that fewer languages relativize direct objects (e.g., the boy whom we know...), that even fewer relativize indirect objects (e.g., the boy whom I gave the book to...), and that even fewer than those relativize oblique objects (e.g., the knife with which I cut the salami...). From these observations, they developed the Noun Phrase Accessibility Hierarchy (NPAH)--- SUBJECT > DIRECT OBJECT > INDIRECT OBJECT > OBLIQUE OBJECT > GENITIVE > OBJECT OF COMPARISON ---which is to be read as follows: subjects are more universally relativizable than direct objects, which are more universally relativizable than indirect objects, which are more universally relativizable than oblique objects, which are more universally relativizable than genitives, which are more universally relativizable than objects of comparison. This is the principle of accessibility, which is that some Noun Phrases are more accessible than others for relativization, and is complemented by the continuous segment principle (see Johnson, 1977), which is such that a language's access to NP's must be continuous. That is, if a language can relativize an NP which is low on the NPAH, then it must also be able to relativize all categories above that NP. English is a perfect example of the continuous segment principle since it can relativize OBJECT OF COMPARISON (the boy whom there was nobody taller than) and everything above that category on the NPAH (GENITIVE: the boy whose book I have; OBLIQUE OBJECT: the boy with whom I went; and so on). But Tagalog and Malagasy can relativize only subjects, nothing lower. Furthermore, languages employ elaborate strategies to promote NP's to higher positions on the NPAH in order to relativize. One common strategy is passivization, which creates a subject out of an object, and many languages (e.g., French, Albanian, Cebuano) employ passivization for this very purpose of the promotion of NP's on the Accessibility Hierarchy.

Now, it is less essential to understand the details of these arguments (some of which have been questioned---see Manaster-Ramer, 1979) than to follow the general principles of the theory: that there exists a universal hierarchy of accessibility for relativization and that languages employ strategies for accessing continuous parts of the hierarchy. It is principles such as these which also operate in the universal distribution of sentential complements. Dryer (1980) has made a survey as extensive as that done by Keenan and Comrie, but focused on the position of sentential complements (i.e., sentences which function as NP's, such as "you said that" in "I don't believe that you said that"). He has found that there is a universal hierarchy for sentential complements: CLAUSE-FINAL > CLAUSE-INITIAL > CLAUSE-INTERNAL. That is, languages "prefer" sentential complements in clause-final position (e.g., I know that you are here), and those are "more preferable" than clause-initial ones (e.g., That you came surprised me), which are "more preferable" than clause-internal ones (e.g., ??*John that you arrived believed---English has no access to clause-internal complements, but some languages, such as Hopi, Lakota, and Tamil, productively employ clause-internal complements). As with the NPAH, the complement hierarchy predicts not only that there are more accessible complements in languages but also that languages develop strategies to promote complements to higher positions on the hierarchy. English, for example, productively employs the Extraposition and Pseudo-Cleft transformations to move sentential complements from clause-initial to clause-final position (or to promote complements on the hierarchy): that you came surprised me → it surprised me that you came (Extraposition); that you came surprised me → what surprised me was that you came (Pseudo-Cleft).

Finally, Ioup (1975) has looked at the universal properties of quantifiers and has found that there are two hierarchies which determine the distribution of quantifiers in sentences. One such hierarchy is the hierarchy of inherent scope, which shows that quantifiers are ordered with respect to each other according to the inherent range of effect which they have on other expressions in the sentences in which they (the quantifiers) occur. Ioup's inherent scope hierarchy is as follows: each > every > all > most > many > several > some > a few. That is, inherent scope of quantifiers decreases as one moves to the right. Thus, "each" has more inherent scope than "every" and so on.

Ioup's second hierarchy is the hierarchy of scope according to grammatical function. This hierarchy is a gradience which captures the scope of a quantifier according to its syntactic function in a sentence: SUBJECT > INDIRECT OBJECT > OBJECT OF PREPOSITION > DIRECT OBJECT. That is, quantifiers in subject position have more scope than those in indirect object position, and so on. This variation in degree of scope according to grammatical function can be seen in the following sentences:

1. Some boys bought every book.
2. Every boy bought some books.

In (1), the preferred reading is that a group of boys performed the act of buying on a totality of books. Note that the quantifier of low inherent scope, "some," takes priority over the quantifier of high inherent scope, "every," because of the former's function as subject: the scope of the subject quantifier is so strong that "every," normally a distributive quantifier, changes to a near-collective quantifier---i.e., the notion in the sentence is that the totality of books was bought, not each one singly. In (2), however, "every" dominates in subject position: the notion expressed is that each, single boy bought an unspecified quantity of books.

Now, Ioup explains the details of the quantifier hierarchies further, but those arguments are not pertinent here. The crucial fact is that the quantifier hierarchies predict quantifier scope universally (she justifies this with data from twelve languages) and that this prediction can be made by using the claims of universal grammar.

Universal Grammar and Composition

What does all of this have to do with writing theory? First, universal grammar is inherently appropriate for use in writing theory because this theory of syntax is a _performance theory_ (in the Chomskyan sense), something which cannot be claimed for _any_ of the other linguistic models which have often been pirated by writing theorists. I have argued this point elsewhere (Frawley, 1980; in press) and will not pursue it here, except to note that since writing is a _production_, it requires a theory of inherently variable choices to explain it (as de Beaugrande, 1978, eloquently argues), not a theory of categorical states of knowledge, or a competence model. Universal grammar, with its "more or less" predictions about syntactic usage, thus embodies the sorts of performance claims needed for a theory of syntactic choice in writing.

But a stronger reason for using universal grammar in writing theory lies in the intralanguage validity that universal grammar has and, in at least one case, in its direct application to written language. As for intra-language validity, the universal hierarchies predict not only more _natural_ syntactic structures across languages, but the more natural ones employed by speakers within any single language. Thus, in the case of the NPAH, the preference in any one language for relativization strategies will decrease as speakers move down the NPAH; similar naturalness claims inside any single language hold for the complement hierarchy. This intralanguage naturalness is justified in several ways, but the most telling evidence comes from Keenan and Comrie (1977), who report that ease of relative clause comprehension for adults decreases as one goes down the NPAH, from Prideaux (1979), who has found that relative clause acquisition parallels the NPAH, and from Limber (1973), whose study of sentential complement acquisition shows that the development of complement structures parallels the complement hierarchy. Thus, naturalness seems to be borne out within language.

Finally, Kennan (1975), has applied the NPAH directly to prose and has found that published writers with intuitively simple styles (e.g., Orwell) relativize more frequently at the higher end of the NPAH than do published writers with intuitively complex styles (e.g., Virginia Woolf), who, as might be surmised, relativize more frequently at the lower ends of the NPAH than those with simple styles. In other words, the naturalness claims that universal grammar makes are valid not only within any single language, but also are valid for predicting syntactic performance in written language.

What all of this amounts to is as follows: universal grammar, because of its cross-language and intralanguage claims about naturalness in syntax, ought to predict the syntactic differences between beginning writers and advanced writers. Beginning writers, since their syntactic performance is limited, ought to access the higher ends of the universal hierarchies since those are the natural and more common syntactic choices in language. Conversely, advanced writers ought to access lower ends of the universal hierarchies more than beginning writers since, by the definition of "advanced," their syntactic performance ought to allow them a broader range of "less natural" choices. These hypotheses are tested below in a consideration of the relativization and complementation habits of sophisticated and unsophisticated writers.

APPLICATION OF UNIVERSAL GRAMMAR

Relative Clause Usage

To check NP accessibility in relative clause usage for sophisticated and unsophisticated writers, I tallied all of the relative clauses from twenty-nine freshman compositions and from seven articles in literary journals. I assumed that these groups represented each of the ends of the writing spectrum: the freshman compositions were first-semester papers and were thus representative of unsophisticated (untrained) writing; the literary papers were from The Journal of Modern Literature, Studies in the Literary Imagination, Modern Language Studies, and PMLA and were thus representative of sophisticated (trained) writing. In my count, I considered as relative clauses only those structures which had overt verbals (finite verbs or participles). I therefore counted as relative clauses such structures as "the man who is sitting in the chair" and "the man sitting in the chair," but not "the man in the chair" or any adjectivals supposedly derived from reduced relative clauses, according to some theories of syntax.

The count of such clauses gave the following distribution for each group of writers: see table 1. The expected trend emerges: high subjective relative clause usage for unsophisticated writers; lower subjective relative clause usage and more access to lower ends of the NPAH for sophisticated writers.

If these findings are graphed according to the NAPH, it is easier to see how the predictions are borne out (I have collapsed the categories of INDIRECT OBJECT and OBLIQUE OBJECT into one according to Keenan's (1975) suggestion since INDIRECT OBJECT derives from a deep structure OBLIQUE OBJECT (to + NP)): see figure 1.

Of particular note is that relative clause usage follows exactly the predictions of the NPAH. Unsophisticated writers have a preponderance of subject relative clauses, and this usage declines rapidly and monotonically as NP accessibility decreases. Quite the opposite, as expected, is true for sophisticated writers, who relativize significantly fewer subject NP's and who have greater access to NP's for relativization at the lower ends of the hierarchy, especially at the middle range of the NPAH, where the differences between the two groups are greatest, suggesting that sophisticated writers become sophisticated, at least with regard to this syntactic variable, by developing oblique relativization strategies at the expense of subjective relatives. In short, the unsophisticated writers can be characterized, in their relative clause syntax, as using the more natural structures in language while the sophisticated writers have a greater range of access to relativization strategies in language.

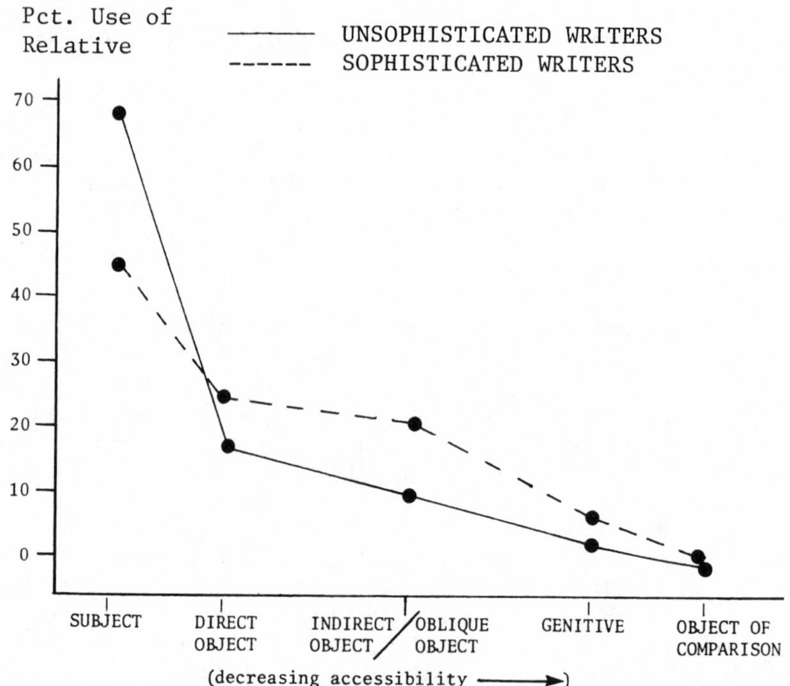

Figure 1. Relative Clause Usage.

Now, one could object, here, and say that all that the above verifies is that sophisticated writers have more strategies than unsophisticated writers, not a novel claim, to say the least. On a very banal level, this is true, but what the above demonstrates, beyond the simple quantitative differences, are the qualitative differences in syntactic strategies employed by each type of writer. The above findings finally allow us to point to the exact differences in syntactic strategies between advanced and beginning writers: we are no longer constrained to ask "How great are the differences between sophisticated and unsophisticated writers?"; we can answer the question "In what ways do these sorts of writers differ in their syntactic choices?" And even if we wanted to insist on answering the quantitative question, we can do so not by claiming that one group has more or fewer syntactic options (which is analytically true), but by demonstrating that the frequency of strategies for each group is distributed differentially and that this differential distribution is accountable to the predictions of universal grammar for naturalness of relativization, which is a rather weighty finding since it means that the differences between each group are quite systematic.

Interestingly enough, similar results emerge from a comparison of the choices of each group for the control NP's of their relative clauses: the control NP is the NP which the entire relative clause modifies---e.g., in "the boy who I know is here," "the boy" is the control NP. The results of a count of control NP usage for the same relative clauses as tallied above can be seen in table 2.

Two things are apparent in the data. Most prominent is that control NP usage follows the NPAH in a pattern similar to the distribution of the usage of relative NP's. A graph of the control NP usage illustrates this (again, INDIRECT OBJECT and OBLIQUE OBJECT are collapsed into one group): see figure 2. As with relative NP usage, control NP usage for unsophisticated writers shows a predominance of subject NP's with a marked decline as accessibility on the hierarchy decreases. For sophisticated writers, access to control NP's at the lower end of the NPAH is continually greater than for unsophisticated writers, with a marked difference between the two in subject usage and in access to the mid-range of the hierarchy, again as if deployment of strategies to access subjective controls by

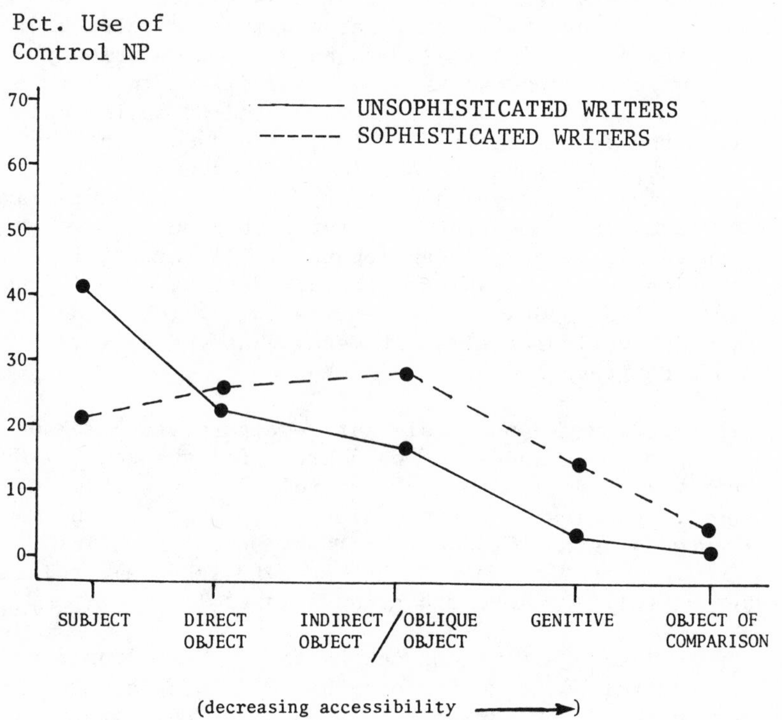

Figure 2. Control NP Usage.

Table 1. Relative Clause Usage.

	Unsophisticated Writers		Sophisticated Writers	
NP	# Relative Clauses	Pct.	# Relative Clauses	Pct.
SUBJECT	129	68.62	66	45.83
DIRECT OBJECT	35	18.62	36	25.00
INDIRECT OBJECT	0	0	0	0
OBLIQUE OBJECT	20	10.64	31	21.53
GENITIVE	4	2.12	9	6.25
OBJECT OF COMP.	0	0	2	1.39

Table 2. Control NP Usage.

	Unsophisticated Writers		Sophisticated Writers	
NP	# Control NP's	Pct.	# Control NP's	Pct.
SUBJECT	77	40.96	31	21.53
DIRECT OBJECT	45	23.94	38	26.39
INDIRECT OBJECT	2	1.06	3	2.08
OBLIQUE OBJECT	33	17.55	39	27.08
GENITIVE	7	3.72	24	16.67
OBJECT OF COMP.	4	2.13	6	4.17
TOPIC	20	10.64	3	2.08

Table 3. Subject Relative Clauses Derived From Passive.

Group	# Subject Relatives	# Passive	Pct.
Unsophisticated Writers	129	22	17.05
Sophisticated Writers	66	5	7.56

sophisticated writers is decreased in favor of access to oblique controls. In short, the NPAH predicts for each group of writers not only access to NP's for relativization, but also access to control NP's.

The second interesting finding is that a new category has emerged and perhaps deserves a place on the NPAH. This is the category TOPIC. A great number of controlling items for the relative clauses in the prose of unsophisticated writers---and a fraction of the controls for sophisticated writers---is the <u>topic</u> of the discourse. Some examples of this sort of access from the freshman papers are below:

3. The bishop handed out diplomas, which I will never forget.
4. Everyone was hugging and kissing, which made me feel good.
5. We could sit with our friends, which made this occasion special.
6. Men encounter feelings of insufficiency during recessions, which creates problems.

There is strictly no head NP for the relative clauses above, other than the theme of the discourse. In (3), the control is the entire event of the handing out of diplomas; in (4), the events of hugging and kissing control the relative; in (5), the act of sitting is the control; in (6), the event of encountering feelings of insufficiency is the control for the relative, as evidenced by the singular verb in the relative clause. These are very peculiar structures and are found, as figure 2 indicates, predominantly in the prose of unsophisticated writers.

One could, of course, explain the use of TOPIC as control in the way that traditional rhetoric books do: as a mistake, an error of vague reference. But this gets us nowhere. There is actually a very straightforward explanation for the use of TOPIC controls in universal grammar, and that is that the category TOPIC is very closely related syntactically to the category SUBJECT. Keenan and Comrie (1977), show that languages which relativize only subjects actually appear to draw no distinction between subject and topic. Ioup's (1975) study of quantifiers in universal grammar indicates that, in quantifier behavior, subject and topic have almost identical functions. Finally,

Givón (1979), reports that, diachronically, the syntactic category SUBJECT evolves from the category TOPIC, and that, ontogenetically, children develop the category SUBJECT as a derivative of the category TOPIC. What this means is that the high frequency of TOPIC controllers in the prose of unsophisticated writers is accountable to the predominance of SUBJECT controls in their writing since the two categories are intimately related syntactically. Likewise, the low frequency of TOPIC controllers in the prose of sophisticated writers follows from their infrequent use of the category SUBJECT. In short, given that universal grammar has identified close connections between the syntactic categories of SUBJECT AND TOPIC, the differential usage of these categories for control items by sophisticated and unsophisticated writers is accountable to the predictions which universal grammar makes for the usage of SUBJECT in general for these two groups of writers.

Up to this point in the discussion, evidence has been adduced that different relativization and control NP strategies for sophisticated and unsophisticated writers are predicted by the NPAH. Now, let us look at the second claim of universal grammar: that unsophisticated writers ought to employ more syntactic transformations than sophisticated writers in order to promote NP's on the hierarchy to relativize them. In particular, let us consider the promotional operation of passivization insofar as it is used by each group to promote objects to subjects inside of relative clauses. If the hypothesis about promotional operations is correct, then unsophisticated writers ought to have a noticeable percentage of their subject relative clauses derived from passives: that is, that there be a noticeable amount of structures such as (7) as opposed to (8):

7. The book which was read by John is here.
8. The book which John read is here.

A tabulation for each group of writers of the percentage of subject relative clauses derived from passives is given in table 3. Although the totals are small, the percentage difference in usage of the passive to promote NP's is revealing. Unsophisticated writers promote to subject via passivization more than twice as much as sophisticated writers. Thus, passivization as a promotional operation is not generally productive for either group, but when it is employed, it is used, as expected, to a much greater extent by unsophisticated writers, thus bearing out the predictions of universal grammar for use of promotional operations in syntax.

Sentential Complement Usage

To establish the distribution of sentential complements in the prose of sophisticated and unsophisticated writers, I counted two hundred sixty-eight sentential complements from thirty freshman compositions and the same number of complements from thirty-seven literary papers in the same journals I used for gathering relative clauses. In this tabulation, I counted as complements all sentences which functioned as nouns, whether the verbals in the complements were infinitives, gerunds, or finite verbs. I counted the complements according to the distributional categories given by Dryer (1980, discussed above): CLAUSE-FINAL > CLAUSE-INITIAL > CLAUSE-INTERNAL. Furthermore, I broke the complements into two other groups: marked and unmarked. Marked complements are those that are syntactically introduced by a complementizer: "to," "that," "the fact that," "-ing," and so on. Unmarked complements are not introduced by a complementizer. Thus (9) represents a marked, clause-final complement and (10) an unmarked one:

9. I know that you are here.
10. I know you are here.

My motivation for looking at the marked/unmarked distinction comes from studies of the ontogenesis of syntactic structures which provide evidence that in the early stages of acquisition, unmarked structures are common (Prideaux, 1979; Potts, et al., 1979). Thus, insofar as the early stages of syntactic acquisition have paralleled the higher, more natural ends of the universal hierarchies, which have paralleled the syntactic usage of unsophisticated writers, differences in marked/unmarked complement usage between the two groups of writers seem possible.

The distribution of sentential complements was as in table 4. As expected, the results follow the predictions of universal grammar, predictions similar to those given for the NPAH: namely that unsophisticated writers have less access to lower ends of the hierarchy. A graph of the complement distribution according to Dryer's complement hierarchy points this out nicely: see figure 3. Unsophisticated writers use ten percent more clause-final complements than sophisticated writers, who use twice as many clause-initial complements as unsophisticated writers do. Neither group uses any clause-internal complements, but such structures are generally unacceptable in English. In short, the predictions of universal grammar are again borne out in that unsophisticated writers use the more natural end of the complement hierarchy while sophisticated writers use more natural structures less frequently and have access to lower ends of the hierarchy.

Similarly, the use of marked and unmarked complements follows the predictions of universal grammar. In syntactic situations where writers had a choice of using either a marked sentential complement or an unmarked one (i.e., in clause-final position), sophisticated writers chose marked clause-final complements ninety-five percent of the time, or about ten percent more than unsophisticated writers, who, interestingly enough, used about three times as many unmarked clause-final complements as sophisticated writers. In other words, marking of clause-final sentential complements is a characteristic syntactic difference between sophisticated and unsophisticated writers, as predictable as the use of natural structures by the latter group and less natural structures by the former.

Just as complement usage follows the complement hierarchy, so does the use of transformations to promote complements on the hierarchy. That is, just as passivization was a device employed by unsophisticated writers to raise NP's to more accessible categories on the NPAH, so too unsophisticated writers employ a large number of transformations (such as Extraposition and Pseudo-Cleft) to move complements from clause-initial to clause-final position, thus promoting such complements on the hierarchy. Sophisticated writers, however, do not employ such promotional operations productively. A count, for each group, of the number of clause-final complements derived from transformations bears this out. The data are in table 5. Almost one-fifth of the clause-final complements of unsophisticated writers were derived from a promotional operation. This may not seem to be a startling number, but given that sophisticated writers use such operations to promote complements only five percent of the time and that

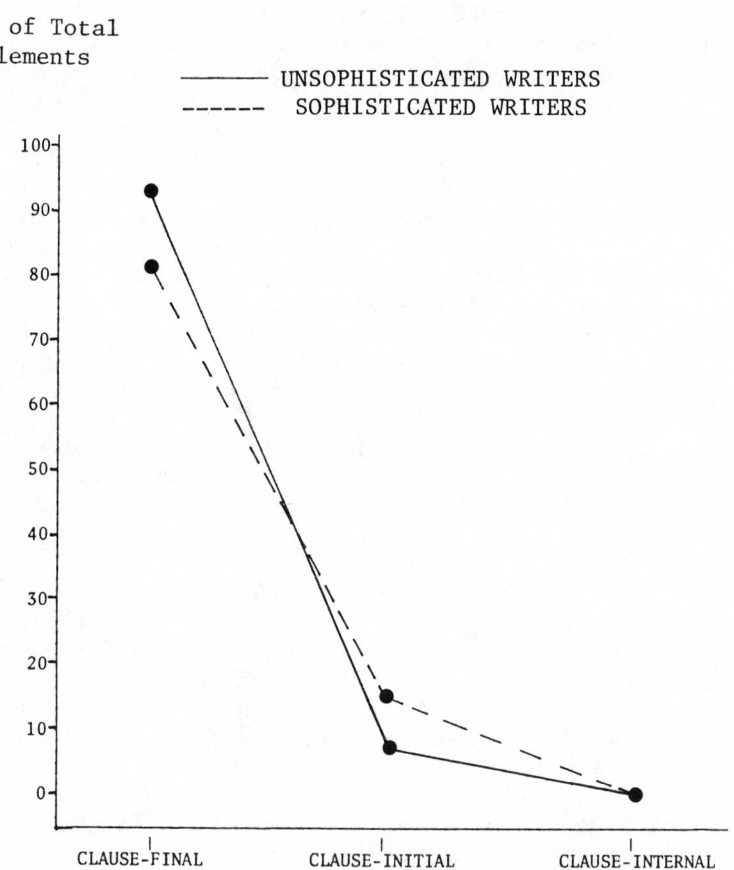

Figure 3. Sentential Complement Usage.

Table 4. Sentential Complement Usage.

	Unsophisticated Writers			Sophisticated Writers		
Complement Type	# Complements	Pct. of Total	Pct. of Final	# Complements	Pct. of Total	Pct. of Final
CLAUSE-FINAL						
Marked	213	79.48	86.59	210	78.36	95.02
Unmarked	33	12.31	13.41	11	4.10	4.98
Total	246	91.79	100.00	221	82.46	100.00
CLAUSE-INITIAL						
Marked**	22	8.21	---	47	17.54	---
Total	22	8.21	---	47	17.54	---
CLAUSE-INTERNAL	0	0	---	0	0	---

**All CLAUSE-INITIAL Complements are marked in English

Table 5. Clause-Final Complements Derived from Transformations.

Group	# Derived from Transformations	Pct. of Clause-Final
Unsophisticated Writers	45	18.29
Sophisticated Writers	11	4.98

this usage is four times as infrequent as the usage of unsophisticated writers, it is a very interesting finding. What it means is that, just as with relativization, unsophisticated writers go to great syntactic pains to access the high end of the complement hierarchy, as predicted by universal grammar.

What is just as interesting as the amount of promotional operations is the range of operations used by unsophisticated writers. Thus, unsophisticated writers used sentences such as the following:

11. What counts most is what shows up on the vinyl (Pseudo-Cleft).
12. It is no surprise that a great number of drownings occur (Extraposition).
13. The device is activated by rotating it clockwise (Passive).
14. Among the ways is committing yourself (Subject-Verb Inversion).

But transformations such as these are evidently unproductive in the prose of sophisticated writers, who predictably avoid clause-final sentential complements and promotional operations to achieve such structures.

Quantifier Usage

In order to see if quantifier usage follows any pattern similar to those outlined above, I counted and categorized one hundred eighty quantifiers from forty-one freshman essays and the same number of quantifiers from fifteen papers published in literary journals. I tabulated these quantifiers according to the two universal hierarchies of quantification which Ioup established. The distribution of these quantifiers for each group of writers is very revealing.

First, consider the frequency of quantifiers for each group, listed in Table 6. These data show a marked difference in usage for each group, a difference which is interesting if the data are graphed according to the hierarchy of inherent scope for quantifiers: see figure 4. What this graph reveals is that sophisticated writers tend to use quantifiers of high inherent scope: the maximum

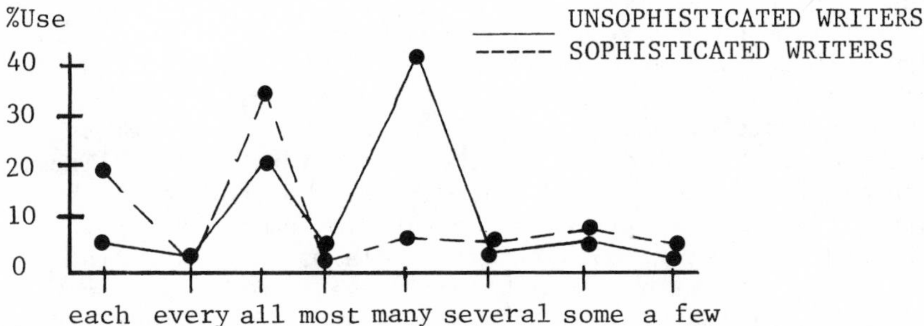

Figure 4. Quantifier Usage by Hierarchy of Inherent Scope.

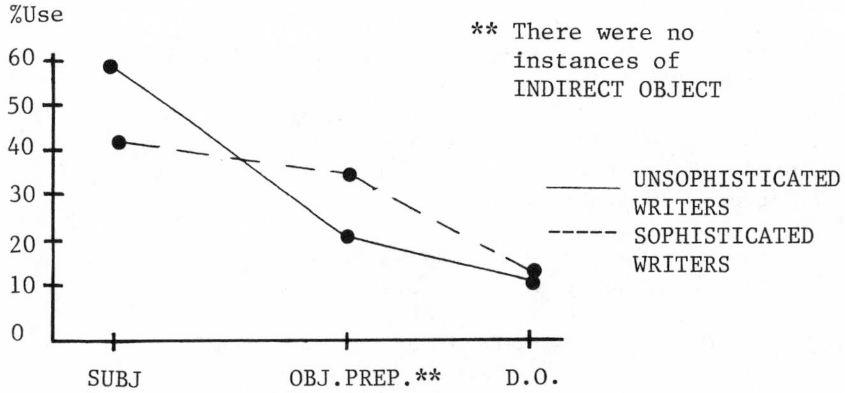

Figure 5. Quantifier Usage by Hierarchy of Scope (Grammatical Function.)

usage for sophisticated writers clusters around the quantifiers "each" and "all." On the other hand, unsophisticated writers tend to use quantifiers of lower inherent scope: almost half of the total usage of quantifiers by this group lies in the use of "many."

Two explanations for this difference come to mind. The first is a semantic, and somewhat speculative, reason. Quantifiers of high inherent scope logically express a prediction which is true or false for the totality of a set: "each," "ever," and "all" distribute the claim of the predicate of the sentence in which they occur across all members of the set which the quantifiers modify. Thus, one might speculate, here, that the marked usage of such quantifiers by sophisticated writers indicates that such writers are making broader claims: claims which are true or false for entire sets. Unsophisticated writers, however, use more collective quantifiers; the quantifiers characteristic of this group of writers logically express a predicate which is true or false for only part of a set: "many," for example, expresses the truth or falsity of the predicate of the sentence in which it occurs only for some of the members of the set which the quantifier modifies. It thus seems that this usage indicates that such writers are not making claims as broad as those of the other group of writers.

Now, the above semantic explanation is admittedly tentative, but a syntactic explanation of this differential quantifier usage is a bit more credible. Quantifiers of high inherent scope have the capacity to be moved variously throughout a sentence and still retain their scope and meaning. Note that all of the following sentences are rather close paraphrases:

15. a. Each of the boys is here.
    b. The boys, each, are here.
    c. The boys are each here.
    d. The boys are here, each of them.

This movement is not available to quantifiers of lower scope:

16. a. Many of the boys are here.
    b. ?The many boys are here.
    c. *?The boys, many, are here.

Table 6. Quantifier Usage.

	Unsophisticated Writers		Sophisticated Writers	
Quantifier	#	Pct.	#	Pct.
EACH	14	7.78	32	17.77
EVERY	9	5.0	5	2.78
ALL	40	22.22	65	36.11
MOST	14	7.78	9	5.0
MANY	71	39.44	17	9.44
SEVERAL	6	3.33	11	6.11
SOME	12	6.67	19	10.56
A FEW	5	2.78	11	6.11
BOTH**	9	5.0	11	6.11

**BOTH was included in the count for other purposes, not to be explained here.

Table 7. Quantifier Usage.

	Unsophisticated Writers		Sophisticated Writers	
Grammatical Function	#	Pct.	#	Pct.
SUBJECT	107	59.44	86	47.78
OBJECT OF PREPOSITION **	43	23.89	60	33.33
DIRECT OBJECT	30	16.67	34	18.89

**There were no instances of INDIRECT OBJECT

d. *?The boys are many here.
e. The boys are here, many of them.

Thus, a syntactic explanation for this differential usage is that sophisticated writers, in using quantifiers of high inherent scope, increase the potential for stylistic variation in their syntax since such quantifiers have rather free movement throughout sentences. Unsophisticated writers, however, have a limited range of stylistic variation available to them with their usage of quantifiers of low inherent scope. In short, the differential usage of quantifiers is, it appears, attributable to the basic difference between the two groups of writers in the freedom of syntactic choice each has, something which is understandable, given that good writers are supposed to have more syntactic options open to them than do poor writers.

If the data are considered in a different framework, however, some other facts emerge. Consider the frequency of quantifiers for each group according to Ioup's hierarchy of grammatical function: see table 7. There is again a marked difference in usage across the groups, and the graphed data show some interesting facts: see figure 5. What emerges, as in the data for relativization and complementation, is the marked tendency in unsophisticated writers to use the natural end of the universal hierarchy. By far, the dominant grammatical function for quantifiers in the prose of unsophisticated writers is SUBJECT, with a monotonic decline in usage as the hierarchy is traversed to the right, to the less natural functions. In other words, the data for this variable follow the exact pattern of distribution for unsophisticated writers as did the other structures considered above. This, of course, provides further evidence for the claim that unsophisticated writing is characterized by the use of natural, more universal syntax.

Sophisticated writers, however, have freer access to less natural quantifier structures, just as in their access to relative and complement structures. For this group of writers, the distribution of quantifiers according to function is more even, with greater access to the mid-range of the hierarchy, as was true in the other data above. Thus, it seems again that sophisticated writing differs from unsophisticated writing qualitatively: in the choices and the range of choices that are available.

But of greatest interest, here, is that these differences are explained (and in some sense predicted) by the conditions of universal natural logic on the form of sentences. The more universally accessible structures are those used by unsophisticated writers: quantifier usage and the logic of quantification bear this out nicely.

CONCLUSION: SOME REMARKS ON WRITING SOPHISTICATION

What all of the above amounts to is that universal grammar provides a new heuristic in identifying writing sophistication. Access to a great part of a relational hierarchy is the predictor of syntactic sophistication, not word choice, T-unit length, embedding depth, or whatever.

Consider the case of depth of embedding as a predictor of syntactic sophistication. According to this theory, which is at the base of such things as T-unit analysis (Hunt, 1965) and tagmemic approaches to writing (Arena, 1975), sophisticated writing is characterized by a large number of embedded clauses for every matrix clause. Thus, a writer who produces a lot of relative clauses or sentential complements (or both) is sophisticated by virtue of sheer number of clauses. This is a misleading measure of sophistication, however. For one thing, embedding depth as a measure of sophistication completely overlooks the fact that there are many writers with very low embedding depths, but who are judged to be sophisticated: Hemingway and Orwell are notable cases in point. For another, it overlooks the fact that it is _not_ the _quantity_ of embedding which separates sophisticated prose from unsophisticated; rather, it is the quality of the embedding which is the indicator. However many clauses a writer uses is unimportant; it is the kind and distribution of them which matter (and tagmemics has helped in this respect---see Arena, 1975).

This point about quality is supported by the data on relatives and complements. In order to locate one hundred eighty-eight clauses in the prose of unsophisticated writers, I had to search through approximately fifteen thousand words, whereas the locating of one hundred forty-four relative clauses in the prose of sophisticated writers required a search of only eight thousand one hundred words, or roughly half that needed for searching unsophisticated prose. In other words, unsophisticated writers use fewer relative clauses, which embedding depth measures predict. But in order to locate two hundred sixty-eight sentential complements in the prose of unsophisticated writers, I had to search through rougly eighteen thousand five hundred words, while locating the same amount of complements in sophisticated prose required a search of approximately thirty-seven thousand five hundred words. In short, sophisticated writers use many, many _fewer_ sentential complements than do unsophisticated writers, quite the contrary of what embedding depth predicts! And this is paradoxical since a relative clause and a sentential complement have the same embedding depth---one---and should thus be used with equal frequency. The point is that it is not the number of syntactic choices which writers make that determines sophistication in prose, but the kinds of choices they make (their performance). When the frequency of use of syntactic structures is held constant for each group, one sees great disparities in the distribution of kinds of constructions. It is this differential distribution which universal grammar predicts.

Consider another heuristic in identifying sophisticated prose---generative rhetoric, or sentence combining (see, e.g., Christensen, 1967)---which is predicated upon the contention that sophisticated writers have access to a broad range of syntactic transformations and permutations while unsophisticated writers do not, and which results in a theory of writing instruction based on teaching students to transform "kernel sentences" in systematic and complicated ways. This heuristic, likewise, suffers from the flaw of syntactic quantity as an indicator of sophistication: that good writers simply have more structures at their command. This is an over-simplification, and, in fact, universal grammar demonstrates the precise opposite: unsophisticated writers use _more_ transformations than sophisticated writers since the former group employs such systematic permutations to promote structures on the hierarchies. Further support of this claim can be found in some data on the use of clause-initial complements by each group. Of the forty-seven clause-initial complements used by sophisticated writers, forty-three were untransformed and four had the form of an "-ing" complement (nominalization transformation); however, of the twenty-two clause-initial complements used by unsophisticated writers, twenty-one were in the nominalized form (i.e., employed a transformation) while only one was untransformed. Thus, on this syntactic variable, unsophisticated writers again used more transformations than sophisticated writers. The crucial issue, here, is not mere numbers, but the function and type of structures and operations chosen by sophisticated and unsophisticated writers: these are things which universal grammar, not sentence combining, addresses.

Insofar as writing theory must look at the kinds of choices writers make and how sophisticated writers make different kinds of choices from other writers, universal grammar provides a new and promising tool for analysis. It predicts differential distribution of structures and operations for sophisticated and unsophisticated writers; it is the nearest thing to a performance theory of written syntax that has been developed.

REFERENCES

Arena, Louis, 1975, "Linguistics and Composition," Georgetown, Washington, D.C.

Christensen, Francis, 1967, "Notes toward a New Rhetoric," Harper & Row, N.Y.

de Beaugrande, Robert, 1978, Linguistic theory and composition, CCC, 29: 134-40.

Dryer, Matthew Synge, 1980, The positional tendencies of sentential noun phrases in universal grammar, Can. J. of Ling., 25: 123-95.

Frawley, William, 1980, The philosophy of composition, Tchng. Writing, 4: 1-13.

Frawley, William, in press, Theoretical linguistics in composition: an exorcism, Pap. in Ling.

Givón, Talmy, 1979, "Understanding grammar," Academic Press, N.Y.

Hunt, K. W., 1965, "Grammatical structures written at three grade levels," NCTE, Urbana.

Ioup, Georgette, 1975, Some universals for quantifier scope, in: "Syntax and Semantics 4," J. Kimball, ed., Academic Press, N.Y.

Johnson, David E., 1977, On relational constraints on grammars, in: "Syntax and Semantics 8," P. Cole and J. Sadock, eds., Academic Press, N.Y.

Keenan, Edward, 1975, Variation in universal grammar, in: "Analyzing Variation in Language," R. Fasold and R. Shuy, eds., Georgetown, Washington, D.C.

Keenan, Edward and Comrie, Bernard, 1977, Noun phrase accessibility and universal grammar, Ling. Inq., 8: 63-99.

Limber, John, 1973, The genesis of complex sentences, in: "Cognitive Development and the Acquisition of Language," T. E. Moore, ed., Academic Press, N.Y.

Manaster-Ramer, Alexis, 1979, The other side of accessibility, CLS, 15: 207-19.

Potts, M., Carlson, P., Cocking, R., and Copple, C., 1979, "Structure and Development in Child Language," Cornell, Ithaca.

Prideaux, Gary, 1979, The acquisition of relative clauses: a functional analysis, Can. J. of Ling., 24: 25-40.

RELATIONSHIPS: WHAT DID I WRITE? WHAT DID I DRAW?

ViLora Lyn Zalusky

The Ohio State University

INTRODUCTION

Separating visual and verbal representations of knowledge is a beguiling fiction, an artificial dichotomy which gives the impression that the two are separate entities. Kolers (1977) makes this point about reading, but it is just as true of writing. Ultimately to create a text or to comprehend one depends upon both visual and semantic properties.

Drawing, like writing, can also be seen to contain both the visual and verbal elements. Often children produce a drawing accompanied by talk. To interpret such a drawing properly, it is necessary to consider it in context, including any verbal information offered by the child (Korzenik, 1977; King and Rentel, 1979-1980). Children, then, tend to offer words or actions to help convey the message of their drawing to the receiver or interpreter of that message: "a child might jiggle up and down while drawing 'jumping' ... In general, subjects' efforts to articulate a symbol sprawled outside the drawing into gestures and words" (Korzenik, in Perkins, 1974: 46). During the course of a data collection in which this researcher served as a scribe for children's dictations, a similar situation arose. Many children, having trouble beginning their texts, chose to first draw a picture. Then, during the process of drawing that picture, they would simultaneously compose an oral text. Interestingly, as their picture became more detailed, so did their story.

Examples such as these are commonplace in the literature. Thus it is possible that children freely generalize across these two modes of production. If this is true, then a relationship can be expected to exist between writing and drawing.

THEORETICAL OVERVIEW

Much work in the area of art education and artistic development has concerned itself with children's perceptions of artists and their work (Gardner and Winner, 1976; Korzenik, 1977; Wilson, 1966a, 1966b), whether or not art training in the schools affects these perceptions (Wilson, 1966b, 1970, 1972), the influence of children's orientations concerning what they draw (Ives and Rovet, 1979; Ives, 1980; Ives and Houseworth, 1980) as well as intelligence measures and their relationship to children's drawings of the human figure (Goodenough, 1926; Harris, 1963; Cellotta, 1973). But comparatively little information exists from which a theory of development might be postulated to explain children's drawings (Lindstrom, 1957; Kellogg, 1970, 1979; Gardner, 1980). King and Rentel (1979-1980:2) argue

> ...writing at this stage in development serves another end. Its purpose is to create a tangible artifact, a drawing, or a display. Langer's (1953) notion of presentational symbolism, as distinguished from representational symbolism, would best characterize children's aims. They frequently tell stories while producing these displays (Britton, 1970). This form of solo discourse between thought and action embodies both elements of dialogue which are less collaborative and elements of narrative which are maintained by particular actions.

Thus while it may be important to look at writing on its own as well as drawing, it may be equally important to look at ways in which they potentially feed upon one another.

Recently, it has been argued that each different medium of communication contains unique characteristics, inherent in that medium, used to convey specific information (Ives and Gardner, 1979; Ives and Rovet, 1979). Certainly research in linguistics has documented many inherent properties in language and has shown how these properties shape communication through language (Halliday, 1976; Olson, 1977). Ives and Rovet (1979) point out that drawing, because it is a two-dimensional and static medium, utilizes communicative devices different from language. To support this notion one study provides intercorrelations of two "families" of media - one represented by language, the other represented by artistic productions (Ives, Silverman, Kelly and Gardner, 1979). These researchers have concluded that because of the rate differences in the trends of the process and production scores of the storytelling, drawing and clay molding tasks, differences in the development of competencies between these two families are supported. However, writing has properties similar to drawing that are not taken into account by this study.

Korzenik (1977:192) states: "Representational drawing is not, as is sometimes assumed, a mere photographic replica of the objective world, requiring only a knowledge of the chosen referent." By the same analogy, the composition of a text is not merely an objective description. In both the case of writing and drawing, there is a composing process with aesthetic elements inherent in that process. Goodnow (1978) observed that young children add features to their standard form for drawing of a person to indicate an action. She offers the example of a child who adds an extended arm to his standard form drawing of a person to indicate that the person is "picking" up the ball. She also points out "the similarity to young children's tendency to simply add units to either end of practiced linguistic units, leaving the center intact, when conveying information as a change from statement to question" (Goodnow, in Ives and Houseworth, 1980:591). Further, it has been argued that the standard orientation of object orientations in drawing is similar to the nominal case in language (Ives and Rovet, 1979). Ives and Houseworth (1980) have suggested that children are initially constrained by their reliance on certain graphic rules as a framework for their organizational strategies in drawing and that only later are they able to move beyond these initial stages to produce more complex configurations.

Citing Pufall's argument, the authors conclude with the possibility that these observed similarities between language use and drawing may indeed be reflective of some "common underlying principles of the semiotic function" (see Pufall, in Ives and Houseworth, 1980:593). On the basis of the previous observations, the following can be posed:

1. Is it possible that oral language, written language, and graphic language are represented in the same symbol system, each existing on different points of one continuum?
2. Or, that each of these may be represented by a distinct symbol system?
3. Or, is it possible that written language may be a point of overlap, sharing properties of two different symbol systems?
4. And finally, does the acquisition of competence in one symbolic process facilitate the acquisition of competence in another?

In order to shed light on these kinds of questions, the following study was designed.

Subjects who were still in the process of developing language, literacy and drawing competencies were selected. Two rating scales, concept of message and elaboration, were constructed to serve as dependent variables to be analyzed individually. It was hypothesized that group differences would be realized with respect to the concept of message and elaboration scales when those groups were based on literacy level. In addition, both King and Rentel (1979-1980) and Pettegrew (1981) found that the use of lexical cohesion was a discriminating factor in text-forming strategies in first grade children. Pettegrew also found that the use of restricted exophora was a significant discriminating factor as well. Therefore the factors of literacy level, proportion of lexical cohesive ties, and use of restricted exophoric references served as blocking variables in this study.

Cohesion, as Halliday and Hasan (1976:4) define it, relates to the semantic element of a text "... it refers to relations of meaning that exist within the text, and that define it as a text." Cohesion is realized when one element in the text is dependent on another element for its interpretation. Halliday and Hasan refer to this dependency of one element on another as presupposition. It is in this manner that cohesive ties are possible. Based on this definition of cohesion and the five different categories of ties, that of reference, substitution, ellipis, conjunction and lexical cohesion, it is possible to analyze a text of discourse and obtain a measure of its "cohesiveness." Again because of the significant results obtained by King and Rentel and Pettegrew, only the categories of lexical cohesion and restricted exophoric reference were used in this study.

A child who has a high proportion of lexical ties is showing a preference for using reiterative strategies to "bind" together his text. Use of restricted exophorics, on the other hand, indicates less sensitivity to the text as a relevant environment. Using the two rating scales constructed (concept of message and elaboration) literacy level, and two cohesive forces (lexical cohesion and restricted exophorics), four specific hypotheses were generated.

1. Fluent readers will evidence higher ratings on concept of message and elaboration than will transitional readers. In addition, transitional readers' ratings on both scores will be higher than beginning readers.
2. The higher the proportion of lexical ties obtained in the oral dictation task, the higher the rating on the concept of message and elaboration scale from the writing task.
3. With the presence of restricted exophoric references in the dictation task, a lower rating will be obtained on both the concept of message and elaboration ratings of the writing task.
4. A positive relationship exists between subjects' ratings on the concept of message scale and their rating on the elaboration scale.

The following section will outline the procedures for the study as well as provide a more in-depth explanation of each variable.

PROCEDURES OF THE STUDY

Subjects

Subjects for this study were drawn from the middle-class first grade population of a suburban school (see King and Rentel, 1979-1980 and Warner, Meeker, and Ellis, 1949). This particular elementary school was an alternative school which implemented an informal or progressive approach to education. In general, instruction was on an individual or small group basis. Curriculum usually consisted of thematic units with a large emphasis placed on literature, reading and writing, using a language-experience type of approach.

Data were collected on 27 male and female students during the first part of the 1979-1980 academic year (early October through November). The 14 female students and 13 male students that comprise the sample for this study are all students in the same first grade class. Data on the entire class were collected although three subjects were eliminated from the sample due to special psychological testing (1 female subject), special reading testing (1 male subject), and incomplete data (1 male subject). The remaining 13 females and 11 males (with a mean age of 80.38 months) comprised the sample that was analyzed in this study.

Writing Task

The task, for the children, was to create a storybook consisting of text on a topic of their choice. Blank storybooks (8 1/2 by 7 inches in size with 32 pages each) were provided for the children but length was not limited since they were told that they could have more than one storybook if they desired. It should be noted that several children produced more than one storybook and a couple of children made additions to their storybooks by constructing their own books out of construction paper or unlined paper. Length of time taken to complete the storybook was uncontrolled, and students worked on their storybooks whenever and for whatever length of time they felt was necessary in order to complete the task. Students continued to work on one or more storybooks throughout the school year. However, for the purposes of this study, a two month time period was sampled. All of the subjects whose storybooks were analyzed produced at least a half of completed storybook during this time frame.

Assistance to the children by the teacher and/or two research assistants was provided only if requested by the student. In addition, a variety of drawing, writing, painting and textured materials was always available to the children for use in their storybooks. Use of these materials, however, was completely on the child's own initiative and not suggested by either the teacher or the research assistants. Thus, use of materials, assistance, or completion was neither encouraged nor discouraged. One teacher and two research assistants were available if any child requested help. It is clear that the children saw this task as part of their classroom experiences and in no way connected it either to an experiment or to the presence or absence of the two research assistants. Also, since children were totally in control of text length, time duration and other aspects of production, the data are more than likely representative of the children's intentions.

During this same time period the children were producing original stories and dictating them to the two research assistants who served as their scribes. In addition, for accuracy, the children's stories were tape-recorded during their dictation session. Most children requested a turn with the scribe. "Generally the order of data collection followed a volunteer pattern, with the scribes working with children who indicated their readiness with a story" (Pettegrew, 1981:56). This dictation task is relevant to the analysis of this study because it is the significant findings from this task (in Pettegrew, 1981) that constitute the blocking variables utilized in following analysis.

Explanation of Variables

Five factors are of interest in this study: concept of message, elaboration, literacy level, lexical cohesion and restricted exophoric reference. The first two factors are used as dependent measures in this analysis and the last three were used as factors on which the subjects were blocked into groups. The following discussion is intended to provide an explanation of each of these individual factors.

Concept of Message

This rating scale is based on the Concept of Message Categories utilized by King and Rentel (1979-1980) in their study. As King and Rentel point out, the categories are to differentiate between (1) those children who have little or no understanding of the relationship between messages that are expressed in the written language, including those combinations of letters necessary for that expression, and (2) those children who have a holistic understanding of that relationship, (3) those who have the ability to represent copied or invented patterns, and (4) those children who are able to produce complete, varied and original messages.

The following is a description of the concept of message rating scale employed in this study.

Concept of Message

Rating	Description
1	Letter strings only; no letter-sound match ups.
2	Letter strings based on letter-sound relationships; word boundaries usually unclear.
3	Simple patterns, labels or clauses utilized in a repeated fashion; word boundaries observed; high frequency words are spelled correctly (e.g., I like my mother, I like my father, I like my dog).
4	Varied phrases and/or sentences - each phrase/sentence being different from the previous. Writing conventions usually include correct use of capitalization. Correct use of punctuation is not of critical importance in this category;

Rating	Description
	however, some use of punctuation generally occurs. Spelling in general is quite accurate.
5	Fluent writing, which includes a wide range of writing as well as storybook conventions; punctuation, capitalization, chapter headings, numerical indicaters for different chapter, use of "the end." As in category 4, spelling is generally quite accurate.

Elaboration

The elaboration factor deals with the degree of complexity or detail of the subject matter or content of the drawing. The purpose of this rating is to differentiate between (1) the child who chooses to represent his figures as simple figures with no detail; (2) the child who begins to elaborate on the chosen subject; and (3) the child who completely embellishes his drawing. The assumption underlying this scale is that the more detail offered by the child in the drawing, the more detailed the information he has communicated in his production. The following categorical descriptions, including a simplified example (drawn by the author for illustration) are extensions of observations made of children's art (Lindstrom, 1957; Kellogg, 1970, 1979; Gardner, 1980).

Elaboration

Rating	Example	Description
1		Human figures represented as stick-like figures with little facial detail or expression demonstrated. Buildings shown as simple structures with lines used to indicate doors and windows. Often the same pictures appear in isolation page after page

Rating	Example	Description
		with little variation.
2		Human figures have distinguishable body torsos. Evidence of hands, feet, and facial expression. The use of props, such as hats and glasses, allow the viewer to begin to distinguish one human character from another. Decorated torsos indicate clothing; however, identifiable clothing pieces are hard to distinguish. Buildings are still shown as simple structures -- only now chimneys, window panes, and door knobs are included.
		Subjects appear in the context of a total picture with human figures evidencing hair, fingers, feet, shoes, eyelashes and eyebrows. Articles of clothing are differentiated. Sex and age differences are clear. Buildings show details such as window decorations, scenes inside the house, roof textures, or smoke emitting from chimneys. Comparison and contrastive drawings appear frequently in the category.
4		Subject matter is very detailed. Human figures are elaborately adorned with hats, head pieces, jewelry and different kinds of clothing. Extreme attention to detail is obvious.

Buildings and structures are very detailed, as evidenced by the boy who drew an aerial view of a football stadium including the different decks for seating, team locker rooms, team benches, flags, and yard line markers.

Literacy Level

Literacy level was used to block the subjects into three reading levels: beginning readers, transitional readers, and fluent readers. This blocking was done on the basis of the administration of the 1978 edition of the Metropolitan Achievement Test - Reading (Primer Level, K.5-1.4) as well as an independent Teacher Assessment administered during the first part of the data collection procedure. (For a more indepth discussion of this assessment, the reader is referred to Pettegrew, 1981.)

Pettegrew (1981) has identified and classified these three levels and provides the following descriptions.

1. Fluent Readers - Those children who could already read books independently.
2. Transitional Readers - Those children who had considerable letter and word knowledge, could predict their way through sentence-length material, but who could not read passages of connected text.
3. Beginning Readers - Those children who were still learning the directional constraints of graphic language, letter and word concepts, and who could recognize only a few words.

Lexical Cohesion

Lexical cohesion is distinguishable by two categories: reiteration and collacation. Reiteration occurs when the "same" word is repeated. "Same" word may be an exact repetition of that word, a synonym, superordinate, or a similar general word. Note the following example:

My <u>dog</u> just died.
My <u>pet</u> was more than just a <u>dog</u>.

"Dog" in the first instance refers to "pet" in the second instance (superordinate). Notice also that "dog" is repeated in the second sentence, but does not involve identity of the referent. Moreover had the second sentence read "My pet was more than just an animal," or "more than just a thing," reiteration would also have occurred through the use of a superordinate or a similar general word.

The second category of lexical cohesion is collocation. Here the referent and the coreferent are members of the same set. These members generally occur in close proximity of each other. "In general, any two lexical items having similar patterns of collocation, that is, tending to appear in similar contexts - will generate a cohesive force if they occur in adjacent sentences" (Halliday and Hasan, 1976:286).

Restricted Exophorics

Exophora is a means of pointing outside the text. In other words, something outside of the text itself is necessary to help with the interpretation of the text. Technically speaking, an exophoric reference is not a cohesive element as defined by Halliday and Hasan (1976) since it does not rely on a presupposed item within the text. Hasan (in press), however, has further classified exophoric references as implicit devices that may be formal or situation, with situational having the option of being either restricted or immediate. Restricted exophorics are categorized as such because "... their intended meanings are limited or restricted to the smallest circle of potentially successful interpreters" (Pettegrew, 1981:41).

Analysis

Each of the 24 subjects was given two ratings on his storybook productions - a concept of message rating and an elaboration rating. Inter-rater reliabilities performed on these two rating systems produced correlations of .95 and .92 respectively. In addition, each subject was placed into the appropriate group for each of the three blocking variables, which were analyzed as separate rather than concomitant blocking variables. As previously stated, literacy level is comprised of three levels - beginning, transitional and fluent readers. Lexical cohesion has two levels derived from the proportion of lexical ties that each subject produced in the dictation task. Those subjects with proportion less than 0.35 constituted one group, and those with a proportion of 0.35 or above comprised the second. Subjects were grouped according to the presence or absence of restricted exophorics, also derived from their dictation measures. In this case, presence or absence was enough to differentiate the groups. Subsequent to computing the requisite group means and standard deviations, six one-way analysis of variances were performed. Adjustments were made in each case for the treatment of unequal cell numbers (Kennedy, 1978), which, according to Kennedy, presents few problems in a one-factor case.

Tables 1 and 2 display the means and standard deviations for literacy level as the blocking variable with concept of message and elaboration as separate dependent variables. Clearly, as evidenced by the cell means, in both cases, an upward trend is occurring from the beginning to the transitional to the fluent reader. Table 3 shows the results of the analysis of variance for concept of message blocked on literacy level. As evidenced by this analysis, concept of message does seem to be a significant discriminator of the three groups ($\underline{F}$ (1,22) = 7.91, $\underline{p} < .05$). However, the analysis in Table 4, with elaboration as the dependent variable, does not achieve statistical significance. But interestingly, this analysis is approaching significance ($\underline{F}$ (1,22) = 2.74, $\underline{p} < .10$), and this questions the influence of the small sample size on the analysis. These two preliminary analyses show that a relationship exists between reading and writing. However, it is equally as plausible that a relationship exists between reading and drawing.

Table 5 and 6 show the means and standard deviations for subjects blocked on proportions of occurrence of lexical cohesion in their dictation task. Again a slight upward trend is seen both with the concept of message factor and the elaboration factor. However, as demonstrated in the two successive analysis of variances (see tables 7 and 8), neither of these trends was significantly different. Still one would expect that a child who choses to use reiteration and collocation in his oral renderings of a story might make use of similar strategies appropriate

Table 1. Group Means and Standard Deviations of Concept of Message Rating by Literacy Level.

	Group 1 (beginning)	Group 2 (transitional)	Group 3 (fluent)	Overall
(n of group)	(5)	(10)	(9)	(24)
Totals	10.00	24.00	25.00	59.00
$\overline{X}$	2.00	2.40	2.78	2.46
S.D.	1.00	.04	.03	.88

Table 2. Group Means and Standard Deviations of Elaboration Rating by Literacy Level.

	Group 1 (beginning)	Group 2 (transitional)	Group 3 (fluent)	Overall
(n of group)	(5)	(10)	(9)	(24)
Totals	12.00	27.00	30.00	69.00
$\overline{X}$	2.40	2.70	3.33	2.88
S.D.	.55	.67	.71	.74

Table 3. Analysis of Variance of Concept of Message Rating by Literacy Level.

Source	df	SS	MS	F
A	1	3.32	3.32	7.91*
S/A	22	9.31	.42	
Total	23	12.63		

*p $<$ .05

Table 4. Analysis of Variance of Elaboration Rating by Literacy Level.

Source	df	SS	MS	F
A	1	2.0	2.0	2.74
S/A	22	15.96	.73	
Total	23	17.96		

Table 5. Group Means and Standard Deviations of Concept of Message Rating by Lexical Cohesion.

	Group 1 (below .35)	Group 2 (.35 and above)	Overall
(n of group)	(13)	(11)	(24)
Totals	36.00	33.00	69.00
$\overline{X}$	2.77	3.00	2.88
S.D.	.60	.89	.74

Table 6. Group Means and Standard Deviations of Elaboration Rating by Lexical Cohesion.

	Group 1 (below .35)	Group 2 (.35 and above)	Overall
(n of group)	(13)	(11)	(24)
Totals	29.00	30.00	59.00
$\overline{X}$	2.23	2.73	2.46
S.D.	1.01	.65	.88

Table 7. Analysis of Variance of Concept of Message Rating by Lexical Cohesion.

Source	df	SS	MS	F
S	1	.31	.31	.55
S/A	22	12.32	.36	
Total	23	12.63		

Table 8. Analysis of Variance of Elaboration Rating by Lexical Cohesion.

Source	df	SS	MS	F
S	1	1.47	1.47	1.96
S/A	22	16.49	.75	
Total	23	17.96		

to his writing and drawing. Even though this analysis does not bear out this hypothesis, it still seems to be a viable avenue of investigation.

Finally, the subjects were blocked on the presence or absence of their use of restricted exophorics in the dictation tasks. Again, the hypothesis was that a child who tended to rely on the use of an outside context, (outside the text that is) might evidence a lower rating on the concept of message and on the elaboration rating. According to the descriptive statistics in tables 9 and 10, children who did use restricted exophorics in their oral dictations did have slightly lower means on both the concept of message and elaboration ratings. But, the resulting analysis of variance did not reveal a significant difference for the concept of message rating (see table 11). However, in Table 12 statistical significance was achieved for the elaboration rating ($\underline{F}$ (1,22) = 5.59 $\underline{p} < .05$). Thus these data partially bear out the hypothesis.

Lastly, a Pearson product-moment correlation was performed on subjects' ratings on the concept of message scale and their ratings on the elaboration scale. This correlation revealed a significant moderate association between these two factors (df = 25, r = .40, $\underline{p} < .05$). Hence the final hypothesis concerning a relationship existing between writing and drawing remains plausible.

From the data presented in this analysis - the trends of the group means, the subsequent analyses, as well as the correlation between the concept of message and elaboration ratings - definitive answers cannot be reached. However, these results do at least lend credence to the kinds of questions and hypotheses posed in section two of this paper. These data help to illustrate that questions of this nature are not only potential routes of inquiry but important questions of future research. To further highlight these relationships between writing and drawing, pages from three storybook productions have been selected for a closer look.

A CLOSER LOOK

Erin

Throughout his storybook, Erin concentrated on Halloween

Table 9. Group Means and Standard Deviations of Concept of Message Rating by Restricted Exophorics.

	Group 1 (absence)	Group 2 (presence)	Overall
(n of group)	(15)	(9)	(24)
Total	45.00	24.00	69.00
$\overline{X}$	3.00	2.67	2.88
S.D.	.76	.71	.74

Table 10. Group Means and Standard Deviations of Elaboration Rating by Restricted Exophorics.

	Group 1 (absence)	Group 2 (presence)	Overall
(n of group)	(15)	(9)	(24)
Total	41.00	18.00	59.00
$\overline{X}$	2.73	2.00	2.46
S.D.	.70	1.00	.88

Table 11. Analysis of Variance of Concept of Message Rating by Restricted Exophorics.

Source	df	SS	MS	F
A	1	.62	.62	1.13
S/A	22	12.00	.55	
Total	23	12.62		

Table 12. Analysis of Variance of Elaboration Rating by Restricted Exophorics.

Source	df	SS	MS	F
A	1	3.63	3.63	5.59*
S/A	22	14.33	.65	
Total	23	17.96		

*$p < .05$

creatures or symbols - like pumpkins or creatures and symbols from outer space. Among the Halloween subject matter Erin chose were pumpkins, devils, ghosts, monsters, mummies and Count Dracula. Included in his parade of scary ghosts and goblins were Martians and spaceships. Erin introduced his characters with a "this is ..." phrase (see Figure 1). Then, in later efforts, he offered his reader added information about these characters. Notice, in figure 2, his comment that "M U M E S R S K A R R E" (mummies are scary). Clearly Erin has achieved a sense of letter-sound relationships in his writing. His word boundaries are not observed, but in figure 1 it is obvious that he is well on his way. Even though his drawings of both the devil and the mummy are isolated from the context of a whole picture, the lines underneath the mummy show an attempt at a ground-sky relationship. Notice also that he has chosen to give the devil horns and a pitchfork - a beginning of elaboration. The mummy is a creative use of a stick figure variation; with the devil, Erin is choosing to represent the torso. This is a nice attempt on Erin's part to distinguish these monsters within his mode of presentation. Erin would receive a low rating on both the concept of message scale and the elaboration scale; however, it is important not to underestimate the power and effectiveness of Erin's productions.

Barbie

Barbie's storybook was very interesting in that in several cases, she offered information and then extended and elaborated on that initial offer through both drawing and writing. Figures 3, 4, and 5 came in immediate succession in her book. She combined the "this is ..." and the "I like ..." pattern to achieve an elaborative effect. Notice in figure 3 she introduced the subject - a flower. In figure 4, she has told us and has shown us that she likes flowers by writing it and putting herself in the context of the picture near the flowers. Then perhaps to elaborate on the aesthetic qualities of the flowers, she has portrayed them, in figure 5, against a blue sky, so perhaps the reader can enjoy them also.

Several pages later, Barbie has done a very interesting comparison and contrastive study (see figures 6, 7, and 8). She has introduced the reader to a house both in writing and in drawing in figure 6. Then through a series of two

Figure 1.

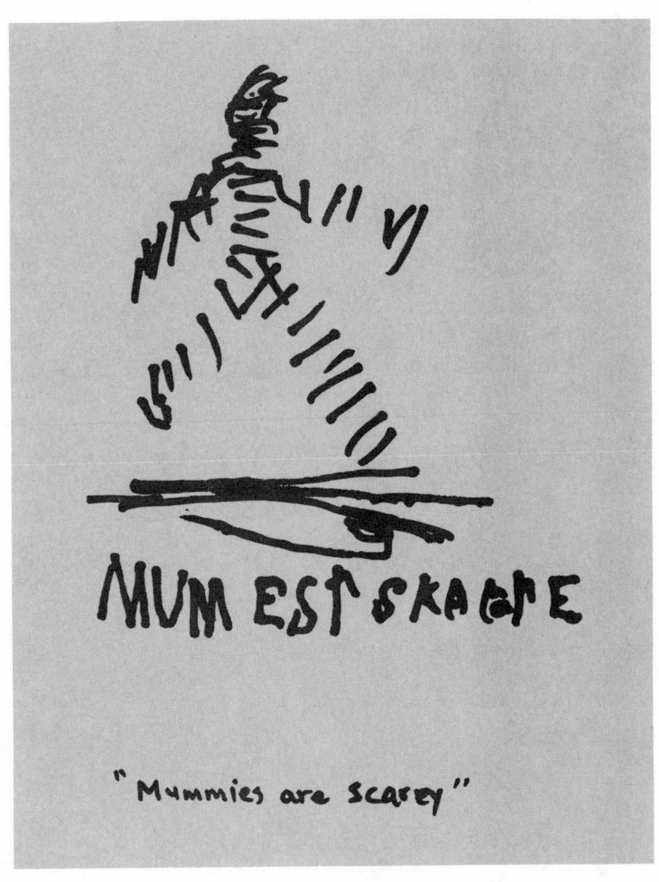

Figure 2.

Figure 3.

Figure 4.

Figure 5.

Figure 6.

Figure 7.

Figure 8.

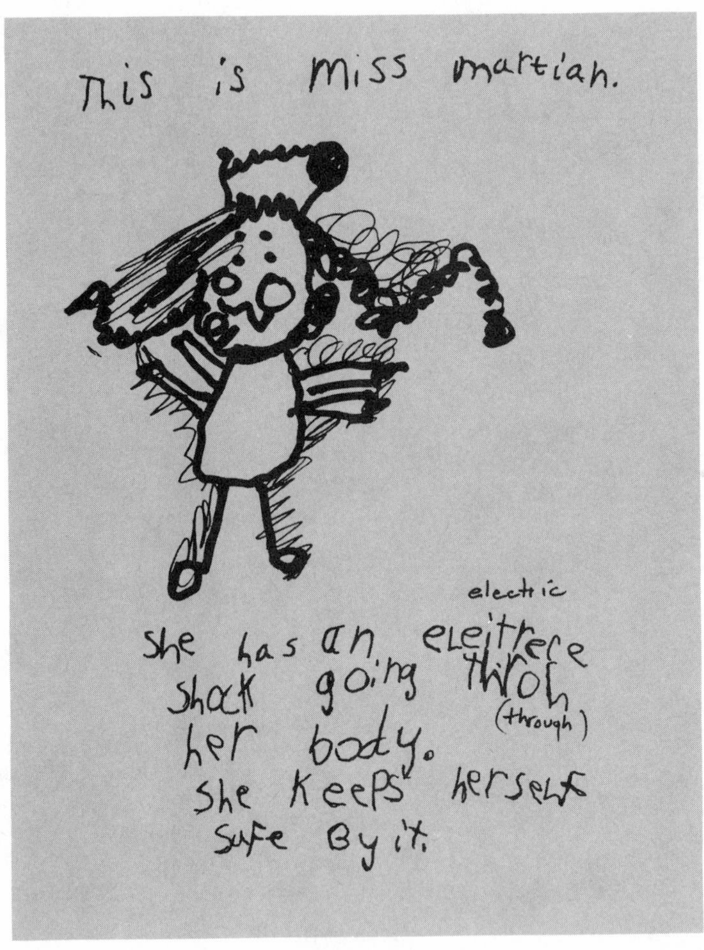
This is miss martian.
electric
She has an eleitrere
shack going throh
(through)
her body.
She keeps herself
safe By it.

Figure 9.

more (figures 7 and 8), "this is ..." phrases, has told her reader that her house is with her mom and the other one is her dad's. Notice however that the striking differences realized in Barbie's drawings are not the same as if <u>only</u> the text were present. Barbie appears skilled at presenting differences and making contrastive statements with her drawing. In addition there seems to be an indication of a similar stage with respect to writing development.

Ellen

In the context of Ellen's storybook she has a brief story about Miss Martian. Figure 9 is a portrait of Miss Martian with the jagged lines representing the electric shock waves that vibrate through her body to keep her safe. Notice how Ellen has utilized disproportioned human features - four eyes, four arms, wide mouth - to make her Miss Martian distinctively "Martian." Her text shows use of original text composed of complete sentences. It is possible that her labeling of Miss Martian is similar in fashion to that of a caption in an illustrated text. Her obvious use of elaboration in the drawing - Miss Martian's crown, earrings, necklace, and hairdo - is illustrative of a child that would receive a high rating on elaboration. Later adventures of Miss Martian give the reader a detailed view of her planet, complete with several kinds of antennae protruding around the planet and a sign indicating the location of her house, as well as a sampling of her school work with her name and an indication of the subject matter.

With Ellen, as with Barbie and Erin, the production is effective as a form of communication. All three subjects are convincing authors both in their use of written language and in the aesthetic language of drawing.

CONCLUSION

This study, the examples of the children's work, and the observations that are now surfacing in the developmental writing and developmental art literatures are all evidence of research concerning the symbol systems. It is not only important for researchers to address themselves to questions concerning the domains of these symbol systems, but to address questions of underlying symbolic processes as well. As Gardner (1979) points out, research into the domains and development of the symbolic processes may be the next step for developmental psychology after Piaget.

The significant findings of this study have implications for future research. More and detailed analyses need to be conducted on different modes of children's production. Just as Clay (1975) has observed links between early writing skills and those skills required in the acquisition of reading, so may writing and drawing be related. Research on the associations between writing and drawing will ultimately shed light on relationships between drawing and general literacy factors as well as the underlying cognitive structures which are employed in the general use of language: oral, written and aesthetic, and their resulting powers of communication.

REFERENCES

Cellotta, B. K., 1973, Knowledge of the human figure as measured by two tasks, Dev. Psych., 8:377:81.

Clay, M. M., 1975, "What did I Write?" Heinemann, Aukland, New Zealand.

Gardner, H., 1980,"Artful Scribbles: The Development of Children's Drawings," Basic Books, N.Y.

Gardner, H., 1979, Developmental psychology after Piaget: an approach in terms of symbolization, Hum. Dev., 22:73-88.

Gardner, H. and Winner, E., 1976, How children learn... Three stages of understanding art, Psych. Today, 42-43: 74.

Goodenough, F., 1926, "Measurement of Intelligence by Drawings," Harcourt, Brace and World, N.Y.

Goodnow, J. J., 1978, Visual thinking: cognitive aspects of change in drawings, Ch. Dev., 49:637-641.

Halliday, M. A. K. and Hasan, R., 1976, "Cohesion in English," Longman, London.

Harris, D. B., 1963, "Children's Drawings as Measures of Intellectual Maturity: A Revision and Extension of the Goodenough Draw-A-Man-Test," Harcourt, Brace and World, Inc., N.Y.

Hasan, R., in press, Ways of saying: ways of meaning, in: "Semiotics of Culture and Language," S. M. Lamb et al., eds., The Press at Twin Willows.

Ives, W., 1980, The use of orientations in children's drawings of familiar objects: percepts versus principles, Br. Jnl. Ed. Psych., 50:295-96.

Ives, S. W., and Gardner, H., 1979, Cultural influences on children's drawings: a developmental perspective, _in_: "Art Education International." A. Hurwitz, ed., Pennsylvania State University Press, University Park.

Ives, W. and Houseworth, M., 1980, The role of standard orientations in children's drawings of interpersonal relationships: aspects of graphic feature marking, Ch. Dev., 51:591-93.

Ives, W. and Pond, J., 1980, The arts and cognitive development, H.S. Jnl., 63:335-40.

Ives, S. W. and Rovert, J., 1979, The role of graphic orientations in children's drawings of familiar and novel objects at rest and in motion, Merrill-Palmer, Q. 25:281-92.

Ives, S. W., Silverman, J., Kelly, H., and Garner, H., 1979, Artistic development in the early school years: a cross-media study of storytelling, drawing, and clay modeling, Harvard Project Zero, Technical Report No. 8.

Kellogg, R., 1970, "Analyzing Children's Art," Mayfield Publishing Co., Palo Alto.

Kellogg, R., 1979, "Children's Drawings/Children's Minds," Avon, N.Y.

Kennedy, J. J., 1970, "An Introduction to the Design and Analysis of Experiments in Education and Psychology," Univ. Press of America, Washington, D.C.

King, M. and Rentel, V. M., 1979-1980, Contextual features produced by children in three modes of discourse: interactive speech, dictation and writing (K-gr. 2). NIE Project Nos. G-79-0039 and G-79-0137.

Kolers, P.A., 1977, Reading pictures and reading text, _in_: "The Arts and Cognition," D. Perkins and B. Leondar, eds., John Hopkins U. Press, Baltimore.

Korzenik, D., 1977, Saying it with pictures, _in_: "The Arts and Cognition." D. Perkins and B. Leondar, eds., John Hopkins U. Press, Baltimore.

Lindstrom, M., 1957, "Children's Art," U. of Cal. Press, L.A.

Perkins, D., 1974, Probing artistic processes: a progress report from project zero, _J. of Aesth. Ed._, 8:33-37.

Pettegrew, B. S., 1981, "Text Formation: A Comparative Study of Literature and Pre-literate First Grade Children." Un. Ph.D. Dissertation, Ohio State University.

Wilson, B., 1966a, The Development and Testing of an Instrument to Measure Aspective Perception of Paintings." Ph.D. Dissertation, Ohio State University.

Wilson, B., 1966b, An experimental study designed to alter fifth and sixth grade students' perception of paintings, St. Art Ed., 8:33-42.

Wilson, B., 1970, Relationships among art teachers', art critics' and historians', and non-art-trained individuals' statements about Picasso's "Guernica." St. Art Ed., 12:31-39.

Wilson, B., 1970, The relationship between years of art training and the use of aesthetic judgmental criteria among high school students. St. Art Ed., 13:34, 43.

THE PRAGMATIC STRUCTURE OF RHETORICAL MATURITY IN THE SCIENCES

Mackie J-V Blanton

University of New Orleans

There is little doubt that successful writing possesses an inherent logic all its own.[1] Our certainty on this point regarding logical, mature writing style reflects our definitions of clear writing, often designed to encourage the novice rhetorician or the teacher of rhetoric. Such definitions, of course, have a centuries-old tradition.

What I intend to report here, however, is logical rhetoric of a specific sort. I would like to look beyond the merely definitional regarding written discourse and examine a particular kind of modern writing to determine an actual or virtual structure of rhetoric. I will limit my investigation to the language found in scientific research reports.

The modern demand in the West for technological advancement has made research one of our larger industries. Since the purpose of research is to add to human knowledge, the modern researcher must be able to communicate subject matter in the most straightforward of formats and styles. My favorite insistence on this point was pronounced some 89 years ago:

> The scientific writer will constantly aspire to reflect objective reality with the perfect serenity and candor of a mirror, drawing with words as the painter with his brush, forsaking, in short, the pretensions of the stylist and

> the fatuous ostension of philosophic depth. Nor would the well-known maxim of Boileau be forgotten: 'What is well conceived is clearly stated' (Y Cajal, 1893:160).

Ramon Y Cajal's description of how the scientist must write rings no less true for today's scientist or engineer or technologist. Consider Britton's opinion on this matter:

> The primary ... characteristic of technical and scientific writing lies in the effort of the author to convey one meaning and only one meaning in what he says. That one meaning must be sharp, clear, precise. And the reader must be given no choice of meanings (Britton, 1975: 9).

Brusaw, Oliu, and Alred have pretty much the same to say:

> Because the focus is on an object or a process, the language is utilitarian, emphasizing exactness rather than elegance. ... Technical writing is direct and to the point (Brusaw, Oliu, and Alred, 1976:475).

Thus, the ability to write clearly is one of the pragmatic requirements for success in today's scientific and technical fields. In fact, in industry the ultimate way of communicating research findings is through written reports; how clear an idea or a significant chunk of technical information appears to any likely reader largely depends on the rhetorical maturity of the researcher doing the reporting.

Hence, the analyst examining scientific and technical rhetoric must reveal the pragmatic structure of scientific and technical communication. The most straightforward way of accomplishing this task is to select essays from a leading specialist journal, assume them to be ideal samples since they have been reviewed and accepted for publication by an editorial board of practicing professionals, and then, finally, by means of some analytic method, discern the rhetorical characteristics common to each of the pieces of writing in order to postulate some generalization regarding the actual and virtual form of any and all such writing.

The language analyst has, indeed, succeeded in discerning the pragmatic nature of rhetorical structure once he has established a set of hypotheses regarding the form of an author's mature style. The procedure for discerning the pragmatism underlying the rhetorical maturity of scientific expression involves approaching the text under analysis as if it were a language informant (see Selinker, 1980).

The procedure I am formulating here is based upon an analogy drawn from how linguistics views speakers of a language community. Each speaker of a language community is representative of the community as a whole. Therefore, the pattern of the speech of any one speaker, theoretically put, will possess structural characteristics similar to that of all speakers of the shared language community. There is no clear reason, then, why one could not view a text to be analyzed as representative of a larger community of all such texts. The "responses" to the question put to an analyzable text constitute in turn a theory not only about the basis for the rhetorical success of that single text, but also of all texts represented by the one analyzed.

Hence, I will make certain observations about sample scientific texts. These observations will in turn result in my formulating a structural description of observable and intuitive aspects of the pragmatic structure of such texts. In order to accomplish my task, I will examine the discourse hierarchy of scientific writing, the rhetorical strategy of scientific writing, the author's intent, the persuasive import of individual sentences, the interpretive force subtly visited upon the reader of scientific writing, and the author's ability to anticipate a reader's potential arguments and questions.

Although I will extract fragment passages from three scientific reports in order to illustrate different aspects of scientific writing, I intend any conclusions I draw regarding scientific rhetoric to be considered as a whole. The sample texts to be analyzed are selected from _Science_. (The texts are: Enright, 1980; Rockley, Davis, and Richardson, 1980; Starkey and Cooper, 1980).

The rhetoric of scientific reports reveals that technical and scientific communication are general models of persuasive communication. We therefore ought to gain some insight into the following questions regarding persuasive communication:

1. Does the science writer's published material reflect the sense of a felicitous schema for developing a rhetorical argumentation?
2. Is there an essential character to how the mature science writer argues?
3. Are there underlying rhetorical primes of organization and development in persuasive argumentation?
4. Do the organization and development of persuasive argumentation suggest that underlying rhetorical primes are ordered according to a particular distribution?

The responses to our questions, of course, ought to be in the affirmative if it is true that:

1. Competent writers have a sense of audience and accommodate the audience in their writing.
2. Strength in rhetorically mature writing results from the writer's sense of data and from the writer's balancing data and hypotheses.
3. Competent writers possess a schema for implicitly developing explicitly organized arguments.

A sense of audience, a rhetorical sense necessary to persuasive writing, can be found in all kinds of writing tasks addressing many different kinds of audiences. Mature writing possesses certain elements essential to its qualifying as an implicitly-developed and explicitly-organized argumentation. Stating hypotheses related to their research, science writers need to support those claims with data and then to support data and hypotheses by allowing the reader (i.e., by convincing the reader) to see how the hypotheses follow logically from the data. This is the nature of making claims and the nature of constructing a justification for such claims.

Mature rhetoric suggests the probabilistic character of a writer's claims and addresses the instances in which the justification for certain hypotheses would apply. Thus, in science writing, hypotheses are of two sorts: those of the writer whose research might be made use of as background or inspiration, or as instigating material. Competent writers initiate a contract between themselves and the reader through hypotheses of the second sort. Hypotheses of the first sort form the reasons why they are writing in the first place. Thus, hypotheses of both sorts carry their own accompanying data.

It goes without saying, then, that the analyst of scientific rhetoric must attribute some sense of creativity to science writing. The creative approach to a writing task reveals:

1. The author's competence to identify the context of purposeful research.
2. The author's competence to draw previous research into question.
3. The author's competence to develop evidence that will establish the originality or uniqueness of new data or new explanatory modellings of scientific subject matter.
4. The author's competence to see beyond the (research) task as given by external circumstances or as generated by one's own personal research.
5. The author's competence to recognize the complexity of the problem, but, nonetheless, not to be led away from the subject matter at hand.

These five factors imply an author's comfort with tasks at hand and ease with experiencing a possible new set of hypotheses. Such psychological relaxation puts the author into an imaginative frame of mind. For scientific expression, no less so than any other mode of discourse, is a way for an author to communicate personal thoughts and opinions to other human beings. The written word is not sacred and must always be used anew under imaginative, personally fresh instances.

Hence, the principle that the results of our linguistic analysis of scientific rhetoric will unencumberingly lead us to is that _pragmatic, mature scientific writing creates itself and in turn creates its own success as rhetoric by holding the reader's attention from its first paragraph to its last with subtle transitions consisting of observable and intuitive shifts in rhetorical mood._

A formal linguistic analysis of scientific rhetoric reveals several interesting findings. These findings account for the comprehensive and comprehensible nature of the format and style common to modern scientific expression in writing.

Understanding the concepts of (author's) intent, persuasive import (of sentences), subtle interpretive force, and author's ability to anticipate any likely reader essentially depends on what the concepts of _discourse hierarchy_ and _rhetorical strategy_ mean. By _discourse hierarchy_, I mean the overarching observable organization that automatically forces the composition of scientific reports. By _rhetorical strategy_, I mean the underlying intuitive development that automatically induces the inherent logic of scientific reports. In successful writing, organization and development are inseparable. Both are discernible by the language analyst's careful linguistic analysis of texts.

Moreover, linguistic analysis of scientific texts reveals that both organization and development serve complementary functions in mature scientific rhetoric; they are complementary ways of achieving the same end: i.e., of compelling any likely reader to participate in a rhetorical reenactment of some particular bit of research and thereby to become convinced by and of the writer's research as if it were one's own. Under the circumstances, both reader and writer are researchers. Thus, my referring to "any likely reader" is not a capricious phrasing on my part. Any Likely Reader (much like the politician's The People or the educator's The Student) is an abstraction; it refers to those individuals who, because of a shared interest in scientific subject matter of a particular sort, are likely to read in the fields of science.

Organization is a function of the spacing of determinable subtopics, such as the need to mention one's own methods, results, and conclusions, in order to convey a total scientific message. Development is a function of the interweaving of deep-level subtopics, such as the need to agree with past research and to coax forth one's own new contribution, as the text constructing itself maintains grammatical meaning.

Organization, or discourse hierarchy, regulates the author's foregrounding both data and the analytic method (or procedure) employed. Because subtitling can be a matter of a particular journal's editorial conventions, the organized components of a scientific report might not be subtitled so as to signal external transitions of the sort peculiar to scientific rhetoric. However, careful observation of when an author is subtopicalizing a new and slightly different treatment of his subject matter compels one to suggest that organization consists of the following possible modulations of the total message:

Introduction	Discussion
Methods	Conclusions
Results	Implications for Further Research

Development, or rhetorical strategy, regulates degrees of commitment on the part of the author to ideas initiating his writing the report now being read by some likely reader. "Ideas" is a rubric here for hypotheses of others and for hypotheses of the author's own. Except for subjoining an abstract at the head of a report, an author, out of respect for peers and for his or her own ideas, apparently never prematurely divulges the hypothesis that a likely reader, by the force of rhetoric, will be invited to consider. Instead, an author uses others' hypotheses, perhaps largely already accepted by the scientific community to cover his own hidden hypothesis. This allows the reader to become psychologically comfortable with being possibly persuaded by new data, a new analytic method, or a new theory or model.

Development is also a matter of transitions within the scientific text, transitions of a subtler sort than those accomplished by organization. Subtitles naming developmental transitions can never surface in a text. The fact of their existence, unlike that of organizational shifts, does not depend on the author's subtopicalizing for the reader the treatment of the subject matter; rather, it depends on the author's competence with the actual idiomatic grammar of English. This is that aspect of writing a text in which variation can take place, where the author's creative, or merely different, use of the language can vary one piece of written discourse from another. Despite the possibility for variation, however, creativity within a text, rudimentary or otherwise, operates within a fixed developmental pattern. The subtler subtopics peculiar to rhetorical strategy are intuitive place holders, so to speak, allowing the author to shift from agreement on an idea to presentation of a new provocative idea to complete (and presumably irrevocable) acceptance (by writer and reader) of a newer idea.

We can give names to these shifts, although we must remember that these labels surface not as subheadings but as manifestations of the writer's mature rhetorical style. Success accorded a writer depends on his or her handling of these shifts. We can call such shifts: Agreed - But - But Suppose - Then - Indeed. An analysis of developmental shifts reveals the following facts:

1. That the author is responsible for arousing reader interest.
2. That, having captured the reader's interest, the author must next persuade.
3. That the author's persuading a reader to believe in a new (initially hidden) hypothesis depends on the author's ability to perform (i.e., to reenact rhetorically) the scientific method.

Around these observations revolve the following two claims: organizational shifts are modulations of the total scientific message; developmental shifts are modulations of grammatical meaning. Hence, the success and logic inherent in a mature rhetorical style are a function of the author's ability to balance message and meaning.

We should now discuss these claims in more detail, placing them well into the context of how the writer modulates message and meaning in the science research report.

Anyone entitled to an opinion regarding the relationship of science, technology, and society agrees that science is truly a human endeavor. The mystery, however, is the process by which individuals contribute to science, and frequent research (by historians of science or psychologists and sociologists of knowledge) characterizing science as a human endeavor continues. Studies of this sort are wonderfully detailed, extrapolative, and revelatory in their own right. Moreover, studies of this sort would seemingly support the opinion of Nobel Laureate of medicine (1960) and philosopher of science, Sir Peter Medawar, who reportedly has cautioned those interested in the topic against assuming that we can plumb the mystery of scientific creativity by studying the form of the scientific paper, recommending instead that we "peer through the keyhole" to see the scientist at work (see Keller, 1981).

There is a lot of truth and much common sense in Sir Peter Medawar's recommendation. However, there is a time when studying the form of the scientific paper is a necessity: namely, that moment when we need to divine what contacts have possibly taken place between writer and reader once the scientist has used language to report personal research findings which the making of science has brought about. Analyzing scientific rhetoric allows us to put aside for a moment the mystery of making science in order to peer more closely at what happens after the moment of scientific creativity. Rhetorical mood captures and frames creativity of all sorts once the created object (in this case, scientific hypotheses) is expressed maturely. Studying the structure of the scientific paper, therefore, can help us to pinpoint the nature and character of the pragmatism underlying rhetorical mood. After all, scientific creativity is a process of conceptualizing; one needs language to conceptualize and, therefore, needs language to give a fixed form to one's own created scientific hypotheses.

The more revealing analysis of rhetoric is one that keeps distinct the details of rhetorical style from the facts of rhetorical effectiveness. Facts underlie detail, as regularity underlies form, structure, and pattern. Knowledge of facts is therefore prior to knowledge of details.

Details of a writing style constitute observable surface syntactic phenomena. Facts constitute the intuitive semantic character of the effectiveness of a piece of writing. The details are often a matter of whether the author defines, analyzes (processually or causally), classifies, compares or contrasts. Facts are a matter of how the writer maintains rhetorical control of the persuasive postulating speaking voice he has created.

Details lend cohesion to the discourse hierarchy, to the outside structure of the speaking voice. Facts lend coherence to the rhetorical strategy, to the inside structure of the speaking voice.

In industry and government today the discourse hierarchy of specialist documents is a matter of convention. However, this is not a trivial observation. For if one follows the conventional rules of external form to compose scientific reports, for example, the rhetorical strategy automatically and logically falls into place. The cohesion characteristic of the discourse hierarchy controls the coherent, developing, modulating rhetorical intuition characteristic of the author's overall rhetorical strategy.

A coherent rhetorical strategy guarantees the success of the author's overall objective, which, in the case of science research reports, is first to present common knowledge, then to discuss theoretical points, and, finally, to do research before the reader, i.e., to reenact the scientific method. Faced with this objective, the author controls his or her reenactment of the scientific method through the pragmatic structure of the discourse hierarchy. The author rhetorically animates the common-sense persuasiveness characteristic of the overall rhetorical mood with a modulating strategy.

As indicated earlier, I will discuss three scientific reports from Science, illustrating different aspects of each. But we should keep in mind that each is a hologram, so to speak, of the pragmatic structure of rhetorical maturity characteristic of science research reports; the structural description of each reflects how the author modulates rhetorical mood in science research reports.

Let us first consider Enright's (1980) "Temporal

Precision in Circadian Systems: A Reliable Neuronal Clock from Unreliable Components." The visual field of the paper, i.e., its discourse hierarchy, is readily evident upon superficial examination: it paraphrases past research, suggesting other possible avenues of investigation (INTRODUCTION); it briefly sketches in the procedure or method to be applied to a general set of observable data, suggesting the possibility of one's being led to new hypotheses (METHOD); it outlines the new hypothesis (no longer hidden or merely suggested), sketching in a new set of data (no longer unapparent even to cursory examination), suggesting the possibility that the new findings will as a matter of fact solve problems heretofore unforeseen (RESULTS); it demonstrates, defends, and elaborates on the generalizations to be drawn from the new findings, ushering in even marginal or earlier unfocused hunches, facts, or hypotheses (DISCUSSION); it briefly paraphrases and summarizes the RESULTS and DISCUSSION sections, rounding out the current implications of the present research (CONCLUSION); finally, it suggests future research, raising questions of theory and potential application (IMPLICATIONS FOR FURTHER RESEARCH).

The observation of this kind of language play at work in the rhetoric indicative of the professions supports a language analyst's hunch regarding the pattern of a deeper-level rhetorical strategy. The grammar of the language employed, although a fixed form, allows and enhances the author's attempt to capture the reader's attention.

The author captures reader attention by stating a factual notion which the reader agrees with completely (AGREED). Then the author suggests that past research lacks the power to produce a significant number of generalizations, prompting the writer (and, by implication, the reader) to wonder why this particular problem exists (BUT). Next, the writer offers a hypothesis that might resolve or explain away the problem with the prior theory, thus safeguarding the scientific method (BUT SUPPOSE). A more complete analysis of some sort is then presented, applying proof to the correctness of the newly proposed hypothesis (THEN). Finally, the author (now the cleverer theorist), to his or her surprise and delight, notices that the new explanation covers an even broader set of data than previously thought possible, solving not only the problems of past research, but also redirecting possibly some, if certainly not all, new research on the same topic (INDEED).

Modulating the mood of the entire text within the fixed form of the underlying grammar, the rhetorical strategy develops against the background of downplaying and highlighting ideas. Downplaying alternative or contrary ideas and assumptions in various sections of the discourse hierarchy of the paper is part of a larger scheme designed to guide the reader's attention and thought through the developmental shifts of AGREED, BUT, BUT SUPPOSE, THEN, INDEED. In fact, it is possible to paraphrase this entire sample scientific paper in light of these shifts:

> AGREED: circadian rhythms of higher vertebrates have (N.B.: _habitual present_) extraordinary temporal precision. BUT single cellular pacemakers by themselves have (N.B.: _habitual present_) widely varying operating cycles. BUT SUPPOSE a number of these pacemakers were (N.B.: _hypothetical present_) coupled together in a manner that produced an operating frequency equal to the mean of the operating frequencies of the individual pacemakers. THEN this frequency would vary (N.B.: _hypothetical future_) very little over long periods of time. INDEED, extensive modeling and testing have shown (N.B.: _immediate past_) that pacemaker coupling will produce (N.B.: _habitual future_) the precision observed in the circadian rhythms of higher vertebrates.

In fact, we see that tense form and implied rhetorical meaning adjust to the overall rhetorical mood: message and meaning shift from hypothetical time to concrete time. The downplaying of an idea leads to the highlighting of an idea.

On the superficial level, the following sentence by the author illustrates how wording downplays contrary ideas:

> It is conceivable that intense natural selection has led to the evolution of extremely precise oscillators in the form of specialized single cells in the nervous or hormonal systems, but such ad hoc explanation has apparently never been invoked for circadian rhythms (Enright, 1980:1542).

The key phrase here is "ad hoc explanation," which implies that the idea of past researchers regarding extremely accurate cellular oscillators was hastily thought out and, therefore, not credible, except perhaps in specialized cases. In science, however, specialized cases are the least favored, for they do not suggest further more universal generalizations or applications.

It ought to be clear that a knowledge of specialist vocabulary is not a necessary prerequisite to knowing intuitively the substance of what is being accomplished by the rhetoric of science research reports. Vocabulary does not constitute the whole of any language: rules do. Once the rules of a language are known, completing a text (i.e., a sentence, a passage, an entire piece of writing) is a matter of resonating the word stock of a language with its rules, thereby generating the rhetoric that will modulate the fixed grammar of the language to accomplish some end. Specialists of scientific fields are first speakers of a language; they learn to know their language before learning the formal vocabulary of their disciplines.

Therefore, the relationship of message and meaning is not a function of specialist vocabulary. The rhetorician must pay closer attention to how mature specialist language modulates rhetorical mood than to the choice of a vocabulary that the specialist's discipline expects. Students of writing, novice rhetoricians, and technical editors can discern the sense of a piece of scientific writing, or the lack of sense and tone, and know - without a schooled knowledge of the formal vocabulary of science - whether a writer is being verbose, imprecise, or unfocused by analytically observing the mature, or otherwise, shifts among the coherent components of rhetorical strategy, AGREED, BUT, BUT SUPPOSE, THEN, INDEED.

As a rule, writers of science research reports do not expect to burden their readers with extraneous, though perhaps otherwise interesting, deliberation and information. The procedure or method of investigation, the emerging results, and the drawn conclusions are the primary focus of one's research. The vocabulary, therefore, is merely a backdrop to these pieces of information. Although the writer adjusts a larger scope around his primary focus in the discussion section of his paper, the results are earlier stated and are to the point. Let us take as an example the findings of Rockley, Davis, and Richardson (1980) in their "Fourier-Transformed Infrared Photoacoustic Spectroscopy of Biological Materials." In their introduction, the authors paraphrase the findings of past researchers and end their two-paragraph introduction by foreshadowing the method they will employ: "By combining these two advances, the technique of FTIR-PAS has been developed" (Rockley, et al., 1980:918). The method section, a single paragraph of five longish sentences, opens with an assessment of their procedure ("The method is simple") and ends with mentioning what the authors' procedure can expect to accomplish:

> The Fourier-transform spectrometer makes these measurements easy because of the multiplexing advantage, the repetitive scanning feature, and the high peak power of the incident infrared light (92 mW for the Digilab FTS-20 spectrometer) (Rockley, et al., 1980:919).

Their results form the major focus of the following paragraph of theirs:

> . . .we measured the FTIR-PAS spectra of protoporphyrin IX, hemin, hemoglobin, and horseradish peroxidase. They are shown in Figs. 1 through 4. The spectrum of protoporphyrin IX dimethyl ester is qualitatively indentical to that reported by Boucher and Katz. ... The only quantitative difference is in the relative absorbance of the methyl propionate ester carbonyl stretch at 1738 cm^{-1} seen by the two methods. By comparison with the rest of the spectrum, the PAS signal strength for this band is much less than that reported by Boucher and Katz (Rockley, et al., 1980:919).

These few observations raise one final issue regarding the pragmatic structure of scientific rhetoric. We need to know how the discourse hierarchy and the rhetorical strategy match up; we need to know to what extent their components have or do not have a one-to-one correspondence.

It is interesting to note, for example, that the introduction section of science research reports suggests the rhetorical strategy in part or in its entirety. If this suggestion is partial, it includes at least AGREED, BUT, BUT SUPPOSE. The two-paragraph opening of "Fourier-Transformed Infrared. . ." typifies a partial introduction.

> AGREED It is common in the study of biochemicals that an infrared spectrum of a lyophilized material or an insoluble material is required ...
>
> ... BUT However, visible and ultraviolet PAS spectra often exhibit broad, structureless features. BUT SUPPOSE Low and Parodi ... extend(ed) ... PAS to the infrared region ... Busse and Bullemer ... obtained(ed) infrared PAS spectra of gases in a spectrophone. (With our) combining these two advances, the technique of FTIR-PAS has been developed.

If the introduction of a science research report reflects the complete rhetorical strategy, it, of course, includes THEN and INDEED. Our third paper under discussion, Starkey and Cooper's (1980) "Perception of Numbers by Human Infants," typifies this extension. I have condensed the first paragraph of the introduction of this report to reveal its underlying rhetorical strategy (see Starkey and Cooper, 1980:1032):

> We AGREE with recent research in cognitive developmental psychology that has shown that 2 to 4 year-olds understand some basic number concepts. BUT the presence of numerical abilities in very young children led us to investigate the possible precursors of these abilities in infants. BUT SUPPOSE, furthermore, that we discover that this ability to discern the numerical value of a set of items may be necessary for a subsequent development of an understanding of number. THEN, given the results of previous research with 2 to 4 year-

olds, and because, in this report, we present data showing that 22-week old infants can also discriminate exact numbers of items - INDEED there is the possibility that the young child's verbal counting abilities grow in part from the infant's numerical ability. All such research, therefore, should first begin with the infant.

Observing the rest of the paper, we discover that BUT SUPPOSE is reiterated again in both the method and results sections, that THEN is developed in the discussion of science research reports, and, finally, that INDEED is confined to the conclusion:

METHOD & RESULTS
BUT SUPPOSE we conducted our experiment and analyzed the data several ways, always having the same pattern of results reveal itself.

DISCUSSION
THEN, because of our experimental controls, a number of potential explanations can be ruled out.

CONCLUSION
INDEED, we think it highly likely that subitizing, a perceptual enumeration process, underlies the ability of infants to discriminate, represent, and remember small numbers of items, and furthermore that verbal counting may have precursors during infancy.

Hence, the entire pragmatic structure of science research reports reduces to five sets summarizing the relationship between the discourse hierarchy and the rhetorical strategy:

AGREED (INTRODUCTION)
BUT (INTRODUCTION)
BUT SUPPOSE (INTRODUCTION (METHOD (RESULTS)))
THEN (INTRODUCTION (DISCUSSION))
INDEED (INTRODUCTION (CONCLUSION))

I have argued elsewhere (Blanton, 1976, 1979, 1980) that the demand for greater scientific and technical information has given rise to different genres of technical communication. The number is not enormous, but significant enough to warrant attention by those interested in the structure of the rhetoric. The basic genres seem to amount to twelve:

1. memos
2. correspondence
3. company catalogs
4. company brochures
5. press releases
6. manuals
7. proposals
8. poster presentations
9. slide lectures
10. technical specifications
11. laboratory reports
12. science research reports

Moreover, when examined in detail, these twelve categories expand roughly into a total of some 35 subgenres; for each basic category can differ not in organization or form (i.e., in discourse frame or hierarchy) but in persuasive, purposeful development (i.e., in underlying rhetorical strategy). Therefore, the structure of pragmatic rhetorical effectiveness needs more investigating (see Locker, 1981).

The discourse hierarchy of science research reports is a matter of convention. No matter which subheadings a writer uses, or whether he or she uses any at all, the discourse hierarchy amounts to a beginning, a middle, and an end. But because the rhetorical mood modulating through the discourse hierarchy is essentially unavailable to superficial observation, one begins to suspect some underlying strategy that controls the external components that introduce, discuss, and conclude the writer's ideas. Upon closer observation, as we have seen in this report, the pattern and structure of the strategy are discernible. Rhetorical success is a function of rhetorical maturity, and rhetorical maturity, though an attitudinal stance or voice of a writer, has a discernible linguistic structure.

However, having discerned a pattern for what we have called a pragmatic structure, we must admit that the investigation reported in this paper has been from the point of view of a reader. What of the writer writing, rewriting, and composing at his or her desk? Surely, no mature writer of science research reports writes first an introduction, then a method section, then a results section, then a discussion, and so forth. One suspects that the discourse hierarchy that is read by any likely reader was differently organized by the specialist writer during the process of research. A writer of science can not construct an actual introduction for actual findings until he has a sizable, replicable, body of data. Results, in turn, are not obtainable until one first has some method which will induce results. One suspects that a science researcher conceptualizes the methods, results, and conclusion sections first; around these the researcher then perceives an introduction, a discussion, and, finally, an implication for further research. This conception-to-perception order seems natural to the science writer; one supposes that further investigation into this order will shed more light on the general principles of natural composition.

Obviously, this is an important research question for those interested in the rhetoric of scientific expression; further research on this matter is necessary so that we might have fewer intuitive conclusions and more discernible data on the differences among prewriting, writing, and composing. We know more about the final product of these processes than about the processes themselves.

NOTES

[1]The research results reported on in this study emerged out of my attempt to test John Lackstrom's suggestions regarding the features of scientific English. I first encountered John Lackstrom's lectures on AGREED, BUT, BUT SUPPOSE, THEN, INDEED at the 1979 Summer Teachers' Training Institute on English for Specific Purposes, Oregon State University, Corvallis, Oregon. I became intrigued by his presentation of these features and felt that some analysis should determine how these rhetorical primes correspond to what I had been referring to in my personal notes as the discourse hierarchy of technical communication. This study is such an analysis. From my analysis also emerges further observations about the Lackstrom primes.

REFERENCES

Blanton, Mackie J-V., 1976, Producing content grammars for advanced learners in the sciences, Ill. TESOL/ Bilingual Ed.

Blanton, Mackie J-V., 1979, English for specific purposes, Am. Soc. Engin. Ed.

Blanton, Mackie J-V., 1980, The Structure of scientific and technical rhetoric, Invited Lecturer Series, SUNY Buffalo.

Britton, Earl W., 1975, What is technical writing?: A redefinition, in: "The Teaching of Technical Writing, Donald H. Cunningham and Herman A. Estrim, eds., NCTE, Urbana.

Brusaw, Charles T., et al., 1976, "Handbook of Technical Writing," St. Martin's, N.Y.

Buchanan, Scott, 1972, "Truth in the Sciences," U. of Virginia, Charlottesville.

Enright, J. T., 1980, Temporal precision in circadian systems: a reliable neuromal clock from unreliable components, Science, 209:1542-44.

Keller, Evelyn Fox, 1981, The Secrets in the tissue of a mouse: a review of June Goodfield's "An Imagined World: A Story of Scientific Discovery," The New York Times Book Review, April 19:80.

Locker, K., 1980, Patterns for organization of business writing, J. of Bus. Comm., 14:35-45.

Rockley, M. G., et al., 1980, Fourier-transformed infrared photoacoustic spectroscopy of biological materials, Science, 210:918-20.

Selinker, Larry, 1980, Some examples of scientific and technical English genres, TESOL.

Starkey, Prentice and Cooper, Robert G. Jr., 1980, Perception of numbers by human infants, Science, 210: 1033-35.

Y Cajal, Ramon, 1893, "Precepts and Counsels on Scientific Investigations, Psychology of Mind Institute Studies, Berkeley.

THE FUNCTION OF A GRAMMATICAL ALTERNATION IN 14 SURGICAL REPORTS[1]

Catherine Pettinari

University of Michigan

INTRODUCTION

Purpose of the Paper

This paper demonstrates that in one particular type of English for Science and Technology (EST) data, surgical reports of cholecystectomies, the discourse function of the alternation between sentences with indefinite subjects and with the dummy subject *there* is to provide an alternation between thematic and nonthematic information. In discourse, thematic information has been generally defined as that knowledge which the speaker assumes is relevant to the goal of the communicative event (Tomlin and Rhodes, 1979). In the case of this data, thematic information is defined as that information which the surgeon assumes is relevant to the goal of the surgical event of removing the gallbladder. Thus, information which is less likely to relate directly to the removal of the gallbladder is usually introduced into the text with a *there* sentence.

Since it has been shown that the proper use of *there* sentences present a problem in written discourse for some ESL students (Schachter and Rutherford, 1979; Rutherford, 1981) this analysis offers possibilities for pedagogical purposes as well as for designing studies for specific purpose acquisition (Selinker, 1980).

The data used in this study comes from fourteen surgical reports of cholecystectomies (an operation to remove the gallbladder) from four surgeons.

Argumentation

In order to provide support for the thesis that the discourse function of the alternation between sentences with indefinite subjects and with the dummy subject there is to provide an alternation between thematic and non-thematic information, I argue that the alternation is ultimately controlled by the extralinguistic situation of the surgery itself. The claim is made that the nature of the surgical procedure, its sequence, and those aspects that are considered to be essential to the procedure determine, in this case, at least, the grammatical form of the alternation. Specifically, I argue that those parts of the surgery that are either essential to the procedure or are considered to be important for further reference can be determined by independent verification to be thematic. The argumentation follows from the general to the specific. I first describe what surgical reports are and what they are used for. Then, I define the notions of thematic and nonthematic information, distinguishing them from shared or nonshared information. As a working hypothesis in this data, I take as given that the surface subject in English represents thematic information (Matesius as cited in Firbas, 1974; Halliday, 1976; Tomlin, 1980b), although in subsequent sections, I question this hypothesis; also, I explain the cholecystectomy surgical procedure and demonstrate how the theme of the discourse can be determined in this data by reference to the extralinguistic situation of the surgical procedure.

Finally, I show that in this data indefinite subjects are thematic and indefinite non-subjects in there sentences are nonthematic, thus demonstrating the discourse function of this alternation in this data. In a concluding section, I discuss some problems about this analysis and further directions for research.

Importance of the Paper

It has been suggested that English speakers have a number of syntactic constructions that allow them to represent relatively unfamiliar information to the right of the verb: existential there, it-clefts, left dislocation (Prince, 1979). Much of the discussion about the function of there constructions has centered around data that has been intuitively generated for the purposes of the argumentation, however. Even in some data which purport to give a discourse explanation for the function of there sentences, one finds that examples have been given with a limited context; often no more than two or three sentences are given.

In this paper, however, I will demonstrate directly with concrete, naturally produced data in a medical context that the alternation between sentences with indefinite subjects and with there is not arbitrary, but is linked to the thematic information which is, in turn, determined by extralinguistic factors, thus providing strong empirical support for a discourse explanation of this particular syntactic alternation.

The type of data used here, which is based on describing a procedure followed, allows for a more precise analysis of this alternation and of thematic information than might other discourse genres. In the first place, in this data, there are both a number of sentences with indefinite subjects and with the dummy subject there. In the second place, the thematic information can be determined precisely with the aid of a specialist informant. Surgical reports of cholecystectomies were chosen because excision of the gallbladder is a routine, relatively standard procedure in which there is little variation in technique, and importantly, little variation in the discourse structure from surgeon to surgeon.

Since the surgical procedure is relatively standard, it should then be a fairly straightforward task to isolate and clearly identify, with the specialist informant's aid, which parts of the procedure are more essential to the cholecystectomy procedure proper than others. My experience with an informant shows that this is so. Thus, I claim that the thematic information of the discourse can be established in a noncircular fashion. And since the format is relatively consistent from one report to another and from one surgeon to another, one can make even stronger generalizations about the syntactic consequences found in this genre. This is an unusual type of text since it breaks the extremities of written and oral discourse. These reports are spoken, in that the surgeon orally dictates the text, and written, in that they are meant to be read.

Data from surgical reports are significant above and beyond their usefulness as confirmation of a discourse function for a syntactic form. Not only do they allow for a more precise analysis of the discourse function of a syntactic alternation, but they offer other possibilities for investigation of both a theoretical and applied nature which will be explored in further research.

Despite the consistency in format of surgical reports, according to the informant, no where in their training or background do surgeons or physicians receive formal training or education on how to do surgical reports or what types of grammatical constructions to use in writing them, so one would eventually wish to ask how they acquire this "shared information" (Carpenter, in preparation).

Because of the nature of the data, this analysis escapes the trap of a circular explanation. In many analyses of discourse, it is difficult to determine thematic and nonthematic information without resorting to introspection on the part of the analyst about what constitutes thematic and nonthematic information, thus resulting in a circular analysis. In these analyses, the theme of the discourse is determined by the linguist and then, in turn, that textual information is labeled as thematic or nonthematic. In this study, on the contrary, thematic and nonthematic information are not determined by introspection. Rather, the theme of the discourse is determined by interviewing a specialist-informant in a more or less disciplined fashion over several interview sessions. He pointed out those elements of the cholecystectomy procedure proper that are essential to the successful completion of the operation and those elements that are more peripheral. From this information, then, the thematic information can be determined, and a noncircular analysis be made.

Methodology

This paper provides a methodology of analysis of EST texts that builds upon other methodologies of this type of data (Tomlin, 1980a; Selinker, 1979; Bley-Vroman and Selinker, 1980; Tarone, 1981) but differs from them in significant ways. As in Tomlin (1980a; 1980b), key syntactic processes are linked to thematicity, but this paper uses a specialist-informant to determine thematicity in an independent fashion and to validate hypotheses.

The specialist-informant is consulted in order to gain access to technical information, as done by Selinker (1979). Selinker's goal was to relate to the problem that many ESL teachers have faced: that of teaching students to read materials in English which the native speaking teachers do not understand themselves. Thus, he attempted to gain as much information as necessary for ESL teachers to understand a text. And so it was not necessary for him to frame questions in such a way as to avoid concentrating on prejudicing the informant. The purpose of this analysis, on the other hand, is different in that my goal was to determine the thematic information in such a way as not to lead the informant to my presupposed conclusions.

The methodology here closely parallels Bley-Vroman and Selinker (1980) in that the analysis proceeds in a cyclic fashion. The analyst has a "preunderstanding" about the nature of a construction in the text, examines that construction in a small number of texts, makes a conclusion, and then gathers more of the same type of data, analyses it, and then continues to refine the conclusions based on findings from more and more data. As in Bley-Vroman and Selinker the analysis here is cyclic as well, but, in contrast, validity is not determined by the incorporation of additional data and retrievability of the cycles alone, but by confirmation by a specialist-informant.

Use of the Specialist Informant

It can be seen, then, that the specialist-informant is essential in order to gain access to the technical information that lies behind texts (Selinker, 1979). Although I have a fairly extensive background in a medical field, in this study the specialist-informant was extremely helpful in filling in gaps in that knowledge by explaining lexis and anatomical relationships.

Informant techniques used in linguistic field methods (see, e.g., Craig, 1979) were utilized in order to determine the most important parts of the surgery and variations in technique and procedure. Three sessions of approximately one hour each were held over a period of nine months with the informant. Also, a questionnaire was also sent to verify information, and, additionally, several phone calls were made and drafts sent to the informant to check final information. The goal of these sessions was to determine thematic vs. nonthematic information plus to validate hypotheses and to gain additional knowledge about the nature of the surgical procedure. The thematic information was determined by asking the informant what is usually done in a cholecystectomy procedure and what is the step-by-step procedure usually followed. Then he was asked to explain problematic areas and questions.

THE DATA

The surgical reports looked at here are dictated by the surgeon who performed the operation immediately following each surgical procedure. The report is required to be filed with each patient's medical report for medico-legal purposes, for hospital accreditation requirements, for research, and, most importantly, for further patient care purposes. Surgical reports also serve as documents to provide proof of correct surgical procedure and adequate technique. They also may be used for research purposes to compare techniques and findings.

Data for this particular study come from 14 reports of cholecystectomies written by four surgeons, all native speakers of English, during a nine month period of time from 1979 to 1980. The reports examined here (see Appendix 1) are each one to two pages in length. The format of each text is highly similar, with little variation from surgeon to surgeon. A number of other aspects of the data are similar from text to text as well. For example, the reporting of the temporal sequence of the procedures followed in the operation is invariable from text to text. One process must precede another in time and space before another can follow. Obviously, because of the nature of the operation, the abdomen must be cut open before bleeding can be controlled, and the cystic duct must be identified (found) before it can be opened. Thus, the temporal sequence of reported events is the same in all texts. In addition, regulations require that the procedure followed, surgical findings, excision of tissue, and abnormalities be reported, and so one can find information of this nature on each report.

Some stylistic variations in the format of the text may be seen, but this does not affect the analysis of the data. For example, one surgeon divided the text into three sections: Summary and Indications, Findings, and Summary. For this surgeon's reports, only the Findings and Summary part of the data was examined because the Summary and Indications section was determined not pertinent to the main procedure. Another surgeon divided the text into two sections: Operative Findings and What Was Done in one report, but reported the data in a sequential text in the other report. The remaining surgeons did not divide the text into sections.[2]

SYNTACTIC FRAMEWORK: THERE SENTENCES

The alternation between sentences such as

1. A book is on the table.
2. There is a book on the table.

has been the subject for discussion in the literature of transformational grammar. Researchers such as Bolinger (1977), Kuno (1972), Prince (1979), and Sheintuch (1980) have speculated about the function of the transformation called "*There* insertion."

Previous explanations of *There* insertion have ranged from those in earlier transformational grammar, in which the form but not the function of *There* insertion was discussed, to tentative explanations based on semantic and/or higher level discourse factors. In transformational grammar, as Bolinger (1977:90) states, "*There* insertion was generally assumed to be an essentially meaningless transformation. *There* insertion added a constituent to a sentence which was complete without it." Conditions affecting *There* insertion were purely syntactic.

In over-simplified terms, I should say that much research (Ross, 1972; Allan, 1972; Sampson, 1972; Rando and Napoli 1978) has dealt with the permissible constituents of *There* insertion sentences. In this paper, I am not interested in expanding upon these analyses of syntactic form; rather, I am concerned with demonstrating the function of *There*-sentences in this particular type of EST discourse by linking it to the informational structure of the text.

More recent explanations have attempted to account for

the inadequacy of the transformational grammar explanation to account for a wider range of data. Explanations based on semantic, discourse, and pragmatic conditioning have been offered.

One way of looking at the semantic nature of There insertion has been to consider the "presentative" nature of the construction. Bolinger (1977) claims that presentative There insertion initiates a line of thought. Kuno (1972) claims that in discourse "the most natural way to introduce an entirely new event in conversation seems to be to talk about the existence or coming into existence towards the speaker, (Kuno, 1972:284) as does Sheintuch (1980), who claims that There insertion functions to introduce certain subjects into discourse.

Further research such as that by Linde (1977) and Prince (1979), has examined the discourse function of There insertion. Prince (1979:276) claims that "speakers seem to have command of a variety of syntactic constructions to remove relatively unfamiliar entities from being represented by subject NPs: existential there, it-clefts, etc." This paper will expand upon this claim by demonstrating that the placement of NPs to the right of the verb in there-sentences functions to provide an alternation for nonthematic information.

DISCOURSE FRAMEWORK, THEMATIC INFORMATION

No accepted definitions exist in the discourse analysis literature of such notions as thematic and nonthematic information, old and new information, given and new information, and shared and nonshared information. These notions are often conflated in one way or another and are not defined clearly. For the purposes of this particular paper, I will accept the derivative of the Prague School tradition (Halliday, 1967; Halliday and Hasan, 1976) of a split in textual information between at least what has been termed (a) thematic and nonthematic information and (b) shared and nonshared information.

The approach to the analysis of discourse organization follows Tomlin (1980b) in its consideration of the extra-linguistic situation that produces the text. In this approach, texts are seen to derive from an overall communicative event. This event consists of the text and the participants in the event, both in the production of the text and the interpretation of it. The entire extralinguistic situation is viewed as influencing the textual organization in significant ways.

The textual organization can be linked to the extralinguistic event in two ways. The first way concerns information that the speaker and the hearer hold in common; this is termed shared information and information that is not held in common is termed nonshared information. For example, consider the following example from one of the texts:

3. A 24 Malecot catheter formed a gastrostomy and the gastrostomy was tacked to the abdominal wall with 3-0 Dexon. (5-B)

The first NP gastrostomy (surgical creation of an opening from the stomach through the abdominal wall) is the first mention of gastrostomy in the text. Thus, at this point in the text, it is nonshared information, is marked with the indefinite marker and is found to the right of the verb. The second time it is mentioned, it is shared information to the technically sophisticated reader because of prior mention; now the technically sophisticated speaker and the potential reader hold this information in common, and so it is shared information. It is now in the subject position and marked with the definite marker.

The second way in which the textual organization is linked to the extralinguistic situation is the consideration of that information which is crucial to the development of a text or subtext. According to Tomlin, in the production of a particular text, the speaker will "build the text around information he assumes to be the most relevant for the goal of the communicative event that he is in" (Tomlin, 1980b:10). This information is termed by Tomlin "thematic information." In prototypical cases, the notions of shared and thematic information overlap and are marked with the definite marker, nonshared and nonthematic information overlap, are represented in one NP, and are marked with the indefinite marker, but they need not be.

In this data, the goal is to describe the surgical

procedure of removing the gallbladder; thus, some medical information is more relevant to that description than other medical information. For example, references to certain procedures and instruments used to carry out these procedures are more relevant to describing this particular operation than are references to the phenomena such as surgeons, their assistants, and organs other than the affected area. Thus, for the purposes of this paper, thematic information is defined as:

> That knowledge which the surgeon assumes is relevant to the goal of the communicative event of describing the surgical procedure for medical record purposes.

Thus, in this data, those parts of the surgery that are more crucial to the main surgical event include the necessary procedures that the surgeon follows in order to excise the gallbladder. In other words, the main thrust of the surgical procedure determines that information which is analyzed as thematic information. As a consequence, areas not directly within the surgical field or the surgical procedure, i.e. peripheral information, are determined to be nonthematic information.

The extralinguistic situation that determines the thematic information is as follows. According to the specialist-informant, the procedure that is followed in the cholecystectomy procedure is relatively standard. Elements of the surgery that are essential to the procedure include:

> An incision is made.
> The abdomen is opened.
> The abdomen is explored.
> The gallbladder is grasped with a forceps and drawn upwards.
> The cystic artery is closed to prevent bleeding.
> After cutting the cystic duct the gallbladder is dissected.
> A tube is then slipped into the cystic duct.
> A cholangiogram is obtained and read by the radiologist.
> The cystic duct is then dissected free to its junction with the common duct and closed.

A drain is placed and the wound is closed.

Other information which is important to include in the report are: what the size of the common bile duct is; whether there are stones in the common bile duct; if any abnormalities are found upon exploration of the abdomen; whether a cholangiogram was taken; and whether any growth was found in the pancreas. Thus, all of the above constitutes the <u>thematic information</u> in this context.

There are some minor variations to this standard procedure, and they include the types of incisions that are made, the direction from which the gallbladder is dissected, the types of drains used, the use of hemoclips or ties and the use of absorbable or nonabsorbable sutures. Sometimes an appendectomy is also performed, sometimes not. Cholangiography (an x-ray procedure to visualize the bile duct) is not always performed.

Finally, it appears that the notions of thematic and nonthematic information, in this case, do not form an either-or dichotomy but, rather, they form a hierarchy, as in Tomlin (1980b). It can be seen in this information structure that some elements of the surgery are more important to the main thrust of the surgery than others and the informant confirmed this. For example, the process of grasping the gallbladder is more important to the development of the surgical procedure than the surgical equipment utilized to do so, whereas the surgical equipment used is more central in some instances than the stones that are found.

ARGUMENTATION

If this type of discourse were to follow the general pattern of English discourse, as discussed in Linde (1977), we would expect that the speaker would use the indefinite article to the right of the verb to introduce the information and then the definite article to mention that information subsequently. For example:

4. Yesterday Anderson kissed <u>a girl</u> with blue eyes. <u>The girl</u> called the police (Sørenson, 1959).

And in these instances, we could analyze the thematic information as that information that contributes to the development of the text. For example, the thematic information is Anderson's actions in the first sentence and the girl's actions in the second sentence.

In surgical reports, this pattern can be seen also. Consider again example (3):

> A 24 Malecot catheter formed *a gastrostomy* and *the gastrostomy* was tacked to the abdominal wall with 3-0 Dexon. (5-B)

In contrast to the introduction of information to the right of the verb and then placement in the subject position, in this data, there are a considerable number of examples of sentences that introduce information with the indefinite article in the subject position. The relationship between these sentences with indefinite subjects and those with the dummy subject *there* will be considered.

Argument 1: Indefinite Subjects are Thematic

The purpose of this section is to show that the alternation between sentences with indefinite subjects and *there*-sentences functions to provide an alternation between thematic and nonthematic information in this data. I first list those sentences with indefinite subjects and demonstrate that they correlate with the theme of the discourse. Next, I list those sentences with *there* and demonstrate that they correlate with nonthematic information. Finally, I examine in detail some apparent counterexamples and show that they do not disconfirm the hypothesis, but provide additional support for it.

57 sentences with NPs in the surface subject position with indefinite markers were found in this data. They can be classified into the following groups of information (see Table 1):

A. Surgical equipment, especially tubes and drains - 27 examples
B. Types of incisions - 8 examples
C. Cholangiograms - 6 examples
D. Adhesions - 2 examples
E. Stones - 6 examples

Table 1

A. Sentences with NPs with indefinite markers in the surface subject position: Surgical implements, especially drains and tubes:

(5) Finally, a stone rasping forceps was placed down...
(6) A #14 T tube was then placed into the common duct and sutured into place using interrupted 4-0 Vicryl.
(7) A Jackson-Pratt drain was placed in the foramen of Winslow through the lateral aspect of the wound.
(8) A large Jackson-Pratt drain was brought into the lateral portion of the wound...
(9) A #8 feeding tube placed in the cystic duct obtained a cholangiogram...
(10) A catheter was left in Morrison's pouch...
(11) A Fogarty biliary catheter passed easily into the duodenum and was drawn back with no evidence of stones.
(12) Running 5-0 Prolene closed the duct completely and no T-tube was used and no repeat cholangiogram obtained.
(13) ...and then a Fogarty catheter was passed.
(14) A #8 feeding tube was then passed into the jejunum about 15 cm. from the ligament of Treitz...
(15) A 24 Malecot catheter formed a gastrostomy...
(16) A Jackson-Pratt catheter was then laid across the anterior surface of the anastomosis...
(17) A 24 red rubber catheter was laid posterior to the anastomosis and through the foramen of Winslow.
(18) A catheter was placed around the stone and into the common duct.
(19) ...and a Jackson-Pratt drain was placed in the foramen of Winslow.
(20) ...and a Jackson-Pratt was placed through the lateral aspect of the wound and into the foramen of Winslow.
(21) The cystic duct was secured distally and a tube inserted through the cystic duct and into the common duct...
(22) A perforated silastic catheter was left in Morrison's pouch...
(23) The cystic duct was secured distally and a tube inserted through it into the common duct...

Table 1, continued

A. Surgical implements, especially drains and tubes:

(24) A tube was inserted through the cystic duct into the common duct...
(25) A Silastic catheter was left in Morrison's pouch and brought out through the lateral extent of each incision.
(26) A large Jackson-Pratt multiperforated siliconized drain was placed in the right hepatorenal recess and exited through a separate skin incision inferolateral to the original skin incision.
(27) A large Jackson-Pratt multiperforated siliconized drain was placed in the right hepatorenal recess...
(28) A pursestring suture of 3-0 Chromic was placed in this region...
(29) and a #14 needle was inserted.
(30) For a few moments, a sterile pack was placed in the right upper quadrant to aid in hemostasis.
(31) A large Jackson-Pratt multiperforated siliconized drain was placed in the right hepatorenal recess and allowed to exit through a separate stab wound lateral to the original skin incision.

B. Incisions

(32) A right subcostal incision was made.
(33) A subcostal incision was made.
(34) To improve exposure, a 2nd transverse incision was made slightly above the first.
(35) A right upper quadrant incision was made.
(36) ...and a right subcostal incision was made.
(37) A right subcostal oblique incision was made...
(38) A right, subcostal oblique incision was made...
(39) A right paramedian incision was made.

C. Cholangiograms

(40) A cystic duct cholangiogram was carried out by small infant feeding tube...
(41) A second film did show it.
(42) Running 5-0 Prolene closed the duct completely and no T-tube was used and no repeat cholangiogram obtained.

Table 1, continued

(43) A cholangiogram to the cystic duct revealed some enlarged common duct and a markedly large and curving pancreatic duct.
(44) After removal of the gallbladder, the entire specimen, with great difficulty a cystic duct cholangiogram was done, as a small stone was impaled in the distal spiral valves of Heister.
(45) After complete removal of the gallbladder a cystic duct cholangiogram was done on two occasions and revealed slight dialtion of the common duct...

D. Adhesions

(46) Numerous surrounding adhesions were freed to expose the gallbladder more completely.
(47) Numerous adhesions, both to the liver and gallbladder had to be taken down.

E. Stones

(48) ...and a small stone about 4-5 mm in size which was a crumbly granular nature was removed and seemed of the size seen on the cholangiogram.
(49) ...and it was not felt by the operator that a further stone was present.
(50) The opening of the pancreatic duct was not visualized, no stones were seen.
(51) The common duct felt to be at the upper limits of normal, but no stones could be readily ascertained.
(52) After removal of the gallbladder, the entire specimen, with great difficulty a cystic duct cholangiogram was done, as a small stone was impaled in the distal spiral valves of Heister.
(53) The common duct was then reopened and the choledoscope was passed. No further stones could be identified.

F. Additional cases

(54) A right rectus was transected and peritoneal cavity was entered.
(55) The cystic duct was identified, doubly hemoclipped and divided and a rather generous cystic duct was then identified and clips placed proximally.

Table 1, continued

(56) Probe was then easily placed into the duodenum, and flushing of the proximal and distal ducts was carried out with saline and no further debris ensued.
(57) Repalpation of the duct was carried out and no foreign object could be appreciated.
(58) A hand within the abdomen revealed no gross pelvic pathology though the entire pelvis was not explored because of adhesions.
(59) In so doing a rent was made in the gallbladder.
(60) The small bowel was run from the ligament of Treitz to the ileocecal valve and no abnormality was identified.
(61) The small bowel was run from the ileocecal valve to the ligament of Treitz and no abnormality was identified.
(62) Small bowel was run from the ileocecal valve to the ligament of Treitz and no abnormality was identified.
(63) Attention was redirected to the right upper quadrant, where an extremely tense and gangrenous gallbladder was identified.
(64) An area on the lower border of the gallbladder, roughly half way down its side, was chosen to deflate the gallbladder, because in this area there appears to be no gangrenous change.
(65) A sample of the bile was withdrawn for aerobic and anaerobic culture and sensitivity.

F. Additional cases - 12 examples

Thematic information, which has been established by specialist-informant procedures independent of syntactic structures, includes: surgical equipment and drains, types of incisions, and cholangiograms. In the above data (A-C), 41 examples of indefinite NPs that are subjects can be classified into one of these categories. Therefore, it can be concluded that indefinite subjects represent thematic information.

In the analysis of sentences with indefinite subjects, however, there are some sentences that cannot be classified into the categories of thematic information of surgical equipment, incisions, cholangiograms, adhesions, or stones, and are what I have called "additional cases." Those sentences in additional cases are problematic and require a text by text analysis and will not be analyzed further in this paper.

Before I go on to argue that indefinite subjects to the right of the verb in <u>there</u>-sentences represent non-thematic information, it is necessary to look at those sentences in which NPs that fall into the categories of thematic information are to the right of the verb and are not in the subject position (see Table 2).

These cases are not problematic to the general point of this section, i.e. indefinite subjects are thematic. As I previously stated, some parts of the operative procedure are more central than others. And so, when the possibility exists of including two potentially thematic NPs in a sentence, the NP which is more central to the main procedure will win out for the subject position (Tomlin, 1980b). For example, in (71) we see the order:

grasping the gallbladder > equipment used

Thus, in examples (71) (73), the location of the procedure, i.e. the gallbladder, is in the subject position and the surgical equipment is to the right of the verb.

In examples (72) and (75) we observe the order:

performing a cholangiogram > equipment used

Table 2. Sentences Representing Surgical Equipment, Incisions, or Cholangiograms with an Indefinite Marker not in the Surface Subject Position.

(68) Saline easily passed into the duodenum, as did a #3 and #4 Bakes dilator.

(69) Bile was emptied with a needle.

(70) The abdomen was entered through a right subcostal incision...

(71) Gallbladder was grasped with a Judd ring clamp and a Pean clamp.

(72) Operative cholangiography was accomplished through a cystic duct, utilizing a #8 infant feeding tube...

(73) The apex of the gallbladder was grasped with a Judd ring clamp...

(74) ...and the Hartmann's pouch was grasped with a peon (sic) clamp.

(75) Operative cholangiography was accomplished through the cystic duct utilizing a #5 infant feeding tube...

In these two examples the cholangiography procedure is in the subject position and the equipment used is to the right of the verb. It is interesting to note that in Table 1, Section A, Surgical equipment, that there are no examples of sentences with the indefinite subjects of Judd Ring Clamp or Pean Clamp.

Argument 2: Indefinite NPs to the Right of the Verb in There-Sentences Represent Nonthematic Information

Those indefinite NPs expressed to the right of the verb in there-sentences (see Table 3 for there-sentences in context) do not fall into any of the above categories that have been determined to be thematic, i.e., they are not surgical equipment, nor cholangiograms, nor types of incisions. That is, according to the informant, those NPs that are found to the right of the verb in there-sentences represent information which is peripheral to the procedure. Thus, we can say that they are less thematic than those other indefinite NPs that appear in the subject position. The discussion of there-sentences may be grouped into three classifications and I will discuss each classification separately: Description of findings, Adhesions, Stones.

Description of Findings

The following there-sentences appeared in the reports:

76. There was nice tapering effect at the ampulla...
77. There was considerable bleeding...
78. There was brisk flow in the duodenum.
79. There was slight roughening suggestive of inflammatory secretion or frons at one area.
80. There were abundant patches of fibrin entrapping stone fragments.
81. There was minimal inflammation.
82. There was some evidence of chronic inflammation in the surrounding tissues.
83. ...there was some chronic inflammation of the pancreas.
84. There was no history of jaundice. (3 times)

Table 3. Sentences with there.

#1

...At completion cholangiography was carried out. The initial film did not show emptying of the duodenum. A second film did show it. The radiologist felt there might be an indication of intramural stone in the duodenum; however on reinspection the duct itself filled nicely and there was nice tapering effect at the ampulla with emptying into the duodenum and it was not felt by the operator that a further stone was present.

#2

FINDINGS: There were some adhesions about the gallbladder which were thickened and one large oval stone measuring at least 4 cm in diameter was easily palpable. The liver, spleen, stomach, pancreas, duodenum, kidneys, large and small bowel and pelvic viscera were either palpated or inspected and found to be normal.

#3

The uterus and tubes were absent. There was an adhesion in the right lower quadrant that was taken down by blunt dissection but appeared to make bowel obstruction possible.

#4a

Bile was emptied with a needle and the gallbladder dissected out from above downward. There was considerable bleeding which was all controlled by cautery and a few hemoclips. A cholangiogram to the cystic duct revealed some enlarged common duct and a markedly large and curving pancreatic duct. The ampulla was not clearly seen but there was brisk flow in the duodenum.

#4b

The cystic duct opening was extended into the common duct and choledochoscope passed in both directions with good visualization of liver and good visualization of common duct down to circular frons which probably represented the ampulla. The opening of the pancreatic duct was not

Table 3, continued

visualized, no stones were seen. There was slight roughening suggestive of inflammatory secretion or frons at one area.

#5a

The choledoscope was passed. The walls of the ducts appeared largely white, but somewhat injected in some areas. There were abundant patches of fibrin-entrapping stone fragments, and clots both above and below. There were no obvious large, single stones seen.

#5b

Tissues were dissected away from the wall of the common duct laterally, and one area contained considerable infiltration with yellowish stone fragments. We looked for a leak in the common duct and could find none, so assumed it was a spillover from irrigation during exploration. The tissues were somewhat infiltrated with it. There was minimal inflammation and it did not look like an old leak.

#6

FINDINGS: The gallbladder was acutely inflated and tense. There was marked amount of small stones and conglomerate of large stones, particularly down in the infundibula. The cyst (sic) duct itself was inordinately large but packed with stones which were impaled in the spiral valves. The common duct felt to be at the upper limits of normal, but no stones could be readily ascertained...

#7

FINDINGS: The gallbladder was huge, distended, and chronically inflammed with granules stuck to the upper one-half of the gallbladder. There was some evidence of chronic inflammation in the surrounding tissues. The limited exploration of liver, pancreas, duodenum, stomach, immediate large and small bowel was unremarkable except for the fact that there was some chronic inflammation of the head of the pancreas and what was thought to be a small stone in the distal intrapancreatic portion of the common bile duct.

Table 3, continued

#8

...Because of its large size and chronic edematous nature the upper half of the gallbladder was removed in toto and the small infundibulum in which there was a packed stone was removed as a separate portion...

#9

...and pancreas were palpated or inspected and felt to be within normal limits. There were large stones in the gallbladder with adhesions between the gallbladder and the duodenum.

...The common duct was not dilated. There was no history of jaundice. The cystic duct was secured distally and a tube inserted through the cystic duct and into the common duct and operative cholangiogram was done.

#10

...The cystic duct was dissected out and traced down to the junction with the common duct which was identified above and below and was not dilated. There was no history of jaundice. The cystic duct was secured distally...

#11

Likewise the cystic duct was dissected out, traced down to the junction with the common duct which was not dilated. There was no history of jaundice or hepatitis. A tube was inserted through the cystic duct...

#12

...The right and left kidney were normal although it was noticed that the left kidney was in a somewhat ptotic position. The small bowel was run from the ligament of Treitz to the ileocecal valve and no abnormality was identified. Similarly, there was no detectable pathology in the colon.

Table 3, continued

#14

...Right and left kidneys, right and left hepatic lobes, right and left colon and transverse colon were identified and felt to be normal. There was, however, in the colon, a rather significant amount of diverticulosis which seemed to involve at least the left and transverse colon.

#14b

An area on the lower border of the gallbladder, roughly half way down its side, was chosen to deflate the gall-bladder, because in this area there appeared to be no gangrenous change.

85. ...there was no detectable pathology in the colon.
86. There was, however, in the colon, a rather significant amount of diverticulosis.
87. ...there appeared to be no gangrenous change.

The informant indicated that the above sentences represent areas not directly affected by the cholecystectomy procedure. These areas are peripheral to the surgical procedure itself and are around the main area of surgery. For example, consider examples (82) and (83). Both indicate areas not directly affected by the cholecystectomy, the pancreas and surrounding tissues. Again, according to the informant, (85) and (86) also clearly denote areas that are not directly affected by a cholecystectomy.

Adhesions

It was pointed out in a previous Section that there were some apparent counter-examples to the main hypothesis of this paper in that sentences that refer to stones and adhesions are expressed both with indefinite subjects and as there-sentences. In this section, I demonstrate that the apparent absence of an alternation is not a counter-example to this hypothesis but, in fact, offers the opportunity to determine thematic information in this data in a more precise way.

The first apparent lack of an alternation concerns sentences about adhesions. Adhesions are abnormal joinings of one part to another (Taber, 1962). In other words, they are like scar tissue that forms between parts. Consider the following sentences:

46. Numerous surrounding adhesions were freed to expose the gallbladder more completely.

47. Numerous adhesions, both to the liver and gallbladder had to be taken down.
88. There were some adhesions about the gallbladder.
89. There was an adhesion in the right lower quadrant that was taken down by blunt dissection.

We see two examples of adhesions expressed as indefinite subject, (46) and (47), and two sentences with the dummy subject there, (88) and (89). It was hypothesized from the data alone that when the adhesions themselves are excised or taken down, they are considered to comprise thematic information. When they are not taken down or excised they are considered to comprise nonthematic information. The informant confirmed that (46) and (47) suggest a more difficult surgery and potential increased problems on re-exploration if needed as compared with (88) and (89). Thus, when particular adhesions are clearly important to the immediate surgical procedure by complicating the procedure or by forcing the surgeon to deal with them, reference to them will be more thematic than when they are not dealt with. The point here is that (46) and (47) show indefinite subjects that appear to be nonthematic in that they are not mentioned in any categories of thematic information. Renewed consultation with the informant confirmed that those adhesions represent, in fact, thematic information, but at a finer delicacy of thematic information (see Halliday and Hasan, 1976).

Stones

The second category of data in which there was no apparent alternation was in sentences discussing stones, in that NPs of stones appear in varying syntactic forms and with varying morphological markings. As with adhesions, examples of stones are expressed as indefinite subjects (see Table 1) and also as there-sentences (90)-(94). In addition, in the data, stones also may occur in the subject position with definite markers or with no markers. They also are found to the right of the verb but not as there-sentences. The following are there-sentences with stones.

90. There was marked amount of small stones and conglomerate of large stones, particularly down in the infundibula.

91. There were large stones in the gallbladder with adhesions between the gallbladder and the duodenum.

92. There were _no obvious large stones_ seen.

93. ...the upper half of the gallbladder was removed in toto and the small infundibulum in which there was _a packed stone_ was removed as a separate portion.

94. FINDINGS: ...there was some chronic inflammation of the head of the pancreas and what was thought to be _a small stone_ in the distal intra-pancreatic portion of the common duct.

In order to determine whether the apparent lack of clear alternation seen in the sentences with _stones_ was indeed a counter example to the hypothesis that the alternation between sentences with indefinite subjects and _there_-sentences functions to provide an alternation between thematic and nonthematic information, first I examined those sentences with _stones_ expressed as indefinite subjects and those _there_-sentences with _stones_. Then in order to confirm and support the observation that _there_-sentences provide an alternation for nonthematic information, I examined all sentences in which stones are mentioned.

At first glance, no explanation of the alternation between _stones_ in the subject position or to the right of the verb, either as _there_-sentences or otherwise, could be determined, since it is not readily apparent why _stones_ may sometimes be thematic and sometimes not. However, after consultation with the informant, the explanation became apparent. According to him, two things that are important to the surgeon here are the location of the stones and their size. Stomes found in the common bile duct are, according to the informant:

> about 20 times more important than those in the gallbladder because of potential future problems. Common bile duct stones can create pain, jaundice, serious or even fatal infections, and may require second surgery in a scarred abdomen. Stones, if small enough, have a tendency to move from the gallbladder through the cystic duct into the common bile

duct. As a result, small stones in the gallbladder are more notable than large stones in the gallbladder, since they can pass more easily out towards the common bile duct. In fact, a large stone in the gallbladder is reassuring negative evidence. The presence of a large gallbladder stone is reassuring in that it makes the presence of common bile duct stones unlikely.

After examining (48)-(53) with the informant in the original context of the respective surgical reports, it was noted that in the six examples in which the stones is in the subject position, five of them are all located in the common bile duct. One example, (52), of a stone is in the cystic duct or infundibula, and is notable because, according to the informant, a small stone in this location can plug the cystic duct, thus preventing other stones within the gallbladder from passing into the common bile duct. Without the informant, this crucial subject matter information which affects the syntactic form would not have been discovered.

In the five examples of there-sentences, three examples of stones are located in the gallbladder: (90), (91), (93). Two examples, (92) and (94), are in the common bile duct. Although the correlation between the extralinguistic situation of location and size of the stones and thematicity is not quite as strong in the sentences with stones as in the other classifications of description of findings and adhesions, we must say that there is once again a correlation between there-sentences and nonthematic information, but of a more subtle type.

If we examine all examples of sentences with stones, not only those with indefinite subjects and there, but all sentences, the same correlations between thematicity and the extralinguistic situation of the size of the stones and their location generally holds true as well. In order to examine this apparent correlation, I have listed each sentence with mention of stones to produce the list in Table 4. In those sentences in which the location is not expressed, I obtained the location from the context, and where the location is not clear from context, I consulted the informant (see Table 4).

Table 4. All Sentences with Mention of Stones.

Stones - thematic

In the gallbladder:

(95) Two or three larger stones could be palpated in the distal part of the shrunken gallbladder.
(96) One large oval stone measuring at least 4 cm in diameter was easily palpable.
(97) Small stones could be palpated within the gallbladder.

In the common bile duct:

(98) Finally a stone rasping forceps was placed down and a small stone about 4-5 mm in size which was a crumbly granular nature was removed and seemed of the size seen on the cholangiogram.
(99) The opening of the pancreatic duct was not visualized, no stones were seen.
(100) Choledechotomy was then made through the cystic duct and by manipulation through a Kocher maneuver and instrumentation a small 8 mm. stone was delivered from the distal common duct.
(101) The common duct was then reopened and the chelodochoscope was passed. No further stones could be identified.
(102) It was not felt by the operator that a further stone was present.

In the cystic duct:

(103) After removal of the gallbladder, the entire specimen, with great difficulty a cystic duct cholangiogram was done, as a small stone was impaled in the distal spiral valves of Heister.

Stones - nonthematic

In the gallbladder:

(104) The gallbladder was quite long and contained several small stones.
(105) FINDINGS: Gallbladder moderately tense and slightly edematous with multiple soft small stones and

Table 4, continued

stone fragments.

(106) FINDINGS: There was marked amount of small stones and conglomerate of large stones, particularly down in the infundibula.

(107) In so doing, accidental transgression of the gall-bladder occurred with spillage of some bile and small stones which were easily aspirated out.

(108) The gallbladder was removed in toto and the small infundibulum in which there was a packed stone was removed as a separate portion.

(109) There were small stones in the gallbladder with adhesions between the gallbladder and the duodenum.

(110) The gallbladder contained stones with a few adhesions about it.

(111) The gallbladder was thick walled with adhesions and contained stones.

(112) Attention was redirected to the right upper quadrant where the gallbladder was palpated and felt to contain small to medium sized stones.

<u>In the common bile duct</u>:

(113) There were no obvious large single stones seen.

(114) Stone forceps and scooper passed with removal of a partially crushed small stone.

(115) A catheter was placed around the stone and into the common duct.

(116) ...there was some chronic inflammation of the head of the pancreas and what was thought to be a small stone in the distal intrapancreatic portion of the common duct.

(117) A cystic duct cholangiogram was done on two occasions and revealed slight dilation of the common duct, good hepatic radical filling and essentially no emptying into the common duct with no maniscus and a flat outoff indicating possible stone or other obstruction.

(118) Operative cholangiography was accomplished through the cystic duct revealing normal ductal architecture and no signs of any common duct calculi.

(119) After this a biliary Fogarty was put through the duodenum and withdrawn back without yield of further stones.

Table 4, continued

In the cystic duct:

(120) The cystic duct itself was inordinately large but packed with stones which were impaled in the spiral valves.

In the ampulla:

(121) Palpation of the ampulla gave the impression of a 1-2 mm, stone in the tip of the ampulla.

Since stones are mentioned in sentences other than in sentences with indefinite subjects and there-sentences, we must examine all sentences in order to determine the correlations between thematicity, size, and location of stones. First, we will examine stone NPs in the subject position to determine if there is a correlation between large stones in the gallbladder, stones in the common bile duct, and expression in the subject position.

Then, we must examine stones to the right of the verb and determine whether they fall into the categories of large stones in the gallbladder or stones in the common bile duct (thematic information). If they fall into these categories as well, then they would constitute counter-examples. If they do not fall into these categories, then the hypothesis of a finer level of delicacy of thematic information is suggested.

First we will examine sentences with stones in the subject position.

All sentences with stones in the subject position (thematic):

Location:		
	gallbladder	3 (two, (95) and (96), are designated as large)
	common bile duct	6
	cystic duct	1
	Total	10

Looking, then, at stones expressed in the subject position (thematic), we can see more examples of common bile duct stones (6) are expressed as thematic information than gallbladder stones (3), and of those sentences discussing gallbladder stones, two sentences have mention of large gallbladder stones. This suggests the reasonableness of the new hypothesis that size and location contribute to the thematicity of stones in that those stones that the informant said would be important (large stones in the gallbladder and small stones in the common bile duct) are expressed as indefinite subjects.

Next, we must examine examples of stones expressed to the right of the verb to determine whether they are counter-examples to the hypothesis.

Stones to the right of the verb (nonthematic):

Location:		
	gallbladder	9 (8 designated as small; 1 (106) is unclear)
	common bile duct	7
	cystic duct	1
	ampulla	1
	TOTAL	18

If we examine sentences in which stones is expressed to the right of the verb, we find that these sentences do not offer concrete counter-evidence to the hypothesis. First of all, of the gallbladder stones, eight are designated as small rather than large, and one sentence is unclear. Thus, these sentences do not contradict the hypothesis. Secondly, the seven sentences with common bile duct stones to the right of the verb are not problematic, either, as again, a hierarchy of thematicity is indicated. Here we see another hierarchy of thematicity. For example, in (114) (115), and (119), we find surgical equipment in the subject position and stones to the right of the verb:

surgical equipment > stones.

In examples (117) and (118), performing a cholangiogram is in the subject position and stones is to the right of the verb:

performing a cholangiogram > stones.

Thus, these examples of mention of common bile duct stones to the right of the verb do not present counter-evidence to the hypothesis that size and location contribute to the thematicity of stones. We may then conclude that with stones, there-sentences provide an alternation for nonthematic NPs which are usually gallbladder stones. Stones in the common bile duct or large stones in the gallbladder can generally be analyzed as thematic. A comparison of all stones analyzed as both thematic and non-thematic confirms this correlation between (a) location and size of stones and (b) thematicity.

Therefore, where stones are found in there-sentences it presents no problem to the hypothesis. It is not that stones are present that is important, but that their location determines their importance. And I have demonstrated that analysis of stones as thematic information depends upon the location.

Limitations of this Study and Suggestions for Further Research

The major limitation of this study is that it proceeds from the "bottom up" rather from the "top down." Because I was interested in analyzing the alternation between sentences with indefinite subjects and there-sentences, the present analysis of this discourse genre is based only on this syntactic alternation. In order to provide a more complete accounting of the data, the next step in this analysis would be to formulate rules to account for introduction of subject matter into this type of discourse. For this type of analysis, consideration of the morphological system and more seemingly relevant phenomena, including NPs with definite markers and with zero markers, would be necessary, as there appears to be a rule of deletion of definite and indefinite markers in this data. If the expanded morphological system is considered, it may turn out that thematicity is only one explanatory factor in the analysis.

Other relationships to consider include the relationship between the passive, there-sentences, and shared and nonshared information. An alternative explanation for the alternation discussed here could be that the apparent general discourse constraint for this type of data is that it be written in the passive. Since many sentences are in the passive, indefinite NPs are more likely to be in the subject position, thereby increasing the likelihood for indefinite NPs to appear in the subject position in this data than in other types of discourse organization. And, although probably an oversimplification, it has generally been shown that indefinite NPs signal nonshared information. It could then be argued that since variation is possible in the type of surgical equipment used, in the type of incision made, and whether or not a cholangiogram is performed, then indefinite NPs in the subject position are merely there because those NPs are nonshared information, and the general discourse constraint of the passive gets it there, not that thematic information is in the subject position.

In addition, it has been suggested (Bley-Vroman, personal communication) that since the nature of this type of discourse genre is to describe a procedure that was followed, it would seem, then, that existential <u>there</u>-sentences are incompatible with action. Further research could examine the reasonableness of this observation more completely in other discourse genres that deal less specifically with a description of action than do surgical reports.

Since I began this research by utilizing this type of text in order to argue for a discourse explanation of a syntactic alternation, I have realized the difficulties in approaching a text with only this one goal in mind. A "top down" analysis would provide, I believe, a more intimate connection between the usage and purposes of this text and its discourse organization. For example, the notions of shared and nonshared information in these data are very interesting and deserve further research consideration, because of the transactional nature of the surgical reports. Some potential readers of these texts may share the same information as the surgeon who performed the surgery, and some potential readers probably will not share this information. Access to the lexis and knowledge of specialized information may vary according to readers, from another surgeon who would presumably have complete access to the technical information to attorneys and third party payers who might have a more limited access to the information presupposed by the surgeon in the reports. For example, further exploration of the use of syntactic means to signal future references might offer additional insights into ways in which these reports are interpreted by different readers who have access to different ranges of medical information. Access to this information might more likely be limited to another specialist than to a lay person.

Finally, expansion of this research into integration of (a) native/discourse, (b) the structure of nonnative discourse and (c) potential misunderstandings in surgical discourse leads me to wish to examine cases of cross-cultural misunderstandings based on written documentation in a hospital setting.

NOTES

[1]I wish to thank a number of people who were very generous with their time and suggestions. In particular, I would like to thank Russell Tomlin for his generous support, patience, and suggestions. In addition, I wish to thank Collette Craig who with her ability to recognize a good informant led me to John Bascom, M.D., without whom this paper could never have come to being. Larry Selinker was very helpful in his patient discussion of all aspects of this paper and Robert Bley-Vroman and Charlotte Linde contributed insightful comments. Also, I would like to thank students in Robert Bley-Vroman's English for Science and Technology Seminar for pointing out possible explanations for deletion rules of definite and indefinite markers. Naturally, all errors are my responsiblity.

[2]In three reports additional procedures are reported on besides cholecystectomies. In two of these reports those sections of text that can be clearly isolated from the section that describes the cholecystectomy procedure are not considered for analysis here. In one report, the section that refers to the additional procedure (choledochoduodenoscopy, gastrostomy, and feeding jejunostomy) cannot be isolated and so the entire text is analyzed. In this report no <u>there</u>-sentences were in this section, however.

REFERENCES

Allan, Keith, 1972, In reply to 'There$_1$, there$_2$,' <u>J. of Ling.</u>, 8:119-24.

Bley-Vroman, Robert and Selinker, Larry, 1980, A pragmatic paradigm for grammatical rhetorical analysis, TESOL.

Bolinger, Dwight, 1977, "Meaning and Form," Longman, London.

Carpenter, Cristin, In Preparation, "A Conversational Analysis of Professor-Student Office Hour Appointments," Ph.D. Dissertation, U. of Michigan.

Chafe, Wallace, 1970, "Meaning and the Structure of Language," U. of Chicago, Chicago.

Craig, Collette, 1979, Jacaltec: field work in Guatemala, in: "Languages and Their Speakers," T. Shopen, ed., Winthrop, Cambridge.

Firbas, Jan, 1974, Some aspects of the Czechoslovak approach to problems of the functional sentence perspective," in: "Papers on Functional Sentence Perspective," F. Danes, ed., Mouton, The Hague.

Halliday, Michael, 1967, Theme and information in the English clause, "System and Function in Language," G. Press, ed., Oxford U., London.

Halliday, Michael and Hasan, R., 1976, "Cohesion in English," Longman, London.

Kuno, Susumo, 1972, Functional sentence perspective. Ling. Inq., 3:269-320.

Linde, Charlotte, 1977, Information structures in discourse, in: "Studies in Language Variation: Semantics, Syntax, Phonology, Pragmatics, Social Situations, Ethnographic Approaches," R. Fasold and R. Shuy, eds., Georgetown U. Press, Washington, D.C.

Linde, C., and Labov, W., 1975, Spatial networks as a site for the study of language and thought, Lang., 51:924-39.

Prince, Ellen, 1979, On the given/new distinction, CLS, 15:267-78.

Rando, Emily and Napoli, Donna Jo, 1978, Definites in there sentences, Lang., 54:300-13.

Ross, John Robert, 1974, There, there (there, (there, (there))), CLS, 10:569-87.

Rutherford, William, 1981, Language typology and language transfer, Conf. on Lang. Transfer, University of Michigan.

Sampson, Geoffrey, 1972, There_1 there_2, J. of Ling., 8: 111-17.

Schachter, Jacquelyn and Rutherford, William, 1979, Discourse function and language transfer, Working Papers in Biling., 19:3-12.

Selinker, Larry, 1980, Les domaines de reference dans une theorie de l'interlangue, Encages - Acquisition d'une Langue Etangere, N. special, 85-86.

Selinker, Larry, 1979, On the use of informants in discourse analysis and language for special purposes, IRAL, 17:189-215.

Sheintuch, Gloria, 1980, The there-insertion construction in English - a pragmatic strategy for promoting certain syntactic structures, Glossa, 14:168-88.

Sørenson, H. S., 1959, The function of the definite article in modern English, English Stud., 40:401-20.
Tomlin, Russell, 1980a, The function of passive in scientific discourse, TESOL.
Tomlin, Russell, 1980b, On the interaction of surface subject, thematic information, and agent in English, University of Wisconsin, Milwaukee, Beyond the Sentence Linguistic Symposium.
Tomlin, Russell, Huckin, Thomas, and Olsen, Leslie, 1980, A functional approach to the analysis of scientific English, TESOL.
Tomlin, Russell and Rhodes, Richard, 1979, An introduction to information distribution in Ojibwa, CLS, 15:307-20.

APPENDIX 1 - Sample Surgical Reports

Report 1

Preoperative Diagnosis: Chronic cholecystitis with cholelithiasis

Postoperative Diagnosis: Chronic cholecystitis with cholelithiasis

Operation: Cholecystectomy and operative cholangiogram

The patient was given a general inhalation anesthetic and intubated. He was prepared and draped in the usual manner with Steri-drape. The abdomen was opened through a right subcostal incision and the peritoneal cavity entered without difficulty. Exploration was done. The rectosigmoid, descending colon, splenic flexure, transverse colon, hepatic flexure, ascending colon and cecum, small bowel, retroperitoneal area, spleen, left and right lobes of the liver, esophageal hiatus, stomach, duodenum and pancreas were palpated or inspected and felt to be within normal limits. The gallbladder was thick-walled with adhesions and contained stones.

The adhesions were taken down from the gallbladder to expose the porta hepatis, and this and the foramen of Winslow were packed off in the usual manner. With tension on the gallbladder, the cystic artery was dissected out, doubly secured with hemoclips and divided. Likewise the cystic duct was dissected out, traced down to the junction with the common duct which was not dilated. There was no history of jaundice or hepatitis. A tube was inserted through the cystic duct into the common duct, and operative cholangiogram done and interpreted as normal by the radiologist, Dr. _____ and myself. Cystic duct was secured flush with the common duct with two hemoclips. Gallbladder was then removed in retrograde fashion, the gallbladder bed closed with running 3-0 chromic. A Silastic catheter was left in Morrison's pouch and brought out through the lateral extent of each incision. The latter then was closed in layers using running 0 chromic in the posterior peritoneum and fascia, running 0 Prolene plus interrupted 2-0 Vicryl in the anterior fascia, 4-0 Dexon subcutaneously and 3-0 polyethylene in the skin.

Blood loss during procedure minimal. Sponge and needle counts correct. All specimens sent for pathologic examination. He tolerated the procedure well and left the operating room in satisfactory condition.

Report 2

Preoperative diagnosis: Chronic cholecystitis secondary to cholelithiasis

Postoperative diagnosis: Chronic cholecystitis secondary to cholelithiasis

Operation: Cholecystectomy and operative cholangiography

SUMMARY INDICATIONS: This lady has had chronic and recurrent right upper quadrant pain with positive test for gallstones. Therefore a cholecystectomy was felt indicated.

FINDINGS: There were some adhesions about the gallbladder which were thickened and one large oval stone measuring at least 4 cm in diameter was easily palpable. The liver, spleen, stomach, pancreas, duodenum, kidneys, large and small bowel and pelvic viscera were either palpated or inspected and found to be normal.

PROCEDURE: The patient was brought to the OR, administered general anesthesia by endotracheal tube. Abdomen was prepared with Betadine and draped in a sterile fashion. A subcostal incision was made. Electrocautery was used for hemostasis. The rectus muscle was transected and peritoneal cavity was entered. After thorough exploration the gallbladder was mobilized with some difficulty as it was partially intrahepatic. With blunt and sharp dissection the cystic artery was isolated, reclipped and divided. The cystic duct which was somewhat enlarged was then mobilized. Clips were placed proximally and cystic duct cholangiogram was carried out which was read as normal with good filling of the duodenum.

The gallbladder was then removed from its peritoneal bed and oversewn with running 0-3 chromic. Good hemostasis was achieved. The cystic duct was then taken down to its junction with the common duct, doubly hemoclipped and divided.

A large Jackson-Pratt drain was brought into the lateral portion of the wound and placed in the subhepatic space to the foramen of Winslow. Wound closure was then carried out with running 0 Vicryl to the peritoneum and posterior fascia, running 0 Prolene anterior fashion, interrupted 0 Vicryl figure-of-8 fashion. Subcutaneous closed with running 3-0 Dexon and skin with running 4-0 Poly. Estimated blood loss 150 cc. None replaced. Sponge and needle count correct.

COMPUTERS AND LITERACY

COMPUTERIZED AIDS TO WRITING

Raoul N. Smith

GTE Laboratories, Inc.

INTRODUCTION

Graduates of our colleges and universities spend more and more of their work time on writing. (For some statistics on technical graduates, see Anderson, 1980.) Yet they, like most other people, feel dissatisfied and insecure with how they write. The process of learning to write which children go through is often accompanied by fear and apprehension. The physically handicapped who can make very few movements or have limited control over their movements find writing time-consuming and frustrating. The problems in writing which these people face (and that includes most of us) vary, of course, in type and in amount. The range is quite wide, running from cognitive linguistic problems in spelling and of cohesive argumentation to physical problems of input where the only possible movement is that of puffing and sipping on a straw or moving one's eyes.

There have been some recent attempts to bring to the writer computerized on-line aids. These have included off-the-shelf text editors and text revising aids. For the disabled there have been letter and word choice systems as aids to generating text (see, for example, Gibler, 1981). Some of these aids are available on microcomputers. Others, such as large meaning dictionaries and specialized updatable thesauri, could be made available on national telecommunication networks. And the cost will decrease as the aids increase in number.

The purpose of this paper is to survey and characterize various computerized aids to writing that are already available and to describe a system being developed for aiding writers in the higher cognitive processes of organization in text production.

EDITING AIDS

One of the areas of computerized aids to writing which has seen the greatest development is that of aids in editing. There is one such system which is operational, namely the Writer's Workbench, developed at Bell Laboratories, and one, called EPISTLE, being developed at IBM.

Bell Labs' Writer's Workbench

The Writer's Workbench (Cherry, 1981) consists of a set of programs and a database to analyze a writer's particular choice of words and sentence forms. It also can perform some of the mechanical tasks of a copy editor. There are three categories of programs that the system has. One category of programs discovers the part of speech of each word in the text. Another set uses this information as input in order to characterize, among other things, the style of the text. The last category of programs is that of copy editing.[1]

Part of speech assignment. PARTS is a set of programs used to assign grammatical tags to the words in a text. It consists of four programs. The first removes section headings, equations, and other non-parsable portions of text. Cherry makes the interesting observation that extracting the headings in a text can at times give an outline of it. Similarly, pulling out the topic sentences of each paragraph (usually the first sentence of a paragraph) gives an abstract that can then be used to check the organization of the paper. The second program looks up each word in a dictionary of 210 function words and 140 irregular verbs. The third checks for the presence of 51 suffixes. These suffixes are used to discover part of speech categories. The last assigns part of speech categories not assigned by the other three programs. It does most of the work. It takes as input the sentence as it has been analyzed up to that point. It breaks the sentences into clauses and uses the clause as the unit of analysis. It looks for the verb first. It then uses rules of English word order to determine the classes of the rest of the words in the sentence. The system is very fast (it can classify 340 words per second), and it is quite accurate (about 95% correct assignment).

Stylistic and Other Characteristics of the Text

Style. The features of style which the Writer's Workbench examines are readability indices (based on sentence and word length), sentence length and type, word usage, and sentence openers. (As by products of these it can be used to locate sentences or words with specific characteristics, such as all sentences longer than some given length, a readability index higher than a given number, or a sentence beginning with an expletive or containing a passive verb.) For input, the system uses the output from the parts-of-speech program.

a. readability. Readability indices are used to estimate the reading skills needed by a reader to understand a document. The Writer's Workbench measures readability four different ways, based on measures of word and sentence length. High values of indices indicate difficulties in reading - long sentences and multisyllabic words are considered difficult to read.

b. sentence variety. The measuring of sentence length and structure is performed in order to get an indication of sentence variety. A wide variety of sentence lengths (short sentence = 5 words less than average; long sentence = 10 words greater than or equal to average, where "average" is defined for a genre) and types, for example questions and imperatives, is considered a favorable characteristic of a text.

c. word usage. This program examines sentences for word types in a text. A high number of a particular word type may be inappropriate. For example, a high number of passive verb forms is often frowned upon. A low number of pronouns may indicate a high lexical repeat rate and perhaps a lack of cohesion.

d. sentences openers. A variety of sentence openers is often considered an indication of "good" style. The type of sentence opener is also an indication of transition between sentences such as with conjunctions and with pronouns. Existential there and it's are often overworked in technical writing.

Prose. This program compares the document that is being investigated with standards determined for technical papers and training documents, the types of papers which the Writer's Workbench is used to analyze. PROSE outputs a comparison of the text to "good" texts in the areas of readability, sentence structure and variation, passive verbs, nominalizations and existentials.

Rewrite. This program implements a theory that sentences with passive verbs, many extra words, and long strings of prepositional phrases should be rewritten. To accomplish this, the program highlights by capitalizing all forms of the verb be, "empty phrases," and all prepositions. The writer can then decide whether he or she wants to rewrite those offending parts of the text.

Topic. This program locates frequent noun phrases in the text. These can be used as key words or indices to the document.

Splitinf. This routine identifies split infinitives.

Copy editing. The last set of programs is used in editing copy. One of them reports all those words which it cannot find in a stored word list and flags them as possible misspellings. (A user's particular exclusion list of acronyms and proper names is also checked.) Another one checks the text for balanced quotes and parentheses and for the correct placement of certain punctuation marks.

The most interesting of the copy editing programs are two that are linked together in their operation. These are DICTION and SUGGEST.

1. diction

A list of 450 words and phrases which are felt to be cliches, are frequently misused, can be shortened, or may be indelicate is stored. (The list can also be supplemented with a user's own set as well.) DICTION brackets all the patterns it finds on the list.

2. suggest

The user enters a word or phrase bracketed by DICTION and calls for SUGGEST which returns one or more alternatives. Examples of this are:

Phrase or Word	Suggested Alternative
A large number of	Many
At this point in time	Now
Utilize	Use
With the exception of	Except
Accounted for by the fact that	Caused by
In light of the fact that	Because

IBM's EPISTLE

The EPISTLE system, as described in Miller, Heidorn, and Jensen (1981), is used to critique the syntax of business correspondence. The system is meant to detect the following syntactic errors:

1. Disagreement in number between subject and verb.[2]
2. Disagreement in person between subject and verb: He never write...
3. Disagreement in number between determiner and noun: These letter...
4. Disagreement in number between quantifier and noun: Each men...
5. Disagreement in number between relative clause and head noun phrase: The men who writes...
6. Use of object pronoun in predicate nominative position: If I were him...
7. Use of object pronoun in subject position: Sally and me wrote...
8. Use of subject pronoun in direct object position: They saw Mike and I...
9. Use of subject pronoun in indirect object position: They told Sam and I the story...

10. Use of subject pronoun in prepositional phrase: Between you and I...
11. Use of "who" for "whom": Who did you give it to?
12. Use of "whom" for "who": Whom did you suppose was coming?
13. Use of "of" for "have": I should of written.
14. Use of improper verb form: The letter was wrote by him.

To catch these errors the system has a parser which checks the grammaticalness of each sentence. The system then highlights the error and makes the correction.

REVISING AIDS

Using the computer to edit texts is becoming more and more routine. Another one of the writing tasks in which the computer is useful is in revising text. An experiment in the use of the computer in writing was conducted with a freshman seminar at Northwestern University. The purpose of the experiment was to determine how the students would use the computer in their writing and what their reactions to the experience would be. Suggestions were made as to the potential use of the computer in their writing tasks, a subset of commands of the FMT text editing system were taught them, and they were required to use the system in producing their texts. Students found the facilities for revising one of the most useful. Although much of the revising itself was done on a hard copy of the text, the changes were made on the CRT. The students were more willing to make changes since changes could be made more easily than to a typed manuscript.

The first and last versions of part of one of the students' papers appear in Figure 1. The revisions made to the original are quite interesting. In the first sentence there is a change from a very marked word order "Little do we know..." to one more neutral. This entails a change in focus: "historic heroes" to "an enigma." In addition there is a change in the syntactic representation of a semantic form of the sentence "we know little" to the nominalized and lexically more mature "an enigma." In the second sentence, word order is again changed in

```
 70 Little do we know about our historic heroes.  Sam
 80 Houston, for example, the commander
 90 responsible for
100 ending the Texas Revolution
110 in the Battle of San Jacinto, is lauded for his
    magnificent
120 command of the battle field.  Where did he acquire
    such
130 momentous knowledge?  [Possibly from our fellow
    Americans
140 the Cherokees.]  Was Houston the admired commander we
150 children of the future believe him to be?  Not in the
    least;
160 his fellow fighters denounced him as a craven because
    he
170 delayed confrontation with the Mexicans.  He mastered
180 extreme discipline and patience to restrain himself
190 from returning the abuse he withstood.  Unfortunately,
    a
200 general knowledge of history glides over such issues
210 as education or experience, popularity, and character.
120 Historic heroes are an enigma to the present
130 general population.  For example, the commander of
    the
140 rebels' Army during the Texas Revolution, Sam
150 Houston, is lauded for his magnificent command in
160 the battle field.  Yet, where did he acquire such
170 momentous knowledge?  [From fellow American soldiers
180 or from his second people, the Cherokees?]  How was
190 Houston admired?  As a courageous officer or as a
    coward
200 who refused to confront the Mexicans?  Unfortunately,
210 a basic  study of History glides over these issues of
220 education and experience, and popularity.
```

Figure 1. Portions of early and late versions of a student paper edited on a CRT.

order to shift focus from the characterization of Sam Houston to that of his name, the introductory phrase being used to create a tension or question about the topic. The fourth sentence contains a new cohesive device, the adversative conjunction "yet." The fifth sentence is changed from a hedged statement to a clear cut question, thereby rhetorically avoiding the hedge and clearly delimiting the scope of the answer.

One could go on with this, but the conclusion to be drawn from this demonstration is that records of the stages in the production of a particular text, especially at the micro-level obtained from intermediate outputs, can be a very useful tool in investigating the actual process of writing. And these will become more available and more useful when better, more user-friendly text editing systems are developed. The results of our experiment, however, convinced us that the students, many of whom were initially hesitant about using the system, became proficient and comfortable in using it, considered it a profitable learning experience, and stated that they would continue to use it in the future.

PRE-WRITING AIDS

Part of the process of writing is preparing for writing. One of the most useful pre-writing tools now available is large bibliographic databases which are accessible online. These can be searched and the resulting hits can be placed in one's own file as part of one's own private database. An example of such a personal database, which was used by the author in writing this paper, appears in Figure 2. These are bibliographic entries gleaned from a set of hits acquired during a search of *Psychological Abstracts* on the subject of writing. These were discovered during a search of that file in the DIALOG Information Retrieval Service from Lockheed Information Systems in California via the GTE Telenet telecommunications network.

In addition to using such commercially available databases, writers can keep their own notes on their reading and thinking in this file or some similar file. These files can then be searched full-text, or if each is organized utilizing the facilities of a database management

```
formulation of real life problems as mathematical story-problem statements,
4th & 5th graders
  Section Headings: 3530 .(CURRICULUM PROGRAMS & TEACHING METHODS)

7/5/21
56-06855 Vol No: 56 Abstract No: 06855
  Using the computer to measure syntactic density and vocabulary intensity
in the writing of elementary school children.
  Kidder, Carole L.
  Pennsylvania State U
  Dissertation Abstracts International  1974 Dec Vol 35(6-A) 3524
  Language: ENGLISH  Document Type: JOURNAL ARTICLE
  Descriptors: ELEMENTARY SCHOOL STUDENTS .(16630),  COMPUTER APPLICATIONS
  (10900), WRITTEN LANGUAGE  .(57230), SYNTAX .(51220), VOCABULARY .(56060),
EDUCATIONAL MEASUREMENT .(16140)
  Identifiers:  development & test of computerized language measures,
syntactic density & vocabulary intensity in writing, elementary school
students
  Section Headings: 3590 .(COUNSELING & MEASUREMENT)

7/5/22
56-05148 Vol No: 56 Abstract No: 05148
  Psychological report writing.
  Tallent, Norman
  Englewood Cliffs, NJ: Prentice-Hall, 1976. x, 262 p. $12.95
  Language: ENGLISH  Document Type: BOOK
  Presents a handbook for those who write, utilize, or supervise the
writing of psychological reports which are viewed as the only meaningful
and effective end result of the psychological evaluation process.  The
purpose and context, responsibility and effectiveness, and
conceptualization of the report are among the topics discussed under Part
One which addresses perennial considerations in report writing.  Part Two
consists of a practicum on this writing.
  Descriptors: BOOK .(06590), SCIENTIFIC COMMUNICATION .(45830), PSYCHOLOGY
  (41760)
  Identifiers: psychological report writing, handbook
  Section Headings: 2160  .(RESEARCH METHODS &  APPARATUS & COMPUTER
APPLICATIONS)

7/5/23
56-05147 Vol No: 56 Abstract No: 05147
  Automated psychophysiology laboratory.
  Stenn, Peter G.; Covvey, H. Dominic; Scase, Carlyle; Heseltine, Gilbert
F.
  U Western Ontario Hosp, London, Canada
  Behavior Research Methods & Instrumentation 1976 Apr Vol 8(2) 235-237
  Language: ENGLISH  Document Type: JOURNAL ARTICLE
  Describes a hospital laboratory which has been recently established based
on a PDP-11/40 processor running a real-time Executive (RSX-11/D) which has
storage and data acquisition peripherals to handle online processing of
```

Figure 2. Selected Records from an online Personal Bibliographic Database on Writing.

system, they can be searched by combinations of keywords. Routine searches for lexical co-occurrences in these texts can lead to the discovery of new relations among ideas and consequently to the discovery of new concepts. (For an example of such a use of lexical co-occurrences, see Smith and Evens, 1977.)

WRITING AIDS

The research, editing, and revising tools just described account for the two ends of the spectrum of the writing process -- essentially planning and changing. They involve the gathering of ideas in preparation for writing and the correcting of the finished text. What aids, however, are available for the central portion of the process involved in producing a finished text, the actual process of writing? Currently there are very few such aids. There are some experimental systems for sentence production (see the recent systems described in Bates and Ingria, 1981, and Matthiessen, 1981) and paragraph generation (see, for example, Mann and Moore, 1981), but there are few aids in helping to produce new ideas and to put them into some standard framework or genre. The remainder of the paper will address these latter two issues.

Guided Writing

One of the areas in writing which is amenable to the quick development of computerized aids is that of writing in standardized genres. Aids for writing in such genres can be used by both novice and infrequent writers. Two useful approaches to guiding such writers in standardized genres are prompts and menus. An example of a relatively standardized genre is that of the monthly report at GTE Laboratories. It has the following text structure:

```
Report → Title + Objectives +  Remainder (Tasksummary*)
                               Taskdescription*
Tasksummary → Title + Summary
Taskdescription → Title + Objectives + Remainder
Remainder → Highlights + Currentmilestones +
  Futuremilestones
Discussion
```

The system of writing aids under development at GTE Labs uses this genre schema to drive a frame filler, utilizing a set of prompts to the user to elicit text. For example, after signing on, the user is asked:

"What is your project number?"

The system accepts inputs consisting of a number, "Project + number, or "Project:" + number (including misspellings of the word "project") and displays and stores

PROJECT ___ title [all in caps]

where the title is retrieved from memory.

The next prompt is:

"Please state the objectives of your project. If the objectives of your project are the same as last month, just input Y. [This will be the majority of cases.] If not, choose one of the following sentence beginnings:

1. To develop concepts for
2. To develop algorithms, devices, and systems for
3. To conceive, develop, and apply

and complete the sentence with your description."

The reason for the form of this prompt is to create a mindset which will force the scientist to state his objectives briefly and in a form which management, the target reader, will understand and appreciate.

The system then prompts for one of the three report formats:

"Do you want to describe the progress on separate tasks?"

If "yes," the system then has to prompt for one of the two task-oriented formats, the one which just summarizes each task without detailing highlights, etc., and the one which does. If no separate tasks are to be described, the case we will assume, the system then prompts for highlights in the form of a query by example.

> "Using one sentence for each, please describe the significant accomplishments of your research project this month. For example, 'Compiled list of human factors issues for AWS.'"

The system then prompts for current and future milestones:

> "You should now report on your research milestones. For each current milestone, you will be prompted to choose from the following set:
>
> 1. Define ________.
> 2. Report on ________.
> 3. Complete ________.
> 4. Final version of ________.
> 5. Presentation on ________.
> 6. Test and application plan.
> 7. None.
>
> If your response is other than "none," you will be asked for the date and whether the task is complete or delayed. Please enter the first current milestone."

After the user has entered the milestone, he or she is prompted for the date and completion, and the system outputs it in a standard format. The system continues prompting until "none" is entered.

A similar menu and set of prompts is used for elciting future milestones:

> "Describe future milestones for the project using the following set of frames:
>
> 1. Preliminary design.
> 2. Design and test ________.
> 3. Assemble ________.
> 4. Report on ________.
> 5. Presentation on ________.
>
> "What is the date of this milestone? What is its status? On schedule, ahead of schedule, or subject to delay?"

This form of questioning is geared to filling in slots of a genre which has a rather rigid form.[3] The last portion of the genre, the discussion section, is not as easily amenable to just filling slots. It is the most difficult part of this genre to write and therefore to guide in writing. The difficulties lie in two related areas--semantic content and rhetorical form. In particular the choices of what to report and how much detail can be delicate questions. In addition, knowing how to present these facts in a persuasive way is not an ability which the majority of scientists have. The purpose of the next section is to explore ways in which writing aids addressing these two problems can be created.[4]

Planning: relations in writing

Hayes and Flower (1980) divide the writing process into three processes: planning, translating, and reviewing. As mentioned earlier, there are computerized aids to reviewing text and attempts at developing aids in translating ideas into text, but there are few computerized aids for the planning process. It is the purpose of this section to propose such an aid.

In an examination of writing protocols, Hayes and Flower (1980:27) observed that "the sequence in which ideas were retrieved...was strongly determined by associative connections." Similarly, Van Nostrand, et al. (1978: 4) define writing as "a process of making and stating relationships." Later they say (1978:6): "Searching for relationships is the essence of writing. What you communicate to your reader is the set of relationships you have found among pieces of information relevant to your subject." They explicitly mention three relations: "relating by classes," "causal connection," and "hierarchy." These are what are referred to in the literature on relations as "set membership," "cause," and "taxonomy." These are of course important, but they are just a small subset of possible relations. There are two major classes of relations that have been proposed in the literature -- rhetorical relations and lexical relations. Rhetorical relations are used to determine the larger, logical, and cohesive structure of a piece of writing. Meyer (1975), for example, describes rhetorical predicates to be used in specifying the larger conceptual structure of text.

Evens and Smith (1978), on the other hand, list a set of lexical relations used in a question-answering system, working lexically at a micro-level but, for some relations, semantically at a macro-level. It is not surprising to find that some relations occur in both lists (although under different names).

The discussion section of the report writing aid is meant to make explicit the relations among a writer's ideas. It begins with a statement meant to instill a mindset in the writer as to the purpose of this section of the report. Its purpose is to motivate the writer to write clearly and persuasively, relying on his or her intuitions as a writer, without having to detail explicitly writing forms which are still little understood. The introduction to this section of the session reads:

> "In the discussion section of the report you are to describe in more detail what you have accomplished in your research this month and where you expect it to lead you. Remember that your readers will probably not know as much about your topic as you do so strike an appropriate balance between too much detail and not enough. In addition you will want to convince management that your progress is sufficient and the results obtained so far are important or at least show promise. Express yourself, therefore, as persuasively as possible. Do you want help in writing this section?"

If the writer responds affirmatively, he or she is then prompted to list the facts to be discussed:

> "What do you want to describe in the discussion section?
> 1. ________"

Continued prompting for additional ideas is varied in order to prevent boredom, as with:

> "What do you want to write about next?"
> "What else do you want to write about?"

Once the writer responds that he or she can think of nothing else, at least for the moment, the system prompts for the relations between the various ideas or propositions:

"How are ideas 1 and 2 related?"

or

"Is there any relation between 5 and 3?
If yes, what is that relation?"

This continues until all the relations among items have been elicited. If the user is having difficulty responding to these questions about the relatedness of the various ideas, a menu of some relations is presented:

"If you can't think of a word or phrase to describe the relation, here is a list which may contain it:
is an alternative to
is a response to
is an example of
is an explanation for
is evidence for
is a quality of
is analogous to
is a way to perform
is a kind of
is the same as
is opposite to
is in a series with
is a member of the set
is part of
is the principal member of
comes from
is the agent of
is the cause of
is an increase in
is a decrease in
occurred when
took place at
represents a case of"

After elicitation is completed, the system then presents in graphical network form each proposition or concept as a node or node number and the nodes to which each is related as well as an explicit identification of the relation between nodes. A sample network, constructed from the responses of a member of the GTE Labs technical staff, appears in Figure 3. The numbered nodes are the ideas generated by the first set of prompts. The solid lines represent the links/arcs connecting the nodes, elicited during the second set. They are explicitly labelled with relations chosen by the user. In this particular case the discussion is about distributed databases. (The subject was explicitly asked what the central or core node in the network was, and he called node 2, distributed databases, the central one.) All of the ideas are related; that is, there are no nodes which are not connected to the other nodes through some path.

As feedback concerning the correctness of the network, the subject was presented with the network that was generated. He made no corrections, but he did add three relations to the existing nodes. These are represented in Figure 3 by dashed lines. What this shows is that the subject understood the network representation and that what he had specified did not capture everything that he wanted to express. The same experiment conducted with other subjects has given similar results. The same result with a larger number of subjects would demonstrate the usefulness of this approach, and this is a task currently being undertaken in this project.

What we are attempting to operationalize is what Flower and Hayes (1980:34) have described as the major task in writing: "transforming incoherent thought and loosely related pockets of information into a highly conceptualized and precisely related knowledge network." How to translate these networks into text is not a simple matter however. The tree structure form derived through the analysis (not synthesis) of text in Meyer (1975:206-235) is a dependency tree with words from a text as nodes and roles and rhetorical predicates as labels on the links. A tree structure has the advantage of being easily linearized, but it has the disadvantage of being uneconomical, potentially repetitious, and relationally obfuscating. Network representations have the opposite attributes. However, the translation process, from network to text, is more difficult than with a tree.[5] Although it is probably the case that nodes in the network of high indegree or outdegree will be indicative of core or central concepts, writing a set of rules for choosing nodes and ordering them are issues of rhetoric

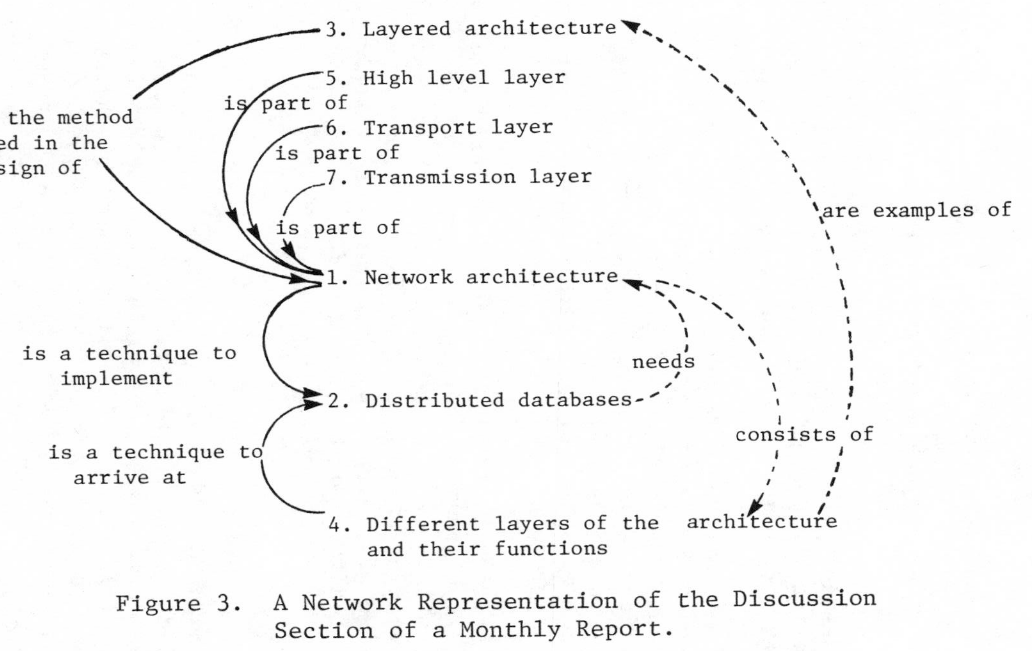

Figure 3. A Network Representation of the Discussion Section of a Monthly Report.

which have not been addressed. At this stage in the development of the system, since this is not part of the planning phase, the task of mechanically producing the written text has not yet been addressed.

SUMMARY AND CONCLUSIONS

The computer has already proven itself a powerful tool in the editing and revising of text. It has also become invaluable in the collecting of information from large databases as part of the text preparation process. It is now showing its potential as an aid in some of the higher cognitive processes of organization in text production.

The techniques demonstrated here for guided writing and planning are new approaches to aiding in the process of writing. Using menus and prompts to elicit text in a standardized genre is a method which can be fruitfully employed in aiding novice and infrequent writers of such texts. An extension of this methodology in the planning process for elciting words and propositions and relations among them is also very helpful. Consistent and extensive use of these methods can be extended in purpose to build large, encyclopedic, knowledge bases which could subsequently assign to the computer a much more active role in the writing process, perhaps some day contributing to the design of an expert writing system which would perform many of the tasks of text production.

NOTES

[1] The Workbench programs run under Bell Labs' UNIX Operating System. It is interesting to note that a UNIX-like operating system is available for 8080/Z80 systems (Libes, 1979). This means that the Writer's Workbench may be transportable to microcomputers. A system, Grammatik, based on the Writer's Workbench and made to run on the TRS-80, is being marketed by Asten Software Co., Tijeras, N. M. (Bruce Wamtler, personal communication).

[2] It is ironic that this very error occurs in the sentence of their article in which they describe the error, namely, "A <u>variety</u> of possible critiques of textual material

are identified in this paper, but the discussion focuses on the system's capability to detect several classes of grammatical errors, such as disagreement in number between the subject and the verb" (p. 649, underscore, RNS). Perhaps if the paper had been processed by the system, as the Bell Labs' one was, the error might have been detected. It is interesting to note that Cherry (1981), which was processed by the Workbench, is much more readable than Miller, Heidorn and Jensen (1981), even though the style is somewhat banal.

3 For somewhat different approaches to the same problem, see Hamilton and Alderman (1978) and Hammer, et al. (1981).

4 For questions of the relation between function and form in written communication, writing as a communicative act, and tools for writing cohesive, compact and persuasive text, see Smith (1981).

5 We are are dealing with the organizing subprocess of planning. The elciting functions are aids to the generating and goal-setting subprocesses. The present approach is much richer than theirs, however, since they account for only two relations, subordinate and superordinate.

An alternative method for guiding the planning process through questioning can be found in Odell (1980:146). It has questions such as for questioning about "Location in physical context" (what Evens and Smith, 1978, refer to as Loc(X)). Odell asks: "Where does X appear? What is its relation to its surroundings? How does it affect its surroundings? How do its surroundings affect it?" This approach is an appropriate one for novice writers.

REFERENCES

Anderson, Paul V., 1980, The amount, importance, and kinds of writing performed on the job, MLA, Session on Technical Writing.

Bates, Madeleine and Ingria, R., 1981, Controlled transformational sentence generation, Proc. 19th Am. Mtng ACL.

Cherry, Lorinda, 1981, A toolbox for writers and editors, Proc. Office Automation Conf.

Evens, Martha and Smith, Raoul N., 1978, A lexicon for a computer question-answering system, Am. Jnl. Comp. Ling., 83:1-98.

Flower, Linda S. and Hayes, J. R., 1980, The dynamics of composing: making plans and juggling constraints, in: "Cognitive Processes in Writing," L. W. Gregg and E. R. Steinberg, Eds., LEA, Hillsdale, N.J.

Gibler, Clint D., 1981, Linguistic and human performance considerations in the design of an anticipatory communication aid, unpublished Ph.D. dissertation, Northwestern University.

Hamilton, Karen K. and Alderman, E. L., 1978, An interactive text generator for the production of standardized medical reports, Computers in Cardiology, Sept., 369-372.

Hammer, Michael, et al., 1981, Etude: an integrated document processing system, Proc. Office Automation Conf.

Hayes, John R. and Flower, Linda S., 1980, Identifying the organization of writing processes, in: "Cognitive Processes in Writing,"L. W. Gregg and E. R. Steinberg, Eds., LEA, Hillsdale, N.J.

Mann, William C. and Moore, J. A., 1981, Computer generation of multiparagraph English text, Am. Jnl. Comp. Ling., 1:17-29.

Matthiessen, Christian M. I. M., 1981, A grammar and a lexicon for a text-production system, Proc. 19th Am. Mtng. ACL.

Meyer, Bonnie J., 1975, "The Organization of Prose and its Effect on Memory," American Elsevier, N.Y.

Miller, Lance A., Heidorn, George E., and Jensen, Karen, 1981, Text-critiquing with the EPISTLE system: an author's aid to better syntax, Proc. Nat. Comp. Conf.

Odell, Lee, 1980, Teaching writing by teaching the process of discovery: an interdisciplinary enterprise, in: Cognitive Processes in Writing," L. W. Gregg and E. R. Steinberg, Eds., LEA, Hillsdale, N.J.

Smith, Raoul N., 1981, The function and form of written communication, Lecture, Symposium on Written Language, Northwestern U.

Smith, Raoul N. and Evens, Martha, 1977, Generating a conceptual network from an index, Information Management in the 1980's, Proc. ASIS An. Mtng.

Van Nostrand, A. D., Knoblauch, C. H., McGuire, P. J., and Pettigrew, J., 1978, "Functional Writing," Houghton Mifflin Company, Boston.

COMPUTER-EASE: A TWENTIETH-CENTURY LITERACY EMERGENT

Carolyn Marvin and Mark Winther

University of Pennsylvania

Several years ago at Smith College in Northampton, Massachusetts, the Standing Committee on Educational Policy convened an informal subcommittee to consider whether all Smith undergraduates should be required to take a course in the art and science of computing. For months the subcommittee considered what it was that every Smith graduate should know about computers to live happily in a world in which their presence would be increasingly felt. The subcommittee's task was nothing less than to arrive at a definition of functional computer literacy, and to decide whether Smith graduates ought to have that degree of literacy or better. This did not turn out to be an easy job. After a year of trying to decide whether computer literacy meant meeting a certain criterion of computing proficiency, or achieving a certain level of social awareness about computers, the committee gave up. At Smith College there are now a number of courses in computing, and there is a concerted effort to introduce students to computers in the context of other courses whenever possible. But for the time being, the attempt to create a uniformly computer-literate class of Smith undergraduates has been abandoned.

The dilemma at Smith reflects a general twentieth-century concern in higher education about the role of technological awareness and competence in the education of a culturally well-equipped modern citizen. Most recently, this concern is a response to the powerful expansion of computing into every aspect of life: political, recreational, productive, public, and private. The

Alfred P. Sloan Foundation has recently thrown its considerable weight behind a proposal broadly addressed to American educators which calls for re-thinking certain aspects of the traditional college curriculum in a vision of the "new liberal arts" that emphasizes applied mathematics, technological literacy, and computing. The Foundation is hosting a series of conferences to consider the merits of its proposal and possible strategies for implementing it (see Koerner, 1981). The Sloan proposal is the most visible recent effort to wrestle with the same issue addressed by the Smith subcommittee on computer literacy--the responsibility of the educational establishment in the large and difficult-to-comprehend transition into a world characterized by what the Sloan proposal calls "new modes of thought."

That an elite institution like Smith College should have difficulty evaluating and prescribing appropriate computer skills is no surprise. After fifty centuries of experience with writing and five centuries of experience with printing, the definition of print literacy continues to plague everyone with a serious interest in it. This is because the only measure of literacy is success in interpreting messages, and success in interpreting messages will always be a socially constructed rather than an objective category. In the twentieth century in the West, literacy has come to denote a consensual level of competence in deciphering and manipulating <u>written</u> material. But literacy may also be thought of in broader terms as decoding or manipulating whatever message systems particular cultures regard as important. It was once taken for granted, for example, that God Himself had inscribed the creation with messages that men must learn to understand, and that time was the unfolding of a divine meaning for man to read and profit from. At any time the definition of literacy and its proper objects is not only a standard of skillful performance but also a social sorting procedure for labeling certain tasks and domains of knowledge as especially worthy of social attention and effort.

Our anxieties about the definition of computer literacy stem in part from our high valuation of print literacy, as so many things about computer literacy do, including the term itself. As a matter of public policy, we have been committed to the effort to achieve universal print literacy, whatever it may be, for roughly a century in the United States. No serious public argument can be made today that teaching literacy is not a primary responsibility of the educational system. Our commitment to universal print literacy is based both on our belief that democracy will not work properly if its individual citizens do not know what is going on, and on our response to historical changes in the condition of Western society. That society is now held together less by families, kin groups, and local neighborhoods (arenas of oral transmission, all) than by abstract bonds of expertise and information which support geographical diffusion and functional specialization. Maintaining social cohesion at this level of size and complexity requires that citizens be able to send messages to and receive messages from those they do not know and who are not present. Written language has become a necessary social cement, and literacy an essential skill of modern citizenship.

Any definition of computing skills in terms of print literacy, therefore, excites our interest because the use of that terminology may imply a public obligation to train citizens in this newest technique of modern life. Since the definition of computer literacy we select (we will argue that computer *literacy* is the best term to describe these skills) will determine who ought to be trained in it and what that training should be, some will resist any comparison which prematurely suggests that computer literacy will become as important as print literacy.

HISTORICAL COMPARISONS BETWEEN COMPUTER LITERACY

Computer literacy may properly be compared with print literacy at many levels, however, and nowhere more so than along a historical dimension. We generally agree that literacy is proficiency in reading and writing the language of preferred communication at some acceptable level. In the United States this is Standard English. But what is the language of computer literacy? Is it FORTRAN, BASIC, COBOL, or LISP? Is it mathematics? Or is it the abbreviated, even pidgin English of the end-user system? Does computer literacy have distinct components of reading and writing? Is it the ability to design systems for others to use, or is it having the presence of mind to type HELP and being able to act on the response? Whatever computer literacy becomes, its present forms include a great range of skills in manipulating hardware and software in different and often incompatible systems among diverse and overlapping user communities who transmit their "literacy" skills to new users in a variety of ways.

The contrasting concept of written literacv as a _uniform_ set of skills is a relatively recent historical development representing the convergence over centuries of widely diverse skills for manipulating various written codes for the separate purposes of church, state, and commerce. Michael Clanchy (1979) has examined this development at length in his account of the painfully slow process by which writing became a routine administrative tool of government in England between the eleventh and thirteenth centuries. Among the circumstances that fashioned and complicated it were the existence side by side of separate sacred, bureaucratic and vernacular literacies involving different languages and performing different functions. Written Latin was the preserve of the clergy and guardian of a sacred tradition; written French was the badge of a dying Norman political aristocracy; English was being transformed from the spoken medium of Anglo-Saxon tribal culture into a full-fledged national written and spoken language.

Not only were there several distinct literacies, but many of the devices of literacy with which we are most familiar were just being invented. Making records, storing records, and retrieving records are not, after all, the logically inseparable, self-evident utilities of literacy we often take them to be. Each of these applications was a separately invented and painfully perfected _program_ for creating, organizing, and using written information. The diffusion of written techniques for handling socially useful information (conventions for dating documents, for example, procedures for validating their authenticity, alphabetizing, indexing) required attentive effort on the part of royal governments able to deploy social resources in behalf of this goal and able to insist on replacing familiar oral customs with innovative written procedures.

The history of early medieval lay literacy has significant parallels with current developments in computer literacy. Just as written literacy began as a variety of specialized literacies using different languages and serving different ends, so computer literacies comprise a variety of languages for a variety of purposes. Just as written literacy moved gradually in the direction of greater uniformity, so we can expect a similar long-range trend in computer literacy. If the varieties of computer literacy are in the meantime more elaborate and more numerous than the varieties of early written literacy, that is because the achievements of written literacy are the starting point for the development of computer literacies. Just as effective computer literacy requires a mastery of the conceptual logic of programs invented by earlier computer literates for organizing and using electronically coded information, so medieval literates had to invent and then master structurally similar (if less complex) techniques for handling written information. And finally, just as official intervention was necessary to move any substantial portion of the population in the direction of acquiring the cognitive habits of the new written literacy, so we may expect the same to be true of computer literacy.

The fact that major transformations in the demography of literacy have always required systematic official intervention makes literacy a political phenomenon as well as a social one. Historians of modern literacy have argued, for example, that nineteenth-century governments in Britain and North America subsidized public education to fuel and promote mass literacy movements that provided more literates to operate the increasingly specialized machine of industrial society, and in North America, to acculturate waves of new immigrants as efficiently as possible (Graff, 1979). A century, more or less, since that effort began, it has been reckoned that one out of five adults in the United States is functionally illiterate (see *N.Y. Times*, 1975). Such figures make it difficult to imagine that computer literacy (for which written literacy is usually a prerequisite) can spread on a mass scale without energetic official efforts. These may be gradually forthcoming, since industrial governments are now irreversibly committed to computerizing records and services, just as twelfth-century royal English governments began to require lesser officials and some citizens to cope with new kinds of records as a matter of practical survival.

But there are many uncertainties. For all the immediacy of computers in our lives, direct hands-on experience with them at more than a trivial level is still rare for most people. Computerized toys and automatic banking may be the opening wedge to mass computer literacy, but their power is to the real power of computing as the ability to sign "X" in lieu of one's own signature is to the real power of the written word. It is more likely that by popularizing and legitimating new technological modes and offering large numbers of people a chance to become rudimentarily acquainted with their operation, computer games and automated banking will play the same cultural role that calendars, chapbooks and almanacs played in the early days of printing. Still another uncertainty is the technology from which current computer literacies flow. Its future development will present at least short-term obstacles to the smooth growth of computer literacy by rendering some existing literacies obsolete, remaking others, and giving rise to others still undreamed of.

On the other hand, there are sturdy and familiar regularities in the shift to a new technology from an old one. New technologies feed on their predecessors by learning forms from them, and organizing around imaginative habits associated with them. New techniques of writing, for example, at first imitated the dominant oral tradition and only gradually asserted their own novel features. In the same way, computer literacies bear the visible stamp of their origins in written discourse and their continuing dependency on it--another good reason for arguing that the term computer "literacy" accurately describes the process now unfolding before us.

Basic end-using terms like PRINT, TYPE, READ, TEXT, and EDIT come directly from print literacy to aid new users in negotiating unfamiliar territory. In the new medium, however, the old meanings have been significantly altered, and these once familiar terms are sometimes confusing to new users who expect them to mean in computing exactly what they mean in reference to written texts. It is quite conceivable, of course, that computers will eventually become the bearers of vast quantities of information that is not alphabetically based. The potential impact of mass interactive computer graphics may be as unimaginable today as the impact of television was to pre-electronic generations, or mass literacy was to the eleventh century. At the present moment, however, the user interface is primarily alphanumeric, and print literacy is the foundation upon which computer literacy must be built.

In the context of a more general decline of interest in books and reading, there are those who see any movement towards computerization as a devaluation of imaginative thinking in favor of the narrowly instrumental, explicit, and rationalized. This is in some ways an inappropriate attempt to equate beginning computer literacy with advanced written literacy. When written literacy passed out of the Church's control, its first important expansion was fueled less by imaginative impulses than by prosaically practical ones. Generally distributed skills in dealing with royal writs demanding money or information long preceded a generally distributed appreciation of great written literature, which is, after all, no more the characteristic form of the written word than the invoice, the laundry list or the calendar.

Now that computer literacy is no longer the exclusive domain of cryptographers, ballistics experts, and other modern priesthoods, the pattern of its diffusion in the population at large is similar to the diffusion of early written literacy. Simple rather than powerful skills are being acquired by airline clerks, secretaries, and others who must master computer procedures to perform their jobs. Like the growth of written literacy before it, the growth of rudimentary computer literacy is by and large a problem-solving response to imposed necessities. Even our popular sense of computer literacy is instrumental. While we speak of _readers_ in discussing print literacy, in computing we speak of _users_.

The comparison of historical similarities between computer literacy and written literacy offers one kind of perspective on current developments. Just as important is the perspective of those who find themselves in the middle of the current transformation. Wittingly and unwittingly, they are its engineers. Whatever computer literacy becomes in the future will grow partly out of how it is now practiced and perceived by those who work most closely with computers as experienced designers and users.

In order to discover what sophisticated users think it means to have facility in computing, we sent electronic mail questionnaires over the Advanced Research Projects Agency network (ARPANET) to a number of different computer systems.[1] Users were notified by an item on an electronic bulletin board that our questionnaire was available for access and voluntary response. With occasional variations, we asked five open-ended questions and invited respondents to answer in any way they thought suitable. These were the questions:

1. How do you conceptualize the major types of skills and levels of knowledge that organize computer users into major classes?
2. If you were to use a metaphor (you may use more than one) to describe the kind of thing a computer is, what would it be?
3. If you were to use a metaphor (one or more) to describe the relationship of power between you and the computer, what would it be?
4. Do you think distinctly different habits of imagination are employed in being comfortable with a book, and in being comfortable with a computer? If so, what are they?
5. How would you define computer literacy?

We received fifty-nine replies from users at a variety of institutions, including the University of Texas at Austin, Columbia, MIT, Carnegie-Mellon, Rutgers, Cal Tech, Harvard, Stanford, Lawrence Livermore Laboratory, Bell Labs, Wright-Patterson Air Force Base, Digital Equipment Corporation, and Bolt, Baranek and Newman. While our respondents were rarely in detailed agreement about very much, certain general themes appeared over and over in their replies. We will typify these in what follows.

WHAT IS A COMPUTER?

We first want to discuss what our respondents think a

computer is, what kind of thing aspiring computer literates have to learn to be comfortable with. Our users generally fell back on the ideology either of (1) the computer as tool (34 respondents selected a description in this category), a malleable extension, when appropriately employed, of their own wills, or (2) as the embodiment of a distinctly independent intelligence or personality--even, in certain circumstances, an opposing one (19 respondents chose a metaphor of this kind). Subscribers to an "ethic of realism," as one respondent labels the moral mode he assigns to those who refuse to mystify or anthropomorphize the machine, emphasize the tool-like computer. For these users the computer has only two states. Either "it is deterministic, or it is broken and inoperable" (35). Put another way: the computer is "like a new kind of clay. Science and art are just now discovering what shapes it can be molded into and what the shapes are good for" (45).

When respondents go beyond the lore of computer-as-machine, which is part of their professional training, to describe the kind of tool a computer is, they often invoke tools that men rather than women use. (Of the eighteen users who offered examples of the kind of tool a computer is, eleven specified one or more tools associated with men's work, three specified tools traditionally associated with women's work, and seven selected gender-neutral tools). For example, "It's like a typewriter, a table saw, or a basin wrench. Actually, it's more like a toolbox or workbench when appropriately organized" (47). Or: "It is a hammer or saw or microscope. It permits me to extend my sphere of influence and improve productivity of real-world problem solvers" (24). It was called "a logical extension of the idea of power tools, like a band saw" (13), a "screwdriver" (21), and "a giant pocket knife with many knives and tools. It is an invaluable tool but sometimes hard to work with. Did you ever try to use all the parts of a pocket knife at once?" (59).

Among the few comparisons to more domestic tools was:

> A computer is just like a meat cleaver: it makes some jobs a lot easier: it's inappropriate for certain other jobs: and you can lose things

> if you're not careful...I think of my computer like a toaster: it'll always work the way I want it to, within its natural limitations, as long as I watch it like a hawk. If I expect it to govern itself, it can waste a lot of time and bread (50).

Other users preferred to personify the computer, or at least to emphasize its approximation to an independent personality. One user described the computer as a "companion," since:

> I don't start from scratch on a computer: someone has already created something out there with which I have to work and which will at least occasionally frustrate me (1).

According to another:

> I guess I consider a computer to be a series of identities. Certainly each different system I "talk" to is a separate identity, and to some extent each of the major sub-systems is a separate identity. I think of the editor and the compiler as different personalities, they were written by different people after all and the method of interaction is very different. But getting a program to compile is much like negotiating with someone for something. You give it a program and it gives it back if it doesn't like some part of it (2).

Another was "comfortable" thinking of the computer as:

> a personal assistant. I tire quickly of programs which remind me that I am dealing with a machine (e.g., the ones that type out how much cpu time they have used or...give numbers instead of text and error messages.) ...When a program does something which I have taught it to do, I am pleased in much the same way perhaps, as I would be if I had taught a person to do such things (34).

Another considered the computer as a "friendly helper," but added a qualification:

> That depends on the computer. I would never call a TRS-80 a friend of mine (38).

Real people are, of course, the valid source of anthropomorphic impressions of encounters with computers--real people who design programs, operating systems, and hardware. For users at most levels, to negotiate any of these is to take account of someone else's intellectual creation made manifest. The sense of the computer as a resistant other, variably helpful and irritating, also surfaced in response to our question about the power relationship between a user and a computer. Some users, of course, deny that the notion of power has any meaning between a user and a computer, but others concede that the computer system represents persons who are in relationships of power to them as users. For example:

> People clearly control the computer. Unfortunately, if I am [directing] it to connect me to another computer and another person (more powerful than me) is [directing] it not to connect me (by disconnecting the wire, for instance), then the computer says, 'Sorry, I can't connect you.' It never says, 'because David won't let me,' so the impression is made that the computer won't let me (33).

Others described the tug of war that sometimes takes between themselves and the computer:

> I pull the strings, but it has a pair of scissors (55).

> I can usually get what I want, but sometimes I have to run around the block first (6).

> I guess it's not too unlike a pet. I have full control over my actions, but I don't always have full control over its behavior. And at times its behavior influences mine... It can be balky at times and extremely cooperative at others (2).

> Sometimes it's the classic pain of dealing with an 'over-literal' child, and cursing your flawed efforts to communicate with it (25).

> [Some] computer systems constantly refuse to trust their users. They are programmed to act as if they always know what is best, and what is right, and will not consider changing their minds. Just like outside bureaucrats. So I don't use those systems if I can help it (46).

LEVELS OF SKILL

There is wide general agreement on levels of skill and areas of expertise that define large classes of computer users. Hard distinctions always oversimplify the real state of affairs, and users are always reminding us of this. But users make such distinctions themselves with some consistency. In general they identify two broad hierarchical categories of ability: being able to build systems for others to use, and being able to use systems one does not necessarily understand. In more detailed schemata, this division also characterizes the relationship of any one level to levels above and below it.

There is also wide consensus on three very general categories of computer-using. There are: (1) end users at the bottom of the scale, (2) programmers who vary in skill from functionaries to hackers, and (3) experts of several varieties. At expert levels there are also divisions in knowledge about hardware and software; moreover, few experts are pure cases. From an infinite number of possible groupings, we can specify five concrete levels of literacy that most of our respondents would recognize:

1. First, there are non-users--people who have daily contact with machines, but do not realize that the candy machine, the microwave, and the grocery store cash register all contain microcomputers (59).

2. Next are data-entry, casual users ("tourists," in

their contemptuous designation), or applications users. These are non-programmers who follow fixed procedures designed by others to accomplish specific tasks. To them the terminal is often the "computer." These users include merchants with point-of-sale terminals, lab technicians for whom the computer is a black box analysis machine, accountants for whom it is a report generating system, travel agents for whom it is a constantly updated reservations system. "Social" users run the electronic mail program or interactive message system. Other users may be civil engineers or secretaries whose jobs are made easier by sophisticated word processing (50).

It is essentially between this level and the next that our respondents debate about where to draw the criterion line for fundamental literacy.

3. Programmers run the gamut of sophistication from "anyone who has ever written a computer program that worked" (53) to someone with "an extremely good model of the domain, including odd boundary cases and details" (47), that is, with an advanced understanding of data structures and algorithms. Programmers specify the procedures by which computers can be used to solve problems assigned by others. Programmers are often referred to as the middle class or clerks of computer using. They are software operatives: white collar workers whose power is sometimes more apparent than real. They work for others, but do not make major decisions because they do not design operating systems, direct computer research, or allocate computer budgets and resources.

4. Hackers appear by name in nearly everyone's list. Hackers are knowledgeable and chaotically creative. "Nothing is sacred, no conventions have to be maintained" (50). The best hackers "tend to know computers totally, from the integrated circuits, to the machine language, to the operating system, to the high-level programming languages" (58). Hackers are also the "trickiest" users. "They like to do things in a new and clever way" (40). The hacker "skillfully alters or extends the domain" of problem-solving performance (47). The hacker mentality is distinguished by its determination to solve all problems without assistance. Because they break bottlenecks and start logjams moving, hackers are a highly valued resource.

For some, the machine is a Faustian challenge to the exclusion of almost everything else. The lore of their obsessiveness sometimes depicts hackers "as having below-normal social skills and concern for personal hygiene--the 'greasy nurd' syndrome" (53). The same inquisitiveness that makes hackers persist in blazing new paths through integrated circuitry may also make them undisciplined programmers, but the very best of them are included in an elite called Wizards.

5. The Wizard is at the top of the literacy pyramid and has "achieved such intense competence that he is capable of amazing feats: wizards make patches, in octal, to running monitors, debug hardware by passing their hands over circuit boards," and so forth (53). Wizards are the most talented and respected members of several high-level expert categories, including hackers, system designers of various kinds, analysts and computer scientists.

A quick summary of the levels of literacy above non-user was offered by one respondent as follows: "can design them, fix them, program them, can't program them" (21). Within this five-level hierarchy, the largest number of our respondents identify themselves as being somewhere between hacker and wizard.

COMPUTER LITERACY

Not all our respondents are sure it is appropriate to speak of computer literacy beyond a definition of skills required to use computers for different purposes. For those who accept the term, the question is whether the criterion definition for literacy should be hard or soft: whether the ability to do simple programming in some language should be the minimum definition of literacy, or whether understanding "enough about computers to approach the subject rationally," a criterion of social awareness, is adequate (2). Soft literacy is frequently defined as being neither in awe or in fear of computers. As one respondent graphically put it in a specifically contemporary context:

> The minimum I would expect in computer literacy in a reasonably well educated person today...is

> [knowing] that computers are complex devices which when properly instructed can do almost anything: that the instructing currently requires very painstaking and meticulous work and may not always be correct: that any one who says, 'We can't do anything about that, the computer (followed by any asinine excuse),' should be told politely that the problems of the computer are something to be resolved by the company's staff on the company's time, and not on the victim's, and you will please straighten this out immediately without any further excuses (31).

The same respondent goes on to argue, however, that "anyone should be able to write a program," even if writing superior programs is not within everyone's ability. This is a widespread view, not least because the special logic system that a computer is cannot really be understood, many respondents feel, without some first-hand experience in manipulating it. In general, however, our respondents are fairly equally divided in their opinions on standards for fundamental literacy. Seventeen of our respondents believe that programming ability is the minimum criterion of computer literacy. Fourteen respondents are willing to settle for some level of end-using skill, and fourteen more believe that social awareness is sufficient.

A few users reject the term computer literacy because it seems to them to focus on narrowly intellectual rather than broadly practical skills. "The analogy [is] to tools not books," writes one respondent (51). These users define computer facility in functional (and frequently masculine) terms "like telephone literacy, or soldering iron literacy, or chain saw literacy" (51) and evaluate it on the basis of how it furthers practical survival. The co-existence of both practical and intellectual-symbolic emphases represents an ambivalance on the part of our users, and in society at large, about whether computers are better understood as a new way to record and exchange ideas--as a new medium of communication --or as a new set of knobs and whistles. "Computers are the new automobile," suggests one respondent. "If you can't drive, you're going to miss a lot" (53). In comparing computers to automobiles, telephones, television, and other technological furnishings of modern life which consumers use successfully without understanding how they work, one user argued:

> Damned few people are electrically literate, yet electricity pervades our society. The electricians have developed some simple user interfaces (plugs and switches and lightbulbs) and it suffices to know only a few trivial rules and to have someone you can call if something goes wrong (14).

A related comment compared computer literacy to "knowing how to mail letters or go shopping, or drive a car. I don't think it's closely analogous to reading" (12). While the notion of computer literacy as a practical survival skill hearkens back to the introduction of written literacy, there is still an important difference between skill in manipulating the physical environment, and skill in manipulating new symbolic forms. Computers are very different from, say, plastic, another versatile product of modern technology. Even when computers are used to facilitate physical operations, their essential feature is always their symbolic power.

DIFFERENCES IN PRINT AND COMPUTER LITERACY

The term "computer literacy" invites comparison with its print counterpart not only historically, but experientially. The sense of the object of computer literacy as a text created and modified by users themselves in real time, in contrast to the fixed text of print, is at the heart of what our respondents consider the essential difference between computing and reading. While printed text seems unalterable and independent of the reader, the computer "text" is a potentiality realized only through the participation of the user and constrained only by a program that sets perimeters for interaction. In two words, our respondents perceive computer literacy as active, print literacy as passive. For example, users occasionally compared books to "television, in that neither makes demands on the user" (35). Alternatively: "With a book one can sit back and let the author's ideas fill your head. With a computer you are sitting in front of a blank blackboard, and must say: 'Now what?'" (54).

In spite of the fact that contemporary literary theory has disabused us forever of the notion of a simplistically fixed text and a passive reader-interpreter, most of our respondents greatly underestimate the amount of interactivity that occurs when a good reader encounters a challenging text.[2] Whatever the interactive subtleties of conventional reading and writing may actually be, success in computing is associated with a level of concentration and a sense of action in the world that is perceived to be very different from conventional reading. Consider these comments from our respondents:

> A book does not force you to react, it presents itself to you and allows the freedom to react. A computer demands that you react to it so it can react to you (37).

> I cannot relax in the presence of a computer as I can relax in the presence of a book. To be comfortable with a computer takes a great effort and patience, while a book can be ignored, read at your own pace, or skimmed (4).

> A computer takes undivided attention to become comfortable. I can have fun writing a program, but I never find programming restful. I almost never enjoy reading a program (18).

> A computer is an interacting component in a complex system of creativity and reinforcement (28).

The generally held sentiment that books do not offer the same degree of creative involvement as computing is based, by and large, on an arguably inappropriate comparison of our users' experiences as <u>readers</u> of books to their experiences as <u>writers</u> of programs and systems. Some respondents do discriminate reading and writing functions in both print and computing on the grounds that there are similarities both in reading books and executing programs written by others, and in writing books and creating programs. "For simple tasks such as using the computer as a mere provider of data, there is no difference between reading a book and 'reading' a computer," argues one (11). Another adds: "To be comfortable with the computer...one needs an active, highly structured imagination. Book readers who have active, highly structured imaginations are latent bookwriters" (55).

A few users see no significant differences at all in print and computer literacy. "Both involve 'picturing' things in one's mind," observes one (57). That comment brings us to our next topic.

SPATIAL VISUALIZATION AS A COGNITIVE COMPONENT OF COMPUTER LITERACY

The power of the computer is its capacity to simulate any machine for which an operation or program can be explicitly articulated, that is, made completely visible. But from its hardware to its logical operations, a computer may be comparatively invisible to its users. We see and hear how many other machines work, but computers sit mysteriously in isolated rooms like closed refrigerators. Often it is not even clear if they are on. Computing mastery, therefore, requires that users have an adequate mental model of the relevant operations.

A number of accounts of teaching software suggest that information processing is often visually conceived by users as a spatial arrangement of letters, numbers, and items moving in three dimensions from place to place. For teaching purposes a computer may be metaphorically represented as a desk or office in which information is created, transmitted, sorted, and retrieved in particular places. An elaborate three-dimensional information model of this kind, "Dataland," is used by Nicholas Negroponte and his colleagues at MIT in a project to teach Spatial Management of Data Systems (SMDS) (Negreponte, et al., 1979). The Director of Academic Computing at Hollins College explained to us recently that she instructs novices to picture the computer as a large cabinet with files, each containing a user's name. Our respondents also frequently use spatial imagery in their descriptions of computer systems and computing.

The spatial conceptualization of information is not

unique to computing, however. In one of the oldest information retrieval systems we know of, the memory system of classical Greece, items for recall were visualized in specific architectural spaces (see Yates, 1966). The spatialization of information is also a structural feature of every typewriter keyboard and of the very concept of moveable type. A typist or compositor physically locates letters and symbols in one place in order to transfer and reorder them in another as text. A fast typist or compositor performs this operation almost automatically. The state and content of information may also be spatially conceived at different levels of computer architecture. (Though its definition varies, this tangibly spatial metaphor has achieved the status of a technical concept.)

Among our respondents, spatial explanations of what the computer is and how it works are very common. Besides demonstrating in operation an imaginative modality that is apparently quite useful with computers, the spatial character of many of these descriptions often suggests the intense intellectual and emotional absorption of their authors in computing, which demands that users "enter its world" (16). According to one such description:

> A suitably rich computer system is a universe to explore, conquer, change and live in part of the time, at least...In some of these universes I am a stranger and easy prey for the hostile local spirits, in others I am a serious explorer, others I know intimately and in these I am a formidable wizard -- if a mountain is in my way, I move it. Some universes are unfit for civilized habitation and I stay out of them unless someone pays me a lot to go in and zap something (14).

In this account the computer constructs the dimensional world in which the user operates. An alternative configuration has the computer operating within a world of shifting spatial contours:

> It would probably be like a car with a small but extremely powerful engine where the outside of the car could change as the terrain required. Sleek and fast for the long flat stretches and high and rugged for climbing over trees and

> rocks like a jeep. With all that power I could drive the car anywhere, even underwater ...If it has power steering I can even get the job done without having to exert much effort (59).

Visual spatialization characterizes descriptions of everything from hardware design, "a row of dominos, set up to do all kinds of tricks that seem intelligent (spelling out words, etc) but which obviously have no innate intelligence" (16)--to definitions of computer literacy, "the ability to be able to find one's way around a computer with minimal effort" (17)--to discussions of skills, "first to be understood as territory" (20) and programming, "I imagine what I am going to build with the computer, what I am going to do" (7), and "programming seems to stress the ability to visualize structural connectivity" (5).

THE POLITICS OF COMPUTER LITERACY

We come finally to a consideration of the political dimensions of computer literacy. To make training in computer literacy generally available would require a considerable and deliberate commitment of social resources. That is why, as Raymond Williams has observed, "the content of education, as a rule, is the content of our actual social relations, and will only change as part of a wider change" (Williams, 1966:310). New symbol systems joined to new technologies have contributed to such change in the past, but are also shaped in turn by complex and not always progressive circumstances.

Because of the dramatic apparent contribution of technology to a rising standard of living in the West since the sixteenth century, most new technology is celebrated as a partner in the development of democracy--certainly democracy conceived, as it frequently is, as a better material life for all. Industrialized Western democracies are ever optimistic that technology will put an end to political strife based in economic scarcity. Accordingly, the computer has been portrayed in the two roles dearest to Western recipes for positive progress: as a booster of economic productivity holding out the promise of affluence for more and more people, and as a serenely impartial accumulator and dispenser of valuable knowledge to all who are skilled in its use or have access to those who are.

There is now some public recognition of the inescapable human costs as well as benefits of the labor-saving effects of the computer, but there has been less examination of the popular and potent image of the computer as a positive, democratizing instrumentality--or at worst, an apolitical one. The ideology of computer literacy as a skill acquired and used by the most diligently energetic and upwardly mobile plays an important part in that democratic image. It helps fit the computer into the familiar, cherished, and anachronistic American mythos of practical technical innovation by individual tinkerers whose self-interested endeavors will coalesce in the common good. The de-anthropomorphized, freely accessible, non-political computer-as-tool does not, however, describe the practical political realities of large present-day computer systems, or prepare people for what will come.

Even if our society were to take an active and successful hand in educating all its citizens in the rudiments of computing, the ranks of computer literates would by necessity be mostly end-users and programmers at fairly low levels of sophistication. This is partly a matter of the vast investment of capital and labor required to support systematic education in computer literacy at even a "functional" level. It is inconceivable that a really large proportion of the population could learn to use computers with great sophistication in the foreseeable future.

The public character of a computer network is expressed in the rules which govern access to it, define permissible claims on processing capacity and memory, and bestow authority to make or use files and program packages. The fact that programs and operating systems, which constitute the intellectual skeleton of computing, are explicit and visible makes tempting but not true the inference by analogy that computer systems can be socially organized in an entirely visible and impartially public manner, guaranteed by the literate participation of all users. The notion of a technological social compact of political accountability based on the availability (in principle) of hardware and software systems for public inspection is a false leap. The social and political organization of any large computer system is much more invisible than this, and has to be.

Computer systems are expensive, multi-purpose, finite resources requiring cadres of human expertise for logistical support. Even the most public-spirited network, a network that is not on the horizon, would be unthinkable without its own technocratic elite charged to maintain, and therefore inevitably to govern it. Some computer users must always be more equal than others by virtue, first, of their knowledge and ability to decode and recode the system, their privilege to do so, and the value of their knowledge to those who can pull the plug. While it is possible to formulate and enforce rules of equal access within a large class of users, it is the definition of fundamental privileges for each class of users that is critical.

It is also difficult to conceive of a functioning computer system of any size and power that does not have behind its declared public system of allocation and access a less visible actual negotiating system for dispensing its resources. This is, of course, true of all other institutionally organized social resources we know of. In any conscientious effort to bring the computer to a wide slice of end-users, such hierarchies of literacy and power seem to be inevitable.

Think for a moment: if it is difficult to establish criteria and curricula in computer literacy for college students, an existing and thoroughly familiar educational elite, how much more difficult will it be to identify and meet the needs of non-elite groups? Instead of democratically leveling differences in social power, the computer may well exaggerate them, since elites are likely to get more and better training in computer literacy sooner than non-elites. At the moment, broad training in computer literacy is institutionalized in comparatively elite sectors--computer science departments in colleges and some other schools with special financial resources, in certain sectors of private industry, and in government research and administration. It is, of course, possible for those who are not formally situated within this web of power centers to manage in one way or another to acquire excellent computer training. But we can generally expect certain socio-economic factors to select this population as well. It is a safe bet that the faculty child will be more likely than the ghetto child to find a way into the computer center of the university where both their parents work.

In the short run, the development of computer literacy also will not de-emphasize print literacy, but will make it more important than ever. Since print literacy is the principal avenue of access to computer literacy for most people in our culture, the extent to which print literacy skills are economically and socially stratified can be expected to shape the acquisition of computer literacy as well. And while new media of communication frequently do democratize old hierarchies of privileged knowledge sooner or later by eroding established intellectual monopolies, they also substitute new ones, and new elites, in their places.

In principle, unlimited computer resources could solve many of these problems. The rhetoric of electronic abundance assumes the continuing capacity of miniaturization to produce significant increase in productivity, the major economic reward of technological innovation. What the limits of miniaturization will be is not clear. That there are such limits is as certain as that there was a limit to productivity increases made possible by the steam engine--increases that fell far short of ending economic scarcity, despite the most hopeful rhetoric of the Industrial Revolution. Although there have been remarkable gains in miniaturization to date, there is no evidence that we will soon be awash in computer capacity, nor, given the history of most developments in communications, is there *ever* likely to be. Innovations in communications technology have always been advertised as far surpassing the capacities of previously existing technologies for transmitting and storing information, but demand for more capacity than there is has always caught up, and rapidly, with each new technology. New communications capacity always generates its own demand, or to say it another way, its own scarcities.

If scarcities are locally regulated by politics at the micro level of the computer system network, they are also politically governed at the macro level through official political channels and institutions like the Federal Communications Commission, the Department of Defense, communications industry manufacturers and vendors, and other groups competing within the known political domain for resources and privileges. We can leave this more familiar political territory to others. Whatever unexpected developments occur in the arena of computer politics are likely to grow out of relationships and structures now existing informally in computer systems.

The presence of these informal communities can be felt in activities like the ongoing, behind-the-scenes, multi-player games that exist in most computer systems. "Gamers" can often make substantial claims on computer resources, selectively socialize members of a system community, and set up rules for access at certain levels of skill or through personal political influence. Often they do so without explicit public organization or recognition. They are officially invisible precisely because conventional vocabularies of political analysis are based on a world in which they did not exist. They may be powerful, nonetheless. The political structure of any computer system is certainly much more complex than this example suggests. But the phenomenon of system games is part of the process by which new classes of computer literates create and organize novel tasks and relationships among themselves with potential consequences for a much larger community.

Games are also important examples of the development of new expressive forms that use the specific technological capabilities of computing. With their multi-interactive structures, fancy displays, elaborate computations and large data bases, games are the indigenous literature of the printing press. Other new art forms to emerge from computing include synthesized music and computer graphics. Significantly, none of them is dependent on print literacy as a mode of expression.

IN CONCLUSION

Because of the growing concern of educators and others with computing, there are now several widely quoted, broadly similar definitions of computer literacy in circulation. One that is fairly well known comes from the Duke University Personal Computing Project, an independently initiated effort, like that at Smith College, to acquaint Duke students with computing. The Duke Project defines computer literacy as

> an awareness of computing capabilities within a discipline or profession, and an ability to recognize and articulate problems that can be solved with the aid of computing technology. The definition does not necessarily imply an ability to program or operate computers (Gallie, et al., 1980:4).

This definition is admirably inclusive in its desire to make the computer age a common resource, but it evades the real issue. No one accepts awareness of what print literacy can do as a substitute for the ability to read or write. Much of the social alarm about our most popular contemporary mass medium, television, concerns its transmission of vicarious experience to passive viewers. It would be unfortunate if our social model of the computer were a kind of television programmed by others. Warner Communications' computer interactive QUBE cable television system in Columbus, Ohio, in which the computer-connected viewer becomes a member of an extended game-show audience, suggests that this familiar impulse will be a powerful one (see Wicklein, 1979).

Definitions of computer literacy by educators and entrepreneurs frequently portray it as a low-level skill for consumers or a medium-level skill for white-collar professionals in a variety of fields. Expert users who value a high level of symbolic skill as a criterion for effective computer literacy may lack an adequate appreciation of the lengthy, thoroughgoing, and inevitably painful readjustment that will be required both in the habits of thought of individual learners and in our most familiar cultural practices of information handling. The social definition of computer literacy will certainly depend on the imagination of all cultural participants, but practically speaking, it will be enforced only at the level of economic commitment our society is willing to make. If that level is low, we will have the option either of training a powerful but tiny elite of highly skilled literates, or of widely diffusing a low-level literacy without true personal and social power.

In our view, the only appropriate social ambition for the introduction of a new and powerful symbol system harnessed to a new and powerful technology is that as many people as soon as possible should be able to make full use of both for themselves. A democratic perspective requires us to make our goal for diffusion as broad as possible. A historical perspective allows us to recognize that reaching that goal will take a long time. While we must be patient, we cannot be satisfied with anything less than universal computer literacy, just as we now insist on and work for a truly universal print literacy. Even though popularly diffused end-user sophistication and programming skills are a very long way off, the implied suggestion in the Duke definition and in many expert definitions that it is acceptable to delegate to others computer tasks one could learn to perform for oneself is not acceptable for the long term. The more disturbing implication of such definitions is that those who have no white-collar power to compel work in their own behalf will be required to plead with the more powerful for consideration of their computing needs. No such surrender of the personal right to manipulate a powerful symbol system can be a realistic democratic goal.

NOTES

[1]Data from our questionnaire results are cited in the text by number of respondent. An appendix following these notes lists, by number, all respondents who replied to our questionnaire; their affiliations are also included.

[2]The widely accepted view of a passive relation to a fixed printed text has an interesting echo, nevertheless, in some recent research about how naive users learn to operate an electronic bibliographic retrieval system. One of the first and most difficult steps is to convince the novice that he or she, and not the computer, is in charge of initiating and maintaining interaction. See Ross A. Bott, _A Study of Complex Learning: Theory and Methodologies_, Center for Human Information Processing Report #82,

(La Jolla: Department of Psychology, University of California, San Diego, March, 1969). The tendency of the naive user to seek direction from the computer may reflect the superficially passive role he or she customarily assumes as a reader of printed text or a viewer of television.

[3]The authors wish to express their appreciation to Henry Dreifus, Wharton Computer Center consultant at the University of Pennsylvania, who assisted in the administration of the questionnaire used in this study and offered helpful advice throughout, and Rob Kling of the University of California at Irvine, who read a draft of this paper and made valuable comments. We are also very grateful to all those users who took the trouble to respond so thoughtfully to our inquiry.

REFERENCES

Clanchy, M., 1979, "From Memory to Written Record, England, 1066-1307," Harvard U. Press, Cambridge.

Gallie, T., et al., 1980, The Duke personal computing project: its strategy for computer literacy, Persp. in Comp., 1:4-8.

Graff, H., 1979, "The Literacy Myth: Literacy and Social Structure in the Nineteenth Century City," Academic Press, N.Y.

Koerner, J., ed., 1981, "The New Liberal Arts: An Exchange of Views," Sloan Foundation, N.Y.

Negreponte, N., et al., 1979, "Spatial Data Management," MIT Press, Cambridge.

N.Y. Times, 1975, 23 million in U.S. found illiterate, Oct. 30.

Wicklein, J., 1979, Wired city, USA: the charms and dangers of two-way TV, Atlantic Mon., Feb:35-42.

Williams, R., 1966, "Culture and Society, 1780-1950," Harper and Row, N.Y.

Yates, F., 1966, "The Art of Memory," Routledge and Kegan Paul, London.

APPENDIX OF RESPONDENTS

The following list of respondents by occupation and

institutional affiliation is summarized from information voluntarily supplied by respondents, consistent with preserving their anonymity.

1. Systems programmer, Digital Equipment Corp.
2. Computer scientist, Lawrence Livermore National Laboratory.
3. Graduate student, Massachusetts Institute of Technology Artificial Intelligence Laboratory.
4. Professor, Temple University.
5. Computer operator, Bolt, Baranek and Newman.
6. Graduate student in theoretical physics, California Institute of Technology.
7. Hardware designer, Raytheon Data Systems.
8. Staff member, Carnegie-Mellon Robotics Institute.
9. Staff member, Massachusetts Institute of Technology Artificial Intelligence Laboratory.
10. Instructor in computer science, United States Air Force.
11. Systems programmer, Stanford Research Institute.
12. Graduate student in computer science, Carnegie-Mellon.
13. Student and programmer, Rutgers.
14. Computer scientist, Carnegie-Mellon.
15. High school student, Los Angeles Unified School District.
16. Graduate student in computer science, Carnegie-Mellon.
17. Programmer, Computer Performance Co.
18. Undergraduate in computer science, University of Pennsylvania.
19. Research programmer, Rutgers.
20. Graduate student in computer science, Carnegie-Mellon.
21. High school programming teacher.
22. Student, Boston University.
23. Research programmer, Rutgers.
24. Research staff member, Massachusetts Institute of Technology Plasma Fusion Center.
25. Graduate student, Massachusetts Institute of Technology Artificial Intelligence Laboratory.
26. Manager of software services, private corporation.
27. Respondent, Stanford.
28. Graduate student, Massachusetts Institute of Technology Artificial Intelligence Laboratory.
29. Graduate student in computer science, Stanford.
30. Research systems programmer, Carnegie-Mellon.
31. Computer scientist, Carnegie-Mellon.
32. Private consultant.

33. Employee, Digital Equipment Corp.
34. Research staff member, Massachusetts Institute of Technology Artificial Intelligence Laboratory.
35. Programmer, Carnegie-Mellon.
36. Respondent, Massachusetts Institute of Technology.
37. Senior Technical writer in computer science, Carnegie-Mellon.
38. Student, Rutgers.
39. Graduate student in computer science, Boston University.
40. Graduate student in computer science, Rutgers.
41. Professor, Carnegie-Mellon.
42. Assistant professor, Massachusetts Institute of Technology.
43. Systems analyst, University of Texas at Austin.
44. Systems programmer, Rutgers.
45. Systems staff member, Massachusetts Institute of Technology Artificial Intelligence Laboratory.
46. Staff member, Massachusetts Institute of Technology Artificial Intelligence Laboratory.
47. Assistant professor, Carnegie-Mellon.
48. Professor, Rutgers.
49. Assistant professor, Harvard Business School.
50. Undergraduate student in computer science, Massachusetts Institute of Technology.
51. Information systems staff member, Bell Laboratories.
52. Undergraduate student, Massachusetts Institute of Technology.
53. Graduate student in computer science, Carnegie-Mellon.
54. Respondent, Rutgers.
55. Graduate student, Carnegie-Mellon.
56. Graduate student in computer science, University of Texas at Austin.
57. Research programmer, Rutgers.
58. Undergraduate in computer science, University of Pennsylvania.
59. Senior systems analyst, private corporation.

A COMPUTER-AIDED STUDY OF CONFUSION IN LATIN MORPHOLOGY

Gerald R. Culley

University of Delaware

The teaching of elementary Latin suffers from the same bane afflicting all language study: attrition is too high. This is generally acknowledged and widely lamented, but efforts to correct the situation have enjoyed very little success. There is good reason for this failure. We simply do not know enough about which areas of the subject are hardest for students to master, so we are unable to restructure syllabi to provide more balanced treatment; nor do we know which learning strategies tend to be most effective for the majority of students, so we are unable to offer sound advice to floundering scholars. The result is that each teacher is left to his or her own devices. The "good" teacher--bless his name--enjoys a high success rate but cannot share his success because it grows more out of instinctive behavior than out of cold choice. The "poor" teacher is doomed to a cycle of high drop rates, frustrated students, and fruitless self-examination. He is helpless and, it seems, unhelpable.

The clear need here is for some reliable study of the learning process. What portions of the elementary Latin syllabus are hard and why? What learning strategies work best for the most students and why? To answer such questions, one must break down the very complex activity we call <u>learning</u> into small units and gather a great deal of information on the relative difficulty of many small tasks. It is a job calling for endless patience, accurate record keeping, nominal arithmetic skills, and an immunity to boredom. In short, it needs a computer.

I started work on this job about five years ago, although I did not know then that that was what I was doing I thought at the time that I was just experimenting with a computer aid to instruction called PLATO^R. This is a system developed at the University of Illinois at Champaign-Urbana and differing from other computers in that it was designed from the ground up to be an instructional system. In brief, for those not familiar with it, it consists of a Control Data Cyber 173 mainframe computer supporting numerous student terminals. The terminals have screens capable of displaying text, non-standard alphabets, graphics, and animation effects. Students enter their responses to the computer by means of a typewriter-style keyset and by touch directly on the terminal's display screen.

It was an exciting opportunity to have access to such a powerful instructional tool, an opportunity made more attractive by a substantial commitment of resources by the University of Delaware. The school, after a time of exploring PLATO as a dependency of the Illinois system, purchased its own PLATO system and pressed ahead with generous support for an Office of Computer-Based Instruction. This office now employs over 30 full-time staff professionals and provides technical and consultative services to faculty members who wish to develop instructional materials on the computer. This kind of institutional support made it possible to develop a series of skill-building lessons to supplement classroom instruction in three key areas: morphology, sentence translation, and grammatical analysis of sentences. The current academic year is the second in which this curriculum of lessons has been available as a whole. It was planned, as I said, as an instructional tool--a means of extending the amount of supervised time my students spent on Latin. As it took shape, though, it soon became obvious that each of the lessons could also be a tool for gathering information on how students learned--or failed to learn--the subject matter. Just how this works will be clearer if we first take a quick look at the lessons.

There are three areas addressed by these lessons: the first is morphology. For the forms of nouns and adjectives, students run Mare Nostrum, a lesson which operates as follows. The computer selects a noun base and adjective base from its memory bank, inflects each to a number and case selected at random, and displays the resulting phrase. The student then has to identify the form by touch on a grammatical chart. A game format is used, with a point value assigned to each form. The name, "Mare Nostrum," suggests the game's object, which is to conquer the Mediterranean world as Rome did--but at 50 points a province. Students use this lesson repeatedly throughout the year, expanding the number of declensions in play as their knowledge grows. Besides this passive format--touching the correct grammatical label--there is an active version in which the machine shows the student a noun and an adjective and asks him to type the phrase in a case and number specified.

A second morphology lesson deals with verbs. In its passive version, the computer draws the principal parts of a verb from its memory and displays them along with one inflected form: for example, scribebamus. The student must parse this form by touching items on a grammatical chart displayed by the computer. When he has finished, the computer inflects the target word using the grammatical identification the student has just provided, and displays the new form under the original one for comparison. If they are identical, credit is assigned and a new challenge is displayed; if not, the student may change his identification of the form by further touches on the chart. If the form above had been wrongly called a third person plural future indicative, the computer would have displayed the result: scribent. Touches on "first plural" and "imperfect" would correct the form. This lesson, like the noun/adjective one, also has an active version. In it, a student works against the clock to type a verb form demanded by the computer.

A second problem area for elementary Latin students is the translation of sentences. A lesson called Translat gives translation practice on the computer. Latin sentences are presented one at a time. As each is displayed, a student may either try at once to type an English translation or he may touch any word in the sentence about which he has a question. A second touch, then, on any of four boxes on the screen, will provide the grammatical form, the dictionary entry, the dictionary meaning, or the function in context of the word in question. The student may interrogate the computer as much as he wishes until satisfied that he is ready to translate the sentence. The object, of course, is to free the learner from the distractions of dictionary, morphology charts, and grammar book by simply providing all that information at a touch. A student is then free to concentrate on integrating that information into a coherent whole. When he feels ready, he then types a translation and the computer judges his answer, marking misspelled words, wrong words, missing words and words out of order.

The third problem area is grammatical analysis of words in context--old-fashioned parsing. A lesson directed to that need presents Latin sentences and challenges the student to parse each word in turn, all by touch on the screen. First he identifies the part of speech by touching one of eight boxes, then goes on to a more precise discrimination (e.g., the _kind_ of adjective involved: interrogative, demonstrative, etc.). At this preliminary level, the computer will not accept an incorrect touch, simply flashing a "no" until the right identification is made. When that is done, more boxes are displayed for parsing appropriate to the part of speech involved: for adjectives, boxes for number, gender, and case. Here, though, the computer will accept any input the student provides, correct or not; when he has finished his identification, it inflects the word as the student has indicated, displaying the new form beside the target form in the sentence. Errors will, of course, produce an improperly inflected form, and comparison with the desired form permits corrections in the identification to be made. When all words in the sentence have been correctly parsed, the computer provides an English translation of the sentence. The thesis of this lesson, then, is that anyone who can analyze the words of a sentence and see their relationships to each other can translate it.

With these representative examples of the computer curriculum in mind, note some key elements in its design:

1. There are only six lessons, so the entire series is available to students at all times; they have free choice among the lessons, though of course a suggested order of use is provided.

2. Lessons are designed for maximum flexibility in two senses. First, their content and scope are largely under student control. For example, a student running the verb lesson decides at each session which conjugation or combination of them he will include in the game, and specifies as well just which tenses, persons, voices, and the like will be used. Therefore, the user can set the level of difficulty to suit his own needs. A second kind of flexibility is found in the kind of feedback given after a wrong answer. Mare Nostrum is an example. Because the computer actually inflects the variable parts of speech, it can judge a student's typed answer in terms of the base or ending of the noun or the adjective. The results of this kind of morphemic analysis are suggested by this chart, where a student fumbling for the dative singular of <u>ager</u> <u>bonus</u> would get responses like these to errors of various kinds (see Chart I).

3. Since the lessons are flexible in terms of content, scope, difficulty and feedback, each of them can be used throughout the semester or the year. Increasing difficulty keeps them challenging, but that is not the only dividend of repeated use. With use, the mechanical details of using a lesson become familiar and no longer are a distraction; the subject matter becomes the center of concentration. And just as a person progresses from being fascinated by a hand calculator as a new gadget to using the calculator as a tool for computation, students soon begin to use the computer as a tool in their acquisition of skill with Latin. It becomes a personal resource which some use more, some less, than the suggested hour a week.

With this background it is possible to discuss some of the answers to specific questions that are accumulating.

A first major question: What portions of the elementary Latin syllabus are really hardest? The lessons provide two kinds of techniques for dealing with this question. The first is morphemic analysis of students' incorrect answers.

PROBLEM: Type the dative singular of <u>ager</u> <u>bonus</u>.

Answer: <u>agro</u> <u>bono</u>

Student Types	Computer Responds (ordinary lesson)	Computer Responds ("smart" lesson)
ager	no	Two words, please.
ager bonus	no	Noun base is wrong. Adjective ending is wrong.
agoro bono	no	Noun base is wrong.
agri bono	no	Noun ending is wrong.
bpno agro (typing error)	no	Adjective base is wrong.
bono agro	no	ok (recognizes either order)
agro bono	ok	ok

CHART I

JUDGING VERSATILITY

Take an instance from a diagnostic verb lesson called Verb Factory. In response to the English cue "you (pl) were calling," a student types vocabis. The computer looks first for the complete correct form, vocabatis; failing to find that, it looks again, this time for the stem of the verb. Had the stem not been in the typed word, the computer would have made a comment to that effect. Since it was, the computer looks yet again, this time for the tense/mood sign. The problem is there, and thus the comment "Check the tense/mood sign" is displayed. If that segment had been correct, the computer would have pointed to the personal ending as the offending part. Feedback of this kind frequently isolates the error (and, notice, all of this is forcing the student to think of the word as a combination of stem, tense/mood sign, and personal ending). But if a student is suffering from selective blindness and still can see nothing wrong with his answer, he has the choice of doing a verb scan. The press of a key will cause the computer to conjugate the target verb in every form based upon the stem in use. Each form--60 for the present stem--is compared in turn with the student's typed answer. If he has in fact typed some legitimate form of the verb in that tense system, the computer will learn what it is and identify it for him. The response for this example would be, "vocabis is 2nd SING/FUT/act/indic."

A truly confused student, after a second wrong answer, can press a key labeled HELP, whereupon he will be taken through a series of leading questions (What conjugation? What mood? etc.) to establish the grammatical identification of the form he is trying to produce. As he establishes the stem, that is displayed for him, gliding by animation out of a cartoon-style factory on the display screen. When tense and mood are correctly identified, the tense/mood sign emerges from the factory. Finally, identification of person/number and voice determine the personal ending, and it is added to the form.

Now, all of that is the experience seen from the student's viewpoint. The computer, meanwhile, is recording errors, and noting the point within the word where the error occurred. After a year of data collection, it was possible to construct a chart (see Chart II). Each bar is a 20-item quiz from Verb Factory. Number 1 included only the present tense of the first two conjugations; number 2

TEST

Test	Stem	Stem Vowel & Tense/Mood Sign	Personal Ending
1	laud	a	t
	19%	15%	66%
2	laud	abi	t
	15%	32%	53%
3	duc duc	i e	t m t
	17.7%	32%	50.3%
4	aud cap	i ie	t t
	7%	30%	63%
5	laudav laudav laudav	 era eri	it t t
	23%	18%	59%
6	laud	aba	t
	37%	30%	33%
7	laud laud mon	a aba ebi	tur tur tur
	17.5%	13.5%	69%
8	laudat laudat laudat	 us era us eri	us est t t
	49%	13%	38%
9	duc aud cap	ī ieba ie	tur tur tur
	20%	33%	47%
10	laud laud	e e	t tur
	15%	31%	54%

CHART II: Relative Frequencies of Errors in Stem, Stem Vowel & Tense/Mood Sign, and Personal Ending.

TEST			
	laud -	are -	t
	laud -	are -	tur
11	15%	28%	57%

	laudav	- eri -	t
	laudav	- isse -	t
12	52%	17%	31%

	laudat	- -	us sit
	laudat	- us esse -	t
13	40%	15%	45%

CHART II, continued

added the future tense; number 3, the same two tenses of the third conjugation; and so on. When students made errors, these were the relative frequencies, broken down by stem, tense/mood sign, and personal ending. Just a few observations will suffice. For the first four quizzes the stem is the source of a relatively small number of errors, decreasing to 7%. Then the perfect system, and a new stem, are introduced; trouble with the stem portion of the form rises dramatically. The confusion carries over into the next quiz, in which the imperfect tense is introduced, and trouble subsides with the quiz following. Then it reappears in quiz 8 when the perfect passive participle is introduced. Clearly, the introduction of a new stem needed to be handled more effectively in class. A similar phenomenon crops up in quiz 7, when the passive voice is first used. Trouble with personal endings suddenly doubles. These figures, and those that follow in this paper, are only preliminary; but they do suggest that the trouble areas can be located by morphemic analysis of students' errors.

I said, though, that morphemic analysis was only one of two techniques for analyzing student errors. The other is the confusion matrix. If a student sees a verb form to identify, for example, and he identifies it wrongly, what did he think it was? Was his error perceptual--a simple carelessness in looking at the word--or was it conceptual--a wrong mental model of the Latin verb itself? One way to try to answer these questions is to construct a confusion matrix. Each time a student identifies a verb form incorrectly, record what the form really was and what the student thought it was. Then construct a chart like Chart III, with 120 finite forms across the top and the same 120 forms down the side. The full matrix is too large for display here, but the small portion shown--the present system, active indicative--shows how the method works. The X's track the line of correct answers where the student's answers on the y-axis meet the correct answers on the x-axis. The "1" at the point circled, for example, means that one student identified a 2nd person singular present active indicative form (perhaps amas) as 2nd person plural present active indicative: plural for singular. Higher numbers will then be frequent errors. These are preliminary figures also; they come from only about five months of data collection, but notice that some patterns are starting to appear. Notice the diagonal pattern

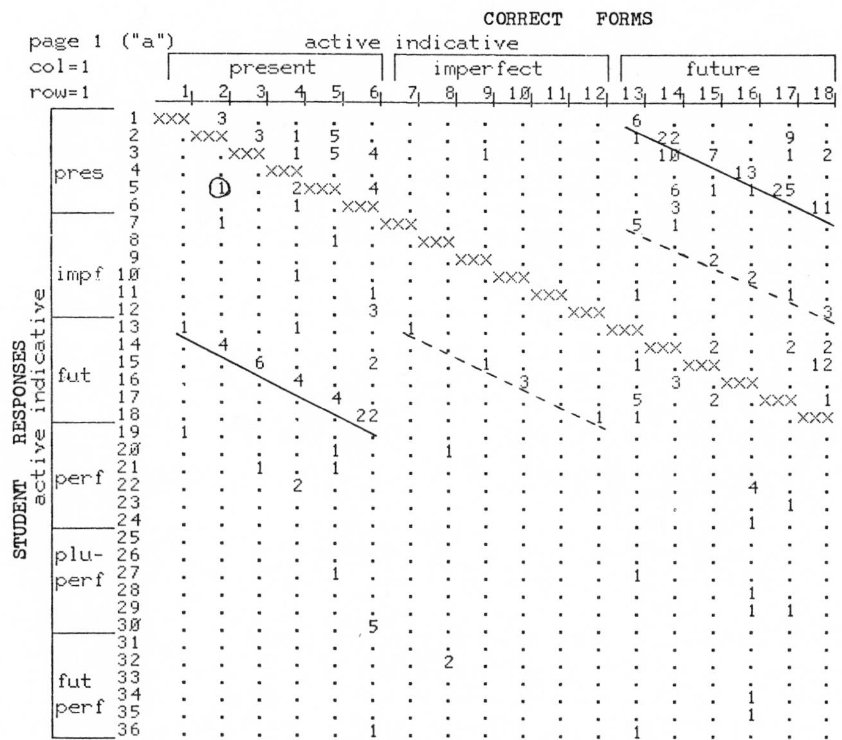

CORRECT FORMS

page 1 ("a") col=1 row=1

STUDENT RESPONSES — active indicative

		active indicative: present						imperfect						future					
		1	2	3	4	5	6	7	8	9	10	11	12	13	14	15	16	17	18
pres	1	XXX	3	.	.	.	.	.	.	.	.	.	.	6	.	.	.	.	.
	2	.	XXX	3	1	5	.	.	.	.	.	.	.	1	22	.	.	9	.
	3	.	.	XXX	1	5	4	.	.	1	.	.	.	.	10	7	.	1	2
	4	.	.	.	XXX	.	.	.	.	.	.	.	.	.	.	.	13	.	.
	5	.	(1)	.	2	XXX	4	.	.	.	.	.	.	.	6	1	1	25	.
	6	.	.	.	1	.	XXX	.	.	.	.	.	.	.	3	.	.	.	11
impf	7	.	1	.	.	.	.	XXX	.	.	.	.	.	5	1	.	.	.	.
	8	.	.	.	.	1	.	.	XXX	.	.	.	.	.	.	.	.	.	.
	9	.	.	.	.	.	.	.	.	XXX	.	.	.	.	.	2	.	.	.
	10	.	.	.	1	.	.	.	.	.	XXX	.	.	.	.	.	2	.	.
	11	.	.	.	.	.	1	.	.	.	.	XXX	.	1	.	.	.	1	.
	12	.	.	.	.	.	3	.	.	.	.	.	XXX	.	.	.	.	.	3
fut	13	1	.	.	1	.	.	1	.	.	.	.	.	XXX	.	.	.	.	.
	14	.	4	.	.	.	.	.	.	.	.	.	.	.	XXX	2	.	2	2
	15	.	.	6	.	.	2	.	.	1	.	.	.	1	.	XXX	.	.	12
	16	.	.	.	4	.	.	.	.	.	3	.	.	.	3	.	XXX	.	.
	17	.	.	.	.	4	.	.	.	.	.	.	.	5	.	2	.	XXX	1
	18	.	.	.	.	.	22	.	.	.	.	.	1	1	.	.	.	.	XXX
perf	19	1	.	.	.	.	.	.	.	.	.	.	.	.	.	.	.	.	.
	20	.	.	.	.	1	.	.	1	.	.	.	.	.	.	.	.	.	.
	21	.	.	1	.	1	.	.	.	.	.	.	.	.	.	.	.	.	.
	22	.	.	.	2	.	.	.	.	.	.	.	.	.	.	.	4	.	.
	23	.	.	.	.	.	.	.	.	.	.	.	.	.	.	.	.	1	.
	24	.	.	.	.	.	.	.	.	.	.	.	.	.	.	.	1	.	.
plu-perf	25	.	.	.	.	.	.	.	.	.	.	.	.	.	.	.	.	.	.
	26	.	.	.	.	.	.	.	.	.	.	.	.	.	.	.	.	.	.
	27	.	.	.	.	1	.	.	.	.	.	.	.	1	.	.	.	.	.
	28	.	.	.	.	.	.	.	.	.	.	.	.	.	.	.	1	.	.
	29	.	.	.	.	.	.	.	.	.	.	.	.	.	.	.	1	1	.
	30	.	.	.	.	.	5	.	.	.	.	.	.	.	.	.	.	.	.
fut perf	31	.	.	.	.	.	.	.	.	.	.	.	.	.	.	.	.	.	.
	32	.	.	.	.	.	.	.	2	.	.	.	.	.	.	.	.	.	.
	33	.	.	.	.	.	.	.	.	.	.	.	.	.	.	.	.	.	.
	34	.	.	.	.	.	.	.	.	.	.	.	.	.	.	.	1	.	.
	35	.	.	.	.	.	.	.	.	.	.	.	.	.	.	.	1	.	.
	36	.	.	.	.	.	1	.	.	.	.	.	.	1	.	.	.	.	.

Chart III. Cursus Honorum Confusion Matrix.

highlighted at the left--a "ghost" of the correct six forms above. These are present indicatives which students thought were futures. The reverse appears at the upper right, where students mistook future indicatives for presents. The latter problem is more severe, as the numbers indicate. There was much less tendency to confuse futures and imperfects; only the faintest "ghosts" of that kind can be seen along the dashed lines. Common sense suggests that there should be little trouble here, and the data verify the assumption. This matrix, even at this early stage, suggests that more work on distinguishing present forms from futures is desirable.

Chart IV is another application of the confusion matrix, this time based on Artifex Verborum, the parsing lesson. The first level of parsing in every case is to identify the part of speech a word is; errors here may be instructive too. If we read vertically, we see that students were able to identify nouns correctly almost seven out of eight times (about 1600 instances), but they only identified pronouns as such about two out of three times. Moreover, when they were wrong about a noun they most often thought it was an adjective. Pronouns also suffered from this same mistaken identity, in fact much more markedly so.

There is one more confusion matrix. Mare Nostrum, the lesson on noun/adjective phrases, collected the data for Chart V. Notice two high-frequency errors. In the first case, students looked at a nominative plural and thought it was a nominative singular. In the other, genitive plurals were often perceived to be accusative singulars. A look at representative forms from the five declensions may show why; see Chart VI. There are the obvious chances to confuse plural with singular in the nominative case of the fourth and fifth declensions, but those are relatively infrequent forms. Something else must be contributing to the frequency of this error. Perhaps forms like <u>dona</u> are being confused with forms like <u>porta</u>--neuter plurals for feminine singulars. In the other columns, one may compare genitive plural forms with accusative singulars. It is easy to see how fourth declension forms might be misread in the way we are considering, and perhaps third declension nouns too, but it looks as if there are too many errors to be explained

correct answers (columns) / student answers (rows)

	noun	pron	adj	verb	adv	prep	conj
noun	1367	8	37	69	4	4	4
pron	2Ø	264	29	1	3	4	4
adj	156	94	57Ø	27	22	2	3
verb	25	3	5	848	7	2	1
adv	8	24	2Ø	2	2Ø4	18	54
prep	Ø	1	5	Ø	19	187	24
conj	3	5	3	Ø	42	28	328

Chart IV. Artifex Verborum Confusion Matrix.

MCONFUS

INCORRECT (columns) / CORRECT (rows)

	Nom S	Gen S	Dat S	Acc S	Abl S	Nom Pl	Gen Pl	Dat Pl	Acc Pl	Abl Pl
Nom S	Ø	5	3	6	2	1Ø	5	7	5	4
Gen S	8	Ø	9	1Ø	13	5	1Ø	15	6	12
Dat S	3	7	Ø	12	12	9	13	17	13	8
Acc S	2	8	9	Ø	6	1	6	3	9	2
Abl S	4	6	7	1Ø	Ø	9	6	13	6	15
Nom Pl	23	3	6	11	14	Ø	9	6	3	4
Gen Pl	11	8	12	23	2	6	Ø	11	14	1
Dat Pl	4	8	18	7	4	4	11	Ø	7	Ø
Acc Pl	18	9	21	22	8	15	13	23	Ø	7
Abl Pl	5	12	13	9	1Ø	6	22	Ø	16	Ø

Usage:

Chart V. Mare Nostrum Confusion Matrix.

	Nom Pl with	Nom S	Gen Pl with	Acc S
I	portae	porta	portarum	portam
II	amici	amicus	amicorum	amicum
II	dona	donum	donorum	donum
III	reges	rex	regum	regem
IV	fructus	fructus	fructuum	fructum
V	dies	dies	dierum	diem

CHART VI. Confusion in Noun and Adjective Forms.

by these two alone. I suspect that the presence of -um in so many of these forms is causing students to see them as forms like amicum and donum and fructum.

Finally, consider a question of learning strategies. Recall the sentence translation lesson in which students are free to ask about any word of any sentence, as often as they like. What do they ask when they have a perfectly free choice without even a proctor peering over their shoulders? The initial figures (Chart VII) show a remarkably consistent pattern: nearly half of the queries for any one part of speech are simply for the English meaning, with its grammatical form and its function in the sentence tied for second place. To most teachers of Latin this is poor strategy; it suggests a "look up every word and then try plugging them together" approach. If students are really approaching a sentence in this manner, more instruction on the nature of Latin syntax seems needed. This chart is in many ways the most provocative, and it raises a number of questions. Which parts of speech were most frequently the objects of questions? Those data exist but have not yet been compiled. Better yet, did the better students have a detectably different style in using this lesson than the poorer ones? Is there a "most efficient" learning style which can be identified and recommended? Finally, there were 73 times that an entire exercise of ten sentences was run without a single question! Were those super-students, needing nothing but running room? Or were they misguided (or lost?) souls, perversely resolved not to do anything that might look like cheating? The answers to these questions will be interesting, without doubt. They may also help us to understand the learning process.

Student Questions About Words in Context

	Raw Figures				Percentages			
	gram form	dict entr	dict mean	func sent	gram form	dict entr	dict mean	func sent
noun	1015	345	1699	837	26%	9%	43%	22%
pron	214	65	361	168	27%	8%	45%	20%
adj	249	97	600	289	20%	8%	49%	23%
part	46	20	69	35	27%	12%	40%	21%
infin	31	23	86	35	18%	13%	49%	20%
verb	538	185	910	394	27%	9%	45%	19%
adv	54	27	189	75	15%	8%	55%	22%
prep	57	40	223	69	15%	10%	57%	18%
conj	27	28	177	44	10%	10%	64%	16%

CHART VII. Translat.

LINGUISTICS AND READING

SPELLING, READING, LANGUAGE VARIATION

Ralph W. Fasold

Georgetown University

Linguists have something to say about reading education, but some of the things linguistic knowledge would suggest do not work when they are tried out. These failures generally happen for reasons that have very little to do with the direct relationship between language and writing: the main thing linguists are in a position to talk about.

One thing linguists _are_ in a position to talk about is how spelling systems are related to phonological systems. In general, there are two points of view on this. The _phonemic spelling principle_ (phonics is one application) suggests that learners should be taught the relationship between letters and phonemes, in something like the classical structuralist sense. The other point of view is that spelling matches phonological units in the underlying forms (the _morphophonemic_ or _systematic phonemic_ level). If this is the correct way to think about phonology and spelling, then _pine_ and _right_ are just as good as _bed_ at representing the sounds in these words. This is true because at the more abstract level, there really is a "silent _e_" in _pine_ (actually [E] according to Chomsky and Halle, 1968) and there is a velar fricative corresponding to the _gh_ in _right_.

A linguist who believes that the relationship between the sound system of a language and writing is best captured by something like the phonemic spelling principle might suggest a particular kind of customized spelling system for teaching reading to speakers of nonstandard English varieties like Vernacular Black English. Where speakers of VBE have different phonemes, it would follow that they would learn better with a different spelling at these points. For VBE speakers who have [f] in word-medial or word-final position where standard English has [θ], for example, it might be recommended that the reading book spell the word with [f]. The word *bath*, then, would be spelled *baf*.

If the relationship between spelling and the sound system is at a more abstract level, then a customized spelling system might not be necessary for VBE speakers. It does appear that there were once profound differences between Black English and standard English varieties. Careful studies of modern VBE, however, indicate that there has been a considerable accommodation of VBE to varieties of American English spoken by whites and that the differences that remain, although they are reflexes of the earlier profound differences, are now rather superficial (Wolfram 1974b; Fasold 1981).

If spelling matches sound at the systematic phonemic level, there is probably no reason to alter conventional spellings. To take the example of words that have [f] in VBE where standard English has [θ], it turns out that VBE speakers are intuitively aware of two kinds of [f]. Wolfram (1974a) was able to show that where [f] in VBE corresponds to [θ] in standard English, it can be pronounced [t], particularly if the next word begins with [n]. A speaker who would have a final [f] in *fourth period* might also say [f ɔ^{ə} t n^{ə}mbə] (*fourth number*), but would never say *[It nat] for *if not*. In other words, some [f]s can be turned into [t] and some cannot. There must be a level at which the two kinds of [f] can be distinguished. It turns out that the best linguistic analysis results if that level is the systematic phonemic level and if the cases in which [f] that *can* become [t] have [θ] in the underlying forms. If this is the case, then the spelling *fourth* is just as good for VBE as it is in standard English, even if a VBE speaker often or usually pronounces the word as [f ɔ^{ə}f]. In general, a customized spelling does not seem to be required if the fit between sound and letter is taken to be at the more abstract level.

The way things are written in reading books is also influenced by grammar. Even if a customized spelling system is found to be unnecessary, reading texts with customized grammar for speakers of VBE might be advisable. The idea here is that even if the neophyte reader can manage the sound-symbol correspondences, the meaning of the text might not come through if the grammar is somewhat foreign. For example, if there is no past tense morpheme in Vernacular Black English grammar, then it might help not to spell verbs with ed in reading books VBE speakers use.

Some of William Labov's early research (Labov, et al., 1968) indicates that some VBE speakers have trouble picking up cues for the past tense of verbs from written material. He examined this question by the judicious use of the homograph read. This is the only word in English that is pronounced differently in the present and past tense, yet is spelled the same way. As a result, it can be used to test whether a reader understands a context to be present or past. Labov had adolescent and pre-adolescent speakers of VBE read the sentence Last month I read five books, in which the adverbial phrase last month shows that the context is past. The readers were quite successful in picking the past tense pronunciation for read in this sentence, and readers with higher reading test scores did better than those with lower scores.

But he also had his subjects read sentences like When I passed by, I read the posters, in which the only clue to the past context is the ed of passed. VBE speakers were far less successful in interpreting read in these sentences. Strikingly enough, there was little correlation between success with these sentences and reading test scores. In other words, individuals who were in general better readers would be just as likely as those who were poor readers to misinterpret read in this kind of sentence. One possible conclusion would be that the problem here is not the process of decoding itself, but a clash between the reader's linguistic system and the one in the reading passage.

But it is very hard to draw conclusions from these results. Labov did not attribute his results to an absence of the past tense category in VBE grammar. It is easy to show that past tense is part of the grammar of almost all varieties of VBE, but that the morpheme can be removed in actual pronunciation by the same rule that removes the [t] in bes(t) man. Instead, the problem in using the morpheme to identify a past context comes from the influence of grammar on this phonological rule. His results are further complicated by the performance of pre-adolescent white speakers on the same test. The final stop deletion rule operates at a far lower frequency in the phonological system of these speakers than it does in VBE. These youngsters also had problems using ed as a past context cue, suggesting that reading ed might be inherently difficult.

Wolfram and I, in a small unpublished experiment, found that presenting adolscent male VBE speakers with text written in VBE grammar did not contribute to fluency in oral reading at all. The research was primarily undertaken as part of a study of the sociolinguistics of Puerto Rican English in New York City and forms much of the basis of Wolfram, 1974a. Although most of the speech samples were from interviews with Puerto Rican male adolescents, a few black adolescents were also interviewed. The bulk of the interview consisted of questions designed to elicit as much narrative as possible, as is usual in research of this type. This narrative material was carefully analyzed for each of the black speakers. Of the nine black young men who were asked to read the VBE passage, six were found to be speakers of VBE by an analysis of the narrative portion of their interviews. In other words, there was evidence that these six readers were actually native speakers of VBE and that the linguistic structure of the reading passage matched their spoken language competence.

We anticipated that these six speakers would be able to read with fluency and accuracy at least those parts of the text which contained the features found in their speech. Surprisingly, there was a strong tendency for them to interpolate standard English features which were neither in the written text nor in their own speech. For example, the six readers had a total of 42 opportunities to read present tense verbs with third person singular subjects (in which the -s suffix was deliberately not included in the printed text). They misread these verbs by stumbling, inserting the -s suffix, or substituting the past tense form of the verb a total of 13 times, or 31% of the potential instances. There were 34 total opportunities to read sentences containing a zero form of the present tense copula (e.g., We know you a teacher...), and eight times (24%), they either stumbled in their reading or inserted the standard form of to be. They performed in this way in spite of the fact that they were chosen precisely because they used these very features in their own narrative speech style.

Five of the six VBE speakers were asked to participate in a cloze reading task which we originally intended to be a test of comprehension of the VBE passage. Because we ended up with so few readers of the VBE passage and even fewer readers of the control standard English passage, this part of the experiment had to be given up. Nevertheless, the cloze test results proved to be enlightening in another way.

The procedure was to have each of the five read the passage twice; once in intact form and the second time with every seventh word omitted. Between the two readings, there was a distractor task involving reading word lists designed to test certain phonological features. In six places, the word omitted involved a VBE construction. For example, the passage included <u>it</u> where it corresponds to standard English <u>there</u> (<u>it</u> <u>was</u> <u>a</u> <u>man</u>...). In four of the six places, there were chronic problems in supplying the original item. The readers either "remembered" a standard English form, could not respond at all, or made several false starts. Again these are features not only well known as features of VBE, but features the readers used in their own speech.

The findings from the experiment Wolfram and I conducted are no more definitive than Labov's findings are. The research was tangential to a data-gathering project for another purpose and was not very well-designed.

The lack of conclusive answers from these instances is, unfortunately, entirely typical. In spite of the common sense appeal of the idea of writing beginning reading texts for speakers of nonstandard English with customized grammar, the research on the topic is scanty and very ambiguous (cf. Sommervill, 1975). There is somewhat more research on a related problem that is faced by educators in other parts of the world. In many countries, the language of education is not the native language of many of the children.

In Tanzania, for example, some 130 vernaculars are spoken as native languages. The language of education in primary grades is Swahili, the national language, but the native language of only about 10% of the population. In India, there are at least 200 languages spoken. Although official policy is to provide initial education in each child's mother tongue, it is obviously impossible to apply that policy to every child. As a result, the school language at the initial level of education will probably be the official language of the state where the child lives, whether it is the native language or not.

In 1951, a committee of language specialists convened by UNESCO recommended that there were great benefits to be derived from providing initial education to each child in his or her native tongue. In the thirty years since then, a number of experiments have been carried out to test that hypothesis. The results of nearly thirty years of experimentation are most eloquently expressed by the following four quotations, each by a scholar who has examined several of these experiments:

> However, in view of the lack of satisfactory evidence, perhaps the wisest counsel to follow at the present time is to say that the linguistic effects of teaching in a second language are unknown (Macnamara, 1966:133; five studies reviewed, including Macnamara's own).

> The evidence about the difficulties of a foreign medium at the school stage thus seems inconclusive. The superiority of the mother tongue has not been everywhere demonstrated... (Dakin, Tiffen, and Widdowson, 1968:27; four studies reviewed).

> The twenty-four studies or reports summarized varied in every conceivable way, and most provided no substantial evidence as to which approach is better (Engle, 1975: 26; twenty-four studies reviewed).

> For a number of years, many educators have accepted as axiomatic the idea that the best medium of instruction for a child is his mother tongue... Are there empirical data which unequivocally support this position? The answer would would seem to be _no_. Does this

> mean the position is untenable? Once again, the answer would seem to be _no_ (Tucker, 1977: 37-38; three studies reviewed).

Thirty years and numerous studies after the publication of the UNESCO Report and the unanimous opinion seems to be that nobody knows whether or not using the mother tongue as the medium of instruction is better than using a second language. It is important to emphasize just what we are talking about. These experiments have to do with cases in which a child walks into a classroom where the teacher speaks a language the child does not understand and the books are all written in a language foreign to him. The children are expected to learn everything, including reading, under these circumstances. It would seem obvious that children would learn better if they _could_ understand the classroom and textbook language than if they could not: so obvious, in fact, that any experiment conducted to test this hypothesis would confirm it. But it simply has not happened that way. Of course, it is not the case that every experiment is inconclusive. A number of them indicate that the idea _does_ work. But an approximately equal number seem to show that learning through a second language is successful and efficient and still others cannot come to a conclusion in either direction.

But there are peculiarities in even those studies that are cited as evidence in favor of the validity of the use of vernacular languages in education. In one carefully designed experiment carried out in the Philippines (Ramos, et al., 1967), an experimental group of school children were taught through Hiligaynon, their native language, in grades 1 and 2 and then switched to English for grades 3 through 6. A control group was instructed in English for all six years. At the end of the first year, the experimental group tested significantly higher in reading and social studies. There was no significant difference in arithmetic. (Both groups were tested in the language they had been instructed in). After four years, when the experimental group had been instructed in English for two years, the control group was slightly better in reading and arithmetic and significantly better in language. The experimental group was slightly better in social studies. One has to wonder if the early success of the experimental group is due to the two years of Hiligaynon instruction or the fact that they understood the test in their native language better. Similarly, the advantage may have gone over to the control group in the fourth grade because they had been dealing with the test language (English) for two years longer than the children in the experimental group. In other words, it is not clear that the results say very much about the efficacy of the use of Hiligaynon as an instructional medium.

If it cannot be demonstrated conclusively that children learn better through their native language than they do through a foreign language -- in spite of the fact that it is only common sense that they would -- then there must be other things going on besides the match between printed text and learner's internal linguistic system. And if this is true when different languages are involved, it might well also be true where different dialects are involved.

In multilingual communities, the various languages that are spoken are normally reserved for particular uses. A language that is used at home might not be the one that is used in church, and the language used in church might not be appropriate for education. In Oberwart, Austria, for example, a town with a substantial population of native speakers of Hungarian, it proved impossible to maintain a Hungarian language school despite the fact that the Austrian government would have supported it. The reason was that even Hungarian-speaking parents believed that only German was the right language for school (Gal, 1979).

In our own country, the same feeling is common in communities where VBE or some other variety of English that is not a standard variety is the usual language of home and neighborhood. Standard English is very definitely believed to be the only reasonable language to be used in school and in textbooks. An attitude study conducted in the black community of East Palo Alto, California by Mary Rhodes Hoover (1978) found exactly that pattern.

Part of the research design involved the subject being presented with a written or oral (tape-recorded) passage in Vernacular Black English and being asked if they would object to their child using the same kind of English under various circumstances. The circumstances involved the setting (School, Community or Home), formality (Formal or Informal) and mode (Reading, Writing, Speaking or Listening). The results were strong approval of VBE (i.e., a large proportion would not object to VBE) for speaking and listening tasks in the home or community (nearly 70% -- I calculated this and other percentages from Hoover's raw data). There was far less approval of VBE for speaking and listening in school (26%) and for reading and writing in any circumstances (30%). Subjects who objected to VBE were asked to explain their disapproval and gave such answers as that teaching the vernacular would take time away from teaching standard English and hurt a child's chances of getting a job or going to college, or that school was the only place for their children to learn the language of education. When asked the advantages of the vernacular, respondents gave such answers as its association with black culture, its value as a means of solidarity and communication among black people, and its use as a means of talking with old people.

Anyone familiar with the typical diglossic distribution of language varieties in various speech communities around the world will find these results very familiar. As long as the domains for the standard language and the vernaculars are established the way they are, the linguistic mismatch that results is of distinctly secondary importance. All else being equal, teaching reading would be more efficient if the grammar and phonology of the learner's mother tongue variety were adequately reflected in written texts. The trouble is that all else is never equal.

Still, even if it is not possible to use reading texts that are customized for speakers of nonstandard dialects because vernacular speech varieties do not seem to belong in school, there are at least two ways that a knowledge of the linguistic relationship between speech and writing can be applied. First, teachers should be able to distinguish oral reading performance that shows the correct rendition of written text in the student's native dialect from oral reading that shows inadequate mastery of reading skill. Some children learn to read, using standard language materials, before they master standard language pronunciation. The result is that they will orally read standard language texts with vernacular pronunciation rules. Far from indicating reading problems, this kind of performance demonstrates success in learning to read. For example, a VBE speaking youngster who reads He's playing with a ball as He playin' wif a ball has read the sentence correctly. When reading is being taught, there is no reason even to comment on the pronunciation of with or playing or the deletion of 's although attention might be called to them when spoken language is the focus.

A second possibility is the use of materials in which some of the dialogue is written in the students' native dialect, while the connecting narrative is in standard grammar and spelling. If the narrative makes it clear that it is appropriate for a certain character to use nonstandard speech, then it might not be so objectionable to see it on the printed page. A little good sense should be used in this connection; it should not be the case, for example, that all and only black people are portrayed as using nonstandard language. Since published readers with nonstandard dialogue might be hard to find, this suggestion can be tried in connection with a language experience approach. Youngsters can be encouraged to tell experiences that involve people talking to each other and these stories can be transcribed exactly as they are told with no attempt to edit the grammar of the dialogue portions. These materials can be presented to learners as text to practice reading skills with. It could be that the linguistic familiarity of the dialogue might help some youngsters see how reading is supposed to work.

Most crucial, of course, is for educators to see non-standard language varieties for what they are. They are fully formed linguistic systems that work well for the affective and communicative tasks they are called on to fulfill. They stand for the personal and social identity of their speakers in the most profound sense imaginable. They would work perfectly well as school languages if their speakers saw them as belonging in that domain; nothing linguistic would prevent it. Quite aside from any techniques that linguistics might indicate, an appreciation for how speech and writing are related and how language varieties fit into the social scheme of things can have a good effect on just how educators go about the business of teaching.

REFERENCES

Dakin, Julian, Tiffen, Brian, and Widdowson, H. G., 1968, "Language in Education," Oxford U. Press, London.

Engle, Patricia, 1975, "The Use of Vernacular Languages in Education: Language Medium in Early School Years for Minority Language Groups," Center for Applied Linguistics, Arlington.

Fasold, Ralph, 1981, The relation between black and white speech in the South, _Am. Sp._, 56:163-89.

Gal, Susan, 1979, "Language Shift: Social Determinants of Linguistic Change in Bilingual Austria," Academic Press, N.Y.

Hoover, Mary Rhodes, 1978, Community attitudes toward Black English, _Lang. in Soc._, 7:65-87.

Labov, W., Cohen, P., Robins, C., and Lewis, J, 1968, "A Study of the Non-standard English of Negro and Puerto Rican Speakers in New York City, Volume I: Phonological and Grammatical Analysis," U.S. Office of Education, Cooperative Research Project No. 3288.

Macnamara, John, 1966, The effects of instruction in a weaker language, _J. of Soc. Iss._, 23:121-35.

Sommervill, Mary Ann, 1975, Dialect and reading: A review of alternative solutions, _Rev. of Ed. Res._, 45:247-62.

Tucker, G. Richard, 1977, "Bilingual Education: Current Perspectives, Vol. 2, Linguistics," Center for Applied Linguistics, Arlington.

Wolfram, Walt, 1974a, "Sociolinguistic Aspects of Assimilation: Puerto Rican English in New York City," Center for Applied Linguistics, Arlington.

Wolfram, Walt, 1974b, The relationship of white southern speech to Vernacular Black English, _Lang._, 50:498-527.

LINGUISTICS AND/OR READING OR IS APPLIED LINGUISTICS A CAVEAT EMPTOR TECHNOLOGY?

Richard L. Venezky

University of Delaware

INTRODUCTION

That linguistics, and particularly applied linguistics, is not viewed with uniform affection, can be deduced from modern literature. Vladimir Nabokov, for example, wrote in Pnin:

> ...nor did Pnin, as a teacher, ever presume to approach the lofty halls of modern scientific linguistics, that ascetic fraternity of phonemes, that temple wherein earnest young people are taught not the language itself, but the method of teaching others to teach that method; which method, like a waterfall splashing from rock to rock, ceases to be a medium of rational navigation but perhaps in some fabulous future may become instrumental in evolving esoteric dialets -- Basic Basque and so forth -- spoken only by certain elaborate machines (Nabokov, 1953: 10).

Similarly, Eugene Ionesco, in a play first produced in the early 1950s, ridiculed modern linguistics through a professor, although in this case a mad, fascist figure, rather than the light-hearted emigre of Nabokov's early novel. To a young, female student he is tutoring, Ionesco's professor addresses the following lines:

> ...in fifteen minutes time, you will be able to acquire the fundamental principles of the linguistic and comparative philology of the neo-Spanish languages.

> ...every tongue is at bottom nothing but language.
>
> ...it takes years and years to learn to pronounce. Thanks to science, we can achieve this in a few minutes.

The Maid, who knows what the horrible outcome of the lesson will be, insists that the philological tutoring not continue.

> No, professor, no!...You must'nt do that!... especially not philology, philology leads to calamity (Ionesco, 1954:60-63).

Whether through association with calamity or frivolity, or with some other undesirable trait, linguistics as a science still has its detractors. Part of this problem stems from a natural hostility that some writers display toward the structured or the scientific, particularly when language is involved. But part also must result from the ambiguous position that linguistics occupies vis-a-vis psychology, and particularly applied linguistics, which brushes up against the full spectrum of human behavior. The role of linguistics in the field of literacy is an instructive locale for observing this problem, especially because philologists and linguists have engaged themselves in the improvement of literacy for almost 200 years, yet the proper role which language science can and should play in this domain remains undefined.

My intentions here are to trace the involvement of philologists and linguists in matters of literacy from the late 1700s until now, and to try to understand both the achievements and the failures of this interaction. If there is any true focus to what follows, it is on the question of how philologists and linguists have dealt with the psychological aspects of language behavior in applying linguistic science to human activities. The focus of concern will be the two primary activities which linguists have pursued in relation to literacy: the design of new orthographies and the design of reading instruction.

DESIGNING ORTHOGRAPHIES[1]

The Nineteenth Century View

The earliest scientific concern for accurate representation of speech was published by Sir William Jones in 1788. Jones, who was also the first to formulate the fundamental postulate of Indo-European comparative grammar, developed a system heavily laden with superscripts to represent the "primary elements of articulation," which he (Jones, 1789: 183) described as the "...soft and hard breathings, the spiritus lenis and the spiritus asper of the Latin Grammarians."[2] Following Jones' lead, Volney in Europe and Pickering in the United States devised systematic orthographies using Roman letters. While Volney, like Jones, was concerned with scientific accuracy in writing Asiatic languages, Pickering was concerned with the practical writing of American Indian languages. "...it never was my plan to give a _universal_ alphabet on strict philosophical principles for the use of the learned, but merely a _practical_ one, to be applied to the Indian languages of North America..." (Pickering, 1820:32). Nevertheless, Pickering made little improvement over Jones' work. The vowels, for example, were viewed as a continuum of sounds, to be represented by the letters a, e, i, o, u, y, plus a bevy of diacritics.

The first guide lines for the design of a universal writing system were developed by Lepsius[3] in 1855 (Standard Orthography for Reducing Unwritten Languages and Foreign Graphic Systems to a Uniform Orthography in Latin Letters). Lepsius, a world renowned Egyptologist, had developed a set of orthographic principles for the Church Missionary Society in 1848, in collaboration with philologists from Cambridge and London. The new system, which was based upon the earlier principles, was sponsored jointly by twelve missionary societies from England, the United States and the Continent, and resulted in a clumsy procedure for recording all known speech sounds according to articulatory movements, regardless of their functional value within any single language. The vowel system was based on the three primary vowels (represented by _a_, _i_, _u_) which Lepsius likened to the three primary colors, and then expanded in the other Latin vowel letters plus an extensive set of superscripts and subscripts, much like Pickering had suggested. The consonants were no less burdensome. As a phonetic transcription system it made little headway, being superseded in time by Sweet's Broad Romic and the International Phonetic Alphabet. As a writing system for preliterate languages, however, it was widely employed, especially in Africa, where the Missionary societies which had sponsored it were the most active.

On the relationship of linguistics to the goals of the missionary societies, and therefore to the design of orthographies, Lepsius was quite clear.

> Hence for many years the Committees of the principal Missionary societies have regarded it an important object to reduce to writing the language of all the nations to which their missionaries have penetrated, and to prepare in all these languages translations of the sacred Scriptures, as well as Christian tracts. This presupposes an accurate and scientific study of those languages, and the preparation of grammars and dictionaries...(Lepsius, 1863:26f).

The Early Twentieth Century View

Concern over the difficulties encountered in teaching reading with Lepsius' system led to the design of a new set of principles for orthographic design, set forth in 1930 by the International African Institute. The basis of the new system was a phonemic representation of speech, using single letters, digraphs, and a minimal number of diacritics. For the first time in print psychological and pedagogical factors were considered, derived primarily from Huey's research on reading (Huey, 1908). This attention to human factors in the design of orthographies for African languages precedes by almost 20 years any similar concern in the United States.

Another innovation in the Institute's principles was the suggested deviation from pure phonemic representation for some instances of tones, a suggestion which had been anticipated by Westermann a year earlier.[4] "In books for Africans, tones...may sometimes be omitted when the context makes it quite clear which word is intended" (from International African Institute, 1930, p. 11). Sir William Jones was the first to enunciate the one-letter, one-sound principle for practical orthographies: "...the orthography of any language should never use the same letter for different sounds, nor different letters for the same sound" (Jones, 1789, cited in Lepsius, 1863: 31).

Summer Institute of Linguistics

The current attitudes in the USA toward orthographic

design were developed primarily by workers of the Summer Institute of Linguistics, and in particular by Pike (1947), Gudschinsky (1953), and Nida (1954), beginning with a one symbol per phoneme concept which has been modified slowly as experience has demonstrated its non-desirability in particular situations.[5] Pike's original position was clearly stated in Phonemics: "A practical orthography should be phonemic. There should be a one-to-one correspondence between each phoneme and the symbolization of that phoneme" (Pike, 1947:208). But within a few years this principle was seriously challenged by Nida (1954) who distinguished between the technical use of an orthography by linguists and the practical use by speakers of the language. Both psychological and cultural factors were cited for deviating from the one-letter, one-sound basis, but even more important for the development of design principles was the description of reading as a "complex series of reactions to visual symbols" and the resulting emphasis on preserving the "unity of visual impressions." Nevertheless, the belief that the ideal orthography (not just "transcription" system) should be a one-letter, one-sound system was still tenaciously guarded. "In an ideal orthography there is a one to one correspondence between the symbols and the phonemes of the language" (Gudschinsky, 1959:68).

Objections to One-Symbol, One-Sound

This "one-symbol, one-sound" principle appears to be derived from three implicit, but generally unstated assumptions: (1) the reading process involves little more than producing sounds from visual stimuli, (2) human language processing is isomorphic to the descriptions of language that structural linguists produce, that is, proceeds from one discrete language level to the next, and (3) there is a psychological reality to the phonemic system which a linguist derives. The first of these assumptions dates in American linguistic writing from Bloomfield (1933); the second and third are somewhat newer; none, nevertheless, is unquestionably valid.

Other objections to the one-letter, one-sound approach to practical orthographies have been expressed by Daniel Jones (1950), DeFrancis (1950), and Hockett (1951). Jones assumes a one letter per phoneme basis for an orthography, but then gives a variety of reasons for departing from this principle, the most important being to (1) distinguish homophones, (2) show popular alternative spellings, and (3) avoid cumbrous spellings. To the horror of most spelling reformers, Jones even countenanced the inclusion of certain silent letters. "It may even at times be found advisable to introduce unpronounced letters into orthography in order to show relationships between words or to distinguish homophones" (Jones 1950:232).

In a discussion of alphabet reform in China, DeFrancis (1950) devoted an entire chapter to the question of whether or not to include indicators for tone in an alphabetic writing system. He concluded that the amount of graphic ambiguity resulting from their omission in Chinese would be small enough to justify such a procedure. This, in essence, is what Westermann stated in 1929 (see footnote 4). Hockett concurs with DeFrancis, but goes one step further:

> So far as possibility is concerned, it can be shown that any established omission of some sufficiently small number of [the operative phonological contrasts] produces a nevertheless workable notation, whether the omission is systematic or haphazard (Hockett, 1951: 444f).

Walker (1969) cites examples of writing systems now used for North American Indian languages which deviate from the one-letter, one-sound principle. Foremost among these are the syllabic alphabets for Cherokee and for Cree, Ojibiwa, Chipewyan, Slave, and Eastern Eskimo.

Failure to Evaluate

What can be said of this 200-year effort to design new orthographies is that although many practical orthographies have resulted, the value of these orthographies for teaching literacy remains largely unknown. Although evaluation has been a formal component of curriculum design in education for the last half-century, no formal evaluation of a literacy program based on any of the missionary orthographies has ever been published.[6] Consequently, a vast amount of experience in the design of literacy programs for preliterate societies remains generally unavailable. This neglect seems to result from the attitude of many linguists that linguistics expertise is not only a necessary but a sufficient basis for designing new orthographies.

Just because linguists, or at least some linguists, analyze language into units like phonemes and morphemes does not necessarily mean that humans process language through such entities. Furthermore, reading, as we have learned from over a century of experimentation, is a far more complex process than simply the translation from visual symbol to sound. The type of orthography that may be optimal for the beginning reading may not necessarily be optimal for the experienced reader. And the approach to teaching an orthography may be more important for the outcomes of learning than the design of the orthography.

What is most difficult to understand about the entire missionary/linguistic effort is how it managed to ignore until recently the field of psychology, and particularly the psychology of reading, which began to develop in the 1880s and has continued to develop ever since. Aside from the International African Institute reference to Huey's text, mention of psychological studies of reading are rare in the orthography design literature. Exceptions to this neglect can be found in Walker (1969), which cites a study on Zuni spelling preferences, and in the work of Grimes and Gordon (1981) which uses reading speed to evaluate orthographic variations. These, however, have been isolated forays into the realm of empirical investigation. The linguistic record that has been established over the past three-quarters of a century, and particularly in the past 40 years, views reading primarily as a letter-sound translation process. Linguistic constructs have been endowed, ex cathedra, with psychological validity and instruction designed more from philological dogma than from empirical data. The causes for these directions are complex, centering as much on the state of psychology over the past century as on trends within the field of linguistics. Nevertheless, it is difficult to deny that the orthography design school was driven by the tenets of twentieth century structural linguistics, and particularly by the work of Leonard Bloomfield, who converted linguistics to a modern science and who also attempted to apply this science to the teaching of reading.

LINGUISTIC SCIENCE AND THE TEACHING OF READING

Many twentieth-century linguists have taken active roles in the design of reading instruction; none, however, has been as influential as Leonard Bloomfield. Yet almost all that we know about Bloomfield's views on reading instruction are contained in word lists he developed for teaching his sons to read, plus an article he wrote on the topic which was published in an abbreviated form in _The Elementary English Review_ (Bloomfield, 1942), and in its entirety in _Let's Read_ (Bloomfield and Barnhart, 1961), a posthumous text compiled by Clarence Barnhart, to whom Bloomfield had given the manuscripts for his reading lessons. Nevertheless, because of Bloomfield's stature as a linguist, his notions about reading received, and continue to receive, serious attention.

Exposure to Wundtian Mentalism

Leonard Bloomfield was born in Chicago in 1887, but grew up in Elkhart Lake, Wisconsin. He attended Harvard, receiving an A.B. degree in 1906, and then did graduate work in Germanic philology, both at the University of Wisconsin and the University of Chicago. He received his doctorate from the latter in 1909 with a dissertation on Germanic secondary ablaut. After instructorships in German at the University of Cincinnati (1909-1910) and at the University of Illinois (1910-1913), Bloomfield continued his Germanic studies abroad, studying at the Universities of Leipzig and Gottingen.

At Leipzig he came strongly under the influence of Wilhelm Wundt, the father of experimental psychology and the dominant figure in European psychology in the first quarter of this century. Although Wundt was 81 years old when Bloomfield arrived in Leipzig, Wundtian mentalism was sufficiently strong to lead Bloomfield to state in his first text on linguistics "It will be apparent, especially, that I depend for my psychology, general and linguistic, entirely on Wundt; I can only hope that I have not misrepresented his doctrine" (Bloomfield, 1914:vi). Whether or not Bloomfield misrepresented these views, he certainly attempted to represent them. Most of the first chapter of _An Introduction to the Study of Language_ was devoted to Wundt's theories on expressive movements, gestures, and language development in the child. Terms like _psychic_, _mental organization_, and _association_ abound, and an entire chapter is devoted to the "Mental basis of language," wherein Wundt's notions on total experience, associative organization of aggregate ideas, and progressive appreception are presented.[7]

Conversion to Behaviorism

But mentalism was not to dominate Bloomfield's views for long. In 1921 Bloomfield accepted a professorship in German and Linguistics at Ohio State University and soon was associated, both academically and socially, with A.P. Weiss. Weiss, who was Professor of Experimental Psychology at Ohio State from 1918 until his untimely death in 1931, helped revive behaviorism in the United States. Weiss's writings on psychology, particularly his 1925 text *A Theoretical Basis of Human Behavior*, rejected "mind" as an explanatory concept in psychology. Thinking was seen as a form of behavior characterized by muscle contractions, a doctrine that Bloomfield readily incorporated into his views on language. On the importance of Weiss's work for linguistics, Bloomfield wrote in a laudatory obituary "Weiss was not a student of language, but he was probably the first man to see its significance. He saw that language supplied the key to those phenomena of human conduct and achievement which hitherto had been attributed to non-physical forces" (Bloomfield, 1931:219).[8]

In *Language* (Bloomfield, 1933), Bloomfield rejected mentalism outright, but claimed also not to subscribe entirely to mechanistic psychology. "We can pursue the study of language without reference to any one psychological doctrine" (Bloomfield, 1933:vii). However, his sympathies were clearly with the mechanistic camp of behaviorism, as revealed by his later writings (Esper, 1968). For teaching reading, Bloomfield suggested that children should first read a phonetic transcription to acquire the "essential reading habit," or be taught initially only with words that had regular letter-sound correspondences.

Bloomfield's Pedagogy

The latter was the direction which Bloomfield pursued in developing materials for teaching his children to read. Lists of "regular" words for various letter-sound correspondences were developed, and a pedagogy similar to the old ABC approach designed. However, contrast of letter-sound patterns was used, along with nonsense words, to focus the child's attention on the important elements of each lesson. On the role of instructional methods, Bloomfield seemed clear. "Pedagogues must determine how reading and writing are to be taught. Their study of eye movements is an instance of progress in this direction" (Bloomfield, 1933:500).

Yet Bloomfield showed no obvious interest in the available psychological or pedagogical literature, either on eye movements or any other topic related to reading.[9] He claimed, for example, that having the "necessary muscular skills" for seeing the small distinctions between the letters was a concern in early reading (Bloomfield and Barnhart, 1961:3). Yet the literature available then showed that by the age of four (at least) children had sufficient control over the optic muscles to make distinctions required for letter discrimination. But the most debilitating failure of Bloomfield's views on reading was his lack of concern with the meaningful components of literacy. Neither in his approach for teaching reading nor in his writings does Bloomfield attend seriously to this issue. C. C. Fries, who unlike Bloomfield rejected eye movement studies as an aid to an understanding of reading, also gave little emphasis to meaning in learning to read.[10] For Fries, reading is primarily a process of building rapid associations between symbols and responses.[11]

Absence of Comprehension

In fairness to structural linguistics, it should be pointed out that comprehension was also largely ignored by educational psychology until recently. Few texts on reading instruction or on the psychology of reading attended to comprehension processes or comprehension instruction until the 1960s and even in the 1980s it received little emphasis in most practical guides. However, the failure of Bloomfield and Fries to attend to comprehension may result from the same causes that kept comprehension out of psychology texts for so long, and that is behavioral psychology.

Behaviorism, with its emphasis on mechanistic explanations, dominated twentieth century psychology until the 1960s. As a science, it led more to observation and classification than it did to experimentation and model building. By defining meaning in neuro-muscular terms, the behaviorists off-loaded the study of higher cognitive processes to physiologists and others who had little interest in this pursuit. Bloomfield even stated (1933: 157) that "The statement of meanings is therefore the weak point in language study, and will remain so until human knowledge advances very far beyond its present state." But so long as description of meaning required "...scientifically accurate knowledge of everything in the speakers' world," little progress could be expected. Innovative approaches to the study of mental processes, such as Bartlett (1932), remained outside of the mainstream of psychology until the last decade. Behaviorism, in crushing mentalism, also eliminated fruitful study of cognition. And both psychology and linguistics suffered for adequate theories of meaning. Bloomfield, in building a science of linguistics, was not able to construct beyond what behaviorist psychology could offer.

EPILOGUE

Present-day psychology is highly cognitively oriented, and instructional psychology, in particular, is attending more and more to memory structures and processing strategies (e.g., Bruner, 1966; Case, 1978). New opportunities exist for finding an appropriate psychology for relating language constructs to human behavior. Behaviorism has been tried and found wanting, as was mentalism earlier in the century. Whether the new cognitive science will be an appropriate basis or not remains to be determined. But linguists can not ignore that linguistic constructs, when applied to literacy, carry psychological implications.

To claim, for example, that reading is best introduced using words with regular letter-sound patterns is to make claims not about linguistics per se, but about human learning. The validation for such claims must, therefore, come from the empiricial investigation of learning, not from linguistic analysis. Similarly, to advocate the teaching of reading in a native language prior to literacy in the majority language of a country is to state beliefs about cognitive behavior and about instructional capabilities. Without serious attention to underlying psychological constructs, such positions have no scientific validity. For nearly 300 years linguists have avoided human psychology in their approaches to literacy. The time has clearly arrived for abandoning what Nabokov called "the lofty halls of modern scientific linguistics, that ascetic fraternity of phonemes," and for building a linguistic basis for literacy instruction that is empirically derived and compatible with the mainstream of psychological theory.

While the new cognitive psychology has not focused too well on instruction, it nevertheless offers a rational set of strategies for developing good literacy instruction, based on objective linguistic principles. What is needed now is not new dogma from linguists on how reading should be taught, but a well defined set of questions about instruction, based upon language analysis.

NOTES

[1]Parts of the section which follows have been adapted from my earlier paper, Venezky (1970).

[2]Jones' system is apparently derived from one designed by Halhead for his Bengal Grammar and was motivated very strongly by the gross distortions made by Classical Greek and Latin writers in writing foreign terms. "The ancient Greeks," wrote Jones, "who made a voluntary sacrifice of truth to the delicacy of their ears, appear to have altered by design almost all the oriental names which they introduced into their elegant, but romantick Histories" (Jones, 1789:175f).

[3]Karl Richard Lepsius (1810-1884) is counted among the founders of modern scientific archaeology. Among his contributions to that field was one of the first chronologies for the ancient history of Egypt, and the excavation (at Tel el Amarna) of the first evidence on the character of Ikhnaton. He also contributed to the study of African languages with a classification system which he published in 1880. Lepsius studied archaeological philology and comparative languages, and obtained both a doctorate of philosophy and a doctorate of divinity. He taught at the University of Berlin from 1846 until his death.

[4]Westerman (1929) suggested the omission of nasalization marks where ambiguity (within context) would not result.

[5]The Summer Institute of Linguistics (S.I.L.), an activity of the Sycliffe Bible Translators, was founded in 1935 by W. Cameron Townsend specifically to involve linguists in the task of Bible translation. The Wycliffe organization draws its name from the Englishman John Wycliffe, a

fourteenth century religious reformer whose teachings inspired the first translation of the Bible into English. Work by members of the Summer Institute of Linguistics is published in a variety of books and journals, including The Bible Translator, which is published by the United Bible Societies of Great Britain.

[6]By formal evaluation I mean something more than the program developer's subjective reports. Summative evaluation in the sense of Scriven (1967) is one widely accepted approach, as are some of the designs summarized by Campbell and Stanley (1963).

[7]For a discussion of Bloomfield's psychology, see Esper, 1968.

[8]In this obituary Bloomfield wrote of the unfortunate last years of Weiss's life, when after a heart attack "for long periods he was denied even the slightest activity" (Bloomfield, 1931:221). Tragically, Bloomfield's life was to end the same way 18 years later. Bloomfield suffered a stroke in 1946 and spent the last three years of his life as an invalid (see Bloch, 1949).

[9]By the early 1940s a voluminous literature on reading existed and the major textbooks on psychology gave considerable space to the psychology of reading (e.g., Woodworth, 1938).

[10]"In spite of the great number of studies dealing with eye movements...very little of a positive nature has been contributed from these studies to our understanding of reading ability and to our knowledge of how to develop it in either children or adults" (Fries, 1962:30f).

[11]C. C. Fries, who was born the same year as Bloomfield but outlived him by 18 years, wrote two texts on reading (Fries, 1963, 1965) and co-authored with his wife and others an elementary level reading series, A Basic Reading Series Developed Upon Linguistic Principles (Fries, et al., 1965). Other linguists have also taken part in the design of reading instruction, but the works of Bloomfield and of Fries remain as the most notable statements by twentieth century linguists on the teaching of reading.

REFERENCES

Bartlett, F. C., 1932, "Remembering," Cambridge U. Press, Cambridge.

Bloch, Bernard, 1949, Obituary of Leonard Bloomfield, Lang., 25:87-89.

Bloomfield, Leonard, 1914, "An Introduction to the Study of Language," Henry Holt, N.Y.

Bloomfield, Leonard, 1931, Obituary of Albert Paul Weiss, Lang., 7:219-21.

Bloomfield, Leonard, 1933, "Language," Holt, Rinehart and Winston, N.Y.

Bloomfield, Leonard, 1942, Linguistics and reading, Elem. Eng. Rev., 19:125-30, 183-86.

Bloomfield, Leonard and Barnhart, Clarence L., 1961, "Let's Read: A Linguistic Approach," Wayne State U., Detroit.

Bruner, Jerome, 1966, "Toward a Theory of Instruction," Harvard U. Press, Cambridge.

Case, Robbie, 1978, A developmentally based theory and technology of instruction, Rev. of Ed. Res., 48:439-63.

DeFrancis, J., 1950, "Nationalism and Language Reform in China," Princeton U. Press, Princeton.

Esper, Erwin A., 1968, "Mentalism and Objectivism in Linguistics: The Sources of Leonard Bloomfield's Psychology of Language," American Elsevier, N.Y.

Fries, C. C., 1963, "Linguistics and Reading," Holt, Rinehart and Winston, N.Y.

Fries, C. C., Fries, A. C., Wilson, M. and Randolph, M. K., 1965, "A Basic Reading Series Based upon Linguistic Principles," Charles E. Merrill, Columbus.

Grimes, Joseph, and Gordon, Raymond G., Jr., 1980, Design of new orthographies, in: "Orthography, Reading and Dyslexia," J. Kavanagh and R. Venezky, eds., Univ. Park Press, Baltimore.

Gudschinsky, Sarah, 1959, Recent trends in primer construction, Fund. and Adult Ed., 11:67-96.

Gudschinsky, Sarah, 1953, "Handbook of Literacy," Summer Institute of Linguistics, Norman.

Hockett, C., 1951, Review of: John DeFrancis, "Nationalism and Language Reform in China," Lang., 27:439-45.

Huey, E. B., 1908, "The Psychology and Pedagogy of Reading," Macmillan, N.Y.

Ionesco, Eugene, 1958, "The Lesson," Grove Press, N.Y.

International African Institute, 1930, "Practical Orthography of African Languages," Oxford U. Press, London.

Jones, Daniel, 1950, "The Phoneme," W. Heffer and Sons, Cambridge.

Jones, Sir William, 1788, On the orthography of Asiatic words in Roman letters. *Asiatic Res.*, 1:1-56.

Lepsius, Carl R., 1855, "Standard Orthography for Reducing Unwritten Languages and Foreign Graphic Systems to a Uniform Orthography in European Letters," Seeleys Fleet Street & Hanover Street, London.

Lepsius, Carl R., 1863, "Standard Orthography for Reducing Unwritten Languages and Foreign Graphic Systems to a Uniform Orthography in European Letters," 2nd ed., Williams & Norgate, London.

Nabokov, Vladimir, 1964, "Pnin," Atheneum, N.Y.

Pickering, John, 1820, "Essay on a Uniform Orthography for the Indian Languages of North America," ms., Cambridge, Mass.

Nida, E., 1954, Practical limitations to a phonemic alphabet, *The Bible Tran.*, 15:35-39, 58-62.

Pike, K. L., 1947, "Phonemics: A Technique for Reducing Language to Writing," U. of Michigan Press, Ann Arbor.

Scriven, Michael, 1967, The methodology of evaluation," *in*: *AERA Monograph Series on Curriculum Evaluation* (No. 1), Rand McNally, Chicago.

Venezky, Richard L., 1970, Principles for the design of practical writing systems, *Anth. Ling.*, 12:256-70.

Walker, Willard, 1969, Notes on native writing systems and the design of native literacy programs, *Anth. Ling.*, 11:148-66.

Weiss, A. P., 1925, "A Theoretical Basis of Human Behavior," R. G. Adams, Columbus.

Weiss, A. P., 1929, "A Theoretical Basis of Human Behavior," 2nd ed., R. G. Adams, Columbus.

Westermann, D., 1929, "The linguistic situation and vernacular literature in British West Africa, *Africa*, 2:337-51.

Woodworth, R. S., 1938, "Experimental Psychology," Holt, N.Y.

THE DEVELOPMENT OF VERBAL REASONING: PRAGMATIC, SCHEMATIC AND OPERATIONAL ASPECTS

Judith Orasanu[1] and Sylvia Scribner

City University of New York

Becoming literate, that is, mastering the use of written language, has been assumed to carry with it consequences for the way people think and how they use spoken language. Havelock (1973) has argued that the Greek's invention of the alphabetic writing system led to new modes of thought because storage of information for later use released "the human brain from certain formidable burdens of memorization while increasing the energies available for conceptual thought" (Havelock, 1973:60). Goody and Watt (1963) contend that literacy led to new regard for "literal" truth and fostered critical analysis because logical inconsistencies became apparent in written prose. Writing permitted the development of the rules of formal logic, as in Aristotle's *Analytics*.

Despite a long history of speculation about the consequences of literacy, empirical examination has been limited. Oral and literate cultures have been characterized by anthropologists (see Akinnaso, 1981; Goody and Watt, 1968); psychologists (Greenfield, 1972); and sociolinguists (Tannen, 1982), but there have been few investigations of the effects of literacy on individuals. One difficulty in any attempt to investigate the consequences of literacy directly is that it is usually embedded in schooling and associated with other cultural factors that could contribute to the effects typically attributed to literacy (Bruner, 1966; Greenfield, 1972; Rogoff, 1981; Stevenson et al., 1978). Recently, however, Scribner and Cole (1981) took advantage of an unusual situation among the Vai people of West Africa to tease apart these factors and investigate the consequences of literacy without schooling. They found these to be less sweeping and universal than previously thought. Under the circumstances of Vai society, literacy *per se* did not confer general advantages on abstract thinking, logical reasoning or memory abilities. Cognitive skills related to literacy did appear in the studies, but these were specific and associated with the culture's literacy practices and methods of transmission. Schooling, and its attendant literacy instruction, was a more potent factor in influencing logical reasoning and ability to provide verbal explanations in situations divorced from practical contexts.

This paper examines the development of logical reasoning ability in U.S. children as they acquire the culture of literacy and schooling. This development is viewed through the lens of cross-cultural research. While logical reasoning has traditionally been treated as an aspect of cognitive development in the Piagetian sense, the cross-cultural work has documented the role of schooling in the development of what we call "formal thought." This work has also yielded insight into the role of language in logical thinking. Some detail will be provided on these studies to create a context for understanding the U.S. study to be reported here.

Working in Liberia, Scribner (1975, 1977) presented logical syllogisms like the following to adults who differed in levels and kinds of literacy.

> All stores in Kpelleland are in a town.
> Mr. Ukatu has a store in Kpelleland.
> Is it in a town?

Performance on these problems varied with amount of formal schooling. In brief, unschooled adults frequently failed to solve the problems correctly because they assimilated the premises to their personal experience and reasoned from their real-world knowledge. This finding does not mean that they did not possess the ability to think logically; to the contrary, Scribner reported that they often provided elaborate and very logical explanations for their conclusions. However, their logic was applied to evidence not presented in the problem; that is, new information was introduced, presented information was neglected or premises were omitted.

Other adults from the same communities who had at least two or three years of Western-type schooling and rudimentary literacy skills approached the problems as hypothetical reasoning tasks, restricted their reasoning to the premise contents, and solved them correctly. Most significantly, justification for their answers referred to the information presented in the premises, whereas the non-schooled adults' justifications referred to their everyday experience (or they rejected the possibility of solution because they lacked relevant personal experiences).

These findings echo with remarkable fidelity those obtained by Luria (1976) more than 40 years ago in Central Asia, just following the socialist revolution in the USSR. He found that different modes of thinking characterized peasants whose daily lives were dominated by concrete practical activities, and those whose lives were transformed by rapid social and technological advances, plus a modicum of education. More recently, Sharp, Cole and Lave (1978) also found schooling effects on reasoning skills among Yucatecan populations.

At issue is the nature of these mental changes documented in diverse cultures at different points in history. Luria concluded that new modes of thought developed as a function of new types of social practices. These include theoretic reasoning skills, or the ability to perform logical operations on abstract propositions, unsupported by concrete referents or immediate experience. However, it is still not clear whether a fundamental restructuring of mental processes occurs or whether the range of application of existing modes of thought is extended to new contexts (see Cole, in Luria, 1976).

What is clear is that new ways of using language emerge. Scribner and Cole (1981) reported that schooling led to more elaborate verbal descriptions of mental processes or strategies, rules and justifications for behavior. In general, schooling fostered explicit expository skills that were not evident in the behavior of the non-schooled (although literate) Vai participants in their study. Scribner (1977) suggested that schooling fosters acquisition of verbal genres not common in everyday language. Viewing logical syllogisms as a particular genre, it is apparent that specific demands are associated with them: a hypothetical attitude, working within the confines of the problem structure and applying rules of logic to the presented information. Such demands appear to be common to the language and tasks of schools (see Mehan, 1979 and Cook-Gumperz & Gumperz, 1982). Much school discourse deals with people, events and objects not physically present, and with problems represented symbolically. Students are encouraged to think and talk about the hypothetical. This distinction between school and out-of-school language has been noted by Olson (1977) and characterized as "text" and "utterance," where text represents that form of language associated with literacy -- explicit, decontextualized, and logical. Utterance refers to implicit, context-dependent, face-to-face conversation more common to social interaction.

THE RESEARCH STUDY

The rest of this paper reports an empirical investigation of the development of logical reasoning in American school children. The focal task was solution of logical syllogisms. However, Scribner's and Luria's cross-cultural research and other studies with adults and children in the United States indicate that successful performance depends on three components.

First, one must know how to approach the problems. They must be treated as hypothetical, abstract reasoning problems. Information in the premises must be taken as true and conclusions based solely on such information rather than on everyday knowledge or belief. This component will be referred to as the _pragmatic_ aspect of syllogistic performance.

Second, one must have a mental schema for the essential components of the problem and the relations holding between them. A schema serves to identify and organize critical information in memory. In the case of syllogisms, the schema must include the quantified class inclusion relation specified by each premise. Linguistic and cognitive knowledge about quantification and negation are essential for accurate representation of the problem. This component will be referred to as the _schematic_ aspect.

Third, one must apply specific rules of logic to derive the allowable inference from the premises. At a minimum, this involves integrating the information contained in the two premises, drawing a conclusion, and checking to see whether other conclusions are possible that contradict and thereby falsify the initial conclusion. This component will be called the operational aspect. It is the aspect usually of concern in studies of logical development and reasoning.

Of particular interest in the present study was the sequence and rate of development of each component as children progress through school and become literate. The clinical procedure initially developed by Luria and subsequently used by Scribner was adapted for this study. In addition to solving a set of logical syllogisms, we also asked the children to tell us how they determined the answers and to repeat back the problems from memory. Justification of their answers was expected to indicate how they approached and solved the problems: from their own experience or on a theoretical basis. The recall task was to tell us whether the children had a mental schema for the essential logical structure of the problems. Distortions in recall are currently viewed as reflections of pre-existing knowledge about the form and content of discourse. Thus, recall was expected to serve as an indicator of the child's knowledge of the form as well as a reflection of the actual problem content on which the child operated. Solution, of course, would indicate whether the child could engage in the appropriate logical operations.

In providing multiple sources of the evidence, the triple procedure strengthened our ability to draw conclusions about the development of logical reasoning skills.

DESCRIPTION OF THE PROBLEMS

First, the kinds of problems used in this study will be described briefly. They are classical syllogisms consisting of two quantified premises, each of which describes a class-inclusion relation between two sets. For example:

> Some of Tom's shirts are in the closet.
> All the shirts in the closet are cotton shirts.
> Are some of Tom's shirts cotton shirts?

For convenience we can label this problem in the following way:

Some A are B
All B are C
Are some A C?

A, B and C refer to the three terms in the problem: A = Tom's shirts, B = shirts in the closet, and C = cotton shirts. This notation will be used throughout the paper.

Quantification in each premise can be either universal or particular (All vs. Some), and aspect can be either affirmative or negative (All vs. None; Some vs. Some not). In addition, relations among terms within the two premises can vary, determining the figure. B always refers to the term repeated in both premises. Four combinations are possible:

	(1)	(2)	(3)	(4)
Premise 1:	A-B	B-C	B-A	A-B
Premise 2:	B-C	A-B	B-C	C-B
	(transi-ive)	(intransi-ive)	(subject repeat)	(predicate repeat)

Factorial combinations of quantifiers, aspects and figures yields 256 different syllogisms, of which only 19 are valid, that is, permit an unambiguous conclusion about the relation between the A and C terms.

Eight valid problems and four invalid ones were used in the present study. These can be found in Figure 1. In each problem one premise was universal affirmative (All A-B), and the other premise was one of four types: universal affirmative (<u>All A-B</u>), universal negative (<u>No A-B</u>), particular affirmative (<u>Some A-B</u>), and particular negative (<u>Some A not B</u>). All the problems contained meaningful but factually neutral content familiar to American schoolchildren.

RESEARCH PROCEDURES

Findings will be reported from one study taken from a set of related developmental studies using similar problems and procedures.[2] This study involved 16 second graders and 16 fifth graders from a public school in New York City serving lower class to upper-middle class children.

1. All sixth grade girls are in the play.
   All girls in the play are tall.
   Are all sixth grade girls tall?

2. All the books on the desk are science books.
   All Janet's books are on the desk.
   Are all of Janet's books science books?

3. None of the Halloween candies are chocolate.
   All of the candies in the dish are Halloween candies.
   Are any candies in the dish chocolate?

4. All of the cats in the house are Mary's cats.
   None of Mary's cats are black.
   Are any of the cats in the house black?

5. Some dogs in the park are the teacher's dogs.
   All of the teacher's dogs are puppies.
   Are some of the dogs in the park puppies?

6. All of Mark's shirts are wool shirts.
   Some of the shirts in the closet are Mark's shirts.
   Are some of the shirts in the closet wool shirts?

7. Some of the Christmas toys are not dolls.
   All of the Christmas toys are in the chest.
   Are all of the toys in the chest dolls?

8. All of Carol's cakes are homemade cakes.
   Some of Carol's cakes are not for sale.
   Are all of the homemade cakes for sale?

9. All maple trees are red in the fall.
   All the farmer's trees are red in the fall.
   Are all of the farmer's trees maple trees?

10. All children from the school are smart.
    No children from the school are on the team.
    Are all children on the team smart?

11. Some boats on the river are sail boats?
    All of Robert's boats are on the river.
    Are some of Robert's boats sail boats?

12. All broken crayons are blue crayons.
    Some blue crayons are not in the box.
    Are any broken crayons in the box?

Note: Problems 1-8 are valid; 9-12 are invalid.

Figure 1. Problem Set.

Participants in the study were randomly selected from their classes, half girls and half boys.

The order of the three tasks was: (1) to solve the syllogisms, (2) to give a reason for the answers, and (3) to repeat the problems from memory.

Working individually with a child, the experimenter read aloud each problem once and asked the child to answer the question. Response alternatives included "Yes," "No," and "No One Can Tell" (the correct answer for the invalid problems). Several practice problems were given first so that the child understood the procedure. They were asked to give a confidence rating to each response: "Very Sure," "Sure," or "Not So Sure." Next, the experimenter asked the student, "How do you know that the answer was ("Yes," "No," or "No One Can Tell")?" Finally, the student was asked to repeat the problem from memory exactly as the experimenter had read it. Then the experimenter went on to read the next problem. No feedback on accuracy was provided.

Findings will be organized to answer three questions: (1) How do students approach the problems--as hypothetical reasoning tasks or as everyday experience problems? (2) How well are students able to solve the problems? and (3) How well do students remember the information given in the problems? Findings that address all three questions are summarized in Table 1.

Approach to the Problems. The first and most striking finding was that by second grade most children knew that they were to seek the answers to the questions in the premises. That is, they had acquired the pragmatic knowledge about the genre, and appreciated the "rules of the game." We determined this from their responses to the question about how they knew the answers. Explanations that referred back to the premises were called "theoretic" responses and signified a decontextualized approach. These responses were in contrast to explanations that referred to prior factual knowledge or belief rather than to premise information, called "empiric" responses (Scribner, 1977). 78% of second graders' and 94% of fifth graders' explanations were theoretic. Examples of theoretic and empiric responses are provided in Figure 2.

Table 1. Performance Measures for each Task by Grade.

	Grade 2	Grade 5
1. Theoretic Explanations		
(% correct out of 12)	78	94
2. Correct Solution - All problems		
(% correct out of 12)	57	69 *
Valid problems only (8)	74	77
Invalid problems (4)	24	52
3. Recall - All 12 problems		
# Sentences recalled (out of 36)	10.1	17.3 **
# Problems (out of 12) recalled with		
3 content terms present (A, B, C)	7.7	10.4 **
Syllogism form preserved	3.9	7.6 **
Both premises correct	1.4	3.1 **

** = difference significant at $\underline{p} < .01$
* = difference significant at $\underline{p} < .05$

Table 2. Mean Number of Narrative Conversions in Recall per Student.

	I	II	III	IV	Total
	Topicalize	Change Verb	Elaborate Content	Pronominal-ize or Drop Modifier	
Grade 2	1.7	1.7	.8	2.5	6.6
Grade 5	.3	.8	0	1.4	2.5

Examples of Empiric and Theoretic Justifications

Empiric

Grade 2

1. (problem 1) I know a sixth grade girl who is not very tall. There are lots of girls in high grades who are not tall.

2. (problem 4) Maybe she doesn't like black cats or something.

3. (problem 9) Farmers usually have maple trees.

4. (problem 10) Because you don't have to be smart to be on the team. You can be a cheerleader and not be very smart; you can be a baseball player and not be very smart.

Theoretic

Grade 2

5. (problem 5) 'Cuz that's what it said in the puzzle.

6. (problem 6) The story said all of the shirts are wool.

7. (problem 9) It says all of the farmer's trees are red, some of the trees are maple trees, and that tells you.

8. (problem 10) If all the kids in school are smart and they're on the team, they must be smart.

Grade 5

9. (problem 2) Because the second clue was, "All of the books on the table were science books." It's logical.

10. (problem 5) If the teacher's dogs are all puppies and they're in the park, or some of them are in the park, well then there's got to be puppies in the park.

11. (problem 9) If the maple trees are red and he only has red trees, then that means he must only have maple trees.

12. (problem 9) There could be another tree, like an oak or a birch, that is red in the fall. That doesn't mean that they are necessarily maple. They could be that other kind of tree.

Figure 2.

Solution Accuracy. While even second graders generally knew how to approach the problems, their ability to solve them lagged behind, as shown in Table 1. Given three response choices (Yes, No, and No One Can Tell), both second and fifth graders solved at above chance levels (chance = 33%). Most of the difficulty was caused by the invalid problems, especially for the second graders. On valid problems second and fifth graders performed equally well (74% and 77% accuracy, respectively). On invalid problem response accuracy dropped to 24% and 52% respectively.

Based on justifications given for their answers, at least some errors on invalid problems appear to result from a failure to check for alternative inferences that contradict the first one generated. Alternative inferences are possible because certain class inclusion premises can represent more than one state of affairs and combinations of these yield conflicting conclusions. An example illustrated through Venn diagrams may clarify this point.[3] Problem 9 was:

All the farmer's trees are red in the fall.	= All A are B
All maple trees are red in the fall.	= All C are B
Are all the farmer's trees maple trees?	= Are all A C?

Each premise can be represented either of two ways: All A are B can mean that A and B are completely overlapping sets (hence All B are A) or that A is a subset of B (hence, Some B are A and Some B are not A), shown in Figure 3.

Combining these alternative representations of the two premises yields six possible combined representations and conclusions, as shown in Figure 4. In order to appreciate that no solution is possible on invalid problems, one needs to generate these alternatives. The distinction between valid and invalid problems is that for valid ones all combinations will yield the same answer to the question posed. Hence, correct solution can be achieved without generating all combinations. Invalid problems are indeterminate precisely because different interpretations of the quantification in the premises or different premise combinations yield contradictory solutions. In order to determine that a problem is invalid, at least two contradictory

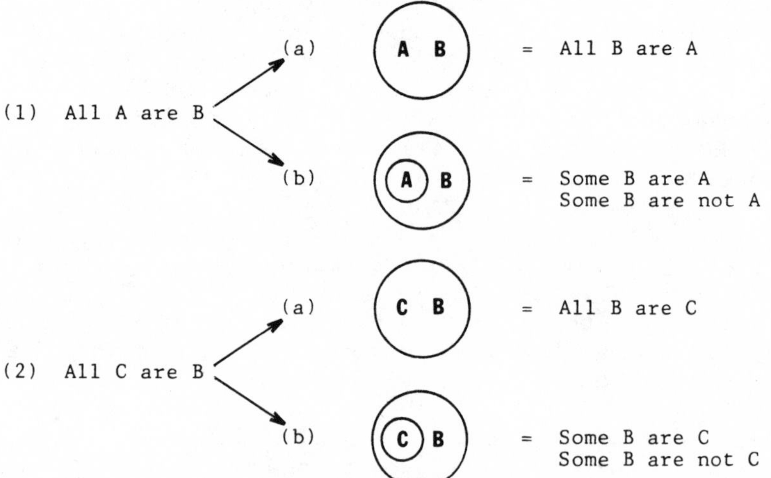

Figure 3. Alternative Representations of Quantified Logical Relations.

Combination	Conclusion	Response (Are all A C?)
1(a) + 2(a) =	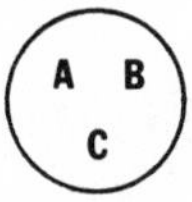 = All A are C	Yes
1(a) + 2(b) =	 = Some A are C and Some A are not C	No
1(b) + 2(a) =	 = All A are C	Yes
1(b) + 2(b) =	 = No A are C	No
OR =	 = Some A are C and Some A are not C	No
OR =	 = All A are C	Yes

Figure 4. Alternative Premise Combinations and Conclusions.

combinations must be generated. Fifth graders' justifications for their answers often reflected this appreciation, whereas second graders' responses rarely did. For example, one fifth grader justified his correct solution of an invalid problem as follows:

> There could be another tree, like an oak or a birch, that is red in the fall. That doesn't mean that they are necessarily maple. They could be that other kind of tree.

In contrast, another fifth grader's justification for a wrong answer to the same problem reflects a failure to appreciate the alternative representations:

> If the maple trees are red and he only has red trees, then that means he must only have maple trees.

This child appears to have represented the problem as 1 (a) + 2 (a) in figure 4, in which the set of red trees does not contain any other trees than maples and the farmer's trees. Based on his justification, it appears that he has applied appropriate logical operations to an incomplete representation of the problem.

Problem Recall. The recall task was designed to provide us with information about the children's representations of the problems. Age differences were most prominent on this task, appearing in both retention of the essential content of the premises and in preservation of the form of the recalled problems. With respect to content, using number of sentences accurately recalled as a measure, older students recalled significantly more than younger (Table 1). By accurate recall here, we do not refer to verbatim recall, but to accurate reproduction of the class inclusion relations, whether or not there were surface variations in the manner of conveying them. Our generous scoring criterion allowed for use of synonyms, syntactic variation and decomposition of the premises. An example of decomposition that preserved the logical relations is the following.

> Presented: None of Mary's cats are black.
> Recalled: Mary has some cats and none of them are black.

A verbatim scoring criterion yielded such low scores that results were totally uninformative.

Looking at recall of each problem as a whole, we find that most fifth graders recalled all three content terms and retained the essential information from both premises more often than second graders. Even when they were wrong about the content, fifth graders more often preserved the essential form of the syllogism. We defined syllogism form as two premises each containing two terms (AB, BC or AC), with one term repeated in both premises (serving as a middle term linking the two). Quantification was ignored for the purpose of the score.

Considering recall from the perspective of information needed for accurate solution, the criterion that is most relevant is accurate recall of both premises. Fifth graders only reproduced the correct information for 3.1 problems (out of 12), and second graders recalled this information for 1.4 problems. For children in both grades there was a relation between accuracy of solution and recall. That is, those problems that were recalled accurately were more likely to be solved correctly. However, it should be noted that this relation was not perfect and does not explain the low solution rates on the invalid problems. As a group the four invalid problems were remembered as well as the eight valid ones (42% vs. 37% of the sentences accurately recalled, respectively).

These low levels of accurate recall are somewhat surprising in light of the relatively high solution levels, particularly for valid problems. Recall protocols were examined more closely to try to determine what information was lost or changed. The nature of the recall "errors" suggested that the syllogism content was assimilated to a genre more familiar to young children, the narrative. Four types of narrative conversions were very common across children and can be summarized as the following rules:

1. Introduce topic, then predicate
2. Change verb
3. Elaborate content
4. Pronominalize

Examples of each type can be found in Figure 5.

I. Introduce Topic (There are...), then Predicate

1. (problem 5) There were dogs in the park.
And some of them were puppies.
And some of the puppies were the teacher's.
Were any of the puppies the teacher's?

2. (problem 11) All of Robert's boats are on the river.
There are some sail boats on the river.
Are some of Robert's boats sail boats?

3. (problem 12) There were crayons in the bowl.
And none of them were blue except the broken ones.
Were any of them blue?

II. Verb Change (to active or possessive)

(Active)

1. (problem 8) Carol made some homemade cakes.
Some of her cakes was for sale.
The cakes was homemade.
Was the cakes for sale?

2. (problem 8) All of Carol's cakes are homemade cakes.
She won't sell them all.
She's not going to sell them all.

3. (problem 11) Robert was sailing boats at the pond.
And some of them were sail boats.
Were any of them sail boats?

(Possessive)

4. (problem 4) Mary doesn't have black cats.
All these cats belong to Mary.
Does Mary have any black cats?

5. (problem 6) Mark had shirts in the closet.
Some of them were wool.
Were any of them wool shirts?

6. (problem 11) All the sailing boats are on the river.
Tom has some boats.
Some of his boats are sail boats.
Are any of Tom's boats sail boats?

Figure 5. Examples of Narrative Conversions in Recall.

III. <u>Elaborate Content</u>

1.	(problem 1)	Some of the sixth graders are tall. Some of them are not so tall. Are all of the sixth graders tall?
2.	(problem 7)	All the presents under the Christmas tree are not dolls.
3.	(problem 8)	Mary baked cakes. Some of them Mary was gonna eat. Some of them Mary was gonna sell. Was Mary gonna sell all of her cakes?

IV. <u>Pronominalize or Drop Modifier (Premise 2 Subject Term)</u>

(Pronominalize)

1.	(problem 2)	All of Janet's books are on the desk. All of them are science books. Are all of the books science books?
2.	(problem 6)	All of Mark's shirts are wool. And some of them are in the closet. Are Mark's shirts wool?

(Drop modifier)

3.	(problem 3)	The candies in the dish are Halloween candies. None of the candies are chocolate. Are any of the candies in the dish chocolate?
4.	(problem 8)	Some of Carol's cakes are for sale. All of the cakes are homemade. Are all of the homemade cakes for sale?

Figure 5.

Introduce topic. The first rule is to introduce the topic of the problem (e.g., candies, dogs, boats) in a narrative-like manner, usually by the assertion that the topic exists, followed by a predicate. The construction "There are X" was universally used to accomplish this. Note that the logical relations between sets can be maintained despite this transformation. Most often topic introduction occurred in problems containing the quantifier "some" (see problems #5, 6, 11, and 12 in Figure 1 and examples in Figure 5).

Change Verb. Every premise in the original problem set included the copula "is a." In recall it was converted to an active or possessive verb. This conversion appeared only in problems offering a protagonist: Robert was sailing boats; Carol baked some cakes; Mark had shirts; Mary has cats.

Elaborate content. This conversion involves addition of content not originally presented in the syllogism but inferrable from lexical or world knowledge. For example, "No children from the school were on the team" became "No children from the school were playing football." Often elaboration consisted of presenting a contrast to what was in the premise, as shown in the examples. Elaborations never incorporated unrelated information.

Pronominalize. All of the problems contained a middle term, that is, the term repeated in both premises. In recall the second occurrence of the middle term was often replaced by a pronoun. This rendered the logical structure of the problem ambiguous because it was not possible to determine whether the pronoun referred to the subject or predicate term of the first premise (see examples #IV-1,2). The interesting aspect of this transformation was that it only occurred with certain figures, namely, the transitive form, AB-BC, or the subject repeat form, BA-BC. In these cases the subject term of the second premise was the repeated middle term, B. By replacing it with a pronoun (e.g., Some of them were X), the problem was made to conform more closely to everyday language use. Pronominalization did not occur in intransitive figures (BA-CB) or in predicate repeat figures (AB-CB); to do so in these cases would not be appropriate because the subject term of the second premise introduces the third term, which is new information. A related change was to drop the modifier of the second premise subject term, rather than using a pronoun, with the same result of making the problem structure ambiguous (see examples #IV-3,4). Both of these conversions represent use of cohesion devices common to everyday language.

The average number of conversions of each type in recall is summarized in Table 2. Second graders' recall contained many more narrative features than did fifth graders'. In recalling 12 problems, second graders used an average of 6.25 narrative features, in contrast to fifth graders' 2.5. In general, fifth graders' recall adhered to canonical syllogism form, that is, two premises constructed with a quantifier, modified subject term, copula, and modified predicate term (negative optional). While fifth graders' recall was by no means perfect, it certainly fit the form. Apart from omissions, most of their errors consisted of mixing up the terms, of recalling the inference as a premise, or combining all three terms in one premise (e.g., "None of the Halloween candies in the dish was chocolate"). The one conversion that was common in their recall was pronominalization (rule 4). The frequency of this conversion is interesting because it is the one that is general across most discourse genres, in contrast to the others which are more specific to narratives.

It is important to note that conversion to a narrative form often resulted in loss of the logical relations among the terms of the syllogism. Canonical form, despite surface errors, was usually associated with preservation of the logical relations. An example of a second and a fifth grader's recall of the same problem will illustrate this contrast.

Original problem: All of Carol's cakes are homemade cakes.
Some of Carol's cakes are not for sale.
Are all of the homemade cakes for sale?

Second grade recall: Mary baked cakes.
Some of them Mary was gonna eat.

Some of them Mary was gonna sell.
Was Mary gonna sell all of her cakes?

Fifth grade recall: Some of Carol's cakes are for sale.
All of her cakes are homemade.
Are all of the homemade cakes for sale?

Just a note about adult performance for comparison purposes: Several groups of American adults were presented similar tasks using similar problems. While their solution rates were not perfect, there was no difference between valid and invalid problems. Their recall conformed to syllogism form precisely, although they sometimes forgot terms, mixed them up or recalled inferences in place of premises. No narrative conversions were made.

Summary of Results

Development of the three components of syllogism knowledge can be summarized as follows:

(1) Pragmatic knowledge was acquired early. By second grade the children had acquired an appropriate "interpretive frame" for the problems (Frederiksen, 1981). They had learned to approach the syllogisms as a genre distinct from everyday conversation, to treat the premise information as hypothetical, and to try to solve the problems based on premise information. In other words, they dealt with the problems in a theoretical manner.

(2) Both grades demonstrated ability to carry out the logical operations, but differed in the range of problems to which they could be applied. Both grades were equally successful in solving valid problems, but fifth graders detected more invalid problems. Fifth graders did not, however, appear to use a systematic checking procedure to confirm the soundness of their deductions, a procedure needed to identify invalid problems.

(3) Schematic knowledge about syllogism form was fairly well developed by fifth grade, but second graders showed little evidence of familiarity with the genre. Rather,

their recall suggested reliance on a narrative schema for interpreting and encoding the problems. Fifth graders' recall generally conformed to syllogism form, but the high incidence of pronoun use in the second premises indicated that their appreciation of the logical structure relating the premises was limited.

DISCUSSION AND CONCLUSIONS

Second graders' theoretic approach to the problems is of particular interest in contrast to that of unschooled adults in traditional cultures (Scribner, 1975, 1977; Luria, 1976), whose performance on similar problems was characterized by failure to adopt a hypothetical orientation. It should be noted, however, that second graders did not respond theoretically 100% of the time. Empiric responding was associated with solution errors. A possible explanation for this inconsistency in approach to the problems is that when the problems were too difficult for the children, they shifted to an empiric mode of responding. This explanation is consistent with Luria's report of shifts among traditional adults. They were able to reason theoretically when the content of the problems was familiar and based on their experience, but when it was abstract or counterfactual, they shifted to an empiric mode.

The important point is that second graders in U.S. schools did not reject the possibility of deriving inferences from hypothetical propositions, as traditional non-schooled adults frequently did in both Scribner's and Luria's studies.

The high solution rates on valid problems is consistent with findings of other investigators, in particular Hill (1960), who reported solution levels of 66%, 75% and 85% for 6, 7 and 8 year olds, respectively, on similar problems. (She presented only valid problems, however, limiting the response choices to "Yes" and "No," and raising the chance level to 50%.)

These findings confirm children's basic logical abilities. However, it is clear that other factors than logical ability _per se_ influenced children's performance on the problems. One factor that has been investigated in other contexts is understanding of quantifiers. This factor would apply to both valid and invalid problems. Neimark and Chapman (1975) provide evidence that children do not understand quantifiers as adults do. Even when the memory demands of a task were minimized, seventh graders in their study did not consider the full range of representations and combinations of quantifier meaning (using Venn diagrams). Neimark and Chapman attributed this failure to the children's concrete level of thinking.

Relations between Operational, Schematic and Pragmatic Factors

An interesting pattern of performance has emerged. Second and fifth graders were equally good at solving valid problems, but fifth graders were more accurate than second graders in detecting invalid problems and were much more accurate in reproducing the problems from memory. While fifth graders' performance on the solution and recall tasks is consistent, the second graders' performance is somewhat surprising. How they could have performed so well in solution of valid problems but so poorly in recall is the issue. This discrepancy calls into question the relation between recall and solution performance and the kinds of inferences one can make from recall about the information on which the students based their solution. At least two alternatives are possible.

First, it may be that the second graders were able to hold the premise information accurately in working memory long enough to draw the inference, but rapidly lost the information because they did not have a syllogism schema to hold it in a stable form. Then, in recall, they reconstruct the problem from whatever information was available, using a narrative schema to structure their production. In this alternative, the information in recall would not correspond to the information on which the solution was based.

The second alternative holds that the premise information was immediately assimilated to a narrative schema. In this case, the narrative conversions evident in recall would be present in the initial mental representation of the problem. The information recalled would correspond to the information used in solution. While critical aspects of the logical relations could be lost immediately, it is possible that correct solutions could still be achieved. Natural-language inferencing is offered as the mechanism that could yield correct solutions based on narrative representations (Johnson-Laird, 1975).

Inferential processes appear to characterize language comprehension, as demonstrated through numerous psycholinguistic studies. An example of the type of natural language inference that has been studied with children is taken from Paris and Carter (1973): "The bird is in the cage. The cage is under the table." In a recognition test even young children falsely "recognized" the inference, "The bird is under the table," even though it had never been presented. Hildyard (1979) reported that even first graders consistently made the kind of inferences necessary to establish coherence in texts. (See Frederiksen, 1981, and Trabasso and Nicholas, 1980, for discussions of various kinds of inferences in language comprehension.) We are suggesting that children could have applied appropriate _operations_ to a problem that differed from the one presented.

In the absence of a syllogism schema, faced with a rather difficult task, it is possible that the second graders assimilated the problems to a narrative schema because (a) it was available, and (b) because of certain similarities between narratives and syllogisms. Both can be treated as hypothetical (although personal narratives are usually experience based); both are integrated discourse forms; and, in the present case, the content of the syllogisms was similar to the content of many children's stories. Narratives are probably the first school and literacy-related genre that children experience. In particular, they probably represent for many U.S. children their first experience with "decontextualized" language.

The important point of the preceding discussion is that both alternatives suggested above implicate schema failure in the discrepancy between solution and recall. Both also suggest explanations for the discrepancy between solution of the valid and invalid problems, but the present study does not support one over the other.

Invalid problems appear to require more work than valid problems because two contradictory inferences must be generated in order to appreciate that the problem is invalid. This requires holding the premises in memory and creating mental alternatives, comparing them with each other. If second graders held premises accurately in mind long enough to draw a single inference, but the information was rapidly lost (alternative 1), it would be impossible for them to generate a second representation. Assuming that the quantifiers were completely understood, students could seek alternative representations and combinations, but the essential information would be missing.

In the second alternative, premise information would be immediately converted to a narrative form, with resulting loss of the abstract quantified relations. Examination of alternative representations and combinations requires the information to be available in a sufficiently abstract form to permit those manipulations. If the information was interpreted in a concrete fashion, generation of alternatives would not be possible. Narratives are usually interpreted by creating a single instantiation of the content (Cf. Anderson and Ortony, 1975; Pichert and Anderson, 1977). Thus, while assimilation of the problems to a narrative schema may have value for the purpose of remembering the content of the problems, it may also have been disfunctional for the purpose of considering alternative representations.

Moreover, if the premises were assimilated to a narrative schema, it is unlikely that the child would entertain alternatives because of pragmatic differences between syllogisms and narratives. In narratives and everyday conversation, one does not normally seek to identify every possible way of interpreting the information. In addition, young children seem to have a propensity to encode propositional information in a concrete rather than an abstract manner (Falmagne, 1975).

An additional factor must be mentioned that could have contributed to the low solution level on the invalid problems. Young children appear to be unwilling to use "No one can tell" as a response. This response alternative was used least often in the present study, which would increase the frequency of errors on invalid problems. Noting the possibility of a response bias does not explain it, however. It may be that children retreated from using this alternative because of the cognitive difficulty involved in appreciating that it pertains to cases where two contradictory states are simultaneously possible.

Whether examination of alternative representations and combinations should be considered a separate factor in syllogism solution is not clear. If a deliberate, conscious effort to falsify an initial conclusion is required, this component should be considered part of the pragmatic knowledge about syllogisms. Natural language inferencing requires no such systematic consideration of alternatives. Systematic consideration of alternatives may be an additional strategic aspect that must be added to our characterization of knowledge about the genre.

Schooling, Literacy and Logical Thought

To return to the original issue posed in the introduction, this study was designed to shed light on the relation between schooling, literacy and logical reasoning. With respect to the logical operations involved in solving the problems, it appears that the children had these abilities by second grade. Other studies have indicated that children as young as 4 years are able to integrate information and draw conclusions, although they do not necessarily do so spontaneously (Bryant and Trabasso, 1971). For young children, keeping the information in memory appears to be a limiting factor in their solution (Trabasso, Riley, and Wilson, 1975; Trabasso and Nicholas, 1980). It would appear that inferential processing is a basic cognitive process that does not depend on schooling for its development. The range of problems and conditions under which it is applied appear to be what is affected by schooling.

Developmental trends were found in both pragmatic and schematic knowledge. The cross-cultural research with adults, in comparison to work with educated Western adults (Johnson-Laird and Steedman, 1978; Sternberg, 1980), indicates that pragmatic and schematic aspects are influenced by experience. Given the relatively high levels of theoretic responding by second graders, it is not possible to say whether that mode of thought was a function of schooling or of pre-school experiences in a "literate" culture (Akinnaso, 1981; Scollon & Scollon, 1981). Schematic knowledge took longer to develop. We may speculate that it resulted from experience with formal instruction in mathematics in school, as most students are not directly taught syllogistic reasoning. Scribner and Cole (1981) highlights the role of language in this development. Both the teacher's questioning and the requirement for the student to provide a verbal explanation are important. Newman et. al's findings are of interest in the context of Scribner and Cole's (1981) observation that schooling fostered skill in providing verbal explanations for principl guiding their behavior on experimental tasks, rules and instructions among the Vai adults they studied, as well as fostering theoretical reasoning.

These findings suggest that neither schooling nor literacy are responsible for logical thought, but that they contribute to the range of problems that can be solved logically. School discourse patterns and the central nature of literacy in school activities provide opportunitie for expanding that range and for teaching new genres that involve the child's logical capabilities.

ACKNOWLEDGEMENTS

We wish to express our thanks to Jeff Woodring who ran this study, and transcribed and helped analyze the data. Thanks are also extended to Michael Cole, George A. Miller, Ellin Scholnick and Warren Simmons for their helpful comments on earlier drafts. Not least of all, we thank the New York City public school and its students who participate in this study. The research was supported by a grant from the Carnegie Corporation to Michael Cole and The Rockefeller University.

NOTES

[1]This article was written by the first author in her private capacity. No official support or endorsement by the National Institute of Education, U. S. Department of Education is intended or should be inferred.

[2]The study reported here is one of a series of studies conducted by the authors on the development of components of logical reasoning. Results reported here were replicated in all major respects in a study involving a low socio-economic school population run by Sharon Lazaroff as her master's thesis research at Yeshiva University.

[3] In using Venn diagrams to illustrate this point, we are not suggesting that people in fact use mental Venn diagrams to solve these problems, although they could. For an alternative system, see Johnson-Laird and Steedman, 1978.

REFERENCES

Akinnaso, F. N., 1981, The consequences of literacy in pragmatic and theoretic perspectives, Anth. and Ed. Q., 12:163-200.

Anderson, R. C. and Ortony, A., 1975, On putting apples into bottles--a problem of polysemy, Cog. Psych., 7:167-80.

Bruner, J., 1966, On cognitive growth, in: "Studies in Cognitive Growth," J. S. Bruner, R. R. Olver and P. N. Greenfield, eds., Wiley, N.Y.

Bryant, P. and Trabasso, T., 1971, Transitive inferences and memory in young children, Nature, 232:456-58.

Cole, M., Gay, J., Glick, J., and Sharp, D. W., 1971, "The Cultural Context of Learning and Thinking," Basic Books, N.Y.

Cole, M. and Scribner, S., 1974, "Culture and Thought," Wiley, N.Y.

Cook-Gumperz, J. and Gumperz, J. J., in press, From oral to written culture: the transition to literacy, in: "Variation in Writing," M. Farr Whiteman, ed., LEA, Hillsdale.

Falmagne, R. J., 1975, Deductive processes in children, in: "Reasoning: Representation and Process," R. Falmagne, ed., LEA, Hillsdale.

Frederiksen, C. H., 1981, Inference in preschool children's conversations -- a cognitive perspective, in: "Ethnography and Language in Educational Settings," J. Green and C. Wallat, eds., Ablex, Norwood.

Gladwin, T., 1970, "East is a Big Bird," Harvard, Cambridge.

Goody, J. and Watt, I., 1968, The consequences of literacy, in: "Literacy in Traditional Societies," J. Goody, ed., Cambridge U., Cambridge.

Greenfield, P. N., 1972, Oral and written language: the consequences for cognitive development in Africa, the United States and England, Lang. and Sp., 15: 169-78.

Havelock, E. A., 1973, "Prologue to Greek Literacy," U. of Cincinnati, Cincinnati.

Hill, S. A., 1961, "A Study of the Logical Abilities of Children," Unpublished Ph.D. diss., University Microfilms, Ann Arbor.

Johnson-Laird, P. N., 1975, Models of deduction, in: "Reasoning: Representation and Process," R. Falmagne, ed., LEA, Hillsdale.

Johnson-Laird, P. N., and Steedman, M., 1978, The psychology of syllogisms, Cog. Psych., 10:64-99.

Luria, A. R., 1976, "Cognitive Development: Its Cultural and Social Foundations," Harvard U., Cambridge.

Mehan, H., 1979, "Learning Lessons," Harvard U., Cambridge.

Neimark, E. D. and Chapman, R. H., 1975, Development of the comprehension of logical quantifiers, in: "Reasoning: Representation and Process," R. Falmagne, ed., LEA, Hillsdale.

Newman, D., Griffin, P., and Cole, M., in press, Laboratory and classroom tasks: social constraints and the evaluation of children's performance, "Everyday Cognition: Its Development in Social Context," B. Rogoff and J. Lave, eds., Harvard U., Cambridge.

Olson, D., 1977, From utterance to text: the bias of language in speech and writing, Harv. Ed. Rev., 47: 257-81.

Pichert, J. W. and Anderson, R. C., 1979, Taking different perspectives on a story, J. of Ed. Psych., 69:309-15.

Rogoff, B., 1981, Schooling and the development of cognitive skills, in: "Handbook of Cross-Cultural Psychology, Vol. 4," H. C. Triandis and A. Heron, eds., Allyn and Bacon, Boston.

Scollon, R. and Scollon, S. B. K., 1981, "Narrative, Literacy and Face in Interethnic Communication," Ablex, Norwood.

Scribner, S., 1975, Recall of classical syllogisms: a cross-cultural investigation of error on logical problems, in: "Reasoning: Representation and Process," R. Falmagne, ed., LEA, Hillsdale.

Scribner, S., 1977, Modes of thinking and ways of speaking, in: "Thinking: Readings in Cognitive Science," P. N. Johnson-Laird and P. C. Wagon, eds., Cambridge U., Cambridge.

Scribner, S. and Cole, M., 1981, "The Psychology of Literacy," Harvard U., Cambridge.

Sharp, D. W., Cole, M. and Lave, C., 1979, Education and cognitive development: the evidence from experimental research, Mono. of Soc. for Res. in Ch. Dev., 44.

Sternberg, R. J., 1980, Representation and process in linear syllogistic reasoning, J. of Exp. Psych., 104:119-59.
Stevenson, H. W., Parker, T., Wilkinson, A., Bonnevaus, B., and Gonzalez, M., 1978, Schooling, environment and cognitive development: a cross-cultural study, Mono. of Soc. for Res. in Ch. Dev., 43.
Tannen, D., 1982, Oral and literate strategies in spoken and written narrative. Lang., 58:1-21.
Trabasso, T. and Nicholas, D. W., 1980, Memory and inferences in the comprehension of narratives, in: "Information Integration by Children," F. Wilkening, J. Becker, and T. Trabasso, eds., LEA, Hillsdale.
Trabasso, R., Riley, C. A., and Wilson, E. G., 1975, The representation of linear order and spatial strategies in reasoning: a developmental study, in: "Reasoning: Representation and Process," R. Falmagne, ed., LEA, Hillsdale.
Vygotsky, L., 1962, "Thought and Language," MIT, Cambridge.
Vygotsky, L., 1978, "Mind in Society: the Development of Higher Psychological Processes," Harvard U., Cambridge.

TEACHING READING IN THE INNER CITY

L. Arena

University of Delaware

The purpose of this paper is to discuss the teaching of reading to a certain segment within the population of bilingual children. Specifically, the paper deals with the teaching of reading to an increasing number of Hispanic children (both elementary and secondary level) who, because of socio-economic determinants, live in urban areas where they acquire a second language that is not only unacceptable in the schools, but also may interfere with the bilingual child's attainment of "reading readiness." I am speaking particularly of the population of Spanish speakers who live in urban environments and who acquire Black Vernacular English (B.V.E.) as their second language. Wolfram (1971, 1972) scientifically points to an increasing number of extremely complex linguistic, cultural, pedagogical, and sociological problems, some or all of which usually interfere with the Hispanic child's learning to read and which subsequently cause him to either fail in or drop out of school. The purpose of this paper is to briefly point out several features of Hispanic students' newly acquired second language which are probably causally related to their reading as well as writing problems.

Throughout this symposium there has been the underlying message that there must be something more going on besides the match between a child's language and his reader's language. Although I acknowledge the attitudinal, social, cultural, and P.T.A. issues as significant in the teaching of reading, they are acknowledged as issues which parallel several linguistic obstacles to the teaching of reading and as issues which are too broad and varied to be covered in a paper of this length. The major thrust of this paper, therefore, will deal with several specific, concrete linguistic features which may influence the teaching or learning of reading.

It is a well documented fact (Baratz and Shuy, 1969; Shuy, 1976; Rystrom, 1970; Wolfram, 1971, 1972) that Spanish-speaking children who live in urban areas will learn English as a second language primarily from their peers. When socio-economic variables determine that Spanish-speaking children transact with children who speaks B.V.E. both in their school and neighborhood environments, the Hispanic child usually acquires B.V.E. as his second language, especially if only Spanish is spoken at home. In fact, the Hispanic child probably learns B.V.E. much better and even faster than he learns S.E. or "academic English," "front-door English," "Green English," or whatever one wishes to label the English that is taught in schools. This facility to learn B.V.E. is due to the fact that a large number of B.V.E. features which are either very similar or identical to features found in the Spanish spoken by the child. The following is a discussion of some of the similarities.

Words in Spanish can be ended by only six consonants: d, s, l, n, r, x; all other endings are vowel endings. While there are consonant endings of words in Spanish, however, there are never any occurrences of double-consonants (or consonant clusters) at the end of any Spanish words. When one observes the Standard features of English, the fact that the majority of regular plurals, possessives, the past tense markers of regular verbs, and third person present singular endings in English are all consonant clusters is easily observed. From the ESL classrooms, we know that such bundles of consonants in English will prove to be very difficult for the Spanish-speaking child to perceive and produce accurately in the early stages of second language acquisition. If much care is not exercised in the classroom, the Spanish-speaking child may not consistently receive or produce these features. These and several other contrasting features are contained in Section I of the appendix. What the lack of consonant clusters in final position of words in Spanish means for the Hispanic student is that, initially in his study of ESL, he may neither receive nor produce plurals, possessives, third person present singular, or regular past tenses with regularity. The fact that the sound /z/ does not occur in Puerto Rican Spanish further reinforces the elimination of three and four of the above features.

It is the position of this paper that some of the problems in learning to read English may result from the lack of consonant clusters in Spanish; such problems are intricate, yet very systematic. In Fasold's (see his paper in this volume) words some reading problems result from "the clash between the reader's linguistic system and the primer's reading system." A further factor which may compound the problems is whether or not the Hispanic child is literate in his native language. If he or she is not, then the illiterate Hispanic student has two problems: (1) to learn English as a second language; and (2) to acquire the skill of reading. The first problem is primary, of course, because in order to achieve the several elements which comprise what may be called "reading readiness" (c.f. Section IV of the Appendix) i.e., auditory discrimination (No. 1), ability to listen with comprehension (No. 3), knowledge of letter-sound relationships (No. 6), and a reasonably large listening (passive) vocabulary (No. 7) - a control of Standard spoken English and grammar is a necessary requisite. It is at this point that the variety of spoken English acquired by the Spanish-speaking child is of paramount importance. When the Hispanic child learns a variety of English such as B.V.E. as his second language, several features which are not found in Standard English may be acquired with facility because of the similarity of some features between Spanish and B.V.E. Five such features of Spanish are listed in Section II of the Appendix.

When the Hispanic child has acquired B.V.E. as his second language, and because Spanish structure accommodates the features of B.V.E. very easily, the Hispanic student who is beginning to learn to read is often perceptually confused by the bundles of consonants which are found at the ends of words in the Standard English primers or basal readers. The child may easily notice, sight-read, and even sound out consonant clusters at the ends of words, but because he has not acquired a knowledge of the letter-sound relationships of Standard English, he may not understand that the bundles of consonants actually carry important meanings and relations such as plurality, possession, subject-verb agreement, and past tense. Further, since Spanish is a syllable-timed language, the child may pronounce the -ed past tense marker as a syllable, e.g., /bərnɨd/, /askɨd/, /tɔlkɨd/, etc., consequently reinforcing a reactive attitude towards his learning ability on the part of some teachers, for the wrong reasons. Further, when markers which carry tense, plurality, etc. are not comprehended by the Hispanic child, frustration-level reading performances often result, which may go unnoticed because the Spanish-speaking child may not express his frustration in a manner that is understood by the American teacher. (The latter may be one of the things which Fasold alluded to (in this volume) when he said that "there must be something more going on in the learning of reading besides the match between a child's language and his reader's language.")

Another possible problem area for the Hispanic student who has acquired B.V.E. as his second language is the large number of new homonyms which English monolingual children do not experience. Because Spanish has no bundles of consonants in the final position of words, this lexical phenomenon is realized by means of a consonant cluster deletion rule. The consonant cluster deletion rule operates in the following manner. The Hispanic child will tend to simplify the clusters of consonants by dropping the last one completely when both are equal in voicing, i.e., both consonants are either voiced or voiceless. Thus, he may say and read "pass" for either "past" or "passed"; "cole" or "coal" for "cold"; "hole" for "hold," which may also be read in a primer as "whole." Consequently, auditory discrimination instruction must be seriously considered at this stage so that the child will not simplify the bundles of consonants found in Standard English, either receptively or productively, thereby obviating some reading and writing problems, respectively.

The fact that the Spanish-speaking child in inner city acquires B.V.E. as his second language is not a matter of controversy. It would seem appropriate that certain features of B.V.E. be discussed at this point. It is well known that B.V.E. has been documented by some linguists as a Creole-based variety of English that manifests many of the same features common to Creole languages throughout the world. (Some of the common features of Creole languages are listed in Section III of the Appendix. They are included only to point out some similarities between B.V.E. and Spanish which may help to account for the facility with which the Hispanic child acquires B.V.E.) B.V.E. has no consonant clusters in word final position, thereby not generating the regular plurals, inflected possessives, third person present singular inflection, and past tense markers of regular verbs as they exist in Standard English. Copula "be" deletion, multiple negation, and pronominal apposition are also features of B.V.E. Except for the copula "be" deletion, the other features could also be descriptive of most forms of Spanish. It is linguistically understandable that the Hispanic speaker may acquire B.V.E. features with facility.

But what do we do with what we have here? First, what do we have? We have a Spanish-speaking child who may or may not be able to read in his native language and who, because of socio-economic variables, lives in an environment where he has acquired a variety of English called B.V.E. as his second language, which is neither accepted by most school teachers nor used in any of the primers to teach children how to read! Next, what do we do with what we have? Despite the conclusions of McNamara (1966), most of the ESL materials and research still hold that success in learning to read in English is greater after the skill of reading has been acquired in the native tongue. One major study by Evelyn Bauer (1968) mentions several experiments involving North American Indians in which superior results were obtained when Indian children were taught to read in their own language before attempting to read the national language. For some Spanish speaking students, such research indicates that they must first learn to read in Spanish. For elementary school Hispanic children who are illiterate, however, and who are acquiring spoken English faster than they are maintaining Spanish, this may not be the better approach. But when the spoken English that is acquired by either of the two populations of children is B.V.E., the question arises as to whether or not <u>spoken</u> Standard English as a second language must first be taught to the bilingual child before he is taught how to <u>read</u> Standard English as a second language in order to achieve reading readiness.

Thus, if either common sense or the hypothesis that success in learning to read is greater when the skill is taught in the mother tongue is valid, then some Hispanic children really have lead-Adidas on their feet when learning how to read today. The typical situation may be described as follows. The Hispanic child speaks Spanish, but due to socio-economic variables which determine his family to live in an urban environment, he acquires a variety of English that linguists call B.V.E. - which is right for communicating with his peers and surviving in the environment. But when the child goes to school, he or she is told in various and sometimes UNTACTFUL ways that _that_ English is not acceptable; this attitude is then reinforced when the Spanish-B.V.E. speaking child cannot find any form of his acquired second language, B.V.E., in any of the primers or basal readers. Further, when he attempts to read along with the rest of the children in his class, he does not do well on comprehension tests because he misses a lot of the information that is carried by those bundles of consonants; what is more, he even sees words "different" from what the other children see because of his new set of homonyms. Such a child will probably be sent to a special education reading teacher who, hopefully, understands as well as accepts the bilingual child's situation, and will do much about it by devising instruction based on a combination of ESL techniques and reading research. However, if the Hispanic child does not encounter the right teacher, he may be viewed as a poor achiever who has learned B.V.E., an English which is both unacceptable and unintelligible to the teacher, and may be assigned to an instructor whose job it will be to _eradicate_ this "bad" English that the student has acquired. The problem with eradication is that, because of the social dynamics involved in an inner city school for example, it is very questionable as to whether or not any Standard English can be taught in the classroom at all. We all know that the most successful language learning has, as a component, meaningful interaction between the learner and speakers of the language he is trying to learn. Most Spanish-speaking children, segregated by race and poverty, will have little opportunity to develop close relationships with Standard English speakers. This means that the Spanish-speaking child will continue to acquire and control B.V.E. to a high degree, and that some teachers, to a proportionate degree, will try to eradicate the Hispanic student's second language. Compounding the psychological damage that is inflicted upon the Hispanic child by this approach to his second language, there are usually no reading materials in Spanish which will permit him to first learn the skill of reading and later on learn to speak, read, and write Standard English.

In conclusion, the purpose of this paper has been to present some of the problems that some Hispanic children experience when learning to read. The presentation and explanations of the problems were predominantly linguistic in approach and point of view. However, educational values and attitudes must be dealt with along with -- perhaps even before -- the linguistic approach to the teaching of reading is implemented. As has been brought out so clearly in the papers in this volume, such values and attitudes are so powerful that they can totally prevent any attempts to teach reading from an approach that makes sense to the linguist. After all is said and done, if literacy is achieved, by whatever approach, at the expense of severe frustration on the part of the Hispanic child, future language development may not come about; if future language development is not realized by such children after literacy has been achieved, the child will fail in, or drop out of, school. At that precise moment, linguistics and literacy will become an anomaly, not a real topic.

APPENDIX

I. Significant Contrasts Between Spanish and English Which May Result in Reading Problems for the Bilingual Student:

English	Spanish
1. 14 vowels	1. 5 vowels
2. 24 consonants	2. 18 consonants*
3. Stress-timed language	3. Syllable-timed language
4. Consonant clusters in final position of words.	4. No consonant clusters in final position of words.

English	Spanish
5. Contraction, but not deletion of copula verb "be"	5. No contraction or dele- of copula verb(s) "be"

*Variety of Spanish spoken in Puerto Rico

II. Reading (and Writing) Problems which May Be Due to No. 4 (No Consonant Clusters in Spanish):

1. No third person, present singular will be produced/perceived by the Spanish-speaking student, e.g., He brings, talks, walks ...

2. No inflected plurals will be produced/perceived, e.g., chairs, dentists, masks, ghosts ...

3. No inflected possessives will be produced/ perceived, e.g., the man's car, my friend's bike, the school's colors ...

4. No inflected past tense of regular verbs will be produced/perceived, e.g., he asked, he burned, he missed, he laughed ...

5. Because there are no clusters of consonants in word-final position in Spanish, there is a tendency to drop the final consonant: e.g., roughly in order of frequency, -st, -ft, -nt, -nd, -ld, -zd, -md, (past/passed, rift, meant, fined, hold/cold, raised, aimed, etc.). One result is that there is generated a different set of homonyms which English monolingual students do not have, and which may cause reading problems when encountered on the written page by the bilingual student. Some examples of homonyms due to consonant cluster deletion are:

   past → passed/pass   told → toll/toe
   hold → hole/whole   wind → wine
   mist → missed/miss   rift → riff
   cold → cole/coal   six → sick
   meant → men

III. Some Features of Creole Based Languages (e.g., Black Vernacular English (B.V.E.)):

1. No consonant "clusters" in word-final position, i.e., third person, present singular suffix, inflected plurals, possessives, and the past tense marker (-ed) of regular verbs may be deleted in speech or writing of B.V.E. speakers.

2. Copula verb "be" may be deleted in certain environments, e.g., "He my brother."

3. Multiple Negation, e.g., "Couldn't nobody never see nothing."

4. Pronominal Apposition, e.g., "John, he don't live here anymore."

IV. Some Reading-Readiness Elements Needed by the Bilingual Student Who is Learning the Skill of Reading:

1. Auditory discrimination (in order to determine differences between letter sounds).

2. Visual discrimination (in order to see differences between letters).

3. Ability to listen with comprehension for a reasonable period of time.

4. Ability to coordinate vision in left to right movement.

5. Desire to read.

6. Knowledge of letter-sound relationships.

7. A store of concepts and a reasonably large listening vocabulary.

REFERENCES

Baratz, Joan C. and Shuy, Roger, 1969, "Teaching Black Children to Read," Center for Applied Linguistics, Washington, D.C.

Bauer, Evelyn, 1968, Teaching English to North American Indians in B.I.A. Schools, Ling. Rep., 10(4):2.

Macnamara, John Theodore, 1966, "Bilingualism and Primary Education: A Study of Irish Experience," Edinburgh U. Press, Edinburgh.

Rystrom, Richard, 1970, Dialect training and reading: a further look. Reading Res. Q., 5:581-599.

Shuy, Roger W., 1976, The mismatch of child language and school language: implications for beginning reading instruction, ms., Georgetown University and Center for Applied Linguistics.

Wolfram, W., "Overlapping Influences in the English of Second Generation Puerto Rican Teen-agers in Harlem," Final Report, Off. of Ed. Grant No. 3-70-003(508).

Wolfram, W., 1972, Overlapping influence and linguistic assimilation in second generation Puerto Rican English, in: "Sociolinguistics in Cross-Cultural Analysis," David M. Smith and Roger Shuy, eds., Georgetown U. Press, Washington, D.C.

EARLY READING EXPERIENCES: SOME LINGUISTIC PERSPECTIVES ON PARENT/CHILD INTERACTION IN BOOK SHARING SITUATIONS

Rosalind Williams, Diane Chapman, and
Ellen Martin-Huff
The Ohio State University

The acquisition of literacy is an important learning for each child's educational process. Students of child language development have focused attention on the early prerequisite behaviors which assist children in beginning to communicate with others. As children learn to read, there are also understandings many children master long before the beginning of school which are essential to the reading process. This report is a portion of a larger study which focuses on several probable precursors to literacy acquisition. These include the child's growing understanding of the use and function of books, the environmental opportunities for reading in the child's home and community, and the nature of the parent/child interaction as parents share books with their children.

The population of interest is two- and four-year-old children from three cultural groups prominent in the central Ohio area. Urban Black, Appalachian white, and mainstream white families were randomly selected from pre-school rosters for participation in the study. A combination of parent interviews, child interviews, and videotapings of parent/child interactions form the data base available. Observations of parents and children as they interact in book sharing sessions show unique linguistic and behavioral components requiring the use of specific analyses. In this report, discourse mappings, analysis of text cohesion, and analysis of questions are targeted as means of enlarging our understanding of the parent/child book sharing context.

Researchers in language acquisition have recognized

the importance of the parent's role in providing a linguistic atmosphere which may be more or less facilitative to language learning. A number of researchers have presented evidence that parents naturally produce a language learning environment which is well-suited to the learning style of the developing child. Snow (1972, 1975, 1976) has shown that mothers modify their speech patterns to children in such a way as to produce consistent and simplified language lessons. They also interact in ways which teach social rules of language and gradually shape more sophisticated language behavior. These and other studies indicate that a critical aspect of parents' language use is calibration designed to fit optimally with the child's current ability to understand. Studies by Frank and Seegmiller (1973), Moerk (1974, 1975), and Cross (1977) have all pointed to the observation that mothers progressively modify their language input as the child's receptive capabilities grow.

A specific instance of parent/child interaction is that found in book sharing situations. Several studies have examined aspects of parents sharing books with children in order to evaluate parental book sharing behaviors or to correlate those behaviors with children's preparation for or achievement of literacy. Guinagh and Jester (1972) and Lamme and Olmsted (1977) developed observational scales for recording parent behaviors during book sharing. Both studies concluded that parents did not always use book sharing to the best advantage in maximizing children's learnings. Flood (1977), focusing on interactions between parents and children in book sharing, identified factors that correlated with children's scores on selected pre-reading measures. Ninio (1980) investigated vocabulary acquisition in book sharing among Israeli mother/infant dyads. She reported correlations between socioeconomic levels and success at adjusting interactive style to infants' vocabulary levels.

Ninio and Bruner (1978) observed labeling during book sharing in a longitudinal study of a child between the ages of eight and 18 months. They reported that the book sharing took on the structure of a reciprocal dialogue in which the child participated first by gestures and babbling vocalizations and later by lexical labeling. They concluded that the achievement of labeling was dependent on the understanding of social rules for participating in such a dialogue as well as on the understanding of the sign/significate relationship.

The present study was undertaken to provide more descriptive information about the nature of parent/child interaction in book sharing. It was based on the belief that analysis of discourse generated in book sharing situations requires a methodology that focuses on the structure of the interaction. This paper illustrates three approaches to the task of describing parent/child interaction in book sharing. The first, cohesion analysis, examines the elements which create a text in the interaction. Book sharing interaction is a unique genre because it includes a text (the book that is read) within a text (the discourse surrounding the reading). The second approach undertaken here to describe book sharing interaction is a form of discourse analysis looking at the text as a whole. This analysis identifies the functions served by text utterances and describes the structure of the text. The third approach to describing the interaction focuses on one type of utterance prominent in book sharing situations: questions. This analysis identifies both the structure and the functions of question utterances and describes the structure of text in which questions occur. Together these three approaches to describing parent/child interaction in book sharing indicate some of the unique features of text specific to the book sharing genre.

Data include transcriptions and behavioral observations made from six video-taped book sharing sessions. The parent/child dyads selected for these analyses include three two-year-olds and three four-year-olds from Appalachian white, urban Black, and mainstream white populations. Each parent was asked to share books with the child for a twenty-minute period, beginning with The Blanket by John Burningham (1975). Parents were not instructed as to how to share the books with their children.

COHESION ANALYSIS

Book sharing is a unique type of interaction because the participants possess a complete text in the form of the book selected. This text in some way influences the interaction of the participants, in this case the parent and child. How then does one determine the text of a book sharing episode? One possibility is that the text of the book is the only complete text in the interaction. In this case all other remarks made by parent and child would be interruptions to the text. Another possibility might be that there exist two or more texts within a book sharing situation. These would be the text of the book and the verbal exchanges of parent and child. A third possibility is that the entire interaction of the book sharing episode is itself a text within which the density of cohesive ties varies.

Before addressing these possibilities it might be useful to review analysis as a means of analyzing texts. Halliday and Hasan (1976) have defined text as "a unity of meaning in context, a texture that expresses the fact that it relates as a whole to the environment in which it is placed" (p. 293). This texture is created through cohesive ties between elements of the discourse. These ties signal that interpretation of some element in the discourse is dependent on that of another (Halliday and Hasan, 1976:4). Therefore, these two elements are cohesively related. There are five categories of cohesive ties. They are reference, lexical cohesion, ellipsis, substitution, and conjunction.

The first category of cohesive tie is reference. Through reference to a presupposed item within the text a relationship between items is established. There are two major types of reference. References to presupposed items within the text are called endophora, and they build cohesion. References to presupposed items which do not exist within the text are called exophora, and they are not cohesive since they do not bind two elements of a text together (Halliday and Hasan, 1976:22).

Cohesion is also created by a lexical repetition. Through the repetition of words, synonyms, or general words of similar meaning, relationships between items are created. One item refers back to another because they share a common referent (Halliday and Hasan, 1976:88).

Ellipsis and substitution are very closely related cohesive devices. An ellipsis is a process within the text whereby a word or clause is omitted, but the meaning is understood. In substitution a word or clause is replaced by something else (Halliday and Hasan, 1976:88).

The final type of cohesive tie is conjunction. Conjunctions specify the way in which what has already been stated is related to that which is yet to come. They serve the cohesive function of relating two elements which occur in sequence but are not otherwise related (Halliday and Hasan, 1976:227).

By analyzing the cohesive devices within a text, it is possible to determine how a text has been created and to determine the boundaries of that text. Halliday and Hasan admit that there are cases in which the textual boundaries are unclear. They suggest that cohesion can be helpful in determining the boundaries of such a text. Book sharing presents such an ambiguous situation. Cohesion analysis of the book sharing situation may provide information regarding the strategies for creating texts that parents and children employ in this interaction.

The cohesion of the interaction of six parent/child dyads sharing Burningham's The Blanket has been analyzed. Transcripts from the videotapes were parsed into units consisting of an independent clause and any related dependent clauses. The cohesive relations between these clauses were analyzed according to Halliday and Hasan's scheme (1976:Chapter 8).

Reference and lexical cohesion were the main types of cohesive ties employed by all of the dyads. All parents used lexical cohesion more often than any other cohesive device. Lexical cohesion, reference, and conjunction were the primary cohesive devices used in the text of The Blanket. Burningham's text contained nine units. The parent/child interactions ranged from 19 to 52 units. All of these interactions contained Burningham's complete nine unit text. Obviously some parents and children interacted more than others during the book sharing episode. Surprisingly, the amount of interaction or number of units in the interaction was not very helpful in determining strategies for creating texts.

The type of reference used in the texts was the critical factor in determining patterns of text construction (see Table 1). By comparing the frequency of endophoric and exophoric reference used in those units which were not part of the text of The Blanket, it was possible to describe patterns of interaction and text boundaries.

The first pattern of text construction (Strategy I) is characterized by a lack of exophoric reference. All

Table 1. Number of Exophoric, Endophoric, and Lexical Ties in Texts produced during Booksharing.

	Reference		Lexical Cohesion
Group	Exophora	Endophora	
Strategy I			
1	0	4	7
Strategy II			
1	2	2	4
2	5	6	1
3	7	4	12
4	16	17	36
Strategy III			
1	11	0	17

Note: Numbers indicate the occurrence of reference and lexical cohesion after the text of _The Blanket_ was omitted from each interaction.

reference items are endophoric. There are few utterances beyond Burningham's text, and those can be tied to his text by lexical repetition and reference. In this type of interaction the parent reads the text of the book to the child with little additional interaction. Any utterances that do occur can be removed from the text without disturbing the meaning of the whole.

The second strategy (Strategy II) for text construction is characterized by a balance of endophoric and exophoric reference. The endophora are the definitive article and references to the main character. The exophora are primarily demonstratives referring most often to aspects of the book or to its illustrations. In this strategy the parent discusses events in the text and illustrations with the child as a complement to the written text. The entire interaction seems to be one text that varies in cohesive density.

The third strategy (Strategy III) contains a high number of exophoric references compared to a very low number of endophoric references. This strategy also relies on lexical cohesion to tie the units to one another and to Burningham's text. This approach might best be described as two separate texts that interrupt one another. One text would be the book and the other text would be the parent/child interaction. This strategy is exemplified by a parent who engages the child in a picture labeling interaction as the text of the book is read.

These patterns demonstrate that in order to determine what constitutes the text of a book sharing situation, it is necessary to uncover the strategies and cohesive devices that are being employed by the participants in the interaction. Parents create patterns of text that relate most closely to the types of references made to the text. The emphasis on endophoric or exophoric reference in the interaction helps to determine the number of texts involved in the interaction and the boundaries of those texts.

DISCOURSE ANALYSIS

After observation of the events making up many parent/child book sharing sequences, the need emerged for a rather broad analysis which takes into account both verbal and behavioral communication elements. The analysis reported in this section depends upon ideas proposed by Hasan (1980a, 1980b) regarding the relationship between text and context of situation. A particular communication context (in this case parent/child book sharing) contains some common elements necessary to recognition of communication of the same genre. In addition the motivation and characteristics of the communicators have a decided influence on the optional segments of the text.

In this case all of the communication related to the sharing of a single book was analyzed as one text. The text was divided into turns, with each turn being defined as the communications which one partner sent before the other partner of the dyad switched to the role of communicator. Verbal, behavioral, and vocal nonverbal communications were considered in defining the turns. Frequently multiple utterances made up one turn, and each of these utterances was assigned a functional category to complete the map of the interaction.

Functional categories were defined after viewing the videotapes of parent/child interaction. Then those categories were piloted and revised by viewing additional samples of book sharing. Major categories were Initiation, Instruction, Maintain Involvement, Text or Picture Read, and Closure (see Figure 1). The major categories are cross referenced with descriptors of the type of utterance (question, response, declaration, etc.), and it was found that infrequent additional categories such as Transition, Expand Text or Picture, Behavior Change, and Reward were needed to describe some interactions.

In this report, analyses of eight instances of parent/child reading of The Blanket will be described. Data from eight interactions involving four two-year-olds and four four-year-olds are discussed. The dyads represent all three cultural groups in the study. One of the major comparisons of interest was the difference between the two-year-olds and four-year-olds observed in the study. It appears that the differences seen from one child to the next are less attributable to age than to the characteristics of a particular parent/child dyad. In some cases parents and two-year-olds engaged in large numbers of interactions focusing on Initiation and Maintaining Involvement. It could be speculated that this was true because two-year-olds are able

Primary Categories	
Transition	T
Initiation	I
Text Reading	TR
Picture Reading	PR
Expand Text	ET
Expand Picture	EP
Maintain Involvement	MI
Behavior Change	BC
Reward	R
Instruct	Inst.
Closure	C

Sub-categories (in combination with Primary categories)	
comment/confirm	c
respond	r
question	q
direct/declare	d
action	a
gesture	g
tempt	t
bargain	b
name	n
check	✓

Figure 1. Discourse Analysis Categories in Parent-Child Booksharing.

to attend to a task for shorter periods of time, and because they may not yet be so familiar with the interactional style expected in book sharing.

Patterns of interaction indicated that there are three basic categories of behavior which are essential to make a book sharing session viable. Those are Initiation, Text Reading (or Picture Reading in the case of wordless books) and Closure. All of the other categories were optional, and although used frequently by parents and children, did not seem necessary for the maintenance of the text (see Figure 2).

Number of turns between a parent and child used to read the same book were widely varied. The range was 4 to 75 turns. Some of the instances of more frequent turns occurred when a child required persuasion to initiate the book sharing situation or when the child was distracted by some other concern during the time a book was being read. The four-year-olds seemed more consistent in their attention to this book since the number of turns used to share it were from 4 to 19 ($\bar{x}$ = 13). The two-year-olds had many more optional types of turns, and their turns ranged from 7 to 75 ($\bar{x}$ = 46).

The Blanket was typically divided into nine utterances by parents as they read. However, the pattern most frequently observed was a lumping of text reading into only a few turns. Turns containing text reading ranged from 1 to 14 ($\bar{x}$ = 4.6). Thus, more parents tended to continue reading the text with few interruptions. This was less likely to be true for two-year-olds whose parents interrupted more frequently to maintain involvement or instruct.

Observations of additional dyads with this and other books would indicate that the interaction pattern of a particular parent and child are likely to remain rather stable. However, the type of book chosen has an influence on the sequence of the interaction and the functional categories chosen by the dyad. For example, alphabet books produce fairly predictable interaction patterns in dyads familiar with that type of book, and wordless books can result in extremely complex interactions with the full range of functional categories being expressed.

This method of analysis seems to have potential for

Text 1: The Blanket

C	1.	Child looks toward father. A book?	I Iq
P	2.	Do you want to read this book with me?	Iq
C	3.	Yeah.	Ir
P	4.	OK. Come up here and sit down.	Ic BC
C	5.	OK	BCr
P	6.	This is about the blanket. See the little boy with his blanket? When I go to bed I always take my blanket. See him carrying his blanket to bed? He's got his robe on.	In PRq TR PRq PRd
C	7.	Yeah.	PRc
P	8.	See, he goes to bed by himself too.	MId
C	9.	Me too.	MIr
P	10.	Yeah. One night I could not find my blanket. Look at that stuff thrown all over the place. Mommy looked in the bathroom. Daddy looked in the cupboard. And I looked under my bed. But we could not find the blanket. So Mommy looked in the washinq. See, she is throwing the clothes all over the place looking for that blanket. And Daddy looked in the car. But I found the blanket under my pillow and went to sleep. Looks to the child for response.	MIc TR PR TR TR TR TR TR PR TR TR MI
C	11.	He went to bed with all his clothes on.	PR
P	12.	Uh huh. No. That's just his pajamas on.	Inst d
C	13.	Oh.	Inst r
P	14.	When Daddy was little, Daddy used to carry a blanket around too.	MI
C	15.	When you was like that? (indicating very small person)	MIq
P	16.	No, not like that.	MIr
C	17.	Big? Like this?	MIq
P	18.	Yeah That's the end.	MIr C
C	19.	Oh.	C

Figure 2. Context of Situation: Parent/Child Booksharing Description of Situation: Experimental with Minimal Social Distance between Communicators but some Environmental Intrusion (Videotape).

examining the overall quality of parent/child book sharing sessions. One notable problem was a difficulty in making distinctions between Maintain Involvement and Instruct categories. Assessing the intent of the parent in some cases is problematic. Clearly, questions are frequently not asked as a true request for information from children. The method has demonstrated that a unique text pattern exists in parent/child book sharing with broad differences possible between dyads engaged in sharing the same material. It would appear from a preliminary examination that differences between dyads are probably greater than differences attributable to age, cultural groups, or type of book chosen. However, age-related differences are evident in the structure of the interactions. These assertions remain to be demonstrated by more extensive analysis. This analysis, although helpful, will need supplementation to provide a more complete understanding of the interaction patterns in this complex context.

QUESTION ANALYSIS

Because questions were a dominant feature of parent/child interaction during book sharing, several analyses of questions were made. First, frequency data for questions were obtained. The number of questions was compared to the number of utterances of all types for each child, each parent, and each parent/child dyad. The percentage of utterances which were questions was computed for each child, each parent, and each dyad (see Table 2). The percentage of utterances and the percentage of questions produced by the parent and by the child was also computed for each dyad (see Figures 3 and 4).

These analyses provided a profile of the role of questions in parent/child book sharing interactions. Frequency data confirmed the observation that questions are a dominant feature of parent/child book sharing discourse. As Table 2 shows, questions comprised 17 to 28 percent of all utterances produced by the six parent/child dyads observed. (Taking into account the number of other utterances which are not questions themselves, but which are associated with questions -- responses, confirmations, etc. -- the role of questions and question-related utterances in book sharing discourse is even greater than suggested by the frequency data.) The number of questions produced in the

Table 2. Frequency of Questions in Parent/Child Discourse during Booksharing.

	Four-year-olds								
	Dyad 1			Dyad 2			Dyad 3		
	Jeff	Parent	Dyad Total	Nikia	Parent	Dyad Total	Richard	Parent	Dyad Total
Number of Utterances of All Types	126	302	428	192	377	569	79	239	318
Number of Questions	16	89	105	18	101	119	4	86	90
Percentage of Questions	12.70	29.47	24.53	9.38	26.79	20.91	5.06	35.98	28.30

Table 2, continued.

Two-year-olds								
Dyad 4			Dyad 5			Dyad 6 *		
Courtney	Parent	Dyad Total	Miles	Parent	Dyad Total	Amanda	Parent	Dyad Total
126	260	386	222	441	663	37	172	209
1	66	67	15	118	133	0	44	44
0.79	25.38	17.36	6.76	26.76	20.06	0.0	25.58	21.05

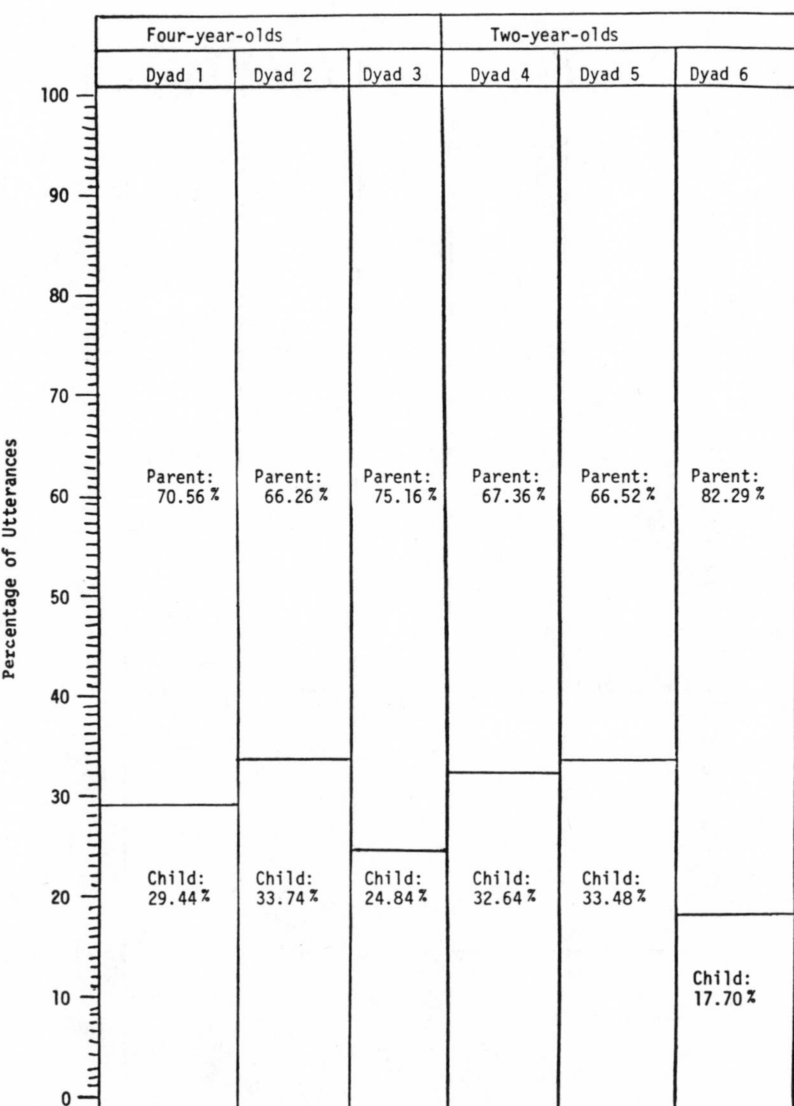

Figure 3. Percentages of Utterances of all Types produced by Parents and by Children during Booksharing.

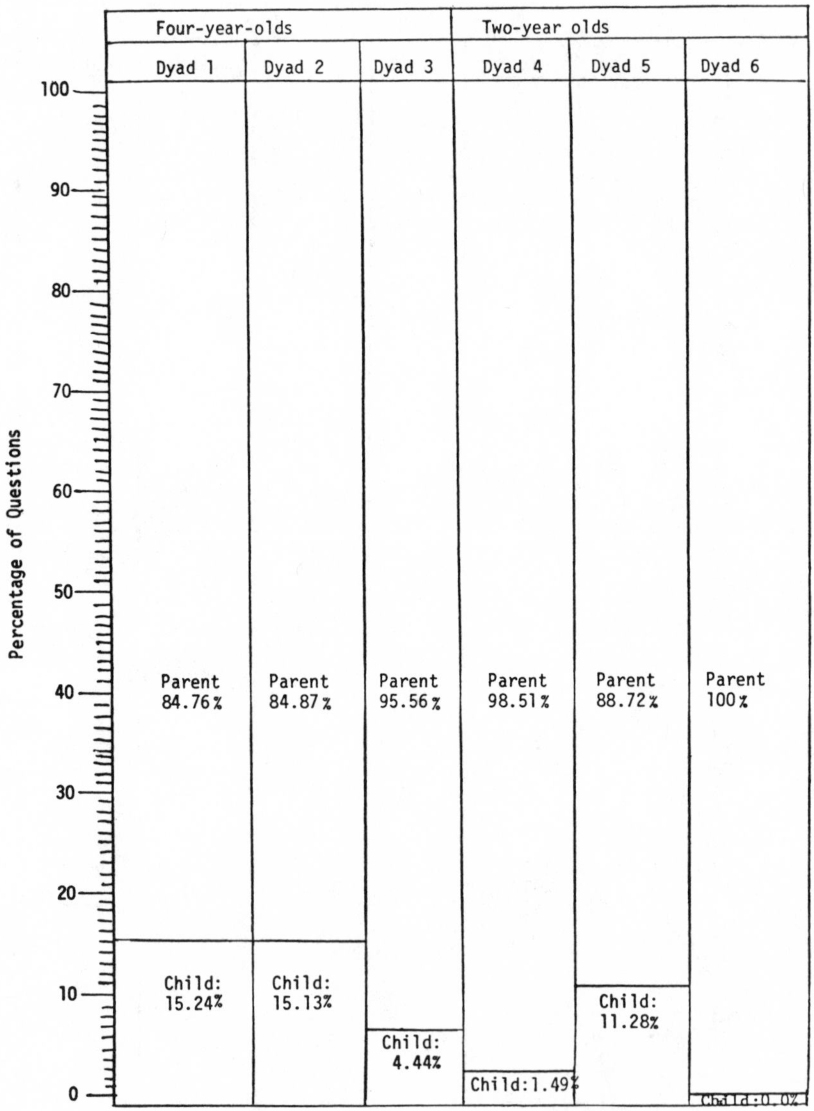

Figure 4. Percentage of Questions produced by Parents and by Children during Booksharing.

twenty-minute book sharing sessions ranged from 44 to 118 for parents and from 0 to 18 for children. The percentages of parents' utterances which were questions ranged from 25 to 36 percent. The percentages of children's utterances which were questions were much smaller, ranging from 0 to 13 percent. Age-related differences among children were suggested by these data, since only one of the three two-year-olds observed produced more than one question. Observation of more subjects would be required to verify this suggested pattern of age-related differences. As Figures 3 and 4 indicate, parents produced larger percentages of utterances of all types and larger percentages of questions than did children. The gap between the percentage of questions produced by parents and by children was larger for questions than for utterances of all types. The percentages of utterances produced by parents ranged from 66 to 82 percent, with children producing the remaining 18 to 34 percent of utterances in the interaction. Of the questions produced, however, 85 to 100 percent were produced by parents, with 1 to 15 percent produced by children.

A second type of analysis focused on the structure of questions. A structural classification schema proposed by Leach (1972) for analysis of parent-produced interrogatives was modified to describe the structural categories observed in the present data. The fifteen categories defined by Leach were collapsed into five broader categories for the present analysis. These categories include:

1. Tag (declarative sentence plus tag element).

   Example: You can run fast, can't you?
   Let's look at this book, o.k.?

2. Auxiliary + (introductory auxiliary verb followed by an infinitive, main verb, embedded wh-modifier, embedded wh-interrogative, or no segment; deletion of the auxiliary verb or the auxiliary verb and the noun or pronoun following optional).

   Example: Do you want to draw a picture?
   Can you write your name?
   Can you tell me what he said?
   Do you know what it is?
   Can you tell me about this book?

Going to leave now?

3. Main verb (introduced by _is_ or _have_ functioning as the main verb; main verb deletion optional).

   Examples: Is this the one you like?
   You there?
   Happy?

4. Wh-interrogative (typically introduced by _who_, _which_, _what_, _where_, _when_, _why_, or _how_).

   Examples: Where is the dog?
   Who is that?
   How do you like that?

5. Conjoined (typically using the conjunction _or_).

   Examples: Are you going or staying?
   Is she happy or unhappy?

In addition to these five structural categories, four additional categories were required to describe the present data. These include:

6. Intonationally-marked (declarative sentence marked by final rising intonation).

   Examples: You're all through?
   That's the one you want to look at?

7. Incomplete sentence (incomplete declarative sentence marked by final rising intonation).

   Examples: This is a ...?
   H is for ...?

8. Interjection (interjections marked by rising intonation).

   Examples: Hmm?
   Huh?
   Uh-huh?

9. Indeterminate (a nonintelligible utterance marked by final rising intonation).

Parent and child questions were classified according to structure using this schema (see Table 3). As Table 3 shows, auxiliary and wh-questions were most frequently occurring for all parents. Certain other structural types (tag, intonational, and main verb questions) were among those idiosyncratically preferred by parents. Wh- and intonationally-marked questions occurred most frequently for most children.

Classification of questions according to function was also done. Functional classification schemas for interrogatives have been proposed by Holzman (1972) and by Shatz (1979). However, it was felt that the parent/child book sharing situation generated the use of interrogatives unique to that genre, so these existing schemas were not used to analyze the data functionally. Instead, the data were examined to identify the functions of questions within the context of the book sharing interactions. This examination revealed sixteen primary functions which were in operation during book sharing. These functions include:

1. Initiating and maintaining the book sharing interaction.

   Example: Would you like to read with me?

2. Focusing the other's attention on some contextual feature or event.

   Example: See the boy?

3. Directing the other's actions.

   Example: Would you like to sit next to Mommy?

4. Testing the other's knowledge of some information already known to the questioner.

   Example: How many strawberries did he eat?

5. Inquiring of the other about some information not already known to the questioner.

Table 3. Classification of Questions according to Structural Types.

		Four - year - olds			Two - year - olds		
		Dyad 1	Dyad 2	Dyad 3	Dyad 4	Dyad 5	Dyad 6
1. Tag	Parent	15	6	1	0	1	3
	Child	0	0	0	0	0	0
2. Aux. +	Parent	23	24	21	25	10	14
	Child	3	0	2	0	0	0
3. Main Verb	Parent	5	0	4	5	1	3
	Child	1	0	0	0	0	0
4. Wh--	Parent	39	49	54	27	88	21
	Child	12	10	1	0	6	0
5. Con-joined	Parent	2	0	1	0	1	1
	Child	0	0	0	0	0	0
6. Intona-tional	Parent	4	5	3	7	10	2
	Child	0	8	1	1	8	0
7. Incom-plete S	Parent	0	15	0	1	0	0
	Child	0	0	0	0	0	0
8. Inter-jection	Parent	1	2	2	1	7	1
	Child	0	0	0	0	0	0
9. Indeter-minate	Parent	0	0	0	0	0	0
	Child	0	0	0	0	1	0
Total	Parent	89	101	86	66	118	44
	Child	16	18	4	1	15	0

Example: Are you getting tired?

6. Clarifying the other's actions or utterance.

   Example: You want to play Patty Cake?

7. Confirming the other's response.

   Example: You were right, weren't you?

8. Relating some feature or event within the book sharing context to some familiar feature or event within the other's life.

   Example: Do you have a blanket at home?

9. Eliciting from the other a feeling-response to some feature or event within the book sharing situation.

   Example: Did you have fun looking at the books?

10. Eliciting from the other an interpretation of some feature or event within the book sharing situation.

    Example: Do you think the boy's upset?

11. Eliciting from the other a statement of preference.

    Example: Which one do you want to look at?

12. Eliciting from the other a prediction related to the book being shared.

    Example: Where could that boy's blanket be?

13. Eliciting from the other a confirmation of the questioner's belief or action.

    Example: She has all those clothes on?

14. Expanding the other's understanding, or instructing the other.

    Example: Any place you got water you need a plumber, right?

15. Challenging a statement or action of the other.

    Example: Cows don't have stripes. What is that?

16. Stating an opinion.

    Example: That's pretty, isn't it?

Parents' and children's questions were classified according to the functions they fulfilled, using the schema described (see Table 4). As Table 4 shows, age-related differences were suggested. Testing, clarifying and expanding/instructing were among the most frequent functions served by questions for parents of both two- and four-year-old children. But parents of two-year-olds produced more initiating/maintaining and directing questions than did parents of four-year-olds. Children's questions fell into only eight of the sixteen functional categories, while parents' questions fell into every category except one, elicitation of confirmation.

A fourth analysis of questions focused on the interactive structures in which questions occurred during book sharing. All connected units of discourse initiated or extended by questions were identified by examination of the data. Initially, these interrogative units were subjected to a method of analysis proposed by Mishler (1978). Individual utterances within each interrogative unit were identified as question (Q), response (R), or confirmation (C). Then the structure of each unit was mapped to indicate the relationship of the constituent utterances, as shown below.

<u>An Interrogative Unit</u>:

Q_1 Parent: Do you know what that is?
R_1^1 Child: Piggy.
C_1 Parent: Uh-huh.

Table 4. Classification of Questions according to Functional Types.

		Four - year - olds			Two - year - olds		
		Dyad 1	Dyad 2	Dyad 3	Dyad 4	Dyad 5	Dyad 6
1. Initiating and maintaining	Parent	5	2	2	3	11	7
	Child	2	0	1	0	0	0
2. Focusing	Parent	1	6	3	0	1	3
	Child	0	0	1	0	0	0
3. Directing	Parent	3	3	1	7	9	4
	Child	0	0	0	0	0	0
4. Testing	Parent	30	62	52	21	76	11
	Child	0	0	0	0	0	0
5. Inquiring	Parent	0	0	3	3	0	2
	Child	11	9	1	0	5	0
6. Clarifying	Parent	10	5	0	10	8	9
	Child	2	3	0	0	10	0
7. Confirming	Parent	1	1	0	1	0	0
	Child	0	0	0	0	0	0
8. Relating	Parent	6	2	3	1	0	1
	Child	1	2	0	0	0	0

Table 4, continued

		Four - year - olds			Two - year - olds		
		Dyad 1	Dyad 2	Dyad 3	Dyad 4	Dyad 5	Dyad 6
9. Eliciting a response	Parent	3	2	0	2	0	3
	Child	0	0	0	0	0	0
10. Eliciting an interpretation	Parent	3	3	3	7	0	0
	Child	0	1	0	0	0	0
11. Eliciting a preference	Parent	2	1	4	5	2	1
	Child	0	0	0	0	0	0
12. Eliciting a prediction	Parent	3	1	0	2	0	0
	Child	0	0	0	0	0	0
13. Eliciting a confirmation	Parent	0	0	0	0	0	0
	Child	0	3	1	1	0	0
14. Expanding or instructing	Parent	10	10	9	3	10	3
	Child	0	0	0	0	0	0
15. Challenging	Parent	10	3	5	1	1	0
	Child	0	0	0	0	0	0
16. Stating an opinion	Parent	2	0	1	0	0	0
	Child	0	0	0	0	0	0

Some interrogative units were preceded and followed by non-interrogative discourse. Others occurred in strings of two or more interrogative units. These strings of interrogative units were examined to determine the modes of connection between them. Three modes of connection described and mapped by Mishler were identified. These included (1) chaining, where the confirmation utterance is also a question, introducing a second interrogative unit that follows the first; (2) arching, where the response utterance is also a question, introducing a second interrogative unit that overlaps the first; (3) embedding, where two respondents offer responses to the same question, creating one interrogative unit super-imposed over another. These three modes of communication are mapped below.

Chaining:

Q_1	Parent:	Which way is that truck going?
R_1	Child:	That way. (pointing)
C_1/Q_2	Parent:	What way is that?
R_2	Child:	Back here. (pointing)
C_2/Q_3	Parent:	Is he going up or is he going down?
R_3	Child:	He's going down.
C_3	Parent:	Uh-huh.

Arching:

	Child:	Mommy.
Q_1	Parent:	What, hon?
R_1/Q_2	Child:	Would you read Bert to me?
$C_1/R_2/Q_3$	Parent:	How about if we read this one first, okay?
$C_2/R_3/Q_4$	Child:	What's that all about?
C_3/R_4	Parent:	I'll tell you in a minute.
C_4	Child:	Mommy.

Embedding:

Q_1	Child:	What's she doing next door?
R_1	Investigator:	Just waiting.
ER_1	Parent:	Uh-huh.
	Child:	(no response)

Of the three modes of connection identified by Mishler, chaining and arching were found in the book sharing data.

The third mode, embedding, occurred only occasionally when a third participant entered the conversation. However, examination of the book sharing data revealed other types of interrogative units as well as other modes of connection among units. Retaining Mishler's definition of question, response, and confirmation, and the approach to mapping interrogative units he employed, five additional types of interrogative units and three additional modes of connection were defined and mapped.

In addition to the basic interrogative unit identified by Mishler (Q, R, C), the book sharing data include interrogative units that are abbreviated, truncated, or extended. An abbreviated interrogative unit differs from a basic unit in that the response is provided by the questioner immediately following the question. In the case of the abbreviated unit, the confirmation is usually made not by the questioner but by the other participant.

An Abbreviated Interrogative Unit:

Q_1	Parent:	Do you know?
R_1		Mousey.
C_1	Child:	Mousey.

Some interrogative units are incomplete. In some cases, a question and a response are present without a confirmation. In other cases, neither response nor confirmation is present. These incomplete interrogative units are called truncated units.

Type I Truncated Interrogative Unit:

Q_1	Child:	And this is Ernie?
R_1	Parent:	No, that's Bert. This is Ernie.

Type II Truncated Interrogative Unit:

Q_1	Parent:	Isn't it pretty? There's our red truck again.

Other interrogative units are extended rather than shortened. Extended interrogative units result when the questioner follows an incorrect response by providing a correct response. In one type of extended unit the provided response (PR) follows the incorrect response and precedes the confirmation. In the second type of extended unit, the provided response follows the confirmation.

Type I Extended Interrogative Unit:

Q_1	Parent:	What's that?
R_1	Child:	See book.
PR_1	Parent:	That's a boy. Look. That's a boy.
C_1	Child:	A boy.

Type II Extended Interrogative Unit:

Q_1	Parent:	Now who is that?
R_1	Child:	Cookie Monster.
C_1	Parent:	No, look.
PR_1		His name is Grover.
C_{1b}	Child:	Grover.

In addition to these additional types of interrogative units, two additional modes of connection among units were identified. Like the chaining and arching modes of connection identified by Mishler, these connections bind two or more interrogative units. Linked interrogative units, specific to book sharing interaction, are those that are connected by text.

Linking:

Q_1	Parent:	Who does that look like?
R_1	Child:	I don't know.
PR_1	Parent:	Timmy, sucking his thumb.
C_1	Child:	Yeah.
	Parent:	"So Mommy looked in the washing."
Q_2		That's where you always put yours, huh?
R_2	Child:	Well, I can't find mine.
C_2	Parent:	"And Daddy looked in the car. But I found the blanket under my pillow and went to sleep."
Q_3		Did you like that one?
R_3	Child:	Uh-huh.
C_3/Q_3	Parent:	Which one do you want me to read next?

Interrogative units can also be related by stacking. Stacked units are not connected like chained, arched, or linked units. Rather, they occur contiguously.

Stacking:

Q_1	Parent:	This is a fox?
R_1	Child:	NVR - nods yes.
C_1	Parent:	You're right.
Q_2		What's that?
R_2	Child:	This is a kangaroo.
C_2	Parent :	Oh, that doesn't look like a kangaroo's tail. You're right!

Using these types of interrogative units and modes of connection along with those described by Mishler, all interrogative units in the first two hundred utterances of each book sharing interaction were mapped. Child-initiated and parent-initiated interrogative units were classified by type (see Table 5), as were modes of connection employed to relate units (see Table 6).

Because the mapping of interrogative types and modes of connection among interrogative units focused on the structure of discourse containing questions, these data were of particular interest for the analysis of interactional elements in book sharing. As Table 5 shows, parents initiated eight times as many interrogative units as did children. That is, they asked many more questions than the children asked of them. One half of all the interrogative units initiated by parents were of the basic type (a question by the parent, followed by the child's response and a confirmation by the parent). One-fourth of all interrogative units initiated by parents were truncated (a question asked by the parent followed by neither a response nor a confirmation). Extended interrogative units (in which the parents followed children's incorrect or incomplete responses with provided responses) comprised one-eighth of the interrogative units initiated by parents. Child-initiated units followed a different pattern. More than one-third of the child-initiated units were basic (Q, R, C) and more than one-third were truncated (both question and response present but confirmation by the child-questioner missing). That is, children responded appropriately to parents' questions about half the time, and parents almost always followed appropriate responses with confirmation of some type. Children, on the other hand, seldom provided confirmations

Table 5. Numbers of Interrogative Units by Type Initiated by Parents and by Children during Booksharing.

		Four-year-olds			Two-year-olds			
		Dyad 1	Dyad 2	Dyad 3	Dyad 4	Dyad 5	Dyad 6	Total
1. Basic (Q1, R1, C1)	Parent	37	17	24	15	15	13	121
	Child	4	5	0	0	3	10	12
2. Abbreviated (Q1, R1, C1a, (C1b))	Parent	1	0	1	2	4	2	10
	Child	0	0	0	0	1	0	1
3. Truncated type I (Q1, R1)	Parent	4	1	4	0	3	4	16
	Child	5	1	2	0	5	0	13
4. Truncated, type II (Q1)	Parent	4	5	14	7	7	18	55
	Child	0	1	2	0	0	0	3
5. Extended type I (Q1, R1, PR1, C1a, (C1b))	Parent	7	1	9	1	7	3	28
	Child	0	1	0	0	0	0	1
6. Extended type II (Q1, R1, C1a, PR1, (C1b))	Parent	0	3	2	0	1	0	6
	Child	0	0	0	0	0	0	0
Total number of units in 200 utterances	Parent	53	27	54	25	37	40	236
	Child	9	8	4	0	9	0	30

Q Question
R Response
C Confirmation
PR Provided response
() Optional element

Table 6. Numbers of Modes of Connection Relating Interrogative Units in Parent/Child Discourse during Booksharing.

	Four-year-olds			Two-year-olds			
	Dyad 1	Dyad 2	Dyad 3	Dyad 4	Dyad 5	Dyad 6	Total
1. Isolated unit of any type	4	4	4	12	5	14	43
2. Chained Q1 R1 C1/Q2 R2 C2 or similar chain of units of other types	16	4	15	2	7	7	51
3. Arched Q1 R1/Q2 C1/R2 C2 or similar arch of units of other types	6	4	1	0	7	0	18
4. Linked Q1 R1 (C1) Text Rdg Q2 R2 C2 or similar link of units of other types	8	0	2	1	3	0	14
5. Stacked Q1 R1 C1 Q2 R2 C2 or similar stack of units of other types	15	15	18	6	13	11	78

for parents' responses to their questions. But parents almost always responded to children's questions. Abbreviated and extended units were produced only once each in child-initiated units, indicating that children seldom provided parents with answers to the questions they had asked the parent.

Finally, as Table 6 indicates, there were also differences in the modes of connection used to relate one interrogative unit to others. Stacked and chained connections and isolated units occurred most frequently in book sharing. More than one-third of the connections made were stacked, with linked and arched connections occurring less frequently. These modes of connection, together with the maps of interrogative units they connect, provide interaction profiles which help to describe the nature of the interaction, at least as it relates to questions and other utterances extending from questions in book sharing discourse.

SUMMARY

Three approaches to the analysis of parent/child discourse in book sharing were used to focus on the interactional elements of the texts created as parents and children share books. Cohesion analysis of book sharing texts revealed several styles, ranging from heavy reliance on the book's text and little exophora to creation of a two-text pattern associated with a high use of exophora. The discourse analysis revealed an interactional pattern unique to the book sharing context with broad individual differences noted. Some age-related trends were seen, particularly with elevated numbers of turns and maintenance involvement functions among younger children. The mapping of interactions initiated or extended by questions constituted a useful means of describing the role of questions and question-related utterances within the structure of book sharing discourse. Preferences for types of interrogative units and for modes of connection among units revealed differences in child-initiated and parent-initiated interrogative units. Together, these analysis reveal some features of parent/child interaction unique to book sharing situations.

REFERENCES

Burningham, J., 1975, "The Blanket." Thomas Y. Crowell, N.Y.

Cross, T., 1977, Mother's speech adjustments: the contributions of selected child listener variables, in: "Talking to Children: Language Input and Acquisition," C. Ferguson and C. E. Snow, Eds., Cambridge University Press, Cambridge.

Frank, S. M., and Seegmiller, M. S., 1973, Children's language environment in free play situation, Soc. Rsrch. Child Dev.

Guinagh, B. J. and Jester, R., 1972, How parents read to children, Theory Into Practice, 11:171-77.

Halliday, M. A. K., and Hasan, R., 1976, "Cohesion in English." Longman, London.

Hasan, R., 1980a, What's going on: A dynamic view of context in language, mimeo.

Hasan, R., 1980b, The structure of a text; the identity of a text, in: Text and Context: Language in a Social Semiotic Perspective, M. A. K. Halliday and R. Hasan, Eds., Sophia University, Tokyo.

Holzman, M., 1972, The use of interrogative forms in the verbal interaction of three mothers and their children, J. Psycholing. Rsrch., 1:311-36.

Lamme, L. and Olmsted, P., 1977, "Family Reading Habits and Children's Progress in Reading," University of Florida, Gainesville, Fla.

Leach, E., 1972, "Interrogation: a model and some implications," J. Spch. Hrng. Dis., 37:33-46.

Mishler, E., 1978, Studies in dialogue and discourse, III: utterance structure and utterance function in interrogative sequences, J. Psycholing. Rsrch., 7:279-305.

Moerk, E. L., 1974, Changes in verbal child-mother interactions with increasing language skills of the child, J. Psycholing. Rsrch., 3:101-16.

Moerk, E. L., 1975, Verbal interactions between children and their mothers during the pre-school years, Dev. Psych., 11:788-94.

Moerk, E. L., 1976, Processes of language teaching and training in the interactions of mother-child dyads, Ch. Dev., 47:1064-78.

Ninio, A., 1980, Picture-book reading in mother-infant dyads belonging to two subgroups in Israel, Ch. Dev., 51: 587-90.

Ninio, A. and Bruner, J. S., 1978, The achievement and antecedents of labeling, J. Ch. Lang., 5:1-15.

Shatz, M., 1979, How to do things by asking: form-function pairings in mothers' questions and their relation to children's responses, Ch. Dev., 50:1093-99.

Snow, C. E., 1972, Mothers' speech to children learning language. Ch. Dev., 43:549-65.

Snow, C. E., 1975, The development of conversation between mothers and babies, ms.

Snow, C. E., Arlman-Rupp, A., Hassing, Y., Jobse, J., Joosten, J., and Vorster, J., 1976, Mothers' speech in three social classes. J. Psycholing. Rsrch, 5:1-20.

A PROPOSITIONAL ANALYSIS OF SPANISH LANGUAGE TEXTS

Guadalupe Valdés, Rosalinda Barrera,

Donald W. Dearholt, and Manuel Cárdenas

New Mexico State University

READING IN BILINGUAL EDUCATION: THE NEED FOR TEXT ANALYSIS

The importance of functional literacy skills for participation in contemporary society is clearly unquestionable. For this reason, research in English language reading has increased and turned its attention from studies which focused primarily on word recognition and word decoding to investigations of higher-level processes of comprehending and recalling written discourse. There is clearly a need, however, to begin research in languages other than English within the current theoretical perspective. It is important to augment current efforts in text analysis and children's comprehension by focusing on a population of young readers whose language experiences and background knowledge differ from those of the educational mainstream. It is especially important to explore the development of reading skills among children involved in bilingual education programs, an alternate form of schooling that seeks to capitalize on native language experience and background in order to insure literacy in a second language.

Unfortunately it is not easy to begin a study of reading comprehension in a minority language. For Spanish, specifically, the type of information taken for granted by reading researchers is not available. There are no measures which can serve as indices of difficulty of any reliability for Spanish language materials. For example, questionable as readability formulas might be in English, at least they have provided a means which researchers and practitioners can use to compare texts. Methods for comparing texts in Spanish, ranging from readability formulas to more sophisticated means of text analysis, are in essence, nonexistent. At the same time, there is an ongoing need for classification and evaluation of materials currently in use in bilingual education programs. To assume that the very existence of bilingual instruction will resolve the educational problems of minority children is naive. No longer is it pedagogically sound to take the position that the mere fact of beginning children's education in their first language will insure that they can succeed in future academic endeavors. Indeed, it becomes more and more clear that academic success and successful learning of a second language are related to the levels of development achieved in a first language: the greater the achievement and learning of L_1, the greater the achievement and learning in L_2.

In order to explore such questions meaningfully, it is clear that researchers must focus more precisely on existing methods, materials and assumptions underlying first language instruction in bilingual education programs. Strategies must be developed which can address the area of literacy in such languages as Spanish by working to ascertain the comprehensibility of materials used for reading instruction and the demands made by them on readers.

The purpose of this paper is to report on research conducted within Phase II of a three-phase project currently funded by the National Institute of Education. As a part of this second phase of the project, a number of strategies have been developed for studying the organization and structure of prose material of the type generally found in children's reading textbooks. Specifically this paper will describe a propositional analysis system developed for the study of Spanish language texts which is based largely on Kintsch (1974) and Turner and Greene (1977). Because, however, the focus on propositional analysis is only a part of the work conducted in the area of text analysis as a whole, this discussion will begin with a brief description of the entire scope of the ongoing project.

PRINCIPAL GOALS OF THE NIE-FUNDED PROJECT: "READING IN BILINGUAL EDUCATION: ANALYZING TEXTS AND CHILDREN'S COMPREHENSION"

The ongoing study "Reading in Bilingual Education: Analyzing Texts and Children's Comprehension" has the following principal goals:

1. To develop strategies and techniques for text analysis which will permit the comparison of Spanish and English language materials used in bilingual education programs.
2. To study the interaction of Mexican-American bilingual children with different kinds of texts in both languages in order to gain insight into the importance of a wide variety of features on the process of comprehension.
3. To establish a basis for assisting teachers in determining how text features and reader characteristics may be either matched or mismatched.

The project involves three distinct phases. Phase I is concerned with the analysis of surface level features of Spanish language texts and seeks to develop a readability formula which may make a comparison with English texts possible at this level. Phase II has as its principal objective the development of strategies for analyzing text semantics; and Phase III utilizes the information obtained in Phases I and II of the project in studying interactions between texts and readers.

PHASE II: THE ANALYSIS OF TEXT LEVEL FEATURES: A GENERAL OVERVIEW

It has become evident that surface level features, that is orthographic, lexical, and syntactic variables, do not account totally for the demands a given text may make upon a reader. Indeed, current research has made clear that the "comprehensibility" of texts is related to such factors as discourse level variables (Halliday, 1970; Halliday and Hasan, 1976; Kuno, 1972, 1975, and 1976; Chafe, 1976; Keenan and Schieffelin, 1976; and Li and Thompson, 1976) and to the textual characteristics and the schematic expectations of the reader (Meyer and McConkie, 1973; Meyer, 1975; Clements, 1975; Marshall, 1976; Marshall and Glock,

1978-79; Rumelhart, 1976; Thorndyke, 1977; Mandler and Johnson, 1977; and Kintsch, 1976). Given this project's goals to develop strategies for studying the comprehensibility of both Spanish and English language texts in order to examine the interaction of bilingual children with such texts, much effort has gone into the exploration of methods which have been used by others for describing the organization of prose. Essentially work has focused on two areas: (1) the analysis of text micro-structure which has involved the exploration and development of methods for coding propositional content; (2) the analysis of text macro-structure, which is concerned with the relationship of propositions to each other within an overall framework. The study of text micro-structure has sought to explore and apply strategies which will permit coding for the following:

a. total number of propositions in text (explicit)
b. total number of propositions in text (implicit)
c. number of propositions per sentence unit.

The study of text macro-structure has concerned itself with seeking strategies useful in describing the hierarchical ordering of propositions within a text. The system proposed by Van Dijk (1977) has been followed closely; while work in this area is not complete at this time, the final version of the system developed for representing the organization of a given text will:

1. permit the study of the staging of propositions (How is importance managed in a given text?)
2. permit the classification of story structures (minimally as familiar/unfamiliar and as requiring or not requiring extensive real-world knowledge in order to explore schema theory)
3. permit the study of the function of dialogue in stories
4. permit the representation of the structure of paragraphs in both narrative and non-narrative prose (for example, to ascertain whether a given paragraph proceeds from general to specific, whether it alternates topics in order to compare and contrast,

whether it presents details in chronological or spatial order, etc.)

The work reported in this paper is concerned exclusively with text micro-structure, that is, with the analysis of the number of ideas contained in a given passage. In the analysis of text level features, the derivation of a propositional text base, that is, the coding of the explicit and implicit ideas contained in a passage, is a necessary first step.

THE STUDY OF THE ORGANIZATION OF PROSE: TRENDS IN PROPOSITIONAL ANALYSIS

A propositional analysis is a description of a text in terms of its semantic content. Its units of analysis are propositions, or in Clark & Clark's (1977) terms, units of meaning which consist of one verbal element plus one or more nouns. More technically, a proposition has been defined by Kintsch (1974) as a unit containing a predicator and *n* arguments. Sentences express propositions and therefore may contain a number of ideas.

The main purpose of a propositional analysis is the derivation of a text base. Propositions in a given text are connected into a cohesive, interrelated whole and include ideas directly expressed as well as those which must be inferred in order to form a logical and connected structure. An ordered listing of all propositions, explicit and implicit, is thus known as a propositional text base. This derived text base presents the total number of units of meaning found in a given passage and, depending upon the level of analysis, information about the relationship of these units to each other.

Recently there has been a increased interest in the organization of prose and therefore in the development of strategies for analyzing the content of specific passages. Studies in the areas of psychology, education, and linguistics have contributed significantly to current views on text analysis. Within each of these areas, it has become clear that research with natural prose is a difficult endeavor. In conducting such research, specific information about text content is needed at a level which will permit, for example, a comparison of different types of passages. At the very least, this presupposes the development of strategies for classifying and coding text meaning consistently.

To date, contributions to the analysis of natural prose have reflected the interest of the three areas delineated above. For psychologists, research using prose has been closely related to the investigation of the structure of memory. Researchers have focused primarily on developing techniques for describing text content as well as the content of recall protocols; much attention has been given to deriving strategies which might make possible the comparison between original passages and texts produced by subjects asked to recall these originals.

Educators, on the other hand, have been particularly concerned with studying learning from reading or listening to prose. Ordinarily, educators have sought to examine an individual's comprehension of a passage by asking questions about the information contained within it. It has become increasingly evident, however, that investigators can seldom describe the information tapped by their questions. Disagreement is prevalent concerning the identification of main ideas in passages as opposed to supporting details. Although Anderson (1972) has recently elaborated strategies for generating several types of questions, these strategies do not provide guidance for deciding which information in a given passage should be selected for focus.

A number of valuable contributions to the study of the organization of prose have come from the field of linguistics. Although there seemed for some time to be little interest in questions relating to meaning among linguists, recently a number of scholars have worked on developing analytical procedures for classifying ideas in a passage, not as subjects or verbs of a specific sentences, but rather according to their role in conveying meaning within the total structure. Work by Propp (1958) on the analysis of the folktale and work by Labov and Waletsky (1967) on narratives focused on functions of segments of information within discourse. Grimes (1972) and Halliday (1967) sought to identify distinct sets of relationships in discourse. Both of these latter researchers attempted to analyze the organization of the content of discourse as well as the presentation of new information within texts. Because of its impact on the development of analytical strategies for the study of prose, however, the outstanding contribution derived from the field of linguistics is the work of Charles Fillmore on case grammar. Three of the major analytical techniques developed to date are based to some degree on Fillmore's identification of the function of information in sentences.

There are essentially four major fully developed strategies which have been used or adapted for use in deriving propositional text bases from natural prose passages. These are: a system developed by Grimes (1972) and further elaborated by Meyer (1975); a system developed by Fredericksen (1972), which is possibly the most complex and detailed of the techniques for analysis developed to date; a system developed by Crothers (1973); a system developed by Kintsch (1974) and further refined and adapted for use with long prose segments by Turner and Greene (1977).

These systems differ as to specific goals and therefore also as to the notational systems used and the level of specificity of the distinctions made. Two of the systems (Meyer/Grimes and Kintsch/Turner & Greene) require one analysis per passage while two others (Fredericksen and Crothers) require two diagrams per passage. In Fredericksen's system, for example, one graph describes the semantic structure of a passage while another reflects the logical structure of the elements within the passage.

Time and space preclude a more detailed discussion of these four systems; however, a sample of three of the notational schemes used is included below.

1. Meyer/Grimes (Sample taken from Meyer, 1975)

CONTENT STRUCTURE OF THE BREEDER REACTOR
HIGH PASSAGE

entitled Fast Breeder Reactors

1 response
2 problem
3 collection
4 NEED TO GENERATE ELECTRIC POWER
5 specific
6 Add (0,4)
7 agent'
8 AMERICAN POWER INDUSTRY
9 patient
10 1600 MILLION KILOWATTS OF ELECTRIC GENERATING CAPACITY
11 benefactive
12 IS PRESENT CAPACITY
13 patient
14 300 MILLION KILOWATTS
15 setting time
16 NEXT 30 YEARS
17 ESTIMATED
18 agent
19 FEDERAL POWER COMMISSION

2. Fredericksen (Sample taken from Marshall and Glock, 1978-79)

1. (#1)--PAT-> (want)--[GOAL2- > ["2]
2. (#1)--PAT-> (represent)--OBJ2- > ["3]
3. (distribution)--ORD@NEG- > (one)
4. (bar graph)--EXT1- > (good)--DEG1- > (#4)
5. (graph.5)--EXT1- > (good)--DEG1- > (#5)
6. (graph.6--EXT1- > (good)--DEG1- > (#6)
7. ["4]--ORD- > ["5]
8. ["4]--ORD- > ["6]
9. ["1] <-IFF- >[["7],["8]]

3. Kintsch/Turner and Greene (Sample taken from Turner & Greene 1977)

1. (POSSESS, A:AUSTRALIA, O:SHEEP)
2. (NUMBER OF, 1, THREE FOURTHS)
3. (QUALIFY, MERINO, PURE)
4. (ISA, 2, 3)
5. (ISA, MERINOS, SHEEP)
6. (QUALITY OF, 3, POPULAR)
7. (QUALIFY, LAND, SEMIARID)
8. (EXTENT OF, 7, LARGE)
9. (CAUS: BECAUSE OF, 8, 6)

10. (QUALIFY, BUSHES, LOW)
11. (CONJ: AND, GRASSES, 10)
12. (QUALIFY, PLAINS, SEMIARID)
13. (LOC: ON, 11, 12)
14. (THRIVE, A:3, I:13)
15. (QUALITY OF, WOOL, FINE-QUALITY)
16. (QUALITY OF, FLEECES, HEAVY)
17. (QUALITY OF, 16, 17)
18. (POSSESS, A:2, O:17)
19. (KNOW, A:$, O:18)
20. (QUALIFY, PRICE, HIGH)
21. (MAKE, A:MANUFACTURERS, O:TEXTILES)
22. (BRING, A:18, O:20, S:21)

THE ADAPTATION OF THE KINTSCH/TURNER & GREENE SYSTEM FOR USE WITH SPANISH TEXTS

Before the Kintsch/Turner & Greene system was selected for use with Spanish texts, extensive experimentation was carried out with the three other systems described above. All experimentation was carried out in English.

In weighing the advantages and disadvantages of the existing approaches to propositional analysis, the following criteria were established: (a) the system selected for transfer to Spanish must have a reasonably simple notational system; (b) it must be efficient, that is, productive of the desired effect without undue loss of time or energy; (c) must be accessible (if simplified further) to practitioners.

The systems requiring two diagrams per passage were eliminated, as was the very complete system developed by Myer. The Kintsch/Turner and Greene system was found to be especially attractive in that it had already been used in the analysis of the popular children's text Freddie Miller, Scientist, by Harste and Feather (1979).

Essentially, within the Kintsch/Turner & Greene system, text meaning is represented by a list of connected propositions. Each proposition contains a single idea. Propositions consist of abstract word concepts (written in capital letters) which may be represented by one or more words at the surface level. Minimally, a proposition must consist of at least two word concepts: the first is a predicator (also called a relation), followed by the argument. Propositions are classified as belonging to one of three types: predicate propositions, modifier propositions, and connective propositions. Table 1 summarizes the elements of the system and includes both definitions and examples of each type of proposition.

It will be noted that several conventions are followed. Word concepts are written in capital letters. The predicator or relation is written first followed by its arguments. When the predicator is a verb, as it is in propositions which use case relations, its arguments fill particular cases. These are written in the order specified by a given relation. Case identification symbols are followed by colons; arguments are followed by commas; each proposition is enclosed by parentheses.

In general, the case system used in the Kintsch/Turner & Greene approach follows Fillmore (1968, 1969, 1971). The following cases are included by Turner and Greene (1977).

1. Agent (A) - typically animate instigator of the state or action identified by the verb
2. Experiencer (E) - experiencer of psychological event
3. Instrument (I) - typically inanimate stimulus of an experience, a force or object causally involved in the state or action identified by the verb
4. Object (O) - object of an action which undergoes change or movement
5. Source (S) - source of state or action identified by the verb
6. Goal (G) - result or goal of state or action identified by the verb

Each case can occur only once in a given proposition.

In addition to propositions which include case relations, the Kintsch/Turner & Greene system identifies the copula "ISA," which expresses set membership, and the predicator "REFERENCE," which identifies arguments as having an identical referent.

Modifier propositions limit or restrict concepts. Qualifiers, quantifiers, partitives and negatives are included as modifier propositions.

Connective propositions express conjunction, disjunction, causality, purpose, concession, contract, condition, and circumstance. These propositions express relationships between facts and propositions in a text.

The Kintsch/Turner & Greene system does not concern itself with the derivation of macro-structure or with making explicit propositions which are implicit. Inferred propositions based on either syntax or world knowledge are not considered to be part of the text base.

The version of Kintsch's system developed by Turner and Greene includes a set of rules intended for use by other researchers, and possibly practitioners, in the construction of a text base. The following algorithm, which contains a nine-branch loop, is meant to serve as a basis for analyzing natural prose according to the Kintsh/Turner & Greene approach (see Turner and Greene, 1977).

1. MODIFIED ARGUMENTS OF PREDICATE PROPOSITIONS
   Write all modifier propositions which are used in a predicate proposition to modify an argument of that proposition. Modifiers of the predicate proposition itself are not included here.
2. CONNECTED ARGUMENTS OF PREDICATE PROPOSITIONS
   Write all connective propositions which are used as arguments for a predicate proposition, and which occupy the same case position.
3. PREDICATE PROPOSITIONS
   Write the predicate propositions(s). There is rarely more than one per clause.
4. MODIFIERS OF PREDICATE PROPOSITIONS
   Write all modifiers of the predicate proposition(s).
5. MODIFIED ARGUMENTS OF CIRCUMSTANTIAL PROPOSITIONS
   Write all modifiers of arguments of propositions of circumstance.
6. CIRCUMSTANTIAL PROPOSITIONS
   Write all connective propositions of circumstance, provided they do not connect arguments between clauses.

7. OTHER CONNECTIVE PROPOSITIONS WITHIN CLAUSE
   Write all connective propositions which connect arguments within the clause, and which have not been transcribed earlier.
8. CONNECTIVE PROPOSITIONS BETWEEN CLAUSES
   Write all connective propositions which connect an argument or arguments from the present clause with an argument or arguments in a previous clause or clauses. Forward-looking connectives from the previous clause are included here.
9. REPEAT
   Repeat steps 1-8 for the next unit of text.

The Kintsch/Turner & Greene system, as adapted for use with Spanish language texts, differs only slightly from the original scheme described above. Essentially, the most important differences involve the elimination of the use of case relations and the attempt to express text meaning while still retaining the syntactic and morphological features of the original text. Table 2 summarizes the adapted system.

It will be noted that the three types of propositions are identical in both the adapted and the original schemes. Predicate propositions are, however, given the name "Base Propositions" in the adapted system in order to emphasize the fact that every sentence will contain at least one basic or core idea. Base Propositions are defined as expressing a relationship between subject and verb (terminology which is thought to be more accessible to practitioners). Base propositions are considered to be of three types: those which express actions or states, those which express set membership, and those which identify the referent of one argument with another. The two latter types, which are termed <u>Nominal Propositions</u> and <u>Referential Propositions</u>, are identical to those described in the original system. Propositions identified in the adapted system as <u>Action/ State Propositions</u> replaced those labeled <u>Propositions Which Use Case Relations</u>. Since preliminary work with teachers has indicated that this level of specificity in the analysis of texts is not practical, case relations were eliminated entirely from the adapted system. Normal word order was followed so that these relationships, while not a part of the analysis, might not be lost.

Modifier propositions and connective propositions are identical in the adapted system to the propositions of the same name described by the original scheme. The examples in Tables 1 and 2 make clear, however, how the adapted notational system sought at all times to focus on the meanings contributed by this type of proposition to the base or core idea contained in the unit of analysis.

One further difference between the two systems involves the listing of both explicit and implicit propositions in the adapted system. Implicit propositions include references which are made logically by most able readers and which result from either syntax or world knowledge. Implicit propositions listed in the adapted system include those which are inferred from the use of pronouns, synonyms, etc. The original system (Turner and Greene: 1977) ignores inferred referents of pronouns rather than including them in the text base. All inferences essentially based on syntax are considered clear and unambigous. For this project's purposes however, which include working with text passages and young children learning to read, it was thought that such distinctions could not be assumed to be totally without problems. The adapted scheme, therefore, contains a listing of such implicit propositions so that they might be studied more carefully.

Summarizing briefly, the adapted Kintsch/Turner & Greene system has retained all of the distinctions made by the original system with the exception of case relations. Work in Spanish has made evident the fact that the use of normal surface structure has made the transfer of the system a less complex process. A number of distinctions not present in English (for example the use of <u>ser</u> vs. <u>estar</u>) could be handled easily using the adapted system. The original system was problematic in a number of ways. A sample of a text base derived using the original system is included in this paper as Appendix 1. It can be compared with a text base derived using the adapted system which is included as Appendix 2.

Preliminary work with practitioners has suggested that the adapted system is less overwhelming. The propositional

Table 1. Types of Propositions and Notational Systems According to the Original Kintsch/Turner & Greene System.

Type of Proposition	Definition	Examples
I. PREDICATE PROPOSITIONS	Express a relation of action or being	(All examples from Turner & Green, 1977)
A. Propositions Which Use Case Relations	Cases are: agent experiencer instrument, object, source, and goal	Betty bought a balloon. (BUY, A: BETTY, O: BALLOON)
B. Nominal Propositions	Express set membership	A collie is a dog. (ISA, COLLIE, DOG)
C. Referential Propositions	Identify referent of one argument with another	Clark Kent is Superman. (REFERENCE, CLARK KENT, SUPERMAN)
II. MODIFIER PROPOSITIONS	Restrict or limit concepts by means or other concepts	
A. Qualifiers	Restrict scope or argument or indicate an attribute	
Adjectival Propositions		Milton is fat. (QUALITY OF, MILTON, FAT)
Adverbial Propositions		The snow is melting slowly. (MELT, O: SNOW) (QUALITY, (MELT, SNOW), SLOW)
Hedges		Richard Nixon is technically a Quaker. (ISA, RICHARD NIXON, QUAKER) (QUALIFY, (ISA, RICHARD NIXON, QUAKER), TECHNICALLY)
B. Quantifiers	Express number	Ed bought three tickets. (NUMBER OF, TICKETS, THREE)
C. Partitives	Express a part/whole relationship	Mike dented the car's bumper. (PART OF, CAR, BUMPER)
D. Negatives	Deny the truth of a proposition or cause it to become invalid	We do not have bananas. (POSSESS, A: WE, O: BANANAS) (NEGATE, (POSSESS, A: WE, O: BANANAS))

Type of Proposition	Definition	Examples
III. CONNECTIVE PROPOSITIONS	Express relationships between facts or propositions in a text	
A. Conjunction	Union or association	Dick and Jane went to the store. (CONJUNCTION: AND, DICK, JANE)
B. Disjunction	Alternatives or opposition	Either Jack or Sarah broke the plate. (DISJUNCTION: EITHER..OR, (BREAK, A: JACK O: PLATE), (BREAK, A: SARAH, O: PLATE)
C. Causality	Cause and effect, correlated events	Merinos are popular sheep because they have fine- quality wool. (CAUSALITY: BECAUSE, A1: (POSSESS, (ISA, MERINOS, SHEEP), (QUALITY OF, WOOL, FINE QUALITY)), A2: (QUALITY OF, (ISA, MERINOS, SHEEP), POPULAR))
D. Purpose	Purpose, reason, intent	Mark went to the beach to swim. (PURPOSE: TO, A1(GO, A: MARK, G: BEACH), A2 (SWIM, A: MARK)
E. Concession	Admission of a point	Although Doug studied for the exam, he failed. (CONCESSION: ALTHOUGH, A1 (STUDY, A: DOUG, G: EXAM), A2 (FAIL, A: DOUG, O: EXAM))
F. Contrast	Divergence, comparison	Milton is fatter than Dan. (CONTRAST: FATTER, A1: MILTON, A2: DAN)
G. Condition	Prerequisites, restriction	If Martha goes, Peter will go. (CONDITION: IF, A1: (GO, A: MARTHA, G:$), A2: (GO, A PETER, G:$))
H. Circumstance	Time, location, manner	Larry went home late. (TIME: LATE, (GO, A: LARRY, G. HOME) Hans is standing behind the counter. (LOCATION: BEHIND, A1 (STAND, A: HANS, A2, COUNTER))

Table 2. Types of Propositions and Notational System According to the Adapted Kintsch/Turner & Greene System.

Type of Proposition	Definition	Examples
I. BASE PROPOSITIONS	Express a relationship between subject and verb	
A. Action/State Propositions	Express action or state	Betty bought a balloon. BASE: Betty bought a balloon.
B. Nominal Propositions	Express set membership	A collie is a dog. BASE/NOMINAL: A collie is a dog.
C. Referential Propositions	Identify the referent of one argument with another	Clark Kent is Superman. BASE/REFERENCE: Clark Kent is Superman.
II. MODIFIER PROPOSITIONS	Restrict or limit concepts by means of other concepts	
A. Qualifiers	Restrict scope or argument or indicate an attribute	
1. Adjectives		Milton is fat. MODIFIER/QUALIFIER: fat
2. Adverbs		The snow is melting slowly. MODIFIER/QUALIFIER: slowly
3. Hedges		Richard Nixon is technically a Quaker. MODIFIER/QUALIFIER: technically
B. Quantifiers	Express number	Ed bought three tickets. MODIFIER/QUANTIFIER: three
C. Partitives	Express a part/whole relationship	Mark dented the car's bumper. MODIFIER/PARTITIVE: bumper- part of car
D. Negatives	Deny the truth of a proposition or cause it to become invalid	We do not have bananas. BASE: We have bananas. MODIFIER/NEGATIVE: We do not have

Type of Proposition	Definition	Examples
III. CONNECTIVE PROPOSITIONS	Express relationships between facts or propositions in a text	
A. Conjunction	Union or association	Dick and Jane went to the store. CONJUNCTION: Dick and Jane
B. Disjunction	Alternatives or opposition	Either Jack or Sarah broke the plate. DISJUNCTION: Either Jack or Sarah
C. Causality	Cause and effect, correlated events	Merinos are popular sheep because they have fine-quality wool. 1. BASE: Merinos are sheep 2. MODIFIER/QUALIFIER: popular sheep 3. BASE: Merinos have wool 4. MODIFIER/QUALIFIER: fine-quality wool 5. CAUSALITY: because #3, #1
D. Purpose	Purpose, reason, intent	Mark went to the beach to swim. BASE: Mark went to the beach PURPOSE: to swim
E. Concession	Admission of a point	Although Doug studied for the exam, he failed. 1. BASE: Doug studied for the exam 2. BASE: Doug failed 3. CONCESSION: although #1, #2
F. Contrast	Divergence, comparison	Milton is fatter than Don. CONTRAST: fatter #1, than #2
G. Condition	Prerequisites, restriction	If Martha goes, Peter will go. CONDITION: if #1, #2
H. Circumstance	Time, location, manner	Larry went home late. TIME: late Hans is standing behind the counter. LOCATION: behind the counter

text base resembles the actual passage closely and most individuals can reconstruct the original sentence from the list of propositions. This was not the case when using the original Kintsch/Turner & Greene system. To date no work has been carried out in teaching practioners to apply the system to brief passages of actual text. A set of rules which complement those derived by Turner and Greene which were cited above is included as Appendix 3. These rules will be expanded as needed after work has been carried out more fully in teaching the adapted system to other researchers and practioners.

SUMMARY AND CONCLUSIONS

The existing need for evaluating and rating Spanish language materials used in bilingual education programs has led to a desire by researchers to analyze both surface level and semantic features of specific texts. Work in the analysis of the organization of natural prose has been carried out in English and includes the examination of both micro-structure and macro-structure. A number of systems have been developed which focus on text content by breaking down passages into propositions. After examining a number of these systems, a scheme devised by Kintsch and elaborated further by Turner & Greene was adapted for use with Spanish language texts. It was possible to retain all but one of the distinctions made by the original system. Preliminary work suggests that the adapted system can be used with Spanish texts of varying complexity efficiently.

REFERENCES

Anderson, R. C., 1972, How to construct achievement tests to assess comprehension, Rev. Ed. Rsrch., 42:145-170.

Chafe, W., 1976, Giveness, contrastiveness, definiteness, subjects, topics, and points of view, in: "Subject and Topic," C. Li, ed., Academic Press, N.Y.

Clark, H. H. and Clark, E. V., 1977, "Psychology and Language," Harcourt Brace Jovanovich, N.Y.

Clements, Paul, 1975, The effects of staging on recall from prose, unpublished dissertation, Cornell University.

Crothers, E. J., 1973, The psycholinguistic structure of knowledge, in: "Cognitive Organization and Psychological

Processes," K. Romney and K. Wesler, eds., National Academy of Sciences, N.Y.

Fillmore, C. J., 1968, The case for case, in: Universals in Linguistic Theory, E. Bach and R. Harms, eds., Holt, Rinehart and Winston, N.Y.

Fillmore, C. J., 1969, Types of lexical information, in: "Semantics," D. Steinberg and L. Jakobovits, eds., Cambridge University Press, Cambridge.

Fillmore, C. J., 1971, Some problems for case grammar, Ohio State Working Papers in Linguistics, No. 10.

Fredericksen, C. H., 1972, Effects of task-induced cognitive operations on comprehension of memory processes, in: "Language Comprehension and the Acquisition of Knowledge," R. Freedle and J. Carroll, eds., Wiley, N.Y.

Grimes, J. E., 1972, "The Thread of Discourse," Cornell University, Ithaca.

Halliday, M. A. K., 1967, Notes on transitivity and theme in English, J. Ling., 3:37-81; 199-244.

Halliday, M. A. K., 1970, Language structure and language function, in: "New Horizons in Linguistics," J. Lyons, ed., Penguin, Harmondsworth.

Halliday, M. A. K. and Hasan, R., 1976, "Cohesion in English," Longman, London.

Harste, J. C. and Feathers, K., 1979, A propositional analysis of Freddie-Miller, Scientist, MS., School of Education, Indiana University.

Keenan, E. O. and Schieffelin, B., 1976, Topic as a discourse notion: a study of topic in the conversations of children and adults, in: "Subject and Topic," C. Li, ed., Academic Press, N.Y.

Kintsch, Walter, 1974, "The Representation of Meaning in Memory," LEA, Hillsdale.

Kintsch, Walter, 1977, On comprehending stories, in: "Cognitive Processes in Comprehension," M. Just and P. Carpenter, eds., LEA, Hillsdale.

Kuno, S., 1975, Three perspectives on the functional approach to syntax, CLS (Parasession on Functionalism), 276-333.

Kuno, S., 1976, Subject, theme and the speaker's empathy, a reexamination of relativization phenomena, in: "Subject and Topic," C. Li, ed., Academic Press, N.Y.

Labov, W. and Waletzky, J., 1967, Narrative analysis: oral versions of personal experience, in: "Essays on the Verbal and Visual Arts," J. Helm, ed.,

University of Washington, Seattle.

Li, C. and Thompson, S., 1976, Subject and topic: A new typology of language, in: "Subject and Topic," C. Li, ed., Academic Press, N.Y.

Mandler, J. M. and Johnson, N. S., 1977, Remembrance of things parsed: story structure and recall, Cog. Psych., 9:111-151.

Marshall, Nancy, 1976, The structure of semantic memory for text, unpublished dissertation, Cornell University.

Marshall, Nancy, 1979, Readability and comprehensibility, J. Rdng., 542-544.

Marshall, Nancy and Glock, Marvin D., 1978-79, Comprehension of connected discourse: a study in the relationships between the structure of text and information recalled, Rdng. Rsrch. Q., 14:10-56.

Meyer, B. J. F., 1975, "The Organization of Prose and its Effects on Memory," North-Holland, Amsterdam.

Meyer, B. J. F. and McConkie, G. W., 1973, What is recalled after hearing a passage? J. Ed. Psych., 65:109-117.

Propp, V., 1958, "Morphology of the Folktale," (translated by Lawrence Scott), Research Center in Anthropology, Folklore and Linguistics, Bloomington.

Rumelhart, David E., 1976, Toward an interactive model of reading, Technical Report 56, University of California-San Diego, Center for Human Information Processing.

Turner, A. and Greene, E., 1977, The construction and use of a propositional text base, Technical Report No. 63, Institute for the Study of Intellectual Behavior, Boulder, Colorado.

Throndyke, Perry W., 1977, Cognitive structures in comprehension and memory of narrative discourse, 9:77-110.

Van Dijk, T. A., 1977, Semantic Macro-structures and knowledged frames in discourse comprehension, in: "Cognitive Processes in Comprehension," M. Just and P. Carpenter, eds., LEA, Hillsdale.

APPENDIX 1

A PROPOSITIONAL TEXT BASE USING THE ORIGINAL KINTSCH/TURNER & GREENE SYSTEM

01. Martín e Isabel, los gemelos Montes, van a cumplir nueve años el domingo.

1. (CONJ: E, MARTÍN, ISABEL)
2. (REFERENCE, MARTÍN & ISABEL, GEMELOS MONTES)
3. (CUMPLIR, A:MARTÍN & ISABEL, O: AÑOS)
4. (NUMBER, AÑOS, NUEVE)
5. (TIME: > EN, (3), (4), DOMINGO)

02. Sus papás los llevarán a pasear.

6. (PASEAR, A: MARTÍN & ISABEL, PAPÁS)
7. (LLEVAR, A: PAPÁS, O: MARTÍN & ISABEL)
8. (PASEAR, A: PAPÁS, O: MARTÍN & ISABEL)
9. (PURPOSE: PARA, (7), (8))

03. Así celebrarán su cumpleaños.

10a (CELEBRAR, A: PAPÁS O: CUMPLEAÑOS)

10b (CELEBRAR, MARTÍN & ISABEL, CUMPLEAÑOS)

11. (REFERENCE, (7), ASÍ)
12. (MANNER: ASÍ, (10a) or (10b)

04. -Nos gusta pasearnos ese día- dice Martín.

13. (PASEAR, MARTÍN & ISABEL)
14. (GUSTAR, E: MARTÍN & ISABEL, (13))
15. (REFERENCE: CUMPLEAÑOS, ESE DÍA)
16. (TIME : >EN, (14), ESE DÍA)
17. (DECIR, MARTÍN, (16))

05. El paseo es siempre una sorpresa.

18. (SER, PASEO, SORPRESA)
19. TIME: SIEMPRE, (18))
20. (DECIR, MARTÍN, (19))

06. -Y siempre nos divertimos mucho-dice Isabel.

21. (DIVERTIR, E: MARTÍN & ISABEL)

22. (QUALIFY, (21), MUCHO)
23. (TIME: SIEMPRE, (22))
24. (CONJ: Y, (16), (19), (23)
25. (DECIR, ISABEL, (23))

07. Todos los años su papá les dice: ¡Fiesta doble! ¡Doble alegría! ¡Ustedes nos han traído doble felicidad a mamá y a mí!

26. (QUALITY OF, FIESTA, DOBLE)
27. (QUALITY OF, ALEGRÍA, DOBLE)
28. (QUALITY OF: FELICIDAD, DOBLE)
29. (TRAER, MARTÍN & ISABEL, (28), G: PAPÁS)
30. DECIR, A: PAPÁ, O: (26) (27) (28)G: MARTÍN & ISABEL)
31. (TIME: > CUANDO, (30), TODOS LOS AÑOS)

08. Por fin llega el domingo del compleaños.

32. (REFERENCE, DOMINGO, CUMPLEAÑOS)
33. (Llegar, (32))
34. TIME: CUANDO, (32), POR FIN)

APPENDIX 2

A PROPOSITIONAL TEXT BASE USING THE ADAPTED KINTSCH/TURNER & GREENE SYSTEM

Explicit Propositions	Implicit Propositions
01. Martín e Isabel, los gemelos Montes van a cumplir nueve años el domingo.	
1. CONJUNCTION: Martín e Isabel	
2. REFERENCE: Martín e Isabel son gemelos	
3. BASE: Martín e Isabel van a cumplir anos.	
4. MODIFIER/QUANTIFIER: nueve años	
5. TIME: el domingo	
02. Sus papás los llevarán a pasear.	
6.	6. Martín e Isabel tienen papás
7. BASE: Los papás llevarán a Martin e Isabel	7. los = Martín e Isabel
8. PURPOSE: a pasear	
03. Así celebrarán su cumpleaños.	
9.	9. Martín e Isabel cumplen años en su cumpleaños
10. BASE ALTERNATE # 1: Los papás y Martín e Isabel celebrarán el cumpleaños. BASE ALTERNATE # 2: Los papás celebrarán el cumpleaños.	

BASE ALTERNATE # 3: Martín e Isabel celebrarán el cumpleaños.
11. MANNER: así

04. Nos gusta pasearnos ese día, dice Martín.

12. BASE: A Martín e Isabel les gusta pasearse. — 12. nos = Martín e Isabel
13. REFERENCE: ese día es el cumpleaños
14. TIME: (durante) ese día
15. BASE: Martín dice # 12, # 13, # 14.

05. El paseo es siempre una sorpresa.

16. BASE: El paseo es una sorpresa. — 16. Martín dice: el paseo es una sorpresa.
17. TIME: siempre

06. Y siempre nos divertimos mucho, dice Isabel.

18. BASE: Martín e Isabel se divierten. — 18. nos = Martín e Isabel
19. MODIFIER/QUANTIFIER: se divierten mucho
20. TIME: siempre
21. BASE: Isabel dice # 18, # 19, # 20.

07. Todos los año su papá les dice: ¡Fiesta doble! ¡Doble alegría! Ustedes nos han traído doble felicidad a mamá y a mí.

22. MODIFIER/QUANTIFIER: fiesta doble

23. MODIFIER/QUANTIFIER: doble alegría
24. BASE: Martín e Isabel traen felicidad a los papás
25. MODIFIER/QUANTIFIER: felicidad doble
26. BASE: El papá dice # 22, # 23, # 24, # 25 a Martín e Isabel
27. TIME: todos los años

24. nos = los papás = mamá y a mí
ustedes = Martín e Isabel

26. les = Martín e Isabel

08. Por fin llega el domingo de cumpleaños.

28. REFERENCE: el domingo es el cumpleaños
29. BASE: el domingo llega
30. TIME: por fin

APPENDIX 3

ANALYZING PROSE USING THE ADAPTED KINTSCH/TURNER & GREENE SYSTEM

Explicit Propositions

1. Read the entire passage.

2. Divide sentences into clauses. Each clause should contain a minimum of one conjugated verb. When analyzing prose which contains dialogue, divide as follows:
   Mary is my sister, said Elise
   Clause #1 Clause #2

3. Write out all embedded propositions in each clause.

   a. connected subjects (Mary and Tom went to the store.)
   b. modified subjects (Mary, Tom's sister, is here.)

4. Write out all base propositions. There is normally one base proposition per clause. Each base proposition includes an expressed verb.

5. Write out/underline all modifiers of the base proposition

6. Write out/underline all connective propositions between/within clauses.

7. Write out/underline all connective propositions between sentences.

Implicit Propositions

1. Write out all information needed to logically follow the ordered set of expressed propositions. Identify all pronouns, possessives, synonyms, etc.; and all conclusions a reader must reach about the passage which are based on real-world knowledge.

SECOND-LANGUAGE LITERACY

STRATEGIC INTERACTION FROM TEXTS: CONVERTING WRITTEN DISCOURSE INTO SPOKEN CONVERSATION

Robert J. DiPietro

University of Delaware

The relationship of writing to language was put simply but eloquently some 15 years ago when William Moulton (1966:117) defined writing as what we put down on paper to remind us of what we know about language. At the time of Moulton's remark, we had only a vague notion of the extent to which written texts mirror language. In the past, linguists and reading specialists saw written symbols basically as reflections of the code-structure of language. But successive stages of the pragmatic analysis of language have led us into considerations of the functionalism that comes from written documents. Previous papers (see, e.g., Holland and Campbell, 1982) have made it abundantly clear that we do not read all written materials in the same way and for the same purposes. We read for definitions, for directions to assemble things, to find our way through a subway system and to determine departure times for airplanes. When it comes time to fill out a tax return we read material presented according to the conventions of a computer programming language (e.g., "enter X in line A and go to Z in paragraph C").

If writing "reminds" us of what we know about language, we can extend the "reminding" to include what written discourse reveals about our knowledge of the functions of language in conversation. With what follows in this paper, we will take a special kind of written text--the one that attempts to record spoken discourse--and show how it can be reconstituted in speech as an aid in learning a foreign language. The model to be followed is one in which conversational language is viewed multidimensionally (see Di Pietro, 1981a). According to this model, all conversations perform three distinct types of functions in communication: (1) an exchange of information, (2) a negotiation through the deployment of verbal strategies and speech protocols, and (3) an interplay of roles. In order to achieve verisimilitude, the author of a written discourse must address all three functional dimensions and find ways to represent them in the text. The well-known playwright Eugene Ionesco has given a good illustration of what can happen when an author attempts to construct a dramatic dialogue from the one-dimensional sentences of a textbook for students of a foreign language. His Bald Soprano was inspired by such a textbook for English. Here are a few lines from the opening scene:

> Mrs. Smith: There it is nine o'clock. We've eaten the soup, the fish, the potatoes fried in lard, and the English salad. The children have drunk English water. We have dined well this evening. That is because we live in the suburbs of London and because our name is Smith.

Mr. Smith, her partner in this dialogue, does nothing but click his tongue in response. No wonder. Mrs. Smith's lines are little more than a series of declarative sentences strung together without strategic or interactional values. Of course as the play unfolds, Ionesco's genius imparts to the dialogue the fullness of natural conversation. But the initial point is made: strings of sentences do not constitute a natural discourse by themselves. Yet, as Widdowson (1981) has so eloquently pointed out, many FL textbook writers persist in filling their materials with dialogue of precisely this type.

How did the profession of FL teaching arrive at its current demotion of the written text as a teaching aid? If we go back far enough into the last century we will find that reading occupied the first position among the four skills. The so-called "audiolingual" movement of the present century brought with it an almost total reversal in ranking these skills. Speaking, albeit in large groups of students parroting drill instructors, reigned supreme while reading was pushed to the back recesses of the methodology. The expectation was that the ability to read extended literary selections would be taken up at the higher levels of instruction, that is, after the students learned how to speak the language. As a consequence, any reading selections introduced at the lower levels were valued only in so far as they promoted the learning of grammar and vocabulary.

The most recent efforts to reconcile the speaking skill with native-like reading and writing have led to the development of instructional materials based on samples of written texts from real-life, such as bus schedules, menus, advertisements, cartoon captions, and want-ads. The intention is not only to teach the structure of the target language as it is expressed in genuine written samples but also to expose students to how native speakers negotiate transactions which are socially important. As welcome as these new materials are, they fall short of addressing the broad range of language use found in literary texts. The reading of a novel or short story entails the skill to reconstitute the speech acts upon which the text is premised. When successful, the text not only conveys a body of lexical information but also allows for the visualizing of believable transactions and role-characterizations. If we, as foreign-language teachers, wish to make native-like readers of our students, we will have to create in the classroom some analogue to how the native reconstitutes speech from literature. The remainder of this paper outlines a proposal for doing just that.

We must first choose a text. As far as the methodology is concerned, the particular theme and author are unimportant. My preference is for a novel or short story that configures, in some way, interactions among various persons, fictional or real. For purposes of illustration, let us consider what could be done with a currently popular novel, *Raiders of the Lost Ark*, by Campbell Black (1981). Judged by its vocabulary and sentence structure, this novel would be a likely candidate for reading in an intermediate or advanced class of English as a foreign language.

The second chapter of the novel takes place in the office of an SS officer named Eidel. A certain Colonel Dietrich has been called in to receive an order transmitted through Eidel from a higher authority. The order is to enlist the services of an impetuous, but expert, archaeologist to locate the lost ark. The scene is not very long, occupying slightly more than four pages of text, but contains several types of written discourse: (a) descriptive narrative, (b) reported conversation, and (c) direct conversation. As the chapter opens, the reader is placed in an onlooker position _vis-à-vis_ the action of the scene:

> In an office on the Wilhelmstrasse, an officer in the black uniform of the SS--an incongruously petite man named Eidel--was seated behind his desk, staring at the bundles of manila folders stacked neatly in front of him. It was clear to Eidel's visitor, who was named Dietrich, that the small man used the stacks of folders in a compensatory way: they made him feel big, important. (p. 29)

At this point, the reader is given access to Dietrich's thoughts by reporting an internal conversation Dietrich is having with himself:

> It was the same everywhere these days, Dietrich thought. You assess a man and his worth by the amount of paperwork he is able to amass, by the number of rubber stamps he is authorized to use. (p. 29)

Then, the author returns to the narrative technique with which he began:

> Dietrich, who liked to consider himself a man of action, sighed inwardly and looked toward the window, against which a pale brown blind had been drawn. (p. 29)

The narrative style continues as the reader is given a description of Eidel's movements around the room. Some direct conversation is embedded in the narration:

> Eidel rose, stretched on his tiptoes in the manner of a man reaching for a subway strap he knows to be out of range, then walked to the window. 'The Führer has his mind set on obtaining this particular object...'

The remainder of the chapter provides direct conversation, interspersed with commentary on how the protagonists deliver their lines and what their intentions are:

> Eidel, in the manner of a small-town university professor, said, 'We come to the matter of expert knowledge now.'
> 'Indeed,' Dietrich said.
> 'We come to the matter, specifically, of archaeological knowledge.'
> Dietrich said nothing. He saw where this was leading. He saw what was needed of him. (p. 30)

The reader must realize that Dietrich's "indeed" is sandwiched between two utterances by Eidel, or more accurately, it interrupts a single, lengthy utterance by Eidel. The line beginning, "we come to the matter..." is not identified as to who says it, but by labeling the previous line as belonging to Dietrich, the reader knows that it is Eidel who speaks last. Closure is achieved in the conversation by paraphrasing Dietrich's reaction in the narrative style. The next stretch of direct conversation begins with the line "I'm afraid it's beyond my grasp." Dietrich is not credited with the line, but it must be his because he was the last to be mentioned in the previous interchange.

The remainder of the chapter continues with the same mix of direct conversation and descriptive commentary. By reporting through Dietrich alone, the reader is led to identify with him, against Eidel, and made to feel a presence in the scene. In addition, more description is given of Eidel than of Dietrich, leaving the reader to fill in a personal interpretation of the latter protagonist:

> Eidel studied the backs of his hands, thin and pale and yet indelicate, like the hands of someone who has failed in his ambition to be a concert pianist. (p. 31)

As far as the interplay of strategies is concerned, it is Eidel who dominates, as shown by the following:

> 'I can find him,' Dietrich said. 'But I warn you now...'

> 'Don't warn _me_, Colonel.'
> Dietrich felt his throat become dry. This little trumped-up imbecile of a desk clerk. He would have enjoyed throttling him, stuffing those manila folders down his gullet until he choked. 'Very well, I _advise_ you...the Frenchman's price is high.' (p. 31)

How does one read the italicized words? In the case of Eidel's _me_, supposedly we raise our voice. In the case of Dietrich's _advise_, however, the voice probably falls. A non-native reader needs to be shown how this intonation works if the subtlety of this interplay is to be understood. The classroom enactment of a scenario derived from this scene, as will be advocated below, provides an excellent means of demonstrating intonational variations as well as other paralinguistic features.

What we have in this scene is a rather complex use of several rhetorical and stylistic devices--to show attitude, movement, strategy, and role-characterization. The reader is involved first as an onlooker and then is placed in the role of one who must deal with an unsavory individual in a position of power. The author skillfully uses paraphrase in the closing lines of the chapter, to show Dietrich's lack of commitment to Eidel's political persuasion:

> '_Heil Hitler_,' Eidel said, raising his hand, his arm rigid.
> At the door Dietrich answered in the same words. (p. 33)

How to get the EFL/ESL students to follow all of the messages conveyed through the text? My answer is to lead the class to transform the scene into a scenario in which they, themselves, take part. To achieve such a transformation entails an analysis of the underlying plot structure and a search for another setting which would generate a parallel discourse. There are three steps to the procedure.

The First Step. A paraphrase is made, either spoken or written, of the information contained in the original text. In the case under discussion here, it could be something along the lines of the following:

> Eidel enlists the aid of Dietrich in contacting an archaeologist for the purpose of locating a missing relic. Dietrich at first expresses some reluctance at becoming involved in the job. Finally, he submits to Eidel's authority and agrees to take on the responsibility of finding the expert.

Depending on the level of the class, the paraphrase can be made more complex or less. The teacher may prefer to pose a series of questions to verify the students' understanding of the scene. I will make no further elaboration of exercises since this step is already well-known to the profession. Starting with the second step, we enter into the novelty of our procedure.

The Second Step. In taking this step, we become concerned with the transactional value of the scene. We inquire into what tactics were used by the protagonists to advance their positions and we seek to discover how the plot developed. The students are led to construct a "transactional grid," that is, a "game plan" of what transpired. The grid can be laid out in terms of phases, such as the following:

Phase One:	Eidel attempts to force Dietrich to do his bidding by making an appeal to a higher authority. Dietrich counters by claiming to be incompetent (the line: "I'm afraid it's beyond my grasp").
Phase Two:	Eidel counters by reminding Dietrich that he has "connections" which can help him. Dietrich defends himself by refusing to give great value to these "connections" (line: "A matter of debate").
Phase Three:	Eidel attempts to override Dietrich's efforts to deny his capabilities by renewing the appeal to a higher authority (line: "I am here, as you are, to obey a certain important order"). Dietrich shows that

he recognizes the significance of that order and his inability to countermand it (line: "You don't have to remind me of that").

Phase Four: Dietrich is now clearly in the weak position and tries to find excuses for not executing the order (line: "The Frenchman is hard to find"). Eidel is unrelenting in exercising his power-advantage (line: "You can find him...You understand where this order comes from?"). Dietrich acquiesces (line: "I can find him") but attaches a condition (line: "The Frenchman's price is high"). Eidel will not accept the condition (line: "No object"). He then reminds Dietrich of the urgency of the order (line: "It must be done quickly...").

The action of the scene comes to a close with Dietrich persuaded to follow the order but disliking the person who gives it to him. The dismissal entails a reference to the nonverbal aspects of the setting. Dietrich sits before Eidel in silence for a brief period. Then Eidel feigns surprise and says to Dietrich: "Are you still here, Colonel?" This remark causes Dietrich to answer, "I was about to leave."

Having clarified the transactions of the scene, the teacher must now ascertain that the students have some idea of the characters being portrayed and how they interact. Eidel and Dietrich simultaneously play two sets of roles. Socially, they interact as subaltern to superior, with Dietrich cast as the subaltern. Psychologically, however, Dietrich remains defiant. In other words he is the professional soldier who knows how to follow orders but dislikes intensely the bureaucrat who gives him the orders (see Di Pietro, 1981b, for a detailed treatment of role interactions). The second step in our procedure comes to an end when the students understand both the role relationships and the transactions which underlie the scene.

The Third Step. To start this final step, the transactional game plan is applied to a different set of circumstances, i.e., to a different setting. In this way, students' attention is focussed on the creative processes which were undertaken by the author. As they cast about for new settings, they become authors themselves. Some new settings might be built around the following: (1) the office worker who is asked to perform a difficult task relayed to him through an underling who is detested; (2) a football player who is made to do exercises passed down to him from the head coach through an assistant; (3) a teacher who must fill out a report intended for the dean but first must pass it through a departmental chairperson who is not liked. In fitting the language to both the roles and the transactions, the students enter into the creative aspect of discourse. Here are some sample lines:

Junior Executive: You know, the boss wants this contract very badly.
Scientific Executive: I know that.
Junior Executive: It isn't that the boss cares about nuclear weapons, it is the symbolic aspect of serving his country that counts.
Scientific Executive: I understand.
Junior Executive: We really need to recruit that specialist.
Scientific Executive: I don't think I can do it.
Junior Executive: But you know all the top men in your field.
Scientific Executive: Well, I'm not sure about that...
Junior Executive: Look, I'm not going to argue with you. You know where the order comes from. Get that fellow.
Scientific Executive: But he's hard to get. He moves around so much.
Junior Executive: Don't worry about having enough money to attract him.

The class can be broken down into smaller groups to prepare the dialogues. Eventually each group should be given the opportunity to perform their dialogues before the class. Following the presentations, the class may engage in a discussion of the relative merits of each one. They can decide among themselves how successful the conversations were and how closely they followed the transactional game plan of the original episode. Comparisons can be drawn, point by point, with the original. In this way, the students bring a document from writing to realization in spoken discourse. The mental exercise for the students is considerable. The rewards are high, however, since each of the three dimensions of conversational language are addressed: the informational, the transactional and the interactional. The example used in this paper is from English, but equally good illustrations can be obtained from other literatures, as well. My colleague, Dr. Mary Donaldson-Evans, has drawn my attention to a story by Guy de Maupassant which is highly adaptable to the three-step procedure outlined above. In Boule de suif, the setting is the Franco-Prussian War. A group of French people are in flight from the invading enemy. In their haste, they have forgotten to take along some food. Only Boule de suif, a prostitute who has fallen in with the group, has remembered to supply herself with sustenance. At first the group is stand-offish. But when they realize that she has food, they change their bourgeois attitudes about her profession. Eventually she is persuaded to share her provisions with them. But as soon as the food is eaten, they return to their earlier moralizing stance. Since the story has the same admixture of descriptive narrative and direct and reported conversation as Raiders of the Lost Ark, it is open to the same type of pedagogical treatment.

In closing I cannot refrain from expressing a personal conviction that the literary worth of a short story or novel is best appreciated when its readers can somehow share in its creation. For readers who are fluent in the language of the text, a direct access to the imagination is assured. For those who are not fluent, the text presents a linguistic barrier that is often formidable. The generation of spoken discourse based on the text and the dramatizations in the classroom are offered as a means to cross that barrier.

REFERENCES

Black, Campbell, 1981, "Raiders of the Lost Ark," Ballantine, N.Y.

Di Pietro, Robert J., 1981a, The many dimensions of conversational language, _in_: "LACUS Forum 1980." J. Copeland and P. Davis, eds., Hornbeam Press, Columbia, S.C.

Di Pietro, Robert J., 1981b, Discourse and real-life roles in the ESL classroom, TESOL Q., 15, 27-33.

Holland, M. and Campbell, L., 1982, Understanding the language of public documents because formulas don't, _in_: "Linguistics in the Professions." R. J. Di Pietro, ed., Ablex Press, Rutherford, N.J.

Moulton, William G., 1966, "A linguistic guide to language learning," MLA, N.Y.

Widdowson, Henry, 1981, The relevance of literature to language learning, TESOL conference.

WORD FREQUENCY AND CONTEXTUAL RICHNESS IN ESL WORD IDENTIFICATION

Kyle Perkins and Sheila R. Brutten

Southern Illinois University

There has been considerable research conducted on the effects of meaning, frequency, context, and redundancy on word identification in first language (hereafter L1) reading comprehension. The first part of this paper will review <u>some</u> of the major research that has been presented concerning each of these factors.

In two independent pieces of research, Davis (1944) and Spearritt (1972) have demonstrated the role of word meanings as a component of reading comprehension. Smith and Holmes (1973) equate meaning to uncertainty reduction:

> Meaning is related to the reduction of uncertainty, and must be defined pragmatically with respect to the perceiver. Meaning and comprehension may be regarded as reciprocal terms: meaning as the input to an information-processing decision-making system and comprehension is the output (Smith and Holmes 1973:59).

Pearson and Johnson (1978:15) state that "there is good evidence that persons at all levels of development have more difficulty understanding passages of infrequently used rather than frequently used words." However, there are no data offered supporting this claim. Smith (1972:22) notes that "there is nothing in psychology that is more firmly established experimentally and more keenly disputed theoretically than that people need less visual information to identify more common words." Empirical studies by Howes and Solomon (1951) and Miller, Bruner, and Postman (1954) indicate that lower thresholds are required for the identification of high-frequency words than for low-frequency words. The Miller, Bruner, and Postman study showed that subjects can perceive and memorize nonword sequences of letters such as vernalit more readily than sequences having lower approximations to English phonotactics.

Context is a widely-researched factor in reading comprehension. It is generally agreed that a meaningful context enhances word identification and reading comprehension. Tulving and Gold (1963) demonstrated that if the context in which a word is contained placed semantic and syntactic constraints upon it, less visual information would be required for that word's identification, or put another way: the more meaning extracted from the context, the lower the visual recognition thresholds. Morton (1964) found that a highly probable context entailed a lower threshold level for word identification. Pierce and Karlin (1957) noted that it took twice as much time to read unrelated sequences of words (word salad) as meaningful material.

Frequency and context are but two components of a much larger determining factor in reading comprehension - redundancy. In language studies, redundancy can be defined as the degree to which language is predictable when only parts of it are known (Kingston 1977:98). Shannon (1951) was the first researcher to estimate the statistical redundancy of language; he concluded that one word in five could be eliminated from most English texts without serious harm to overall comprehension.

Reading researchers such as Goodman (1973) and Smith (1971) have investigated the effects of sequential redundancy in visual, orthographic, syntactic, and semantic cues in language. There is another kind of redundancy - distributional redundancy. It is a function of the relative number of times each of the alternatives (e.g., letters, words, slots and fillers) that constitute the uncertainty of a particular situation can probably occur (Smith 1971:21).

Cherry (1957) viewed language as a set of constraints

which operate at the semantic and syntactic levels of redundancy. The semantic level of redundancy is concerned with the repetition of denotations and connotations of words while the syntactic level of redundancy entails additions to a text. Function words are usually cited as additions to a text because they are not as strictly necessary to convey the message as are content words.

Weaver (reprinted as Kingston, 1977) discussed the effects of a different kind of constraints - what he called horizontal and vertical constraints on reading:

> If a sentence which contains a deleted word (marked by an underline) is presented to a subject who has been instructed to supply the word which he best thinks fits the blank, the response of the subject may seem to be affected by certain characteristics of the sentence itself. For example, the word class of the deleted word, the position of the deleted word within the sentence, or the amount of context preceding or following the deletion appear to function as constraints which partially act to affect the word a subject supplies from his repertoire. These constraints are spoken of...as horizontal constraints. Just as certain aspects of horizontal constraints operate independently (sequential redundacy, for example), aspects of vertical constraints have been studied most often under the label "association studies" and have been completely divorced from their relationships to natural language. Horizontal and vertical constraints apparently function in "context" reading, for the highly able reader seems to be aware of not only the specific textual setting of a word, but also associates the inputs from previously learned concepts and verbal learnings.... Completion of a deleted language unit at a particular point in a sentence is based upon sequential-syntactical relations at that point (the horizontal constraints), upon the associational relationships exhibited by the distribution of words

> with a privilege of occurring at that point (the vertical constraints), and upon the interaction between the two types of constraint (Kingston 1977:183-184).

Frequency, context, and redundancy directly affect the process of word identification (recognition). Obviously one factor that must be considered in a discussion of word identification in a text is the eye. Jacobson (1951) estimated that the eye can process 4,300,000 bits per second, a bit being defined as the information contained in a binary decision, e.g., a yes or no answer to a question.

Smith (1971) stated that there are two sources of information available for the identification of words:

> One is featural, the visual information available to the eye, and the other is sequential, our knowledge of the way words are constructed. When there is an overlap between featural and sequential information -- when both sources can be used to eliminate some of the same alternatives -- redundancy exists. And because redundancy exists, the skilled reader can trade off between the two sources -- he can make identifications on less featural information because he can make use of his knowledge of sequential constraints (Smith 1971:134).

In another paper, Smith calculated that "constraints in the structure of words make 50% of the visual information redundant, and constraints in the structure of phrases and sentences make 75% of the visual information redundant" (Smith and Holmes 1973:62). It seems to be the case that much of the redundancy in a word is found in its medial and final positions because Broerse and Zwaan (1966) found that the initial letters of a word contain more information calculated in terms of sequential probabilities and consequently contribute more to word identification.

The first half of this paper can be well summarized by the following quote from Pearson and Johnson:

> While the ability to identify words accurately and automatically has a direct effect on comprehension, it must be remembered that comprehension affects word identification.
>
> Factors in the written message affect comprehension. Word frequency, ... sentence complexity, ...thematic information, ...can all be manipulated to increase or decrease comprehension (Pearson and Johnson 1978:20).

Pearson and Studt (1975) conducted a systematic, empirical study in which they manipulated word frequency and contextual richness to determine their effects on children's word identification abilities. They examined the effects of word frequency and contextual richness on word identification. Their subject pool was 36 first-grade and 36 third-grade pupils who were asked to guess a word that fit into a blank space in sentences of varying contextual richness. Pearson and Studt found significant main effects for grade level, word frequency, and context and a frequency-by-context interaction.

This paper reports the results of a study using Pearson and Studt's elicitation sentences on an adult English as a second language (hereafter L2) subject pool. The purpose of the study was to investigate the effects of word frequency and contextual richness on word identification by L2 readers. It is hypothesized that: (1) the mean percentage of a word needed for identification by the Course 2 subject pool (described in a later section) will be significantly higher than the percentage needed by the Course 4 subject pool (also described in a later section); (2) the mean percentage of a word needed for identification of high-frequency words will be significantly lower than for low-frequency words; (3) context will have a significant effect - a lower mean percentage will be needed for the identification of rich context words than will be needed for the identification of poor context words. These hypotheses evolve from Pearson and Studt's findings with L1 child subjects.

PROCEDURES

This study was conducted at the Center for English as

a Second Language (hereafter CESL) at Southern Illinois University. The sample consisted of 36 Course 2 subjects and 36 Course 4 subjects. Each of the Course 2 subjects was matched for sex and nationality with the subjects used for the Course 4 sample. Six languages were represented in each of the groups.

Descriptively, a Course 2 reader is one who reads best when the subject matter is familiar. The reading materials for this level are usually short (under 500 words), and have a limited vocabulary. Students at this level tend to confuse their own thoughts with those of the author and are, therefore, assigned materials that are non-inferential and deal with concrete rather than abstract ideas.

A Course 4 reader is able to read the same general non-technical materials as a native speaking college freshman. The reading materials for this level of student are about the length of a short story, and incorporate a broader vocabulary as well as context clues. Students at this level can cope with both concrete as well as abstract ideas, and are able to distinguish between their own ideas and those of the author.

MATERIALS

The same stimulus materials used by Pearson and Studt were utilized in this study. Pearson and Studt selected the target word pairs from the Thorndike-Lorge (1944) list using three criteria: (a) the members of each pair were reasonably synonymous; (b) within a synonym pair, each member had the same number of letters; (c) each word contained four or more letters. They developed three levels of sentence context for each pair of target words.

1. Rich context was highly definitive and specific.
2. Moderate context was definitive.
3. Poor context level was non-definitive, i.e., any word could fit.

As in the Pearson and Studt study, context levels and frequency levels of the target word across serial position in the 12-item test were balanced. Six text forms were required; each test form had 12 sentences. This is consistent with the procedure used by Pearson and Studt (1975: 92; see Table 1). All subjects received an equal number of items from each context and frequency level. Each test form contained 2 each of the following types: high frequency-poor context; high frequency-moderate context; high frequency-rich context; low frequency-poor context; low frequency-moderate context; low frequency-rich context. Each subject was tested individually. Subjects were told that they were going to be asked to word-guess. They were given one example as practice. The experimenter read each sentence aloud. If the subject correctly supplied the target word, the test progressed to the next item. If the subject guessed incorrectly, the experimenter supplied the first letter of the word, and the subject was asked to guess again. This procedure of supplying letters continued until the correct word was identified or until all letters in the word had been identified by the examiner.

ANALYSIS

An analysis of variance was used to evaluate the percentage of the total word needed to achieve recognition. Since directional hypotheses were made, these data were evaluated using a .01 significance level, one-tailed.

RESULTS AND DISCUSSION

Before any analyses were conducted, the researchers determined that the six different tests were equal in difficulty. The Kruskal-Wallis one-way analysis of variance by ranks indicated the absence of a statistically significant difference among the tests used.

The mean percentage of a word needed by the Course 2 and Course 4 subjects to achieve identification for frequency and context levels is reported in Table 2. Cutting across frequency and context levels, the mean percentage required by the Course 2 subjects for identification was 70.03%; for the Course 4 subjects, it was 63.09%. This difference was significant at the .01 level, $F(1,862)=8.14$. The mean for all high frequency words across course and context levels was 51.88%. For low frequency words, it

Table 1. Materials.

Word Pairs	Context Level	Sentences
HF battle	P	The men just returned from __________.
LF combat	M	The men just marched back from __________.
	R	The soldiers just marched back from the bloody __________.
HF change	P	The children decided to __________ sides.
LF switch	M	Father had to __________ the tire before we we left on our trip.
	R	The football teams __________ sides at half time.
HR hurry	P	I will ride there in a __________.
LF jiffy	M	In order to make the flight, we had to drive to the airport in a __________.
	R	If we run we'll get there in a __________.
HF break	P	Did you __________ my candy cane?
LF crack	M	Which leg did you __________?
	R	Will you __________ the candy cane in two for us?
HF dirty	P	After being outside, many children get __________.
LF muddy	M	Children who play outside often get __________ clothes.
	R	Come in immediately and wash those __________ hands of yours.
HF dangers	P	This story tells of the __________ of the water.
LF hazards	M	One of the __________ of driving is having a blowout.
	R	The sign warned us of the __________ of skating on thin ice.
HF build	P	The men came to work to __________ the school.

Table 1, continued.

Word Pairs	Context Level	Sentences
LF erect	M	The workers started to __________ the school.
	R	The birds gathered materials and began to __________ their nest.
HF song	P	In school today we voted for our favorite __________.
LF tune	M	The choir got to choose its own __________.
	R	In music class we chose to sing a happy __________.
HF pain	P	Mother complained about her __________.
LF ache	M	Do you still have the __________ in your head?
	R	Mother took a pill for the __________ in her broken finger.
HF talk	P	John, take time to __________ with us.
LF chat	M	Let's sit down and __________ over that question.
	R	John wants to __________ with you on the phone.
HF look	P	Will you help me __________ now?
LF peek	M	Will you quietly __________ in and see how the baby is?
	R	John, come over and __________ at what I've got.
HF stop	P	We decided to __________ for a while.
LF halt	M	The men were ordered to __________.
	R	You had better decide to __________ for that red light.
HF = high frequency LF = low frequency		P = poor context M = moderate context R = rich context

Table 2: Cell Means: Percentage of Word Needed for Identification

	High Frequency			Low Frequency			
Subjects	Rich Context	Moderate Context	Poor Context	Rich Context	Moderate Context	Poor Context	
Course 2	42.04	54.54	66.73	82.33	83.97	89.90	$\bar{X}$=70.03
Course 4	35.94	42.13	69.95	76.66	75.45	80.83	$\bar{X}$=63.09
	Overall $\bar{X}$ = 51.88			Overall $\bar{X}$ = 81.52			

was 81.52%. The difference between these means was significant at the .01 level, $F(1,862)=216.75$. The mean for identification of poor context words across course and frequency levels was 76.67%; for moderate context words, 64.11%; for rich context words, 59.24%. There was a significant difference at the .01 level between the three means when considered together, $F(2,861)=23.29$.

In order to determine if these findings were consistent for the L2 subjects coming from different language groups, a post hoc analysis was made to see if there were significant differences in the mean percentage of a word needed for identification by the various language groups represented in the subject pool. The Turkish data were not included because of the small sample size. It was hypothesized that each of the language groups would exhibit higher mean percentages for poor contexts than for moderate and rich contexts and that these differences would be significant. These hypotheses evolve from the fact that each language group would have had different amounts of exposure to English, amounts and types of training, and different amounts of interlanguage interference.

Tables 3 and 5 provide the cell means of the percentage of the word needed by course levels to identify low frequency words. As Table 3 indicates, there was no significant difference in the percentage of word needed for the different language groups. Cutting across the language groups, no difference was found among the three contexts. Put another way, there was no significant difference between the means for rich, moderate, and poor contexts, for each language group when the means are considered together. This finding appears to be due to the depressed variability for all subjects in all contexts. The low frequency words were so novel for all subjects that they needed about 85% of each word supplied for recognition in all contexts. There was no significant difference in the mean percentage needed in each context by the different language groups.

As Table 5 shows, Thai was the only language group in Course 4 to exhibit a significant difference in the mean percentage of word needed when cutting across context levels. Looking vertically at all context levels, we see the effect of contextual richness. There was also a

Table 3: Cell Means: Percentage of Word Needed for Identification.
Course 2 - Low Frequency Words.

Language Group	Rich	Moderate	Poor	F-ratio
Arabic	83.25	93.75	100	.67
Japanese	87.5	87.5	85.12	.03
Malaysian	77.5	61.25	84.25	.90
Spanish	83.45	86.47	90.5	1.27
Thai	83.75	78.5	100	4.12
F-ratio	.20	2.01	1.18	

Note: All F-ratios are non-significant.

Table 4. Cell Means: Percentage of Word Needed for Identification.
Course 2 - High Frequency Words.

Language Group	Rich	Moderate	Poor	F-ratio
Arabic	12.25	22.25	82.25	24.73**
Japanese	39.37	44.75	73.62	3.09
Malaysian	36.41	53.66	75.5	4.95*
Spanish	45.45	60.97	63.26	3.67*
Thai	58.5	33.75	31.0	1.03
F-ratio	1.12	2.15	2.64	

*p < .05

**p < .01

Table 5. Cell Means: Percentage of Word Needed for Identification.
Course 4 - Low Frequency Words.

Language Group	Rich	Moderate	Poor	F-ratio
Arabic	86.16	83.33	95.83	.51
Japanese	66.75	83.37	72.87	.84
Malaysian	61.7	58.6	63.4	.07
Spanish	78.5	78.24	83.64	.62
Thai	95.0	67.5	100.0	5.47*
F-ratio	2.03	1.25	4.86**	

*p < .05
**p < .01

Table 6. Cell Means: Percentage of Words Needed for Identification.
Course 4 - High Frequency Words.

Language Group	Rich	Moderate	Poor	F-ratio
Arabic	24.16	37.66	75.5	3.70*
Japanese	33.12	16.87	69.75	8.80**
Malaysian	35.3	57.4	73.8	3.22
Spanish	37.57	43.40	70.85	15.36**
Thai	58.25	65.0	59.75	
F-ratio	.61	2.47	.30	

*p < .05
**p < .01

significant difference in the mean percentage needed by the different language groups. When a poor context was provided, it is interesting to note that the Malaysians needed 63.4% of a word, while the Thai subjects could not identify a single word.

There is no single explanation that can be offered for these findings, but the answers could lie in the effects of exposure to English, previous training, years of study, unilateral and bilateral constraints in context for the various language groups. On the other hand, the variability of the Thai scores in the other contexts may make these explanations meaningless.

Tables 4 and 6 contain data for the high frequency words. As Table 4 shows, the Course 2 group evidenced significant differences in the mean percentage of word needed across the context levels for the Arab, Malaysian, and Spanish speakers, with striking descriptive differences across context levels for the Arabs. There are significant differences in Table 6 (the Course 4 group) for the Arabic, Japanese, and Spanish groups. For the subjects in both course levels with respect to high frequency words, there was no significant difference in the percentage of word neededed for the different contexts.

The findings indicated that all three variables-- course level, context, and frequency -- affect word identification. The fact that Course 4 subjects could identify the target words, particularly those of high frequency-rich and moderate contexts, with fewer visual cues than Course 2 subjects indicates that the ability to use context is a function of increased attained ESL proficiency. The influences of contextual richness and frequency noted in this study are consonant with the finding of the L1 studies. The low-frequency words were so novel for the L2 subjects that the variability was depressed for all language groups. For the high frequency words, variation in L2 competence, previous training, and the effects of various bilateral and unilateral constraints produced different effects among language groups.

Further research remains to be done with these data. Various regression analyses will be conducted to tease out the interaction effects that frequency, context, and proficiency levels have on the word identification process.

REFERENCES

Broerse, A. C., and Zwaan, E. J., 1966, Informative value of initial letters in the identification of words, JVLVB, 3:441-46.

Cherry, C., 1957, "On Human Communication." MIT, Cambridge.

Davis, F. B., 1944, Fundamental factors of comprehension in reading, Psychometrika, 9:185-97.

Goodman, K. S., 1973, Psycholinguistic universals in the reading process, in: "Psycholinguistics and Reading," F. Smith, Ed., Holt, Rinehart and Winston, N.Y.

Howes, D. H., and Solomon, R. L., 1951, Visual duration threshold as a fraction of word probability, J. Exp. Psych., 41:401-10.

Jacobson, H., 1951, The informational capacity of the human eye, Science, 113:463-71.

Kingston, A. J. (Ed.), 1977, "Toward a Psychology of Reading and Language: Selected Papers of Wendell W. Weaver," U. of Georgia Press, Athens.

Miller, G. A., Bruner, J. S., and Postman, L., 1954, Familiarity of letter sequences and tachistoscopic identification. J. Gen. Psych., 50:129-39.

Morton, J., 1964, The effects of context on the visual duration threshold for words. Br. J. Psych., 55: 165-80.

Pearson, P. D., and Johnson, D. D., 1978, "Teaching Reading Comprehension," Holt, Rinehart and Winston, N.Y.

Pearson, P. D., and Studt, S., 1975, Effects of word frequency and contextual richness of children's word identification abilities, J. Ed. Psych., 67:89-95.

Peirce, J. R., and Karlin, J., 1957, Reading rates and the information rate of a human channel. Bell Sys. Tch. J., 36:497-516.

Shannon, C., 1951, Prediction and entrophy of printed English. Bell Sys. Tch. J., 30:50-64.

Smith, F., 1971, "Understanding Reading." Holt, Rinehart and Winston, N.Y.

Smith, F., and Holmes, D. L., 1973, The independence of letter, word, and meaning identification in reading, in: "Psycholinguistics and Reading," F. Smith, Ed., Holt, Rinehart and Winston, N.Y.

Spearritt, D., 1972, Identification of subskills of reading comprehension by maximum likelihood factor analysis, _Rdng. Rsrch. Q._, 8:92-111.

Thorndike, E. L., and Lorge, I., 1944, "The Teachers Word Book of 30,000 Words," Columbia University, N.Y.

Tulving, E., and Gold, C., 1963, Stimulus information and contextual information as determinants of tachistoscopic recognition of words. _J. Exp. Psych._, 66:319-27.

SOME REFLECTIONS ON ERROR ANALYSIS IN THE SPEECH OF NEAR-BILINGUALS WHOSE MOTHER TONGUE IS ITALIAN

Carlo Fonda

Concordia University

The reflections I would like to submit are the result of a study I have conducted to see which errors, if any, could be attributed to a direct interference of the mother tongue (Italian) in the learning process of a foreign language (English). The field of error-analysis in foreign language acquisition being a vast one, I have confined my study to an analysis of syntactic and phonetic errors which tend to become fossilized, more particularly to those errors which, because of their extrinsic pecularities, seldom fail to distinguish the speaker of English whose mother tongue is Italian from other anglophones. The informants I have used for this investigation (six males and six females) are all mature people between the ages of 26 to 65 who came to Canada at an adult age, after acquiring their formal education in Italy. Their cultural background is fairly homogeneous: evenly distributed between white and blue collar workers, they were all born and grew up in either central or southern Italy.

Among the many errors that a learner of English is bound to make, a faulty pronunciation of English obstruents is most conspicuous. What is not clear, however, is as to whether this is the result of interference of the mother tongue or of some other cultural, educational, psychological, physiological factor. From a phonological point of view, English and Italian share the same stops (k, p, t, g, b, d) although in English the spectrum of the allophones is, in each instance, much wider than in Italian. It is this feature of the English occlusives which represents a serious difficulty for the near-bilingual, for it involves not only the articulation of these sounds but also their perception. English discriminates its stops or occlusives between aspirates and unaspirates, exploded and unexploded, glottals, taps and so on. Conversely, in Italian, stops, whether voiced or voiceless, do not offer such a gamut of phonetic variations. Indeed, their striking characteristic is that they are always exploded. This, because of Italian syllabication which demands that all syllables be always stressed, although one syllable is more stressed than the others (see *vacca* pronounced /vaeh-kae/, *gigante* /ǰi-gáen-te/. As a result, co-articulation, syllabicity, consonantal and vowel coloring, nasal and lateral plosion and the like, which play such an important role in English pronunciation, are of no consequence in Italian. It suffices to mention that slurred vowels or consonants such as in American r-less dialects simply do not exist in Italian, for also unstressed vowels, although pronounced more rapidly than the stressed ones, keep their pure sound. Should we lend a careful ear to the anomalies of the so-called Italian accent of near-bilinguals, we would quickly discover that, among the most striking, there is an indiscriminate, universal use of exploded stops, that brings about a considerable phonetic shift, particularly in the case of words ending with a stop (for example, monosyllabic *big* shifts into bisyllabic /bih⊥ga/, *spot* into /spah⊥ta/). Such shifts of course alter not only the phonetic quality of the stops involved, but the phonological structure of the word itself, as we have seen in the two examples above. In English too, of course, stops in word final position may be either exploded or unexploded. The point is, however, that in the mouth of the anglophone the difference between the two is marked, as in the case of voicing, by the length of the preceding vowel rather than by the presence of a short vowel-like sound after the exploded stop which with most speakers is hardly audible.

This indiscriminate use of exploded stops is responsible for other phonetic changes, some of the most striking being the loss of aspiration of all stops in syllable initial position; the lack of lateral plosion in words such as *bottle*/ba?l/, *little*/li?l/, which brings about a different syllabication as witnessed by /bah-tal/ and /lih-tal/, thus replacing the glottals of English with apico-alveolar /t/; the absence of nasal plosion and the resulting loss of syllabicity in words such as *sudden*

/sadn̩/, kitten /ki?n̩/, leaden /ledn̩/, which the near-bilingual pronounces as /sah-ˈdan/, /kih-ˈtan/ and /le-dan/. These peculiarities in the pronunciation of English stops by the near-bilingual seem to suggest that the negative transfer that takes place in these instances does not operate at the level of the individual phoneme as, to quote one example, the replacement of aspirates with unaspirates, but it involves the entire syllabic system. What appears to support this is the reverse process whereby English words, once adopted by the near-bilingual as part of his own Italian lexicon, undergo exactly the same process of phonetic adaptation: tap/taeh-ˈpa, /elevator /a-li-veh-tae/, plumber /plam-bye-re/, garbage /gae-rae bih-ˈča/, forget /far-gehˈtae-re/. Not without humour, Professor Cro of Toronto University has suggested that the use of such phonetically re-structured loan-words from English has brought into existence a new language which he called Italese or Italish. Further evidence that the near-bilingual is transferring the syllabic system of his mother tongue rather than individual phonemes seems to be supported by the peculiar treatment of English inter-vocalic/s/. In Italian, voiceless/s/ in intervocalic position shifts into voiced /z/. It is not so in English where the shift is not positional, as witnessed by pose /powz/, and result /rizalt/, where intervocalic /z/ coexists with intervocalic /s/ as in case /keys/ and base /beys/. As a result, the near-bilingual is always at a loss before these English alternations. His own syllabic system being of no avail in these instances, he perceives the alternation s/z as arbitrary and subjective. The phonetic alternations operated by my informants seem to confirm this by their need to regularize the occurrence of these unpredictable English phonemes. Their mother tongue being of no avail in this case, they produce some remarkable rules of their own. For example, six of my twelve informants would alternate /s/ and /z/ quite capriciously, sometimes pronouncing case and base as /keys/ /beys/ and sometimes as /keyz/ and /beyz/; four would alternate /z/ and /s/ by using the former in simple words and the latter in compounds as follows: /keyz/ /briyfkeys/ /beyz/ /beysbol/, and two operated quite a complex transfer in the sense that when they were speaking English intervocalic /s/ would shift into /z/, and when they were speaking French no such shift would take place. In this regard, I would like to point out that all my informants speak reasonably good French and, finally, that the failure to operate the shift of intervocalic /s/ into /z/ in French is not an uncommon mistake among Italian trilinguals (Italian-English-French) in Quebec. As additional evidence that the Italian near-bilingual attempts to cope with the complexities of English phonetics by transferring into English the syllabic system of his mother tongue can be found in the manner in which he bypasses the difficult pronounciation of English dorso-velar /ŋ/. English has three nasals n, m, ŋ. Of these, apico-alveolar /n/ has a velar allophone /ṇ/ as in con-globe /kaṇ-glowb/. Italian has only two nasals /n/ and /m/. Of these, Italian /n/, like its English counterpart, has a velar allophone /ṇ/ as in ven-go, fun-go, con-glo-ba-re. It should be noted that in these instances, Italian syllabication coincides with English as far as sequence /ng/ is concerned. This feature allows the near-bilingual to cope quite successfully with the difficult pronounciation of English /ŋ/ either by using velar /ṇ/, as in /bay-liŋ-gual/ pronounced /bay-liṇ-gual/, or by alternating velar /ṇ/ with apico-alveolar /n/ in syllable final position, in words such as sing /siŋ/ prounounced rarely as /sin/ and quite often either as /siṇ/ or as /siṇga/.

Among syntactic errors committed by near-bilinguals, there are some which are obvious negative transfers of syntagmatic forms from the mother tongue. This is the case of the speaker of English who says I have sixty years and my wife has fifty. Other syntactic errors, however, are more complex and it is not always easy to establish as to whether they are the product of negative transfer or oversimplification or analogy. A typical error committed by Italian as well as Québec French near-bilinguals consists in the failure to discriminate between the relational prepositions marking place in and place to, as follows:

ITALIAN	Ogni anno andiamo in un paese diverso.
FRENCH	Tous les ans nous allons dans un différent pays.
ENGLISH	Every year we go in a different country.
ITALIAN	L'anno scorso siamo andati nella Cina di Mao.
FRENCH	L'année dernière nous sommes allés dans la Chine de Mao.
ENGLISH	Last year we went in Mao's China.
ITALIAN	Mio padre è ritornato a Montreal nel 1970.
FRENCH	Mon pere est rentré à Montréal en 1970.

<u>ENGLISH</u> My father returned <u>in</u> Montreal in 1970.
<u>ITALIAN</u> Vado <u>in</u> Italia ogni due anni.
<u>FRENCH</u> Je vais <u>en</u> Italie tous les deux ans.
<u>ENGLISH</u> I go <u>in</u> Italy every two years.
<u>ITALIAN</u> I miei genitori volevano emigrare <u>in</u> Canada molti anni fa.
<u>FRENCH</u> Mes parents voulaient émigrer <u>au</u> Canada il y a longtemps.
<u>ENGLISH</u> My parents wanted to move <u>in</u> Canada many years ago.

This intriguing kind of error has attracted the attention of several linguists. Jack C. Richards (1971) flatly rejects the presence of a negative transfer. According to him, errors of this kind are the product of analogy, as proven by the fact that while in all these instances, English systematically requires the same preposition <u>to</u>, French is totally inconsistent with its variety of <u>dans</u>, <u>en</u>, <u>au</u>, <u>à</u>, and so are other Romance languages. (See above Italian with its variety of <u>in</u>, <u>nella</u>, <u>a</u>.) Ronald Sheen (1980) argues to the effect that such errors are the result of both analogy or oversimplification and negative transfer:

> I would suggest that both factors are involved. I maintain that the basic cause of the error is the fact that as far as prepositions are concerned, French does not differentiate between stative and directional verbs. Thus one can say 'Je suis à Québec' and 'Je vais à Québec,' whereas in English one must change 'at' to 'to' when one switches from a stative to a directional verb. This causes the French speaking student learning English to extend his learning of such forms as 'I live in Québec' to 'I am going to Québec.' Thus NT and overgeneralization are contributing factors (Sheen, 1980:195).

It is clear that what Sheen means by negative transfer as a contributing factor is the lack of discrimination between stative and directional verbs in both French and Italian and the ensuing error which the near-bilingual (French or Italian) makes by using the same preposition <u>in</u> with both verb <u>to be in</u> and verb <u>to go to</u>, made on the analogy of French être à, aller à and/or Italian essere a, andare a. Without denying the validity of the argumentations of my learned colleagues, I am inclined to believe that in these instances, the Romance-speaking near-bilingual's error does not consist in a negative transfer of a syntactic relational preposition whose function he then extends to all English verbs either stative or directional through analogy, but in the fact that he is transferring the meaning of this preposition which in Italian, like in French but not in English, is both stative and directional. The error, I submit, rests on the similarity of form and meaning between Romance stative/directional in, en and English stative in and on the contiguity of form and meaning with English directional into. Romance historical grammar seems to support our contention here where Latin stative/directional in retains its meaning and coexists with directional Latin intus, vulgar Latin deintus, which will give Old French enz, denz, up to Modern French dedans, dans.

In the same above-quoted article, Professor Sheen classifies errors such as "I am here since two days" as the result of a direct transfer of an element or rule from the mother tongue:

> Errors of this type...clearly demonstrate the necessity for a more precise definition of NT which reflects more faithfully its actual functioning. I would suggest that more precision might be attained by including in the classification NT two distinct types: one, the type of NT seemingly manifested in the direct transfer of an element or rule from the mother tongue or some other foreign language as, for example, ... 'I am here since two days,' 'I only got two good notes from that professor' committed by French-speakers and resulting respectively from the direct influence of... 'Je suis ici depuis deux jours' and 'Je n'ai eu que deux bonnes notes de ce professeur' (Sheen, 1980: 195).

As to the error in "I only got two good notes ...," I believe that Professor Sheen is wrong in assuming that the French student is transferring, into English, lexical element *note* from his mother tongue. This, he does not need to do as the same word exists in both English and French. The error, I believe, consists in the fact that the speaker, in this instance, is transferring the meaning of French *note* into English word *note*. As to "I *am* here *since* two days," the error has much deeper roots than we suspect. Among its verbal categories, English includes the category of aspect that indicates continuing action or state as *he is doing*, *he has been sick since yesterday*. In Romance languages, aspect as a verbal category does not exist. In its stead, other cumbersome devices may be used as, for example, the periphrastic forms of French *être en train de* or colloquial *être après* or of Italian *stare per*. Conversely, Romance tense categories can be used with wider connotation than in English as in the following:

PRESENT (TENSE CATEGORY)		
French	Il travaille dans la cave.	ASPECT
Italian	Lavora in cantina.	PRESENT PROGRESSIVE
English	-----------------	He is working in the basement.

PRESENT (ASPECT CATEGORY)		PRESENT PERIPHRASTIC
French	-----------------	Je suis en train de te parler.
Italian	-----------------	Ti sto parlando.
English	I am speaking to you.	

PRESENT (NOMIC)	
French	Au Québec on parle francais.
Italian	In Québec si parla francese.
English	In Québec they speak French.

PRESENT (EXTENDED)[1]		
French	Je parle français depuis la fin de la guerre.	
Italian	Parlo francese dalla fine guerra.	
English	-----------------	ASPECT PRESENT PERFECT I have spoken French since the end of the war.

I believe that in the case of errors such as "I *am* here *since* two days," we are certainly in the presence of a negative transfer as suggested by Sheen, but the error does not consist in a transfer of rule or element, but in a transfer of meaning. The use of adverb since as well as the widespread occurrence of errors of this kind by near-bilinguals point out, unequivocally I believe, to a transfer of meaning of the verbal categories of French and Italian into English.

NOTES

[1]By present (extended) I mean, in addition to the above, other usages of the present tense such as, for example, to mark a near future: French "Attendez-moi, je viens," or Italian "Aspettatemi, vengo subito" (Wait for me, I'm coming), a recent past: French "il sort à l'instant" (he just left).

REFERENCES

Richards, Jack C., 1971, Error analysis and second language strategy, Lang. Sci, 17:12-22.

Sheen, Ronald, 1980, The importance of negative transfer in the speech of near-bilinguals, Langue et ling., 6: 191-214.

NON-NATIVE SPEAKERS OF ENGLISH AND THEIR COMPOSITION ABILITIES: A REVIEW AND ANALYSIS

Judith D. Kaplan and Eduarda M. G. Palhinha

Georgetown University

INTRODUCTION

Writing is a creative process that requires not only the mechanical skills that transfer language forms to paper, but also the linguistic and cognitive skills which underlie the production of these language forms. Linguistic skills for the writer include the knowledge of and ability to manipulate language to produce the idea units that represent that which a given individual wishes to express. Cognitive skills for the writer include patterns of logic and rhetoric -- patterns which shape idea units both in the speaker's mind and in their production and, in addition, patterns whose acquisition is far given in the process of learning a second language.

Our interest in the acquisition of writing skills by second language learners arose out of first-hand knowledge of the problems many non-native speakers of English encounter when writing compositions or answering essay-type exam questions in English. To determine possible sources for the writing problems of non-native English speaking college students, we decided to conduct a survey and ascertain their attitudes about their English language education. As we began our search of the literature we found our interest was far from novel in the field of second language literacy. Underlying all the literature is, as Anderson and Wrase (1976:1) state, the responsibility of universities that admit foreign students "...either to require (and enforce) a certain level of English proficiency or to provide the means for the student to get the special training in English which he needs to survive -- and succeed -- in school." Pavelich (1978), Dubois (1976), Henner-Stanchina (1980), Pytlik (1978), Bruder and Furey (1979), Weissberg and Buker (1978), and Kobler (1976) are among the many scholars who have discussed the need for special writing courses for non-native English speaking students and have suggested educational programs designed to combat any deficiencies in composition skills. According to Frestedt and Sanchez (1980), these programs should not be aimed at segregating foreign students, but they must be designed to meet their special needs. In addition, the programs should not aim to "standardize" the writing of these students. Instead, as the authors suggest, the programs

> ...should emphasize cultural and linguistic options in writing in relation to an audience. They should work toward enabling the student to discern and utilize language alternatives and to develop expressive abilities capable of reflecting well each individual's diverse cultural and linguistic identity (Frestedt and Sanchez, 1980:16).

Composition problems that are due to the differing phonological, grammatical, syntactic, and semantic structures of an individual's native and second languages are typically addressed in the second language classroom. However, as Taylor (1981:10) suggests, in dealing with a "process [that] is only partially linguistic, ...a writer also needs to master the essentially nonlinguistic intellectual and cognitive skills which underlie writing." More than a visual representation of thought, writing, as a "creative discovery procedure characterized by the dynamic interplay of content and language" (Taylor, 1981:6), reflects and facilitates thought.

Concern with writing as a process demanding the interplay of language and thought necessarily involves concern with the context in which a written message is presented. Long ago, Aristotle assigned a tripartite composition to spoken messages. In his terms, the context of any speech may be understood as consisting of the speaker, the subject on which he speaks, and the audience he is addressing (Rhetoric I.3). We need not struggle, of course, to assign this tripartite distinction to written messages as well. In doing so, we in turn realize that whether attempting to persuade, inform, instruct, describe, or aesthetically please, all oral and written language cannot progress without an awareness of the different ways in which logical and rhetorical patterns and structures may combine in accordance with the situation in which a message is framed.

The rules of rhetoric aid in the formation of a literate tradition -- a tradition from which the good writer is said to start off but not follow (Cox 1947). According to Cox (1947:3), "... the significance of a writer is in the unpredictable pattern made by the opposing pull and tug of wayward impulse." This impulse is reflective of point of view - the factor underlying the speaker/writer's individual discourse style. To Grierson (1945:23-24), style "...bears the mark of [an individual's] intellectual and moral constitution." To Cox (1947:48), style "... is the way a man takes himself." Finally, to Valéry,

> ...style signifies the manner in which a man expresses himself, regardless of what he expresses, and it is held to reveal his nature, quite apart from his actual thought - for thought has no style. It is in the act of expression that the man distinguishes himself... Thus what makes the style is not merely the mind applied to a particular action; it is the whole of a living system expanded, imprinted, and made recognizable in expression (Valéry, 1966:18).

For the foreigner attempting to learn a language, attempting to gain all the language and culture-specific rules for communication, the matter of style becomes a common, but too often unrecognized, problem. In learning a second language, individuals must acquire the rhetorical traditions on which the stylistic use of the language is based and the logical patterns around which these traditions take shape. In defining rhetoric as "a mode of thinking or a mode of 'finding all available means' for the achievement of a designated end," Oliver (1965:x-xi) concerns himself with those activities that precede vocalization and composition in the human mind. Similarly, Baker, in discussing second language teaching materials, notes that "the highest function of language is not communicative but conceptual" (Baker, 1976:7) - i.e., the means by and manner in which the speaker addresses her/himself. The 1966 Conference on College Composition and Communication also addressed the cognitive aspects of rhetoric in defining rhetoric as "...the act of discovering and choosing from the available means of developing subject matter, organizing the results, and expressing them so that the whole composition will affect the writer's purpose in his chosen audience" (Workshop Reports, 1966:176). With rhetoric grounded in the cultural identity of an individual or group, logic, "...the basis of rhetoric, is [necessarily] evolved out of a culture" (Kaplan 1981:2).

To gain a fuller understanding of the problems inherent in the teaching of composition skills to and the development of these skills in non-native speakers, it is helpful to discuss some of the vast amount of research that has been undertaken. This discussion will focus on (1) the differences between written and spoken language, (2) the question of transfer between spoken and written language skills, (3) the question of transfer between native and second language written and spoken language skills, (4) existing methods of ESL composition instruction, and (5) the place of reading and the importance of cultural awareness in composition instruction.

WRITTEN AND SPOKEN LANGUAGE

Recent characterizations of written language have been set in the comparison of written language to oral language (see Chafe, 1979; Goody, 1977; Tannen, 1980; Keenan, 1979). According to these comparative analyses, oral language tends to be context-bound, multi-channeled, involved, formulaic, concrete, and non-autonomous, whereas written language tends to be decontextualized, integrated, depersonalized, analytic, abstract, and autonomous. Further characterizations have stressed that an individual is typically more concerned with the form of the product when writing than when speaking. Writing has also been characterized as an anchor of performance for language and thought as it preserves ideas over time while leaving them readily available for reflection, revision, and transmission (Goody, 1977). Yet when concerned with writing, one is not concerned with the product (or composition) alone. With its inescapable ties to logic, writing must also be separated into its mechanics (spelling, punctuation, capitalization, etc.) and its content (creativity, tone, organization, coherence, style, etc.).

This specification is beneficial for the understanding of the writing process, but may prove problematic if over-stressed in its teaching. As Shuy (1976:12) points out, "the gestalt of reading and writing will probably not be measured by questions which address isolated component skills at various stages in the acquisition of these gestalts... One should not confuse component skills with the gestalt." Similarly, in discussing writing assessment, Myers (1980) promotes holistic scoring and stresses that "the whole of a piece of writing is greater than the sum of its parts" (Myers, 1980:1).

Similar arguments may no doubt be advanced for the gestalt of speaking. However, because oral language skills are typically acquired before written language skills in both one's native and second language, and typically with less obvious difficulties and a lesser degree of overt learning, the components of speaking may need not be as actively stressed. (We may say, in Krashen's (1976) terms, that the oral language is acquired while the written language must be learned.) Therefore, the point to remember here is that although speaking and writing may share some obvious similarities, differences do exist which define their acquisition in both process and product.

TRANSFER OF SPOKEN AND WRITTEN LANGUAGE SKILLS

The preceding discussion has illustrated that, as Stubbs (1980) concludes, writing is not

> merely a visual representation of spoken language [or]...simply a way of reordering speech... [I]t has its own distinctive forms and functions. Nor is writing merely parasitic: for once a writing system exists, it takes on something of a life of its own, becomes partly independent of speech, and it is then often writing which influences speech, rather than the reverse (Stubbs, 1980: 23).

With this in mind, the difficulties inherent in teaching writing are even more apparent. Without the visible audience (present except perhaps during broadcasting, recording, thinking aloud, etc.) of the spoken message providing encouragement and showing interest, individuals engaged in writing must be taught (as Aristotle so long ago noted) to recognize and address both a purpose and an audience.

Because "writing skills do not transfer automatically from speaking skills, ...students who are explicitly taught to write, write better than those who are not" (Paulston, 1972:36). This sentiment is echoed by Ingram (1973), who states that the fact that students learn precisely what they are taught indicates that one's competence in written language is not assured by concentration on spoken language. In addition, competence in some written language skills does not guarantee competence in all such skills. Kaplan (1967) notes that

> because a student has learned to control the phonology and the syntax of a second language, it is not fair to assume that he is able to write that language. (It is, in fact, 'a fallacy of some repute' (Kaplan 1966:3).) Any language has to be learned as an entity whose only logic is internal. The student needs to be taught the 'logic' which is reflected in the rhetoric in the same way that he has had to learn the 'logic' reflected in the grammatical patterns (Kaplan, 1967:16).

If oral language skills are not directly transferrable to one's ability in written language, just how does an individual acquire the ability to compose and how may second language programs best be organized to aid in this acquisition process? We may begin our answer with a look at Shuy's (1981) discussion of the developmental process of language acquisition. His discussion is based in part on Joos' (1961) designation of five language styles -- frozen, formal, consultative, casual, and intimate. Shuy states that for spoken language, the sequence of acquisition from birth to adulthood is from the intimate end of the spectrum to the formal end. The individual progresses from conversation among friends and family to speaking alone before an audience. In other words, the individual, as he or she develops physically and cognitively, develops also in his/her ability to manipulate language. However, with written language the sequence is not quite so developmental. In fact, Shuy (1981) points out that "initial instruction and experience in writing requires students to begin writing at the formal level without having passed through the casual and consultative stages which prepare them for the monologuing ability to communicate with an unspecified and non-responsive audience" (Shuy, 1981:6).

Arapoff (1969) also addresses the transfer of linguistic and psycholinguistic abilities between spoken and written language within a developmental framework. She begins her argument by stating that " ...competence in the spoken language has little to do with competence in the written one" (Arapoff, 1969:298). Just as every native speaker is not necessarily a "native writer" at the same time, a second language learner, having gained some degree of competency in the spoken skills of that language, will not necessarily have the same degree of competency in the written skills of that language. Many individuals are proficient in the grammatical skills of their native language, yet their writing reflects anything but proficiency. If some native speakers lack the ability to write competently in their native language, "it therefore seems that we are on the wrong track in expecting foreign students to learn to write by learning to produce grammatically correct sentences when native speakers don't seem to learn it that way" (Arapoff, 1969;298).

Arapoff suggests that individuals learn grammar and the skills for writing in a similar way - i.e., through a process of discovering and internalizing rules followed by a process of transforming these rules as illustrated in their use of language. It is a process in which communicative competence precedes communicative performance. With spoken language, sentences are heard in context and fluency is demonstrated by one's "ability to respond appropriately within a framework of a discourse or conversation" (Arapoff, 1969:299). Before one can demonstrate fluency in written language, he or she must have input similar to that which the speaker receives but different enough to provide him/her with an understanding of how written forms combine to form a coherent discourse. Therefore, as Arapoff recommends, "reading must play as important a role in a writing course as listening does in an oral production one" (Arapoff, 1969:299).

We need not delve too deeply for the implications research in the transfer and development of oral and written language skills brings to second language teaching. If as Stubbs, Paulston, and Ingram indicate, spoken language cannot be expected to transfer to and aid writing skills and if, as Shuy and Arapoff indicate, there are developmental sequences for the acquisition of oral and written skills, it seems only fitting that oral language skills and written skills be taught and acquired simultaneously. According to Taylor (1976), because the skills that go into writing involve more than linguistic ability and, more specifically, require intellectual and logical skills, "there is no theoretically sound reason to wait for a student to acquire advanced English proficiency before starting composition training" (Taylor, 1976:309). Taylor insists that because writing requires practice, the sooner students are exposed to free composition exercises, the sooner they will learn to write. The ESL composition program he discusses is said to be highly effective when coordinated with grammatical instruction. Similarly, in the beginning second language courses they organized at CRAPEL, Cambalo, et. al. (1976) sought to teach their students to read and write as they were learning to understand and speak.

Because linguistic abilities alone do not provide an adequate basis for writing, "specific training in composition skills and rhetoric is also required. These skills can be taught to low level ESL students because they are largely logical and do not necessitate advanced linguistic abilities" (Taylor 1976-77:73). As Taylor (1981) states,

> ...writing as a process is only partially linguistic. Regardless of language proficiency, a writer also needs to master the essentially non-linguistic intellectual and cognitive skills which underlie writing... Once students are accepted into academic programs, they need to start producing content in writing well before we may feel their language is ready (Taylor, 1981:10).

NATIVE TO SECOND LANGUAGE TRANSFER

The above discussion has stressed that although skilled in the grammatical intricacies of a given language, many individuals may still lack the skills necessary for written proficiency in that language. However, even when a high degree of written proficiency is demonstrated by an individual in his/her native language, this does not guarantee an equal level of proficiency in his/her second language. While native speakers must make choices about content, organization, vocabulary, and structure when writing, second language learners must do this plus deal with a new language and its associated logical thought patterns. According to Raimes (1979),

> ...students who are not skilled readers and writers in their first language have to learn not only a new language but new basic skills as well. The students who are fully literate come to English composition armed with the skills of reading and writing, but their strategies, based on familiarity with the rhetorical structure of the prose of their first language, are not necessarily directly transferable to the rhetorical structure of English (Raimes, 1979;3).

INSTRUCTIONAL METHODS FOR ESL COMPOSITION

Numerous articles and texts have presented guides and plans for ESL composition training. These works deal with the "mechanics" of writing (Blanton, 1981; Cooper, 1980), rhetorical and cognitive skills (Shwabe, 1978; Kaplan, 1966), assessment (Myers, 1980; EPT, 1977), suggestions for composition activities (Blot and Davidson, 1980; Rivers and Temperly, 1978; Buckingham and Pech, 1976; Paulston and Bruder, 1976), or offer sample programs (Kessler, 1974; Bruder and Furey, 1979). Still others provide lists and/or evaluations of texts related to ESL composition (van Schaik, 1978; Macha and Angelis, 1976).

Van Schaik's comparison of university level ESL and English composition textbooks suggests, in fact, that ESL students may not be receiving composition instruction necessary for survival in American universities. Valette (1973) agrees and places the blame for the language learner's failure to achieve communicative competence on the second language teacher. In failing to present situations as composition topics that are of interest to the student, the instructor fails to teach and test for communicative competence. The Rouchette Plan, as discussed by Aup'ecle (1973), is also concerned with encouraging students to set a direction for their writing. The Plan recommends that speaking and writing tasks be set in real life situations so as to increase the student's motivation to communicate. Similarly, Raimes (1979) suggests that in order to keep students interested in learning how to write, teachers must present topics that will motivate each student toward his/her individual concerns and thereby ease the problem of finding a purpose.

While writing about personal interests may induce students to create, organize, and write, over-emphasis on such activities does not provide practice in all of the writing needs demanded at the college level. According to J. F. Green, it is expository writing that is typically required for college level courses, while "imaginative, narrative, or informal personal writing is rarely required" (in Henner-Stanchina, 1980:66). Henner-Stanchina adds that

> [t]his emphasis [on descriptive and narrative writing], then, must be construed as a failure to recognize learner's needs and prepare them adequately for the demands of college writing [,] as a babying tendency in the nature of the tasks we expect learners to be able to perform and, as such, as a perpetuation of the gap that now exists between ESL writing and writing for a real university situation (Henner-Stanchina, 1980:60).

This again echoes van Schaik's original concern that ESL students are not obtaining adequate training in composition. Faced with the realization that it is a "major task in teaching literacy to get [students] to understand the purpose and conventions of written language" (Stubbs 1980:115), we are also faced with a decision as to what course need be taken if students are ever to reach this goal. Perhaps here too the educator's framework is to be a developmental one as students' interests are initially aroused with suggested topics of personal concern and, later, after confidence and ability have increased, directed toward increasingly more technical and expository writing styles.

THE PLACE OF READING AND CULTURAL AWARENESS IN COMPOSITION INSTRUCTION

Reading

As previously mentioned, the teaching of composition need not, and indeed should not, be limited to the teaching of writing skills. As the Conference on College Composition and Communication (Workshop Reports, 1966) points out, literature offers a valuable component to composition instruction. In providing the language learner with an awareness of writing styles, literature also provides examples of structure, style, and the use of rhetorical devices. In so doing, literature serves as a "...controlling world of experience accessible to each student in the class as well as to the instructor" (Workshop Reports, 1966:177). Expanding on this notion, Taylor (1981) credits reading with providing exposure to content and

> ...a variety of culturally appropriate rhetorical and stylistic writing options, organizational patterns, and patterns of logic and support. [In addition, reading] fosters vocabulary growth and the acquisition of syntax, all in context. Developing personal intuitions about what good writing looks like through reading, and then practicing and applying those intuitions in writing is probably the best way for a student to become a self-reliant writer (Taylor, 1981:12).

Reading is not only valuable for the patterns to which it introduces language learners but also for the intellectual activity it encourages. According to Raimes (1978:13), learning how to locate the main idea when reading a given passage may help the language learner organize his/her thoughts as he or she constructs a main idea for a written passage.

CULTURAL AWARENESS

Because written communicative competence in one's second language entails the acquisition of the logical and rhetorical patterns of that language, it is essential that the language learner be exposed to all levels and degrees of cultural knowledge that are shared by the native speakers of that language. To help students address both their subject and their audience in a manner which guarantees the message fits the context, composition instructors need to acquire and practice multicultural teaching strategies. For example, Rodrigues (1977) suggests that before attempting to teach Spanish-speaking Mexican-Americans compositional English, it is highly advisable that the instructor be aware of the learning styles that differentiate these individuals from English-speaking Anglo-Americans. Each cultural group typically operates within a specific culturally-determined style which Rodrigues has labeled field-independent for the Anglo-Americans and field-dependent for the Mexican-Americans. According to Rodrigues, their field-dependency tends to cause Mexican-Americans to rely more greatly on their instructor's support than do field-independent Anglo-Americans.

Similar cultural differences were identified by Frestedt and Sanchez (1980) and Angioletti (1979) in their research on Navajo and Chinese, respectively, in ESL programs. Frestedt and Sanchez stress that in gaining a knowledge of Navajo language and the conventions of Navajo world view, one becomes able to compare linguistic and cultural aspects of Navajo with those of English and, therefore, possibly to explain the English writing language problems of Navajo students. Angioletti points out that aside from the problems Chinese students of English have with the mechanics of English, such as left-to-right orientation, capitalization, and punctuation, their cultural background encourages them to remain quiet in the classroom and to depend greatly upon group efforts in classroom activities. These cultural tendencies no doubt reflect in the students' stylistic approaches to oral and written language activities.

Arnow (1977) also addresses the need for cultural awareness programs for individuals learning a second language. She states that Spanish-speaking migrant children in the United States have special physical and social needs which may only be met by programs that concentrate not only on academic needs and classroom activities, but also on family and community interaction patterns. These programs aid educators in pinpointing the different learning strategies children bring with them to their bilingual/ESL programs.

When cultural awareness programs are combined with second language composition training, the difficult road leading to the acquisition of non-native logical patterns and rhetorical structures is more easily traversed. Kaplan (1966) suggests that individuals learning to write in a second language be exposed to a contrastive analysis of rhetorical patterns such as the one he presents for English, Russian, and the Semitic, Oriental, and Romance languages. Exposure to these patterns aims at enabling the individual to become aware of and eventually overcome (blind) dependence on native rhetorical constraints. According to Kaplan (1966), it is due to the fact that the non-native "student is employing a rhetoric and a sequence of thought which violate the expectations of the native reader" (Kaplan, 1966:4) that the student's written work is so often judged inappropriate.

As cross-cultural awareness is a goal towards which both students and teachers must strive, contrastive-type programs such as those discussed by these and other researchers must be given a definite place in all ESL/bilingual education curricula. Once these strategies are defined, it is essential that educators work with students and, if possible, their families and communities in presenting English cultural values and logical patterns as they are reflected in rhetoric. However, these efforts must be undertaken with extreme caution, for it is at this stage, according to Kaplan (1967), that "...you are not merely teaching [the student] to see the world through English-colored glasses. [You are running] the very serious risk of being legitimately accused of brainwashing" (Kaplan, 1967:16).

THE STUDY: RESULTS AND ANALYSIS

Having reviewed only part of the great range of research that has been undertaken in the area of second language literacy, our direction now turns to the second major concern of this paper - a discussion of the attitudes of a group of non-native speakers of English toward their writing abilities in English. These attitudes were obtained through a questionnaire designed to provide information about each respondent's (1) personal background, (2) native language abilities, (3) English language education, (4) English language abilities, (5) reading habits, and (6) attitudes toward his/her personal education and toward ESL composition instruction in general. A stratified random sample yielded responses from sixty-seven, non-native English speaking students currently enrolled in undergraduate and graduate programs.

For comparative purposes, informants' responses have been separated into two groups according to the age at which the respondent began formal study of English. The results of these groupings -- into pre-adolescent (12 years and younger) and adolescent or post-adolescent (13 years and older) -- may provide further insight into the question of cerebral lateralization and second language learning. In particular, the findings may lend support to the view that adolescence marks a critical point after which learning a second language is "unnatural" and "imperfect" (see Penfield, 1965; Lenneberg, 1967).

Although the majority of the findings that will be discussed herein have been set in relation to these two age groups, two other variables -- graduate versus undergraduate standing and the physical setting of initial English language study -- also provide some significant results on which to base correlations. One variable we had thought might prove fruitful in terms of differences in respondents' attitudes -- level of native language written competence -- failed to produce any significant results.

As we begin our discussion of the results of the questionnaire, we emphasize once again that our interest was in gathering the respondents' attitudes so we might identify possible sources of and solutions for any writing problems present. We do not intend to evaluate existing ESL writing programs or teaching methodologies. Instead, our aim is to provide suggestions, based on the results, for educational practice and for future directions in second language research.

Based on the review of second language research presented in this study and the information gained through the questionnaire, we shall address the following questions as we enter into our analysis:

1. What area of composition rates as a strength for the greatest number of respondents?

2. What area of composition rates as a weakness for the greatest number of respondents?
3. Is there a relationship between the strength of a given composition skill and whether that skill had been stressed during composition instruction?
4. How do the respondents rate the adequacy of their English language programs' teaching of writing style?
5. Is there a relationship between the adequacy of an ESL composition program and the existence of general writing problems in a given individual?
6. What is the relationship between the physical setting (native country or U.S.) of initial English language study and the presence of writing problems?
7. Is there a relationship between the amount of reading an individual does and his/her composition abilities?
8. Do the respondents believe that an awareness of the beliefs and values of the culture whose language one is learning aids one's ability to write (positively affects writing style) in that language?
9. Are the majority of respondents satisfied or dissatisfied with their English language composition skills? To whom or what do they attribute their success or failure?

COMPOSITION STRENGTHS

In terms of composition strengths and weaknesses in the second language (English), there was no significant differences between the responses of the informants based either on their initial age of formal English study or on their level of educational attainment. Both graduate and undergraduate students who had begun formal study of English either at age twelve or earlier or after age twelve most often rated grammar as a strength. In fact, two thirds (66.7%) of the sample listed grammar as a composition strength. Vocabulary and sentence structure[1] were rated as strengths by 41.2% and 35.3% of the respondents, respectively. Only 19.6% of the respondents rated style, defined here as the expression of ideas in terms of (native and/or acquired logical and rhetorical structures, as a strength.

COMPOSITION WEAKNESSES

As may be expected from the above results, style was rated as a weakness by the greatest percentage of respondents. Some 56.9% of the sample rated style as a weakness, whereas grammar, vocabulary, and sentence structure were rated as weaknesses by only 9.8%, 25.5%, and 33.3% of the sample, respectively. For 23.5% of the sample, stylistic ability falls somewhere between a strength and a weakness. Either this proportion is unaware of any strong stylistic abilities or difficulties they might have or they are aware of their stylistic tendencies yet fail to see in them any attributes or failings.

THE RELATIONSHIP BETWEEN SKILLS STRESSED AND THEIR REALIZATION AS STRENGTHS

After noting the areas of composition in which the respondents experienced strengths and weaknesses, we wondered whether there might be a relationship between the stressing of a particular skill in its teaching and the realization of that skill as a strength or weakness. Of those skills rated as strengths by the greatest number of respondents, grammar, vocabulary, and sentence structure all were also rated as having been greatly stressed in the respondents' English composition instruction. Respondents rated vocabulary as the skill most greatly stressed (82.4%), with grammar second (70.6%), and sentence structure, though third, still having been stressed in the majority (56.0%) of the respondents' classes. With these skills so greatly stressed it is not a surprise that they have become strengths for the respondents (see Fig. 1a).

Is there a similar relationship between the degree to which style is realized as a strength and the degree to which it was stressed in the education of the respondents? The results reveal that style was not stressed for and was not realized as a strength by 72.6% of the respondents. For 7.8% of the respondents, style was stressed but was not rated a strength. For the remainder of the respondents,

a.

Skill	Strength	Stressed
vocabulary	41.2%	82.4%
grammar	66.7%	70.6%
sentence structure	35.3%	56.0%

b.

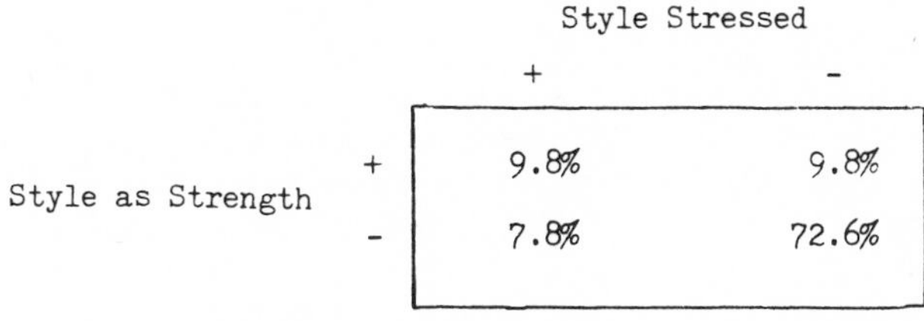

		Style Stressed +	Style Stressed -
Style as Strength	+	9.8%	9.8%
Style as Strength	-	7.8%	72.6%

Figure 1. The Relationship Between the Realization of Skills as Strengths and their being stressed as reported by Respondents.

style was a strength, but for half of these respondents (9.8%) style was stressed while for the other half (9.8%) style was not stressed. Therefore, the stressing of style in composition instruction has only a slight relation to style being a strength. However, the failure to stress style does have a strong causal relationship to style not being considered a strength (see Fig. 1b).

How can we explain the fact that style was rated a strength for as many respondents for whom it was stressed as for whom it was not stressed? There are a number of possible explanations. First, there is the question of self-reported data and with that the degree of teaching a given skill which qualifies it as having been "stressed" and the degree of ability in a given skill which qualifies it as being a "strength." Second, for those for whom style was not stressed yet was realized as a strength, style may have been taught at a degree less than "stressed" yet great enough to have positively affected the respondents' abilities. Third, the strength realized may be the result of informal exposure to style rather than the result of style being stressed in the respondents' formal education.

In review, then, there exists a positive relation between the stressing of vocabulary, grammar, and sentence structure and their being realized as strengths. The only positive relation holding in terms of style is that between style not being a strength and its not being stressed. Stressing style, in fact, makes it no greater a strength than not stressing style. However, the fact that there is a correlation between "style stressed" and "style strength" for some respondents and between "style unstressed" and "style not a strength" for the vast majority of the respondents points to the need for style to be taught in all ESL composition courses. If one may assume that stressing some elements of composition (vocabulary, grammar, sentence structure) may cause them to be strengths, one may also assume that stressing style may cause it to be a strength. Therefore, style instruction must be as great a component of composition instruction as any and all other components. However, to insure that the stressing of style positively affects stylistic performance and provides, as it failed to do for 7.8% of the respondents, more than a slight benefit to stylistic performance, diverse and comprehensive instructional methods must be employed.

Following Kaplan (1966), instructional methods need to be geared towards the rhetorical and logical patterns of each student's native language and, therefore, toward at least some degree of each student's native cognitive processes. Similarly, following Raimes (1979), Taylor (1981), Blot and Davidson (1980), and numerous others, instructional methods, reading assignments, and composition assignments must be varied enough so as to (1) motivate students to participate and to (2) stimulate all of the individual capacities and habits composing the individual's means for learning. In this way, the cognitive modalities of each student may be addressed and activated to their fullest so the acquisition of style may be more greatly guaranteed (cf. Whitaker, 1978). At this stage, reception may well receive greater concentration than production so stylistic patterns may be discovered before they are actively transformed (see Arapoff, 1969).

ADEQUACY OF INSTRUCTION IN STYLE

With the results indicating that style may be stressed yet not guarantee its position as a strength in a large number of non-native students, we wondered whether it was the ESL composition program itself that was responsible or whether the inadequacy rests with the students and their abilities to learn and/or to compose. We have already discussed a few ways in which educational programs may be structured so as to increase student writing abilities. Of course, there do remain individual difficulties with writing that may never be addressed or lessened no matter the instructional program. These difficulties, lying well below the conscious level, are not readily available for discussion by the individual or by anyone attempting to discern them from the outside. However, difficulties arising from the programs may be discovered and the place to start is with the students' attitudes toward the overall adequacy of their programs' teaching of style.

Once again the results reveal no significant differences in terms of the age at which formal study of English began or present level of educational attainment. Only 14.9% of the total sample rated the adequacy of their English language programs' teaching of style as excellent. Program adequacy was rated average by 23.4% of the sample. The final 61.7% of the sample rated their programs as inadequate.

If we remind ourselves that 82.4% of the sample indicated that style was not stressed in their English composition training and of the important place of style in writing education, it is not surprising that the majority of respondents did rate their programs inadequate. The realization that style is a necessary and vital aspect of writing instruction makes its failure to be stressed in that instruction definite grounds for labeling that instruction inadequate. It is obvious that for those who believe in the importance of style-instruction, program adequacy ratings will rise with greater attention paid to style. Yet, as we have seen, it is not the stressing of style alone which will guarantee its becoming a strength or a program reaching adequacy. For any program to be adequate, the very teaching of the subject matter included in that program must itself be adequate. Therefore, whether or not an individual skill is stressed or whether or not that skill becomes a strength is not the sole significant question of education. Rather, attention must be paid to bringing the program to a level of adequacy acceptable to all the students thereby fostering motivation, dedication, and involvement and, thereafter, enlivening and proliferating the individual strengths that combine to mark the success of any effort at composition.

THE RELATIONSHIP BETWEEN PROGRAM ADEQUACY AND DEGREE OF WRITING PROBLEMS

Addressing next the area of general writing problems, we sought to determine the relationship between <u>overall</u> program adequacy and these problems. Of those respondents rating the overall adequacy of their English language programs as inadequate, 72.4% realized some problems in writing. Of those respondents rating their programs average, 50.0% realized some writing problems. Finally, only 14.3% of those respondents rating the adequacy of their programs as excellent realized problems in writing. Therefore, as problems decrease with program adequacy increase, we see a negative correlation between the adequacy of a program and the amount or degree of writing problems which exist.

However, we may still need to question why 14.3% of the respondents found their program to be excellent yet still experienced difficulty and why 27.6% realized no writing problems yet received inadequate writing instruction.

For this latter group, as we shall see later, the role of self-instruction may provide the answer. However, for the former group we must again appeal to the fact that the adequacy of a given program cannot guarantee that a student will gain everything he or she needs to gain to write without problems. Both the psychological and physical environments play significant roles in the education process. We must also recognize again that asking an individual to rate a program in terms of its adequacy involves many personal as well as global judgments. Perhaps for some members of this former group who experience writing difficulties yet have rated their program highly, the program may have indeed been an excellent one in terms of its focus, organization, etc. and yet have still failed to meet the very individual needs of these respondents.

THE RELATIONSHIP BETWEEN PHYSICAL SETTING OF INITIAL ENGLISH LANGUAGE STUDY AND THE PRESENCE OF WRITING PROBLEMS

The results obtained on physical setting of initial English language study reflect some significant differences in terms of age. Of the total sample, 23.5% began formal study of English in the United States. Of the 25.0% who began this study after age thirteen, 66.7% indicated problems with writing style. Of the 75.0% who began this study at age twelve or earlier, only 11.1% indicated problems in style. The fact that respondents who began formal study of English in the United States before age twelve have less problems with writing style points to the important role of cultural awareness in language acquisition. Having been immersed in the culture of their target language at an early age (and, as Lenneberg (1967) indicates, before the learning of a second language becomes "unnatural"), these respondents realized an integrative need for English. This need led them to acquire a variety of values, traditions and customs for the ability to function fully (both linguistically and non-linguistically) in their new society. With the intense dependency of style on culture-specific logical and rhetorical structures, it is understandable that individuals acquiring knowledge of a language in the home of the native speakers of that language will also acquire (all or a degree of) those logical and rhetorical structures that make problems in writing style all the less extreme (see Fig. 2).

		Age of Initial Formal Study of English and the Realization of Writing Problems			
		% of Respondents			
Physical Setting	% of Respondents	Age 12 or <	With Problems	Age 13 or >	With Problems
U.S.	23.5	75.0	11.1	25.0	66.7
Native Country	76.5	43.6	78.5	56.4	54.5

Figure 2. The Relationship Between Physical Setting of Initial English Language Study and the Presence of Writing Problems.

The results dealing with the 76.5% of the respondents who began formal study of English in their native countries prove to be contrary. Of these respondents, 56.4% began formal English study after age thirteen and 43.6% began at age twelve or earlier. Of the former group, 54.5% noted problems in English writing style while of the latter group 78.5% noted problems. Therefore, we see the opposite of what held for students who began formal English study in the United States. With native country as the site of initial English study, it is not the older beginners who realize the most problems, but the younger beginners. What can account for this difference in age groups due to physical setting of initial formal study? One explanation points to the role of time of exposure to one's native language and its logical and rhetorical patterns before the introduction of English. With this longer exposure, the older beginners were able to acquire a degree of written competency in their native language (perhaps greater than that of the earlier beginners) that included a firm grasp on both mechanical and cognitive processes. This competency, if not directly transferrable to a second language, may at least provide the necessary practice in the actual process of writing that is needed before one may attempt to write in a second language. With this practice, one may experience the expectations involved in writing including how to address different audiences and different purposes. When transferred to one's writing in a second language, this ability aids one in applying newly acquired/learned thought patterns in addressing a new audience. Therefore, we see that while age of initial formal study affects composition abilities, the cultural and psychological tie-ins to the physical setting of this initial study also play an important role in the composition acquisition process.

READING AND COMPOSITION ABILITIES

With the apparent prominence of reading as a guide to writing patterns, vocabulary, and syntactic structures and as a stimulator of cognitive activity, we wondered whether the amount of time the respondents spent reading in English had any effect on the quality of their English composition abilities. The results reveal that of the 11.8% of the respondents who rated their English composition skills as "excellent," 100% did a high degree of ("very much") reading in English. As attitudes reflecting a lower degree of proficiency in composition were voiced, reading quantity decreased. Of the 43.2% of the respondents who rated their English composition ability "good," 63.6% read "very much" while 36.4% read "somewhat less," "Average" composition abilities were reported by 31.3% of the respondents as 43.8% of them said they read "very much," 31.2% said "somewhat less," and 25.0% said "only occasionally." Of the 13.7% of the respondents who rated their composition abilities as "fair," 28.6% said they read "very much," 28.6% said "somewhat less," and 42.8% said "only occasionally." No respondent rated his/her composition skills in English as "poor" and similarly no respondent characterized his/her reading activity as "minimal" or "nonexistent." Therefore, there is a positive correlation between the amount of reading in English undertaken and the rating assigned to English composition ability (see Fig. 3).

Because of this positive relationship and because of the recognized need for receptive skills to precede productive skills, we suggest that as listening must precede (as well as accompany) speech, reading must similarly precede (and accompany) writing. In this way, the student acquires receptive and productive skills continuously and once again activates a number of modalities simultaneously.

CULTURAL AWARENESS AND COMPOSITION ABILITIES

Great unity of response was evident in the replies of the informants to the question of whether cultural awareness is an aid to writing. The vast majority of the respondents (91.7%) supported the view that an awareness of the culture whose language one is learning contributes to one's writing competence in that language. Among the comments of those who agreed with the majority opinion were: (1) "I write English better in the U.S.A. then when in Costa Rica;" (2) "Cultural awareness helps me understand why and when certain forms of language are and should be used;" (3) "Knowing which words are polite or not is essential. Ignorance in this area could lead to embarrassing situations;" (4) "The audience is the most important element [when writing]. If you don't know who you're writing to, you're in trouble;" and (5) "A better perception of the beliefs and of the culture one learns helps us <u>feel</u> that language when we write it."

Composition Ability	% of Respondents	Frequency of Reading: % Very Much	% Somewhat Less	% Only Occasionally	% Minimal
excellent	11.8	100	--	--	--
good	43.2	63.6	36.4	--	--
average	31.3	43.8	31.2	25.0	--
fair	13.7	28.6	28.6	42.8	--
poor	0.0	--	--	--	--

Figure 3. The Relationship Between Composition Ability and Frequency of Reading.

With respect to the results of this question and to the literature dealing with the awareness of cultural differences, it is clear that cross-cultural awareness must be fostered in all second language education as well as in all teacher education. For students, the awareness of cross-cultural differences in thought patterns will lead to an understanding of how and where to point their writing. Often, this will necessarily entail switching to some non-native thought patterns in order to produce and transmit the message clearly. For instructors, this awareness will promote better communication between self and student both when teaching and conversing, and also when evaluating any written language. Cross-cultural awareness must be stressed in second language education as much as is any other component of that education. It is this awareness alone that allows the writer to understand fully his/her audience -- to understand how that audience will process the message, what they will expect of it and of its producer, and, finally, how they will likely respond to its content. Because, as Kaplan (1978) states, "...the native speaker and the non-native speaker differ in their ability to determine what suppositions may be shared between speaker/writer and listener/reader in a given communication situation" (Kaplan, 1978:10), the role of cross-cultural awareness instruction in addressing this important difference cannot be understated.

SATISFACTION WITH COMPOSITION SKILLS: CONTRIBUTORS TO SUCCESS AND FAILURE

The final discussion deals with the respondents' satisfaction or dissatisfaction with their English language composition skills. Only 9.8% of the respondents were totally satisfied with their skills. The majority (70.6%) of the respondents were moderately satisfied with their composition skills, and the remaining 19.6% were dissatisfied. Those satisfied with their composition skills rated the biggest contributors to their success as the school system, reading, self-motivation, positive attitudes toward language learning, individual instructors, and English-speaking friends and relatives. Those dissatisfied with their composition skills placed at fault the school system, inadequate English language courses, the lack of diversified reading assignments, individual instructors, lack of self-motivation, and lack of instructional concentration on style.

Among the suggestions offered by the respondents for improving ESL writing/composition education were:

1. use updated materials dealing with current events pertinent to students,
2. motivate students to improve their skills,
3. introduce composition instructors to effective teaching methods,
4. introduce composition instructors to the writing norms of the students' native languages,
5. expose students to the American way of thinking,
6. increase reading and writing assignments,
7. teach style and thought coordination,
8. provide contrastive analyses of ways of speaking and writing,
9. contrast the composition styles of the students' native and target languages.

CONCLUSIONS AND RECOMMENDATIONS

In concluding this report, we remind ourselves that the results of this study have been gathered from questionnaires in which non-native English speaking students were asked to rate their English composition abilities and discuss various aspects of their English language education. As the questionnaire sought to elicit attitudes -- i.e. subjective reactions -- it is essential to remember that the task of rating oneself consistently within a single survey and appropriately within a given population is a difficult one. Not only must the respondents react to the situation of the questionnaire, but they must also react to its content. In terms of a language attitude survey, responses will undoubtedly reflect personal motivation and interest in learning and using the language and, at the same time, personal feelings about those individuals and traditions associated with its use natively. Yet these subjective responses, these attitudes, are specifically what all education must address. Educators must realize what it is that lies at the core of one's desire to learn and what it is they must undertake to take advantage of this desire.

While we have succeeded in identifying some major sources of composition difficulty, our work has encouraged us to question beyond these sources and to discuss further areas of inquiry. Among these will be to compare the attitudes of non-native English speakers with those of native English speakers toward non-native writing samples. In addition, we hope to compare the attitudes of native speakers of English toward their English composition abilities with the results discussed herein. Finally, we plan to discuss whether attitudes toward composition abilities are related to the linguistic and logical structure of respondents' native languages.

In focusing on the attitudes of non-native speakers of English toward their composition abilities in English this study has gathered responses on such topics as (1) composition strengths and weaknesses, (2) adequacy of and skills stressed in composition instruction, (3) physical setting of initial English language study, and (4) the role of reading and cultural awareness in composition education. These responses point to possible sources of writing difficulties and, also, to possible means for their solution. Primary attention has been given to writing style and the related roles of rhetoric and logic in the acquisition of stylistic abilities.

Identified sources of stylistic difficulty in English composition include low frequency of English reading and the inadequacy of ESL composition instruction in general and, in particular, the failure to stress style in ESL instruction. In addition, both age and physical setting of initial English language study contribute to composition capabilities. To combat the problem of ESL program inadequacy and student difficulty with writing style, it is recommended that ESL composition instruction address the logical and rhetorical patterns of both the student's native and target languages. This will necessarily involve interlinguistic and cross-cultural awareness instruction. Focus on cross-cultural awareness is to include instruction in the expectations holding for both writer and reader, the social function of writing in different contexts, and the variety of forms writing may take according to these contexts. Varied and suitable reading assignments are essential for the transmission of the understanding of cultural and individual differences in writing style.

If the aim of ESL composition instruction is to foster the ability in non-native speakers to "write like a native," instruction must be based on those aspects which identify any piece of writing as having been produced by a "native." Aside from the grammatical, orthographic, syntactic, and semantic aspects that identify a sample of writing as "English," there are intellectual and logical nuances which lie below the surface of the sample and yet which are essential for its identification. While English composition instruction cannot provide the student with creativity and imagination, it can provide the student with a knowledge of the form his/her message should take and the conditions for its appropriate dispersal throughout the target audience.

Writing, with its umbilical ties to logic and rhetoric, is both a creative procedure and a generator of cognitive processes. One can neither hope to write without an awareness of his/her audience nor without the knowledge of the way in which to process, organize, and present his/her ideas in a way both understandable and stimulating to the audience. To insure the acquisition of this awareness and knowledge, second language composition instruction needs to borrow both from the process of first language composition instruction and from the process of oral language acquisition. Writing is the result of progressive attainment of individual yet interdependent skills. Therefore, as one's native language and as one's oral language, writing must be taught and acquired in progressive stages which, while building on already acquired abilities, continually stimulate cognitive capacities and motivational tendencies to learn.

NOTES

[1]For purposes of this study, grammar is defined as the knowledge of the composition of and relationships between idea units. A strength in vocabulary is defined as the knowledge of a relatively high number of lexical items and the ability to use them appropriately. A strength in sentence structure includes a knowledge of and ability to manipulate a combination of lexical items.

REFERENCES

Albert, M. L. and Obler, L. K., 1978, "The Bilingual Brain: Neuropsychological and Neurolinguistic Aspects of Bilingualism," Academic Press, N.Y.

Anderson, M. L. and Wrase, J., 1976, What's really basic about teaching composition to foreign students? ms.

Angioletti, P. J., 1979, "Teaching ESL Writing to Chinese Students," M. A. Thesis, Hunter College, City University of New York.

Arapoff, N., 1969, Discover and Transform: a method of teaching writing to foreign students. TESOL Q., 3: 297-304.

Arnow, B., 1977, "Bilingual/ESL Programs for Migrant Children." ERIC, Las Cruces.

Aup'ecle, M., 1973, La langue francaise écrite en milieu étranger à l'école primaire [Written French in primary schools abroad], Francais dans le Monde, 99:20-27.

Baker, S., 1971, The literate imagination. in "The Written Word," S. Baker, J. Barzun, and I. A. Richards, eds., Newbury House, Rowley, Mass.

Blanton, L. L., 1981, "Intermediate Composition Practice: A Text for Students of ESL, Book 1," Newbury House, Rowley, Mass.

Blot, D. and Davidson, D. M., 1980, "Put It In Writing: Writing Activities for Students of ESL," Newbury House, Rowley, Mass.

Bottum, C. T., 1981, Children: writes of passage, Washington Post, June 16, B5.

Bruder, M. N. and Furey, P. R., 1979, The writing segment of an intensive program for students of English as a second language, J. of Basic Writing, 2:67-84.

Buckingham, T. and Pech, W. C., 1976, An experience approach to teaching composition. TESOL Q., 10:55-65.

Cambalo, M., et al., 1976, L'apprentissage des langues au niveau debutant: le problème des supports écrits, [Teaching languages to beginners: the problem of written back-up], Mélanges Pédagogiques (Université de Nancy), 49-69.

Chafe, W., 1979, Integration and involvement in oral and literate culture, ms.

Cooper, T. C., et al., 1980, "Sentence Combining in Second Language Instruction," ERIC, Washington, D.C.

Cox, S., 1947, "Indirections for Those Who Want to Write," Knopf, N.Y.

Dubois, B. L., 1976, British-tradition English in the American university, Lektos: Interdisciplinary Working Papers in Language Sciences, Special Issue, U. of Louisville.

"English Placement Test (EPT) Project Technical Report for May Test 1977," 1977, Educational Research Institute

of British Columbia, Vancouver.
Ewer, J. R., 1974, Note-taking training for non-English-speaking students of science and technology, RELC J., 5:41-49.
Frestedt, M. and Sanchez, M., 1980, Navajo world view harmony in directives for English texts, ms.
Genzel, R., 1981, Review of workshop on composition, TESOL News., 15:31.
Goody, J., 1977, Memory and learning in oral and literate culture, ms.
Grierson, H. J. C., 1945, "Rhetoric and English Composition," Oliver and Boyd, Edinburgh.
Henner-Stanchina, C., 1980, From reading to writing acts, Mélanges Pédagogiques, (Université de Nancy), 65-80.
Holzknecht, S. and Smithies, M., 1980, The errors in written English made by students at the Papua New Guinea University of Technology, ms.
Ingram, E., 1973, Differences of opinion, Times Educ. Sup., March 2, 3013, Extra, 12.
Joos, M., 1961, "The Five Clocks," Harcourt Brace, N.Y.
Kaplan, R., 1967, Contrastive rhetoric and the teaching of composition. TESOL Q., 1:10-16.
Kaplan, R., 1968, Contrastive rhetorics: further speculations, Conf. of Am. Asso. of Applied Ling.
Kaplan, R., 1966, Cultural thought patterns in inter-cultural education, Lang. Learning, 16:1-20.
Keenan, O., 1979, Why look at unplanned and planned discourse? in: "Discourse and Syntax," T. Givón, ed., Academic Press, N.Y.
Kessler, C., 1974, Developing an ESL program in a small two-year college, ms.
Kirkwood, J. M., 1976, Reading and writing in Russian: the neglected skills? J. of Russ. Stud., 32:13-23.
Kobler, J. F., 1976, Basically, graduate students need individual attention, ms.
Krashen, S., 1976, Formal and informal linguistic environments in language acquisition and language learning, TESOL Q., 10:157-68.
Kroll, B., 1979, A survey of the writing needs of foreign and American college freshmen, Eng. Lang. Teaching J., 33:219-27.
Larsen-Freeman, D., 1978, An ESL index of development, TESOL Q., 12:439-48.
Lenneberg, E., 1967, "Biological Foundations of Language," Wiley, N.Y.

Macha, D. and Angelis, P., 1976, An annotated bibliography of materials for teaching advanced written skills in English as a second language, ms.

Mason, C., 1971, The relevance of intensive training in English as a foreign language for university students. Lang. Learning, 21:197-204.

Moirand, S., 1977, Communication écrite et apprentissage initial [The place of the written language in the early stages of language learning], Francais dans le Monde, 133:43-4 and 53-7.

Myers, M., 1980, "A Procedure for Writing Assessment and Holistic Scoring," ERIC, Urbana.

Oliver, R., 1965, Foreword, in: "Philosophy, Rhetoric and Argumentation," M. Nathanson and H. Johnson, Jr., eds., Penn. State, Univ. Park.

Paulston, C. B., 1972, Teaching writing in the ESOL classroom: techniques of controlled composition, TESOL Q., 6:33-59.

Paulston, C. B., and Bruder, M. N., 1976, "Teaching English as a Second Language. Techniques and Procedures," Prentice-Hall, Englewood Cliffs.

Pavelich, J. L., 1978, Organizing special classes for foreign students in the technical writing course, Tech. Writ. Teacher, 5:55-58.

Penfield, W., 1965, Conditioning the uncommitted cortex for language learning. Brain. 88:787-98.

Pytlik, B. P., 1978, Teaching technical writing to foreign graduate students. Tech. Writ. Teacher, 5:53-54.

Raimes, A., 1979, "Problems and Teaching Strategies in ESL Composition," Center for Applied Ling., Arlington.

Rivers, W. M. and Temperly, M. S., 1978, "A Practical Guide to the Teaching of English as a Second or Foreign Language," Oxford U. Press, N.Y.

Rodrigues, R. J., 1977, Awareness of multicultural language and learning styles research: an urging, ms.

Shuy, R., 1976, Confronting the literacy crisis, ms.

Shuy, R., 1981, Relating research on oral language function to research on written discourse, ms.

Shwabe, T., 1978, Survival English for ESL students in American educational institutions, CATESOL Occasional Papers, No. 4.

Stubbs, M., 1980, "Language and Literacy: The Sociolinguistics of Reading and Writing," Routledge and Kegan Paul, London.

Tannen, D., 1980, Spoken and written language and the oral/literate continuum. Berkeley Ling. Soc.

Taylor, B. P., 1981, Content and written form: a two-way street. TESOL Q., 15:5-13.

Taylor, B. P., 1976-77, Teaching composition to low-level ESL students. CATESOL Occasional Papers, No. 3.

Valéry, P., 1966, Style, in: "The Problem of Style," J. V. Cunningham, ed., Fawcett, Greenwich.

Valette, R. M., 1973, Developing and evaluating communication skills in the classroom, TESOL Q., 7:407-24.

van Schaik, J. D., 1978, "A Comparison of ESL and English Composition Textbooks at the University Level," MA Thesis, UCLA.

Vigner, G., 1976, L'initiation à l'expression écrite dans les langues de specialité. L'objectivation [Initial training in writing in a specialist register. Objectivising], Francais dans le Monde, 122:26-42.

Vigner, G., 1974, Techniques d'apprentissage de l'argumention écrite [Techniques for learning written argument], Francais dans le Monde, 109:60-67.

Weissberg, R. and Buker, S., 1978, Strategies for teaching the rhetoric of written English for science and technology (EST). TESOL Q., 12:321-29.

Whitaker, H., 1978, Bilingualism: a neurolinguistics perspective, in: "Second Language Acquisition Research," W. Ritchie, ed., Academic Press, N.Y.

Wigfield, J., 1976-77, ESL adult literacy. CATESOL Occasional Papers, No. 3.

Workshop Reports of the Annual Conference on College Composition and Communication, 1966, CCC, 17:175-200.

FRENCH VERB FORMS SIMPLIFIED

Theodore E. D. Braun

University of Delaware

Why bother trying to simplify French verb forms for our students? I have two responses to this question, psychological and statistical. Let us glance at the psychological aspect of the problem first. A typical French beginning textbook presents the student with a frightening and bewildering list of regular and irregular verbs. By the end of the first two levels (two high school years or two college semesters) a student is expected to know 40 or 50 irregular verbs in at least ten tenses, along with a host of verbs classified in three major regular conjugations. In addition, three or four types of first-conjugation orthographical-changing verbs are usually presented as irregular, so that the appendix contains a list extending for a dozen pages, charting countless forms of scores of verbs.

The reason for this situation is easy to understand: French conjugations are viewed as direct descendants of Latin conjugations, and any verb not fitting into a pre-determined category is declared irregular (ironically, verbs like dormir--"irregular"--are closer to the Latin than "regular" verbs like finir); since many verbs escape easy classification, the number of irregular verbs is, from the students' point of view, overwhelming. Sometimes, too, rules-of-thumb for deriving or predicting stems of various tenses tend to create irregularities where in fact none exist. For instance, if we say that the stem of the present subjunctive can be found by dropping the ending of the third-person plural form of the present indicative, a veritable army of irregular forms is created. A restatement of this rule could significantly reduce the number of irregularities. But I am sliding here from introduction to presentation; we will return to the subjunctive in a few minutes.

The second aspect of the problem of French verb forms is statistical. Without discussing _whether_ we should teach paradigms and conjugations to first-level students, I am starting from the premise that _in fact_ the vast majority of teachers teach conjugations and virtually all textbooks present paradigms, drill on them, and expect students to learn them. Besides, the system I am suggesting can be used equally well to teach paradigms in advance of usage, to tie the students' acquired use of verbs into a neat package when they ask for it, or even to review verb forms in more advanced courses (I use this system myself in all levels of instruction, up to a senior level course on advanced grammar).

Let us turn to the so-called regular conjugations. I assume that students will acquire or at least learn a vocabulary of about 400 words a level, giving them active command by the end of the fourth level of some 1600 words, more than enough to carry on a reasonable conversation on general topics. Now, as Table 1 indicates, the first 400 words[1] (see Savard and Richards, 1970) include 126 verbs, 73 of which (58 percent) are -_er_ verbs. Of these, 15 have some kind of orthographical change in the present tense. The second 400 words include 109 verbs, 88 of which (81 percent) are -_er_ verbs; there are 19 orthographical-changing verbs in this group. In other words, over two-thirds of the first two levels' worth of verbs are in the -_er_ conjugation, and include 34 orthographical-changing verbs. Of note also is the fact that at the 800-word or second level, no other traditional conjugation or "irregular" verb family is as large as, for example the _jeter/répéter_ group (15): the nearest are the _attendre_ group with nine, the _venir/tenir_ group with seven, and the _dormir_ group with six. This would seem to indicate that most of our teaching/learning energy should go into the two-thirds of the basic verbs that are in the -_er_ conjugation; this is especially true of the second level, with four out of five verbs in the -_er_ conjugation.

What about the other two traditionally "regular" conjugations in French (the _finir_-type and the _attendre_-type verbs)? The statistics on Table 1 indicate that we need desperately to overhaul our thinking and our categories. Of the first 400 words, 15 are -_ir_ verbs, only two of which (_finir_ itself and _réussir_) are of the _finir_-type: only 13 percent of the -_ir_ verbs are "regular". Of the first 800 words, 25 are -_ir_ verbs, only five of which are "regular" (_agir_, _choisir_ and the neglected _nourrir_ join the group): 80 percent of verbs in this category are defined as irregular! Clearly we need to change our thinking on this, all the more so since seven _venir_/_tenir_-type verbs (28 percent), six _dormir_-type verbs (24 percent) and five _ouvrir_-type verbs (20 percent) appear among the first 800 words, all at frequencies equalling or surpassing the _finir_-type verbs. But none reaches majority status, which must surely be the main criterion for achieving recognition as regular, that is, as the rule to follow.

The -_re_ verbs present statistics at least as convincing and almost as dramatic. Here, too, no verb family reaches majority status. At the 400-word level, there are seven _attendre_-type verbs, or 24 percent of the total of 29 -_re_ verbs; at the 800-word level, only nine of the 41 -_re_ verbs fall into the so-called regular category, leaving a total of 31, or 78 percent, of -_re_ verbs irregular.

Is it any wonder that students are frustrated when faced with such facts? We have so narrowly defined what is regular that in the first two levels of instruction four out of five -_ir_ and -_re_ verbs are irregular! Is it possible to construct a system of conjugations that confers regularity on most verbs? If so, what is it? What are its strengths and its drawbacks?

My answer to the first question, as I have already indicated, is that such a system exists. The other question deals with the substance of this paper. The strengths of this system will be apparent in a brief demonstration of its simplicity--to know it is to love it--but I am unaware of any drawbacks except the lethargy of tradition.

I posit first of all the existence of only four

Table 1. Distribution of Verbs at the 400 and 800 Word Levels.

	1-400	401-800	1-800
-er Verbs/Total Verbs	73/126 (58%)	87/109 (81%)	160/235 (68%)
jeter/répéter	5	10	15
-cer, -ger, -yer	10	9	19
-ir Verbs/Total Verbs	15/126 (12%)	10/109 (9%)	25/235 (11%)
finir	2	3	5
dormir	5	1	6
venir	5	2	7
ouvrir	1	4	5
others	2	0	2
-re Verbs/Total Verbs	29/126 (23%)	12/109 (11%)	41/235 (17%)
attendre	7	2	9
others	22	10	32
-oir Verbs/Total Verbs	9/126 (7%)	0/109 (0%)	9/235 (4%)

Source: Savard, Jean-Guy and Jack Richards: _Les indices d'utilité du vocabulaire fondamental français_ (Québec: Les Presses de l'Université Laval, 1970).

irregular verbs: _être_, _avoir_, _aller_ and _faire_. All other verbs are by definition regular, falling into the -_er_ conjugation and the -_s_ conjugation, the latter being named after the present indicative first person singular ending.

Everyone who has ever studied French knows that, despite differing verb endings (_e_, _es_, _e_ or _s_, _s_, _t_), all forms of the singular of the present indicative sound alike. Furthermore, the third person plural ending (_ent_) is not pronounced; with -_er_ verbs and their analogues, this form sounds exactly like the singular (_aime_/_aiment_, _ouvre_/_ouvrent_); with the other verbs, there is usually a change in the stem vowel or consonant or both (for instance, _assied_/_asseyent_, _rend_/_rendent_, _vient_/_viennent_). The first and second person plural forms regularly share the same stem (among the regular verbs, only _dire_ is an exception).

From both the phonetic and the written points of view, then, we can establish that if three stems and their associated endings are learned, the conjugations of verbs and verb groups or families can be mastered easily: _je_ for the singular, _nous_ for the first and second persons plural, and _ils_/_elles_ for the third person plural. Table 2 illustrates this with a few examples. A clear benefit to the students is that these forms occur in regular and therefore easily-remembered patterns. Psychologically, since there is less apprehension about what is regular and what is irregular, the learning task is simplified even though the mass of forms to master remains constant. This is true whether conjugations are presented as initial learning guides or as a review. And the statistics here are all on our side. Table 3 shows _all_ the irregular forms of the present indicative; note that except for the _dire_ form mentioned above and for the substitution of x for _s_ in two forms of _vouloir_, _pouvoir_ and _valoir_, all these irregularities occur in irregular verbs, thus only eight verbs show irregular forms in the present indicative.

A side benefit of this system of looking at the present indicative is the more predictable derivation of stems for other verb tenses, in particular the present subjunctive and the future. "Derivation" is a purely fictitious term in the first case and a partly fictitious one in the second: it is better to speak of a rule or a rule of thumb enabling us to predict a stem. This is not mere nit-picking, as I

TABLE 2: Examples of Three Basic Stems in the Present Indicative

-er Conjugation

aimer		répéter	
aime	aimons aiment	répète	répétons répètent
employer		**jeter**	
emploie	employons emploient	jette	jetons jettent
manger		**acheter**	
mange	mangeons	achète	achetons achètent

-s Conjugation

dormir		prendre	
dors	dormons dorment	prends	prenons prennent
finir		**venir**	
finis	finissons finissent	viens	venons viennent
attendre		**boire**	
attends	attendons attendent	bois	buvons boivent

TABLE 3: Irregular Forms in the Present Indicative

SINGULAR

	être	avoir	aller	vouloir	pouvoir	valoir
je	suis	ai	vais	veux	peux	vaux
tu	es	as	vas	veux	peux	vaux
il	est	a	va			

PLURAL

	être	avoir	aller	faire	dire
nous	sommes				
vous	êtes			faites	dites
elles	sont	ont	vont	font	

hope my discussion of finding the stems for these two tenses will make clear.

In the early 1960's, most textbooks taught that one can derive the stem of the present subjunctive, as I stated at the outset, by using the stem of the third person plural of the present indicative (some authors preferred the first person plural, but they were in the minority). In an article published in the *French Review* in 1967 (see Braun, 1967; see also Barrette and Braun, 1968, 1970), I showed that the use of both these forms would predict the present subjunctive forms with such a high degree of accuracy that only eight or ten verbs, rather than legions, would present irregularities. Most authors today have adopted the two-stem formula. The system is simple: we use the *nous* stem for *nous* and *vous*, and the *ils*/*elles*/stem for all the other persons, which are in the present subjunctive phonetically identical. As a result, verbs such as *acheter*, *venir*, *boire* and *prendre* are regular in this tense. Only our four irregular verbs and a handful of others do not follow this rule, or more correctly stated, this rule can predict with accuracy all present subjunctive forms except for the four irregular verbs and a handful of others. Table 4 illustrates these points. I need not point out to classroom teachers and to language learners how much relief can come from discovering a reliable form-predictor, especially one that leaves the verb fully recognizable.

In the future tense, this fictitious derivation has not always been the case, since *in fact* the future was historically formed analytically by adding the present indicative of *avoir* to the infinitive, probably with a meaning akin to the modern English "I have some work to do." But in the twentieth century, with obsolete forms of the infinitive used as the future stem with some verbs (*courir*/*courre*) and modified forms of the infinitive with others (*venir*/*viendr*, *asseoir*/*assiér*, *voir*/*verr*, *aimer*/*aime̸r*, *acheter*/*achèter*), the original relationship is not always apparent, all the less so in that the *av* has been dropped from *avons* and *avez*.

The most efficient way I know of formulating a rule with a reasonably effective rate of predicting the future stem is to establish two rules. The first rule covers *-er*

TABLE 4: Examples of Forms of the Present Subjunctive

A. Regular Forms

<u>acheter</u>		<u>arriver</u>	
achet~~ons~~	nous achetions	arriv~~ons~~	nous arrivions
achèt~~ent~~	j'achète	arriv~~ent~~	j'arrive
<u>finir</u>		<u>dormir</u>	
finiss~~ons~~	nous finissions	dorm~~ons~~	nous dormions
finiss~~ent~~	je finisse	dorm~~ent~~	je dorme
<u>venir</u>		<u>attendre</u>	
ven~~ons~~	nous venions	attend~~ons~~	nous attendions
vienn~~ent~~	je vienne	attend~~ent~~	j'attende
<u>prendre</u>		<u>boire</u>	
pren~~ons~~	nous prenions	buv~~ons~~	nous buvions
prenn~~ent~~	je prenne	boiv~~ent~~	je boive

B. Irregular Forms

<u>aller</u>	<u>valoir</u>	<u>vouloir</u>
nous allions	nous valions	nous voulions
j'aille	je vaille	je veuille
<u>faire</u>	<u>pouvoir</u>	<u>savoir</u>
nous fassions	nous puissions	nous sachions
je fasse	je puisse	je sache

TABLE 4: (continued)

avoir and être are irregular in both stems and endings:

j'aie	je sois
tu aies	tu sois
il ait	il soit
nous ayons	nous soyons
vous ayez	vous soyez
elles aient	elles soient

TABLE 5: Future Tense of -er Verbs

<u>aimer</u>	<u>jeter</u>
j'aime+r+ai	je jette+r+ai
j'aimerai	je jetterai
<u>manger</u>	<u>acheter</u>
je mange+r+ai	j'achete+r+ai
je mangerai	j'achèterai
<u>employer</u>	<u>répéter</u>
j'emploie+r+ai	je répète+r+ai
j'emploierai	je répèterai*

<u>Irregular Forms</u>

<u>aller</u>	<u>envoyer</u>
j'irai	j'enverrai

TABLE 6: Irregular Future Stems of -ir, -re and -oir Verbs

A. -ir Verbs

venir/tenir

je viendrai, elle tiéndra

courir

nous courrons

mourir

vous mourrez

cueillir

tu cueilleras

B. -re Verbs

être

elles seront

faire

je ferai

C. -oir Verbs

avoir	tu auras
savoir	il saura
devoir/recevoir	elle devra, nous recevrons
pouvoir	je pourrai
vouloir	vous voudrez
voir	ils verront
s'asseoir	elles s'assiéront, elles s'assoiront
falloir	il faudra
valoir	il vaudra

verbs and is stated as follows: use the entire first person singular of the present indicative and add r and the future endings, as is illustrated on Table 5. This rule allows for but two irregularities, aller (j'irai) and envoyer (j'enverrai). It not only confers regularity on all verbs of the jeter and répéter[2] types, but has the added advantage of correctly predicting the pronunciation of all verbs in the class (we do not say /ʒɛmee/ or even /ʒɛmeRe/ but rather /ʒɛmRe/). The rule thus covers the oral as well as the written forms of the language.

The second rule, covering all other verbs, is more-or-less the standard rule we find in grammar books today: the future stem can be predicted by using the infinitive; all irregularities are easily demonstrated to be alterations of the infinitive, or to be based on alternate infinitive forms. Applying this rule by sub-classes, we find all -ir and -re verbs to be regular, except those on Table 6. The -oir verbs, on the other hand, all have modified forms of the infinitive, and might all be considered irregular. All exceptions taken into account, we have with this system not scores of irregular forms in the future tense, but only 17, or 13 in addition to the four irregular verbs.

I do not have the space here for a fuller demonstration of this system applied to other tenses, such as the passé composé and the passé simple. I hope to have shown, however, that a phonetically and morphologically accurate system of presenting and predicting French verb forms is possible. The system that I have described, dividing French verbs into two conjugations, eliminates all but four verbs from the classification "irregular". And while several other verbs present irregular forms, the two-conjugation verb system eliminates most irregularities, thereby greatly reducing the complexity of French verb forms and simplifying the learner's task. Simple rules with predictable results and few exceptions. Can Paradise be far away?

NOTES

[1]Savard and Richards (1970:17) note that: "les échelles de vocabulaire oral contiennent environ 1500 mots. L'élève ne peut profiter d'un cours de conversation s'il n'apprend pas le vocabulaire de base." They are referring to an

active command of 1500 words; in a four-level sequence, this means an average of about 400 words per level.

[2]The future form of this class of verbs, although usually written with e in the stem (je répéterai), is pronounced as though it were written with è (je répèterai). Maurice Grevisse (1964: sec. 629a) says: "Il y a, pour ces verbes, une tendance assez marquee à conformer la graphie à la prononciation et à mettre un è au futur et au conditionnel." He cites several modern authors in support of this statement.

REFERENCES

Barrette, Paul and Braun, Theodore, E. D., 1968, "Second French," Scott, Foresman, Chicago.

Barrette, Paul and Braun, Theodore E. D., 1970, "First French," Scott, Foresman, Chicago.

Braun, Theodore E. D., 1967, Making the subjunctive easier to learn, Fr. Rev., 40:810-13.

Grevisse, Maurice, 1964, "Le bon usage," Duclot, Gembloux.

Savard, Jean-Guy and Richards, Jack, 1970, "Les indices d'utilité du vocabulaire fundamental francais," U. de Laval, Québec.

DISCOURSE CONTENT STRUCTURES IN BEGINNING SPANISH LEARNERS

Angela Labarca

University of Delaware

INTRODUCTION

This study attempted to explore the nature of memory structures for discourse set up by beginning Spanish learners reading a text in the second language. Research efforts were specifically directed toward the determination of the time when these memorial structures are set up. The hypothesized facilitative effects of two kinds of word diagrams were also assessed in a recall measure of reading comprehension. A factorial analysis was done on the data.

On the basis of current theories of discourse comprehension, it was hypothesized that the provision of the text's macro- or superordinate content structure would not only serve as a probe of learners' memorial constructions, but also as an aid for comprehension. The text's content structure--obtained by applying Meyer's technique of content analysis--was used both to generate the text's superordinate diagrammatic representations and to score the recall measures for number of idea-units present.

The main effects analyzed were statistically significant and results suggest that the content structure schemata provided probably matched the subjects' own memory schemata and enhanced recall when they were used as retrieval aids. Moreover, given the evidence collected, it seems as if the organization of the information from a reading passage is apparently realized by mental representations that more often than not share the visual-spatial characteristics of a boxed diagram.

THE PROBLEM

The main research questions addressed in this study are:

1. What is the nature of the memory structures for written course set up by beginning learners of Spanish?
2. When are these memorial traces set up?
3. What are the effects of providing selected kinds of word diagrams to support comprehension?
4. Is there a relationship between the kind of memorial construction and the time when it is set up?

Within the domain of second-language acquisition, questions such as the ones formulated above remain unanswered. Much research is needed in order to determine the nature of the memorial constructions set up by subjects learning vocabulary, listening to or reading the foreign language, and in order to assess the degree of effectiveness of selected aids used as memory probes. Omaggio (1979), for example, examined the effects on comprehension of presenting six selected pictures to French learners. She found that the pre-thematic picture significantly enhanced the comprehension of a narrative passage. The pre-thematic visual was therefore proposed to function as an advance organizer, in accord with the meaningful learning theory developed by Ausubel, et al. (1978).

Given the perceptual features of word diagrams, one of the questions to be answered is whether or not visuo-spatial word arrays are to the descriptive text as Omaggio's pictorial contexts are to the narrative passage. Furthermore, if such a relationship can be detected, the stronger contention would be to presume that the organizational array provided matches the learners' mental constructions in a closer way.

Since there is a paucity of information on the topic, it is expected that the answers to the above questions will produce valuable evidence both at the theoretical and the practical levels. On the one hand, information on the memory structures set up by learners in the process of acquiring a foreign language code can improve our understanding of the acquisition process and help to refine research procedures. On the other hand, this knowledge can be readily used both in materials design and in the formulation of instructional procedures.

SUMMARY OF RELATED RESEARCH

Current theories of memory for discourse propose that text material is the input for the laying out of hierarchically-organized mental networks of concepts and their interrelationships in the readers' memories.

Crothers (1970), Grimes (1972), Fredericksen (1972), Kintsch and Van Dijk (1975), Kintsch (1974, 1977), Van Dijk (1977), and Rummelhart, Lindsay and Norman (1972) have not only proposed the existence of such schematic constructions but have also argued that such structures are dependent upon and integrated into even higher-level networks of analysis called frames, schemes, or macro-structures (Van Dijk, 1977).

While there has generally been a lack of supporting evidence in the case of Crother's and Fredericksen's studies, data gathered by Kintsch (1977), for example, have shown that the probabilities of recall are a function of the level of a given proposition in a hierarchically organized outline of the text's content.

Meyer's texts (Meyer, 1975a, 1975b) of the theory also represent an important advance in the study of memory for text. Her data amply support the hypothesis that memorial traces are hierarchical or "staged" in the sense that lowering the height of macro-propositions in a piece of discourse impairs recall, while raising subordinate propositions does not improve their chances of being recalled by subjects. The notion of "staging," as formulated by Grimes (1972), claims that human connected discourse is organized hierarchically. Thus, Meyer's data point toward the psychological existence of staging, since it was demonstrated that staging manipulation affects content recall in the predicted direction and magnitude.

Work on memory for discourse has invariably led researchers to conclude that the memorial construction tapped in experimental studies is similar to a schematic representation of the piece of discourse prepared by the researchers themselves. It is virtually impossible to describe mental schemata without postulating that they in some way replicate pencil-and-paper outlines of the information contained in a piece of discourse. Herein lies the problem. In addition, there is the added convenience that the outlines are also used to score subjects' protocols for quantity and kind of propositions recalled. Consequently, the researchers mentioned above have devised techniques of content analysis that are often based on the researcher's overall view of a passage.

Grimes' and Meyer's techniques for content analysis stand out, however, because they do not rely on subjective conceptions of a text. Grimes' (1972) procedure is based on Fillmore's (1968) case grammar model as well as on a semantic analysis of the propositions in a passage and their interrelations. Grimes' procedure is commonly referred to as semantic grammar of propositions.

Meyer's (1975a) procedure is based on that of Grimes and has been refined as a result of extensive research. It yields one hierarchical diagram of the ideas in a passage showing their rhetorical connections and their subordination to other superordinate ideas. For its objectivity and relative ease of manipulation, Meyer's procedure was used as an analytical tool in the study reported here.

Another kind of data that lends theoretical support to this study comes from varied experimental manipulations in perception and thinking studies. These data also point to the existence of central organizing principles that regulate the construction of memory traces for verbal materials in the native language. This research focuses more on the physical aspects of memorial constructions. Huttenlocher (1968), for example, proposes that reasoning processes in three-term series problems correspond to the setting up of mental spatial arrangements that are memory representations of verbal descriptions read to subjects. It was shown that it takes longer to answer questions on "John is taller than Pete, and shorter than Ed" than on "Ed is taller than John, and John is taller than Pete." This evidence points to the psychological reality of such spatial arrangements. In fact, subjects themselves claimed that they did arrange the series on a mental space. Furthermore, a clear preference for the setting up of rightward and/or downward mentally ordered arrays has been detected. Handel, et al. (1968) and Huttenlocher (1968) have very thoroughly described the physico-spatial properties of these mental diagrams.

Other work by Bower, Clark, Lesgold and Winzenz (1969) demonstrates the facilitating effects of presenting word lists in already organized hierarchies displayed spatially in tree form. Recall was found to be from two to three times higher with this hierarchico-spatial presentation, and the evidence led the researchers to conclude that the provision of structured retrieval schemata was sufficient to produce such impressive enhancement of recall. According to Bower (1972:116) the "subject could...use a conceptual hierarchy as a retrieval plan, beginning his recall at the top node and unpacking it recursively from the top down." The latter comment connects his results to Handel, et al.'s (1968) explanation of a downward preference when recalling hierarchically arranged conceptual layouts. Bower's explanation of gradual downward unpacking of nodes of nested categories is also related to Grimes' "staging" notion, in which the nodes are represented by the succeeding episodes in a story. Pylyshyn (1973) adds to all of the above by focusing on the contents of these mental constructions and characterizing them as symbolic descriptions of what is known. He believes that these descriptions contain highly abstracted and interpreted propositional knowledge that "is not very different from the kind of knowledge asserted by a sentence (Pylyshyn, 1973:7)." Since the data appeared to point toward the organizing potential of spatial arrays, several researchers set up studies to further test this hypothesis. Studies by Gagné and Wiegand (1970), Rothwell (1974), Barron and Stone (1974), Rosenblatt (1975), Hall (1976), Glynn and Di Vesta (1977), Kuhn and Novak (1979) seem to corroborate the hypothesis. The findings also tend to indicate that the locus of the effect is at retrieval, immediately before subjects are tested for content recall.

Of particular interest is Glynn and Di Vesta's (1977) study. In this study the provision of a pre-reading diagram significantly facilitated factual recall, while a post-reading or retrieval diagram significantly enhanced inferential tasks. The absence of diagrams resulted in a generalized inhibition of productive inferences in the control group, in accordance with the theory.

Because all of the data described above have been collected in studies of reading in the native language, the field is missing one important aspect of the problem. Learners reading in a foreign code may see their predictive abilities (see Smith, 1973) and their capacities to interpret and organize content seriously impaired, so that the provision of an organizing device may or may not facilitate comprehension. The present study was thus designed to investigate the effects of providing a text's superordinate structure on recall of a Spanish passage.

METHOD

Design

A one-between-one, within-groups, partial hierarchical design (see Kennedy, 1977: 520-30) was used in the study, in which the effect of classes was controlled by nesting them into the levels of the main variable. This factorial design had two independent variables: *time of presentation* (reading and retrieval conditions) and *kind of scheme* (indented and boxed diagrams). The dependent variable was a 15-minute summary of the passage written in English by the subjects, which was considered to be a recall measure of comprehension.

Subjects

The sample consisted of 161 second-semester students enrolled in twelve traditional-track classes of the Elementary Spanish Program at The Ohio State University during the Winter of 1979. The sample was divided into two groups by randomly assigning six classes to each of the two treatment conditions.

Materials

The reading passage was in Spanish and was designed to conform to the linguistic and instructional restrictions imposed by the course materials. The reading dealt with the social classes in the Inca empire, but no title was provided.

Diagrams

The superordinate structure of the content was schematically presented in Spanish to the subjects in one of two forms: as an indented word outline, or as a tree diagram of the box-and-arrow format. (See figures 4 and 5.) The diagrams form the two levels of the kind of scheme variable described above. The content structure of the passage was obtained by applying Meyer's (1975a) procedure of content analysis. This method yields a complete mapping of the content, hierarchically depicting both super and subordinate propositions and indicating both the informative and rhetorical relations among them. (See figures 2 and 3.) The content structure was also used as the criterion for scoring the recall measures. Each idea unit in the subject's summary was located in the content structure and counted as recalled.

Instrumentation

A criterion measure consisting of a 15-minute summary written in English by the subjects after they had read the passage and studied the diagrams was used to assess recall knowledge of content. Two scorers tallied the total number of idea-units in each summary. Inter-scorer reliability was found to be .98.

Experimental Procedures

There were two conditions in the study, and six intact classes were randomly assigned to each one of them: (1) Reading Condition - subjects received the passage along with a diagram and were instructed to read both; (2) Retrieval Condition - subjects received the passage, read it, the passage was collected, and then a diagram was provided for study. Each class was further divided into two groups by randomly distributing either one of the diagrams to each subject. All experimental events and data collection took place in a single 45-minute period on the same day for all classes.

Analysis

Data were submitted to an analysis of variance (ANOVA) appropriate for the study's design. This analysis is an option of the Balanova program of SOUPAC. In light of the fact that main effects for the random variable (classes) were found to be non-significant ($p < .15$) and also because a pattern was detected when examining the descriptive statistics, data were collapsed over this variable and another ANOVA test was done taking subjects as the unit of analysis. SPSS (Statistical Package for the Social Sciences) was the program used in this case.

Discussion

An examination of the descriptive statistics reveals a 10-point difference between the levels of the main factor, i.e., Time of Presentation. The mean for the reading condition is 54.90, whereas the mean for the retrieval condition is 65.20 points. The highest mean (68.06) is observed in the retrieval condition among subjects using the boxed diagram. (See Table 1.)

A smaller difference (6.5 points) is observed between the indented diagram group (57.71 points) and the boxed diagram group (64.22 points). There also is a 12-point difference between the reading-indented group (50.51) and the retrieval-indented group (62.57). A smaller 9-point difference is noted between the reading-boxed group and the retrieval-boxed group (59.14 and 68.06 respectively). In both conditions, subjects using the boxed diagram outperformed subjects using the indented one. In summary, higher means occurred in the retrieval condition for both kinds of diagrams.

Results

As shown in table 2 and figure 1, the main effects analyzed were significant beyond the .05 level (see table 2 and figure 1). Thus, results suggest that the locus of the effect is the retrieval condition and that a visually

Table 1. Summary of Weighted Means and Standard Deviations of Main Effects on the Recall Measure.

Time of Presentation (A)	Classes (B)	Kind of Scheme					
		Indented (C_1)		Boxed (C_2)		A Totals	
Reading (A_1)	n=6	n	33	n	34	n	67
		mean	50.51	mean	59.14	mean	54.90
		S.D.	19.20	S.D.	17.75	S.D.	18.85
Retrieval (A_2)	n=6	n	49	n	45	n	94
		mean	62.57	mean	68.06	mean	65.20
		S.D.	25.78	S.D.	24.30	S.D.	25.10
	C Totals	n	82	n	79	n	161
		mean	57.71	mean	64.22	mean	60.91
		S.D.	22.04	S.D.	20.28	S.D.	23.21

Table 2. Anova of Recall by Time of Presentation, and Kind of Scheme.

Source	df	MS	F
A (Time)	1	4,299.0568	8.4266**
B (Type)	1	1,950.0306	3.8223*
A x B	1	96.1324	0.1884
S/AB	157	510.1739	
Total	160		

$^{**}p < .004$

$^{*}p < .05$

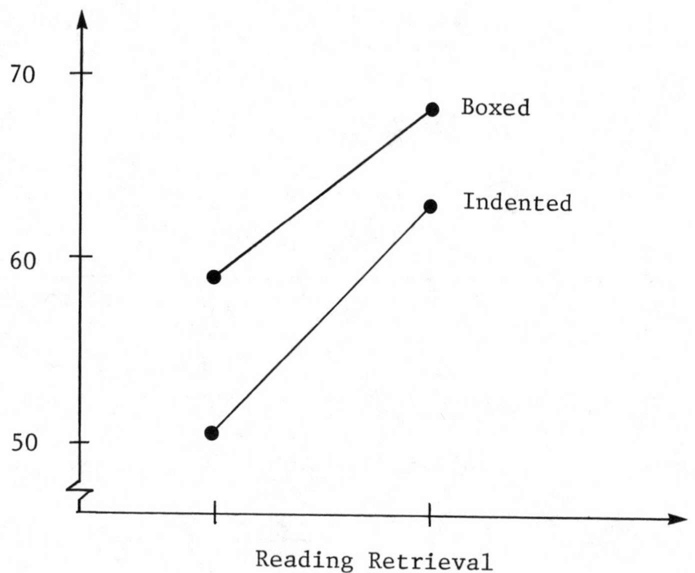

Figure 1. Treatment-Group Weighted Means for Recall Measure. Time of Presentation by Kind of Scheme.

structured scheme significantly facilitates comprehension.

Subjects in the retrieval condition outperformed subjects in the reading conditions by an average of ten points (see figure 1). This finding can be related to similar evidence in studies by Gagné and Wiegand (1970) and by Glynn and Di Vesta (1977). It would seem that subjects reading in a foreign language profit more from the organizing effects of a schematic outline once their attention is free to be devoted to diagram study only. In the reading condition, on the other hand, the provision of the schematic outline may have seemed irrelevant to the subjects who were busy reading the passage. On this basis one could conclude that subjects set up their memorial traces for foreign discourse only after having completed the reading and before being asked to recall the information in it.

According to the results of the analysis, it also seems apparent that a visually structured, box-and-arrow diagram supports the construction of mental schemata in a more effective way by perhaps replicating more closely the subjects' spatio-visual mental networks. Subjects using a traditional indented outline containing exactly the same information produced fewer idea units in their summaries (see figures 4 and 5). The effect may therefore be a function of the physical features of boxed diagrams, which might support or promote a quasi-perceptual scan of the information. It could be that the structure of a boxed diagram not only facilitates the gradual node-unpacking proposed by Bower (1972) but also enhances the hierarchical organization of the information and its "staging" in discourse, in accord with Grimes' proposal. Finally, it could also be speculated that the effect detected might be related to "gestalt" notions, but no strong claims can be made in this direction as yet.

In summary, the results of this study seem to indicate that the provision of schematic verbal arrays of the ideas contained in a foreign text enhances comprehension significantly.

The organization at the top of the content structure of this passage consists of a result relationship between complex propositions stating information about the features contributing to the success of the Empire and a complex proposition stating information about the Empire itself.

The antecedent-consequent rhetorical predicates of the top structure of this passage are hypotactic, because they are not of equal weight. Paragraphing and signalling indicate that the author centered the passage on the antecedent's development, which branches down into a series of specific, collection, attribution rhetorical predicates.

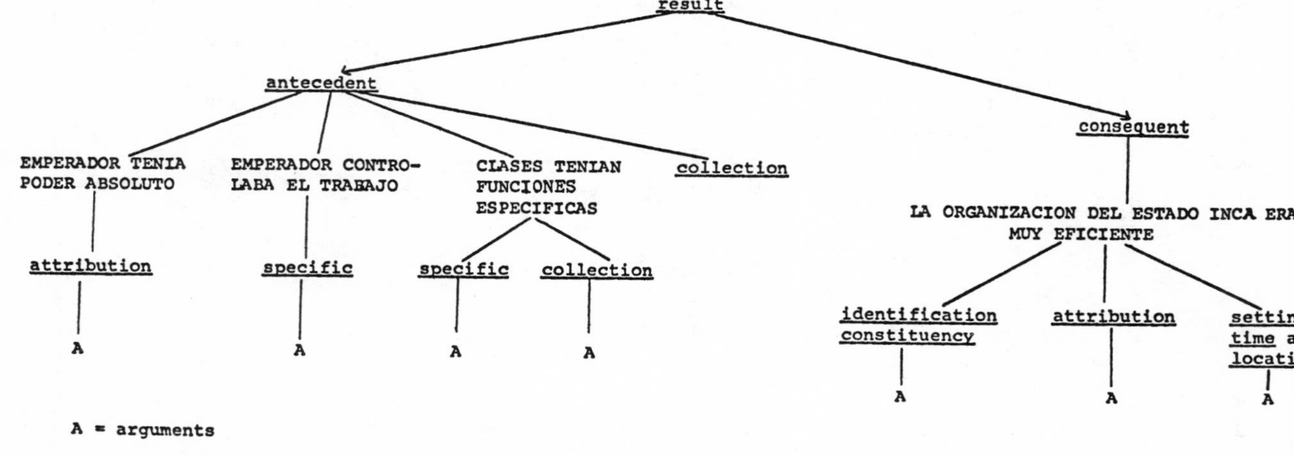

Figure 2. Top Level Structure of the Main Study Passage: "Las clases sociales en el imperio Inca."

result
PORQUE EL EMPERADOR TENIA PODER ABSOLUTO, covariance, antecedent

PORQUE EL EMPERADOR CONTROLABA EL TRABAJO DE TODOS LOS GRUPOS SOCIALES, covariance, antecedent

PORQUE CADA CLASE SOCIAL TENIA FUNCIONES BIEN ESPECIFICAS, covariance, antecedent

specific
HABIA TRES CLASES ALTAS

range
EN EL ESTADO INCA

specific
collection
SU (LA) FAMILIA
EL INCA

equivalent
EMPERADOR

setting location
VIVIAN EN EL CUZCO

equivalent
LA CAPITAL

attribution
collection
SU PODER ERA ABSOLUTO
ADMINISTRABA

patient
EL ESTADO

agent
EL INCA

POSEIA (ERAN DE)

specific
collection

EDIFICIOS PUBLICOS
MINAS DE ORO
PLANTACIONES
LA TIERRA

benefactive
EL INCA

RECIBIA

specific
collection
GRAN PARTE DE LAS COSECHAS
GRAN PARTE DE LA PRODUCCION

equivalent
COMO TRIBUTO

benefactive
EL INCA

TENIA QUE AYUDAR A

patient
TODA LA GENTE

range
DEL IMPERIO
specific
collection
SEGUN SU CLASE SOCIAL
SEGUN SUS MECESIDADES

agent
EL INCA

TENIA QUE DEFENDER DE OTROS INDIOS HOSTILES

patient
EL IMPERIO

agent
EL INCA

LES DABA TIERRA A LOS CAMPESINOS, covariance, consequent

A CAMBIO DE UN SERVICIO EXTRAORDINARIO, covariance, antecedent

ERA TAMBIEN EL JEFE MAXIMO

Figure 3. CONTENT STRUCTURE OF THE PASSAGE. SAMPLE PAGE.

I. ORGANIZACION DEL ESTADO

-muy eficiente porque:
-el Inca tenía poder absoluto y
-controlaba el trabajo de todos
-las clases sociales tenían funciones especificas

II. INCA (emperador)

-administraba el Estado
-poseía tierras y edificios
-recibía cosechas como tributo

SACERDOTES

-influencia en la política y en la educacion
-adoraban al Sol

NOBLES

-aplicaban la política del Inca

III. SOLDADOS

-defendian el imperio
-controlaban el trabajo

EMPLEADOS DEL ESTADO

-median y dividían la producción y la tierra

CAMPESINOS

-vivian en comunidades
-cultivaban la tierra

Figure 4: INDENTED DIAGRAM

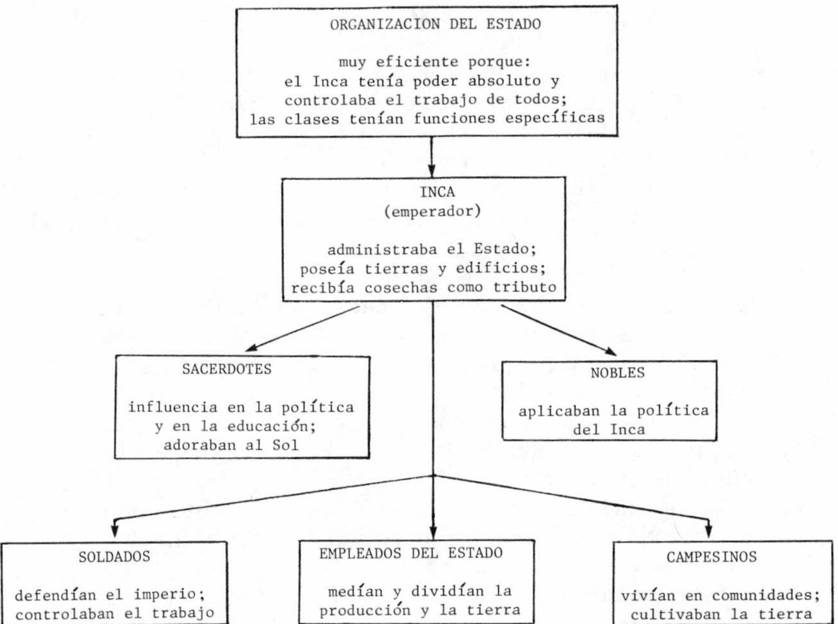

Figure 5. Boxed Diagram.

REFERENCES

Ausubel, David P., 1978 "Educational Psychology: A Cognitive View," Holt, Rinehart and Winston, N.Y.

Barron, R. F. and Stone, V. F., 1974, The effect of student-constructed graphic post-organizers upon learning vocabulary relationships, in: "Interaction: Research and Practice for College Adult Reading," P. L. Nacke, ed., Clemson U., Clemson.

Bower, G. H., 1972, A selective review of organizational factors in memory, in: "Organization of Memory," E. Tulving and W. Donaldson, eds., Academic Press, N.Y.

Bower, G. H., Clark, M. C., Lesgold, A. M., and Winzenz, D., 1969, Hierarchical retrieval schemes in recall of categorized word lists, JVLVB, 8:322-43.

Crothers, E. J., 1972, Memory structure and the recall of discourse, in: "Language Comprehension and the Acquisition of Knowledge," R. Freedle and J. Carroll, eds., Wiley, N.Y.

Fillmore, C. J., 1969, The case for case, in: "Universals in Linguistic Theory," E. Bach and R. Harms, eds., Holt, Rinehart and Winston, N.Y.

Fredericksen, C. H., 1972, Effects of task-induced cognitive operations on comprehension of memory processes, in: "Language Comprehension and the Acquisition of Knowledge," R. Freedle and J. Carroll, eds., Wiley, N.Y.

Gagné, R. M. and Wiegand, V. K., 1970, "Effects of superordinate context on learning and retention of facts, J. of Ed. Psych., 61:406-09.

Glynn, S. M. and Di Vesta, F. J., 1977, Outline and hierarchical organization as aids for study and retrieval, J. of Ed. Psych., 69:89-95.

Grimes, J. E., 1972, "The Thread of Discourse," Cornell U., Ithaca.

Hall, C. K., 1977, "The Effects of Graphic Advance Organizers and Schematic Cognitive Mapping Organizers upon the Comprehension of Ninth Grade Students." M.A. thesis, Rutgers U.

Handel, S., London, M., and Desoto, C., 1968, Reasoning and spatial representation, JVLVB, 7:351-57.

Huttenlocher, J., 1968, Constructing spatial images: a strategy in reasoning, Psych. Rev., 75:550-60.

Kennedy, John J., 1977, An introduction to the design and analysis of experiments in education and psychology, Wa. Univ. Press of America, Washington, D.C.

Kintsch, W., 1974,"The Representation of Meaning in Memory," Wiley, N.Y.

Kintsch, W., 1977, On comprehending stories, in:"Cognitive Processes in Comprehension," M. Just and P. Carpenter, eds., LEA, Hillsdale.

Kintsch, W. and Van Dijk, T. A., 1975, Comment on se rapelle et on résume des histoires, Languages, 40: 98-116.

Kuhn, D. L. and Novak, J. D., 1979, A study on varying modes of topical presentation in elementary college biology to determine the effect of advance organizers in knowledge acquisition and retention, J. of Rsvch. in Sci. Tchng., 7:249-52.

Meyer, Bonnie J. F., 1975a, "The Organization of Prose and its Effects on Memory," North Holland, Amsterdam.

Meyer, Bonnie J. F., 1975b, Identification of the structure of prose and its implications for the study of reading and memory, J. of Rdng. Beh., 7:7-47.

Omaggio, Alice C., 1979, Pictures and second language comprehension: do they help? For. Lan. Annals, 12: 107-116.

Pylyshyn, Z. W., 1973, What the mind's eye tells the mind's brain: a critique of mental imagery, Psych. Bull., 80:1-24.

Rosenblatt, W., 1975, "The Effects of Written Advance Organizers and Schematic Cognitive Mapping Organizers upon the Comprehension of Seventh Grade Social Studies Students," M.A. thesis, Rutgers University.

Rothwell, A., 1974, "Sentence Outlines and the Comprehension of Connected Text," Ph.D. Dissertation, Harvard U.

Rumelhart, D. E., Lindsay, P. H., and Norman, D. H., 1972, A process model for long-term memory, in: "Organization of Memory," E. Tulving and W. Donaldson, eds., Academic Press, N.Y.

Smith, F., 1975, "Comprehension and Learning," Holt, Rinehart, and Winston, N.Y.

Van Dijk, Teun, A., 1977, Semantic macro-structures and knowledge frames in discourse comprehension, in: "Cognitive Processes in Comprehension," M. Just and P. Carpenter, eds., LEA, Hillsdale.

INDEX